ETFs for the Long Run

What They Are, How They Work, and Simple Strategies for Successful Long-Term Investing

LAWRENCE CARREL

WILEY

John Wiley & Sons, Inc.

Published by John Wiley & Sons, Inc., Hoboken, New Jersey.
Published simultaneously in Canada.

For general information on our other products and services or for technical support,
please contact our Customer Care Department within the United States at
(800) 762-2974, outside the United States at (317) 572-3993 or fax (317) 572-4002.

Wiley also publishes its books in a variety of electronic formats. Some content that
appears in print may not be available in electronic books. For more information about
Wiley products, visit our web site at www.wiley.com.

Library of Congress Cataloging-in-Publication Data:

Carrel, Lawrence, 1963–
   ETFs for the long run : what they are, how they work, and simple strategies for
successful long-term investing / Lawrence Carrel.
       p. cm.
   Includes bibliographical references and indexes.
   ISBN 978-0-470-13894-6 (cloth)
  1. Exchange traded funds.   2. Stock funds.   I. Title.
   HG6043.C37 2008
   332.63'27–dc22

                                                                    2008016817

Printed in the United States of America.

10 9 8 7 6 5 4 3 2 1

To Theo and Jackson for their inspiration and to Judy and Jerry for making an investment in me.

Contents

Preface   ix

Acknowledgments   xiii

CHAPTER 1   ETFs—The Newfangled Mutual Funds   1

                 How ETFs Stack Up against Mutual Funds   2
                 Greater Flexibility   3
                 Lower Fees   4
                 More Tax Efficient   5
                 Greater Transparency   6
                 Precise Allocations   6
                 Investment in Alternative Asset Classes   7
                 One Caveat   7
                 Summary   8

CHAPTER 2   ETF History Lesson: How a New Type of Fund
                 Was Born   11

                 A Short History of the Amex   13
                 The Father of the ETF   17
                 Philly Strikes First   18
                 Back to the Drawing Board   21
                 Along Came a Spider   26
                 The Birth of an Industry   27
                 Let's Do It Again   29
                 What Tangled Webs We Weave   30
                 Building a Business   33
                 Shine On, You Crazy DIAmonds   34
                 Arachnophobia?   35

Wedding Bells   35
The Biggest ETF Launch   37
All in the Family   41
The First Assault   45
If You Can't Beat 'Em, Join 'Em   46
Builders and Bonds   47
Free Again   49

CHAPTER 3   The Evolution of the ETF   51

The Importance of a Broadly Diversified Portfolio   53
The Appeal of Investment Companies   55
Types of Investment Companies   56
Types of Mutual Funds   58
Running a Mutual Fund   60
The Creation of an ETF   63
Summary   67

CHAPTER 4   Index Fund-amentals   69

Why an Index?   70
Fund Management Options   72
The Rise of the Index Funds   76
The Big Index Companies   79
Indexes from the Stock Exchanges   82
Actively Managed ETFs   84
Summary   84

CHAPTER 5   Fee Bitten   87

Wall Street Produces Vintages   87
Looking for Low Management Fees   89
Summary   92

CHAPTER 6   The Better Mousetrap: How Can ETFs Charge So Little?   95

Transparent Costs of Mutual Funds   96
Hidden Costs of Mutual Funds   105
The Creation Unit: How They Make ETFs So Cheap   110

So Long, Transaction Costs 114
So What Costs *Do* ETFs Have? 119
Why Would I Ever Buy a Mutual Fund? 123
Summary 127

CHAPTER 7 The New Indexers 129

Missed Opportunity 132
Unfair Fight 136
BONY Builds a BLDR 137
The Name Is Bond 138
Rydex Rides In 140
Vanguard Makes a Splash 142
There's Power in Them There Shares 144
Mutual Fund Scandal Helps ETFs 145
PowerShares Becomes a Powerhouse . . . and Other
    Important Developments of 2005 147
The Buy-Out 148
Opening the Floodgates 149
The Fundamentalists 155
Grow, Baby, Grow 163
Summary 168

CHAPTER 8 The ETFs That Aren't ETFs: ETPs, ETVs, and ETNs 171

You've Got a HOLDR to Cry On 174
Exchange-Traded Notes 176
Commodity-Based ETVs 180
Money Makes the World Go 'Round 199
Summary 204

CHAPTER 9 Putting the "Trade" in Exchange-Traded Funds 217

Discount Brokers 219
The Actual Trade 220
Going Long to Go Short 226
Options on ETFs 229
Summary 232

CHAPTER 10   Building Your Own ETF Portfolio   235

The Simplest Portfolio   237
Assessing Your Risk   237
Strategic and Tactical Asset Allocation   241
Foundation Portfolios   248
Not Following the Herd   258
Tax-Loss Harvesting   265
Hiring an Investment Adviser   267
Summary   269

CHAPTER 11   The Future of ETFs   273

The NYSE-Amex Merger   274
Specialists and Seed Capital   275
Actively Managed ETFs   279
Entering the 401(k) Market   281
In Conclusion   283
APPENDIX :   How to Decide Which ETFs Are Best for You   285

Notes   289

About the Author   300

Index   301

Preface

The exchange-traded fund, better known as an ETF, is the mutual fund for the twenty-first century. Like mutual funds, ETFs hold a diversified portfolio of stocks, bonds, or some other asset class. Yet, their structure is different enough that almost every ETF is less expensive, more tax-efficient, more transparent, and more flexible than any comparable mutual fund. That means more money for you. And in the end, isn't that what investing is all about, having more money in your pocket?

There are other books on the market that explain exchange-traded funds. But most of them are for a professional audience of investment advisors and institutional portfolio managers. This book is for everyone else, anyone who is in charge of his or her personal or household finances. So, if you are an individual investor, whether a buy-and-hold investor in stocks, bonds, mutual funds, commodities or currencies, or even a day trader, this book is for you.

You need to prepare for retirement. You might need to save for your child's education. You might just want to grow capital to buy some other big expenditure, such as a house, a boat, or a vacation. Whether you're the kind of person who likes to manage his or her own finances or who just wants to understand what your investment advisor is talking about, this book is for you. I will explain, in easy-to-understand language, why you should be investing in ETFs over almost any other investment vehicle. I promise not to use any mathematical formulas.

Investing and increasing your assets is difficult. It means having to choose from a multitude of choices and decide which will be a winner. It's taking a risk on the unknown and then waiting. Basically, it's predicting the future, and that's hard to do well. Wall Street investment advisors tell you this is a very complex process, and thus individual investors need their services to navigate these difficult waters. But it doesn't have to be that way. It can be very simple if you follow a systematic approach. One way to simplify your investing life is to buy ETFs.

Let's face it, if you wanted to spend hours each day researching the price/earnings ratio and the return on investment of public companies, you would have gone for a career on Wall Street. Whether you do or don't work on Wall Street, I'm assuming that reading financial statements in your free time sounds like about as much fun as getting a foot amputated.

Even if you like picking stocks, unforeseen circumstances burn the best stock pickers. You can be right in forecasting an industry's rise, but you could own the one company in that industry that was posting a loss or suffering from a scandal. By owning a fund, you could own the entire industry; making one company's troubles just a small stain on your profits.

For this reason, mutual funds have flourished.

Mutual fund investors know that funds are great investment vehicles. Buying mutual funds is much easier than buying individual stocks. You get a professional manager to do the hard work for you. Plus, they offer diversification with a low minimum investment.

With more than 8,000 mutual funds on the market, you can buy a portfolio to suit any strategy. A single fund can hold as few as 20 underlying securities or thousands.

It's a wonderful concept. You don't have to pay attention to the financial news. You don't have to spend time doing scads of research on a wide range of stocks and industries. You just have to pick a few funds, then save the money to put into them. The fund manager takes care of all the rest. He researches stocks, decides what to own, and then buys and sells in order to maximize profits. You don't have to get your foot amputated.

Consequently, mutual funds are the premier savings device for Americans. According to the Investment Company Institute, the mutual fund industry's trade group, 44 percent of all U.S. households own mutual funds or a similar investment device. For nearly 70 years, mutual funds have served the needs of individual investors. For the most part individual investors have been served well, but not always.

High fees are a huge offense mutual funds commit against their own shareholders. In investments, high fees can mean the difference between earning an annual profit or a loss. And the more fees decrease the size of your investment, the longer you will need to save. So, if you found an investment very similar to a mutual fund for a much lower price, would you buy it? Of course you would.

ETFs are that product.

ETFs offer everything a mutual fund does, and usually cost less to own. With the flexibility to trade during the hours of the stock market, and daily portfolio transparency, an alternate title for this book could have been *Mutual Funds Are Good; ETFs Are Just Better.*

If you're one of those hedge fund investors who believe that you get what you pay for, then ETFs are not for you. Unregulated hedge funds offer the potential for huge profits for people who can make a minimum investment in the millions of dollars and stomach massive amounts of risk. With no transparency, the hedge fund investor has no idea what he owns and it can often take weeks or months to get his money out. You need to be rich to invest in hedge funds because there is a much greater risk of their blowing up.

Most investors can neither manage the minimum investment nor stomach the risk of a hedge fund. ETFs are the opposite of hedge funds. These highly regulated funds are much safer than hedge funds. They are open to anyone, very liquid, highly transparent, much cheaper to own, and filled with the potential to beat hedge fund returns with much less risk. And if that is what you're looking for in an investment, then this book is for you.

This isn't to say ETFs have no risk. Like hedge funds and mutual funds, ETFs are as risky as the assets they hold. So an ETF tracking the broad market benchmark, the S&P 500 Index, would be much less risky than an ETF with just companies from the biotechnology industry. The ETF tracking the S&P 500 would have the same amount of risk as a mutual fund tracking the same index, while a biotech ETF would be just as risky as any biotech sector mutual fund. Meanwhile, an ETF holding bonds would typically have less risk than a mutual fund owning equities, and vice versa.

I became a financial journalist in 1995 at the start of what became known as the Information Age. During that time I reported on the rise of the Internet economy, the inflating of the stock market's dot-com bubble, and its subsequent popping. I wrote and edited stories about Wall Street investment banks bringing to the stock market companies with no profits, no sales, and sometimes no products. As the Wall Street community hyped the growth potential of every new stock, mutual fund companies launched new funds filled with these hot stocks and sold them to investors just as the market was peaking.

After the stock market crashed in 2000, I reported on the rash of scandals left in its wake, how companies named Enron, WorldCom, Adelphia, and Tyco defrauded their shareholders. Soon after that I reported on the scandal in which many mutual funds let market timers, hedge funds, and speculators get an unfair advantage to maximize profits over the funds' own shareholders. Recently, I've reported on the subprime mortgage crisis and how some of the brightest minds on Wall Street got ensnared by their own creative schemes for making money off of unsuspecting homeowners.

Reporting these stories left me with the impression that Wall Street is an extremely hostile environment for the small investor. I'm a naturally skeptical person, and these experiences only heightened that sensibility. As I moved into writing about personal finance, I became a different kind of investigative journalist. My job was to cut through the hype and figure out if investments and financial products were a good deal for the individual investor.

In general, there's not much on Wall Street that I get effusive about. However, I like revolutionary ideas, especially when they help the man on the street. So the fact that I became a fan of ETFs soon after I started writing about them isn't to be taken lightly. I immediately liked that they offered a low-cost alternative for mutual fund investors. And unlike most things on Wall Street, the more I learned about ETFs, the more I liked them.

As the ETF industry expanded, it broke down some of the walls Wall Street had built between institutional investors and the little guy. Suddenly individuals found doors opened to investment ideas, assets, and pricing levels that had previously only been available to large institutional investors, such as hedge funds, endowments, and pension funds. Small investors now had a choice. Instead of getting fleeced, they could buy an ETF and get the same advantages as the big boys.

This book tells the story about how ETFs were invented and how they are built, and explains in detail how they can offer investors so many benefits. In the end, it tells you how to build your own ETF portfolio. I've come away from this project believing ETFs are one of the best, if not *the* best, investment vehicle available to the small investor. I hope you find this book helpful and catch my enthusiasm for ETFs.

Acknowledgments

I'm especially indebted to Bill Falloon of John Wiley & Sons for suggesting the idea for this book, offering me the chance to write it, and having the faith that I would finish it. My editor, Emilie Herman, deserves much praise for her patience and support. I am also extremely indebted to Kathleen Moriarty of Katten Muchin Rosenman for taking time out of her busy schedule and vacation to read over most of this book. Bob Tull of Macro-Markets and Arlene Reyes of ExchangeTradedFunds.com were instrumental for their willingness to take many late-night phone calls and answer many basic questions.

I want to thank the following people for not only taking the time to talk to me, but also for reading and fact checking individual chapters or selections: Rob Arnott of Research Affiliates, Hank Belusa of the DTCC, Bruce Bond of PowerShares Capital Management, Steven Bloom of the NASDAQ Stock Market, Dave Hooten of Claymore Securities, Ben Fulton of PowerShares, Doug Holmes of Rydex Investments, John Hyland of Victoria Bay Asset Management, John Jacobs of NASDAQ, Joe Keenan of The Bank of New York Mellon, Wayne Lee of NASDAQ, Steve Letzler of the DTCC, Tim Meyer of Rydex Investments, Sonya Morris of Morningstar, J. Parsons of Barclays Global Investors, James Ross of State Street Global Advisors, and Cliff Weber of the American Stock Exchange.

I'm grateful to Jim Kelly of Kelly Capital Management for his advice on how to build a portfolio, and to Ron Delegge of ETFguide.com, Kevin Maeda of Natixis Funds, Burton Malkiel of Princeton University, and J.D. Steinhilber of Agile Investing for contributing sample portfolios.

I also want to thank the following people for helping me acquire the information necessary to write this book: Darwin Abrahamson of Invest n Retire, Michele Allison of Deutsche Bank, Stuart Bell of WisdomTree Investments, Lance Berg of Barclays Global Investors, David Blitzer of Standard & Poor's, John Bogle of the Bogle Financial Markets Research Center, Renee Calabro of Deutsche Bank, Amy Chain of Vanguard, Mary Chung of the American Stock Exchange, Rebecca Cohen of Vanguard, Bill Conboy of BC Capital Partners, Lisa Dallmer of NYSE Euronext, Courtney Dobrow of Morningstar, Scott Ebner of the American Stock Exchange, Philippe

El-Asmar of Barclays Capital, Jeffrey Feldman of Xshares Group, Kristin Friel of Barclays Capital, David Fry of ETFDigest.com, Gary Gastineau of ETF Consultants, Ed Giltenan of the Investment Company Institute, Tucker Hewes of Hewes Communications, Matt Hougan of IndexUniverse.com, Christine Hudacko of Barclays Global Investors, Dawn Kahler of Rydex Investments, Lori Klash of Rydex Investments, Mark Komissarouk of Morningstar, Joseph LaCorte of S Network, Annette Larson of Morningstar, Gary MacDonald of State Street Global Advisors, James McGowan of JPMorgan Chase, Mike McNamee of the Investment Company Institute, Sam Scott Miller of Orrick Herrington & Sutcliffe, Howard Monahan of Hewes Communications, Peggy Mu of Barclays Global Investors, Melissa Murphy of SunStar, James Pacetti of ETF International Associates, Alvin Rapp of RPG Consultants, Kevin Rich of Deutsche Bank, Tom Roseen of Lipper, Eric Ryan of NYSE Euronext, Kristin Sadlon of Porter Novelli, Shawn-Laree de St. Aubin of Dobbins Communications, Michael Sapir of Proshares, Steven Schoenfeld of Northern Trust, Stephanie Scotto of NYSE Euronext, Luciano Siracusano of WisdomTree Investments, Pam Snook of JPMorgan Chase, Joe Stefanelli of the American Stock Exchange, Jeff Tjornehoj of Lipper, Bari Trontz of the American Stock Exchange, Jim Wiandt of IndexUniverse.com, Chris Wloszczyna of the Investment Company Institute, and Nadine Youssef of Morningstar.

My editors at TheStreet.com, Dave Morrow, George Moriarty, Allison Bisbey Colter, and Brian Cronk, deserve thanks for their patience, understanding and support. I want to thank my family and friends for their love and support, Judy Carrel, Jerome Carrel, Janice Carrel, Marc Carrel, Sterling Barrett, Steven Fox, Darrin Greene, Jennifer Love, Tricia Pool, Mike Rosenband, Eliane Viera, Nick Wade, Jeff Wolfer, and any other friends I may have neglected to mention. Finally, I want to thank three people instrumental to my career, and without whom I would never have reached this point: Kevin C. Fitzpatrick, the impetus for my becoming a financial journalist and the source of some of my best stories; Ezra Palmer, who taught me how to be a financial journalist while I was at The Wall Street Journal.com; and Steve Sakson, who made me a better one while I was at SmartMoney.com.

CHAPTER 1

ETFs—The Newfangled Mutual Funds

Diamonds and Spiders and Cubes, oh my.

Upon reading such things in the financial press, individual investors familiar with stocks and bonds can't be blamed for wondering if some weird menagerie was let loose upon Wall Street. When names like iShares and PowerShares float by in articles and ads, investors may think that typical shares of company stock have undergone some strange mutation into bigger and better shares. And, in a manner of speaking, they would be right.

All of these are brand names for an investment vehicle known as the exchange-traded fund (ETF), one of the hottest products on Wall Street. At the end of 2006, there were 359 exchange-traded funds. In 2007, 270 new ETFs were launched, increasing the industry by 75 percent for a year-end total of 629. Over that same time, the industry's assets under management surged 44 percent to $608.4 billion.

Despite their phenomenal growth and the fact that ETFs have been on the market for 15 years, many investors still are not aware of them. Ask the average person on the street what an ETF is and you will get answers such as the electronic transfer of funds, an enriched text format for computer documents, or the president's energy task force.

While these terms all share the same initials, you can be sure that whenever someone you know is excited about ETFs, they're talking about exchange-traded funds. A simple way to understand the acronym is to recall that it refers to newfangled mutual *funds* that *trade* on a stock *exchange*.

Much like any other industry, such as automobiles or laundry detergent, Wall Street needs to come out with new and improved products to continue attracting clients and investments. Not all new products are improvements: for example, New Coke, Coca-Cola's reformulation of its flagship product in the 1980s, was one of the biggest marketing failures in history. ETFs are Wall Street's new and improved *mutual funds*. They could even be called the mutual fund for the twenty-first century. Both are vehicles that offer individual investors the ability to own a *liquid, diversified portfolio* for a minimal investment. But the differences between them are vast enough to make them very different products. Individuals need to consider how they will be investing before choosing which product to buy.

How ETFs Stack Up against Mutual Funds

ETFs combine many features of a mutual fund into a tradable stock, making the claim "new and improved" much more than a marketing ploy. The top six benefits that exchange-traded funds offer over mutual funds:

1. greater flexibility
2. lower fees
3. increased tax efficiency
4. greater transparency
5. ability to invest in more asset classes
6. ability to create more precise tactical investment strategies

Of course, new and improved implies that mutual funds, like last year's cars, are now relegated to the investing world's back lot or are no longer worthy of our attention. That's not always the case: With more than $12 trillion in more than 21,000 different products at the end of 2007, mutual funds won't be leaving Wall Street anytime soon.

Neither will ETFs. First issued 15 years ago, ETFs aren't some fly-by-night products that will soon become last year's model. The flexibility to be bought and sold during the trading session helped the product gain an enthusiastic following among institutional investors, such as the managers of hedge fund managers and other portfolios. In contrast, during the product's early days, buy-and-hold investors found little imperative to buy ETFs when they could purchase mutual funds that followed the same indexes.

Yet, over the past five years, this financial innovation has developed in such a way that makes it unique on Wall Street. In addition to its flexibility and low costs, the ETF can track asset classes besides stocks and bonds—such as commodities and currencies—in a simple and easy format. This has gained ETFs wider recognition among retail investors, and they have become a staple in the portfolios of many individuals. However, despite growing interest in this area of the investment world, the workings and benefits of ETFs remain a mystery to many.

Perhaps you have heard about ETFs while researching other investments, or from a friend or investment adviser who recommends that you look into them. This book aims to help the individual investor understand the benefits of ETFs and how he or she can best use them in his or her personal portfolio.

Greater Flexibility

The biggest improvement and most important benefit that ETFs offer over mutual funds is the ability to be traded on a stock exchange. This is a huge advantage. Trading offers greater flexibility by allowing individual investors to buy and sell when they choose, as opposed to the once-a-day option offered by mutual funds. Because they trade on a stock exchange for the entire market session, the price of an ETF fluctuates all day long. This may seem like more of an advantage to *day traders* and *institutional investors*, who are most likely to hold funds less than one day, but in fact this flexibility is a great benefit for buy-and-hold investors. The ETF investor can pinpoint the exact price at which he or she wants to buy or sell their investment.

That's not the case with mutual funds. Mutual funds can only be bought or sold from the fund company once a day—after the 4 P.M. market close—at one price, the *net asset value,* or NAV. The NAV is basically the average price of all the shares in the fund, but it isn't calculated until after all the stocks have closed for the day. This leaves mutual fund investors at a distinct disadvantage. Investors must decide during a trading session to buy or sell a fund without knowing what the price will be.

For example, say the stock market receives a very negative economic report at 10:00 A.M. Most likely the market would begin a drastic move lower. Now compare the different experiences on that same hypothetical day of an ETF investor and a mutual fund shareholder, who each have portfolios of $100,000. Both investors are tuned into the financial news, so both become aware of the report at the same time. The news provides the catalyst for a major market sell-off that by the end of the day will send the Standard & Poor's 500 index 2 percent lower.

At 10:05 A.M., the mutual fund investor calls his fund company and says he wants to sell all the shares in his fund. The company tells him that they will be sold at the NAV calculated after the trading session ends. So, even though the mutual fund investor tried to get out quickly by calling his fund company early in the day, it doesn't matter. The fund calculates the sale price after 4 P.M. By that time, the market has already fallen, and the NAV is calculated with all the lowered stock prices. The likelihood is that the fund sells the investor's shares at the lowest price of the day.

Meanwhile, the ETF investor calls his stockbroker at 10:05 A.M. and tells the broker to sell all his shares. Because the ETF trades all day long, the broker makes a market order to sell the shares immediately. Even though the market falls 2 percent by the end of the day, the ETF investor gets out before most of the damage occurs, locking in a price near the high of the day. With our hypothetical portfolios, the ETF investor walks away with nearly $2,000 more than the mutual fund investor. The same scenario would also apply in an up market. The ETF investor buys early in the rally and profits from the day's rise. Meanwhile the mutual fund investor may see the rally, but cannot enter during the trading session. Instead, his share price is determined after the market rallied. Essentially, he buys near the top.

This ability to catch the beginning of a market move rather than only its conclusion gives investors greater profit potential. This flexibility also allows ETFs to be bought or sold with a *market, limit,* or *stop-loss order,* or on *margin.* Many ETFs also offer tradable *put* and *call options.* Another option not available to mutual fund shareholders is the ability to sell short. An investor can sell short an ETF or stock in anticipation of a downward move in the shares. The investor borrows the shares from a broker, then sells the shares first with the hope of closing the transaction by buying them back later at a lower price.

Greater flexibility gives the investor both more control over the purchase and sale price of the investment and an opportunity to take advantage of market moves.

Lower Fees

ETFs are essentially *index funds.* Index funds track a particular market by holding a basket of the exact same securities as the index, or an extremely close approximation.

The first ETF, the Standard & Poor's Depositary Receipt (better known as the *SPDR,* or Spider) began trading in 1993. It tracked the S&P 500, the very vanilla, U.S. large-cap stock index. Subsequent ETFs followed other major market indexes, such as *DIAmonds,* which follows the Dow Jones Industrial Average, and the PowerShares *Triple Qs* or *Cubes (Qubes),* which track the NASDAQ 100 Index. At the end of 2007, all ETFs were required to follow an index.

Because these baskets of stocks follow indexes, they are *passively managed* with infrequent asset turnover. Like index mutual funds, this results in extremely low annual *expense ratios*; in addition, the fees for ETFs are often lower than even those for the corresponding index funds. For instance, the Vanguard 500 Index fund, the largest and oldest index fund available to retail investors, tracks the S&P 500 Index. It has one of the lowest annual fees among mutual funds: only 0.18 percent of assets. Compare that with two ETFs, the Spider and Barclay's iShares S&P 500 Index, which charge a minuscule expense ratio of 0.08 percent and 0.09 percent, respectively. These are half Vanguard's fee. And Vanguard's tiny fee is the exception among mutual funds. Most mutual funds charge management fees of more than 1 percent, and some are as high as 5 percent. Currently, no ETF charges more than 1 percent. Fees are one of the biggest wealth destroyers for investors, so small fees add up to significant savings over time.

"Why is it so difficult to capture the market's returns? Because the market returns we read about ignore the costs of investing," says John Bogle, the founder and former chairman of the Vanguard Group, and the creator of the Vanguard 500 fund. "In the search for the Holy Grail of superior returns, real-life investors incur heavy costs—fund management fees, operating costs, brokerage commissions, sales loads, transaction costs, fees to advisers, out-of-pocket charges, and so on. Performance comes and goes, but costs roll on forever."[1]

More Tax Efficient

The third major benefit that ETFs hold over mutual funds is greater tax efficiency, primarily by delaying taxes on capital gains. Whenever a mutual fund, even an index fund, sells a security, it is a taxable event. All profits are capital gains. Profits earned by mutual funds, pass through the fund to the individual shareholders. And when a shareholder earns capital gains, he or she must pay *capital gains taxes*. Even if index-fund investors hold their funds for decades, every year they must pay taxes on the capital gains that the funds incur during the previous 12 months.

Capital gains taxes can be especially onerous when many investors pull their money out of a fund, as occurred in the wake of the stock market's dot-com crash in 2000. As investors pulled their money out, mutual funds were forced to sell their underlying assets in order to cash out these investors. To add insult to injury, the investors who chose to stay in the funds took a double hit. Not only had their investments fallen in price, but as the other investors left, the ones who stayed were stuck with paying the capital gains taxes from all the stock the fund needed to sell.

Meanwhile, because ETF investors own shares in their own personal accounts, rather than investing in a fund's pool of assets, their investment isn't connected to any other shareholder. ETF investors therefore only pay capital gains taxes when they sell *their* shares. Delaying the payment of taxes can make a significant difference in overall returns. When an investor isn't forced to pay out part of their principle in taxes every year, that means there is more principle to grow. In addition, the buy-and-hold investor who doesn't sell his ETF until after retirement may find himself in a lower tax bracket.

These three benefits—flexibility, lower fees, and greater tax efficiency—are what you will hear about from anyone advising you to look at ETFs for an investment, whether they are an industry insider, investment adviser, or even a financial journalist. But there are three other benefits ETFs offer that add to their luster.

Greater Transparency

Transparency means that at any specific moment, investors have the ability to see the price and holdings of the ETF.

Because they are index funds, it's reasonably easy to determine what stocks are included in an ETF or index mutual fund: simply look at the index. Of course, sometimes ETFs and index funds don't hold every single stock in the index. How far an index mutual fund veers away from the index is not apparent, but with ETFs you always know what stocks are held.

Due to its unique structure, the ETF must make available every day a list of all the securities that make up the fund, so that new shares can be created.

Mutual funds have a measure of transparency, but even that is a bit dubious. The portfolios of mutual funds are not transparent on a daily basis. Every six months the mutual fund is required to send to its shareholders a list of its holdings. This means shareholders see what's in the fund only twice a year, and even then, the report is suspect. Funds are given 60 days to deliver this list to shareholders. Because mutual funds are allowed to buy and sell securities every day, the portfolio documented at the end of the six-month period is often not the same as the one actually held 60 days later.

The transparency of the ETF's portfolio during the trading session gives the investor the ability to see the ETF's share price in real time. As mentioned above, the ability to see the share prices gives the investor greater control over the purchase and sale of the investment.

Precise Allocations

Transparency allows investors to create precise *strategic asset allocations* and *tactical investment strategies*. While all mutual funds have an investment strategy they must follow, it's not uncommon for a fund manager to sometimes stray from the strategy. This can happen for a variety of reasons. If the investment strategy is out of favor, the manager might want to hold some stocks on the rise in order to boost his returns.

Transparency allows the investor to see exactly what his holdings are on a daily basis. This is important because a group of mutual funds with different investment objectives may actually hold the same or very similar securities. Thus, with mutual funds the investor could inadvertently be overweight in areas of the market that are not advantageous to the portfolio.

For example, you own a large stock mutual fund and a small stock technology fund. However, small stocks aren't doing well, so the mutual fund manager buys some large tech stocks that are doing well. However, this could cause the investor's portfolio to have a greater weighting in large tech stocks than he wanted. Because fund managers have a lot of leeway and their portfolios are typically hidden from view, the investor is at a disadvantage.

Most ETFs track an index. This is an advantage because it restricts what the ETF can hold. By knowing exactly what each ETF holds, the investor can make very precise *asset allocations* for his or her portfolio. The investor can fine-tune the portfolio to hold the exact amount of large stocks, small stocks, and international stocks he or she wants, without overlap or overweightings.

Investment in Alternative Asset Classes

Finally, ETFs offer another big benefit for individual investors—the ability to buy *alternative asset classes* as easily as stocks. This benefit doesn't easily roll off the tongue of the person advocating ETFs, but it may be the biggest boon to individual investors since the creation of the original ETF.

In the past, commodity and currency markets were difficult for individual investors to enter. But as the world economy changes, these asset classes have taken on greater significance. To not have the opportunity to take advantage of these asset classes is a severe disadvantage to small investors. But companies using the ETF structure have given the investor the ability to participate in these markets with the same ease and minimal investment as the ETF itself.

With increased demand for gold, oil, and other commodities, as well as foreign currencies, investors have more tools with which to create more diversified portfolios.

One Caveat

For all the laudatory benefits of ETFs, in some cases mutual funds may actually be preferred. ETFs have one big drawback: the price of admission. Because they trade like stocks, they can only be bought or sold through a stockbroker, who, of course, charges a commission. Even with a discount broker, these transaction costs can eat into principle, making ETFs prohibitively expensive for adherents of *dollar-cost averaging*, one of the mainstay strategies for *long-term investing*.

While mutual funds sold through brokers carry commissions, known as loads, savvy investors know to stay clear of those and invest in no-load funds. With no-loads, every investment dollar lands in the fund and not in a broker's pocket, maximizing the investment. And no-loads don't charge a fee to sell. So dollar-cost averaging remains the index funds' ace in the hole.

Summary

ETFs aren't only for the big boys anymore. They offer buy-and-hold investors many benefits over regular index mutual funds.

This book is written for the average buy-and-hold investor: the man or woman who takes care of their individual or family's investments. It will make the case for why ETFs are the mutual funds for the twenty-first century, and the best investment vehicles currently available for individual investors. The theme of the book is that mutual funds are good, but ETFs are even better.

The following chapters will help the individual investor understand mutual funds and ETFs from the bottom up. Even if you don't create your own portfolio, investors need a clear understanding of what they are buying and why. Chapter 3, "The Evolution of the ETF," will explain the similarities between ETFs and mutual funds and describe the benefits they both provide over buying single-company stocks. Chapter 4, "Index Fund-amentals," will advocate for indexing as an investment strategy, by explaining the advantages of investing in indexes over actively managed portfolios. This will lead to Chapter 5, "Fee Bitten," a deeper examination of how fees hurt returns and why investors should always look for the lowest cost alternative. Once you have seen the effect that fees have on profits, the book will examine the nuts and bolts of mutual funds and ETFs. Chapter 6, "The Better Mousetrap," shows how the ETF achieves its greater efficiencies. Finally, Chapter 8, "The ETFs That Aren't ETFs," will examine the new exchange-traded vehicles that are similar to ETFs, and highlight the important differences between them. In the end you should have a greater understanding of these kinds of investments, both their benefits and their costs. The book will then explain how to build your own ETF portfolio, from the mechanics of trading to designing asset allocation strategies.

Sometimes, the most important factor in understanding something is to gain insight into how something came about and what contributed to its current form. Your journey starts with the history of the ETF, who the industry leaders are, and how they got there. Chapter 2, "ETF History Lesson," will cover the ETF industry's first ten years. Chapter 7, "The New Indexers," will examine the main drivers of the industry's incredible growth since 2003. The book ends with an analysis of the main issues that will affect the industry in the future.

CHAPTER 2

ETF History Lesson

How a New Type of Fund Was Born

The history of the exchange-traded fund begins with the stock market crash of 1987.

On October 19, 1987, better known as Black Monday, the Dow Jones Industrial Average plummeted 508 points, or 22.61 percent, to 1,738.74. With a loss of $500 billion in assets, it was the largest one-day crash in U.S. stock market history.

> *While Black Monday was the biggest stock market crash in the U.S., it was only the second largest one-day percentage drop in the Dow Jones Industrial Average. Nor did that occur in the Stock Market Crash of 1929. That crash started Black Thursday, October 28, 1929, with the Dow tumbling 12.82%. The next day it sank 11.73%. Together, that two-day drop decimated 23.1% of the Dow's value. The Dow's largest percentage decline actually occurred Saturday, December 12, 1914, when it plunged 24.39%. That day the stock market opened for the first time since the outbreak of World War I, five months earlier.[1]*

There are competing theories about why the U.S. market crashed. I won't go into those. Whatever the catalyst was, the result was the same: Once investors heard that the market was falling, they panicked. Everyone wanted to sell simultaneously. This triggered the program trading: computerized signals programmed by arbitrageurs to create sell orders at certain prices in the market. The program trading flooded the market with more sell orders, exacerbating an already bad decline. Prices plummeted. The plunge spread, causing stock markets around the world to collapse.

"It's really the first time that Johnny Retail realized that when he sells his mutual fund he doesn't get out until the end of the day," said Bob Tull, a member of the team that created the first international ETFs.[2]

Up until that moment, retail investors didn't comprehend that the fund's price, the net asset value (NAV), is calculated on the close. On the day of the 1987 crash, everyone who tried to sell their funds thought they would get out when they called the broker. Only later did they realize that they got the price at the end of the day, after all the stocks had fallen. The funds structure locked the retail investor ("Johnny Retail") into the worst price of the day.

While everyone lost money in the crash, retail investors ate the biggest losses. The institutional investors—pension funds, insurance companies, university endowments, and any other large investors—got out intraday. But most small investors were in mutual funds, many within a 401(k) plan. Unable to access their money until after the damage had been done, they suffered the most. None of this should have surprised anyone: Wall Street hadn't been created for the investor. It was created for the banks to make a profit from other people's money.

The story of the ETF is one of competition, redemption, and comeuppance. It's about how the American Stock Exchange, suffering a long, slow, debilitating decline in business, reversed what many considered a terminal situation by devising the small investor's revenge for the '87 Crash. It's the story of how a financial invention put "Johnny Retail" on the same level playing field with the institutional investors. It not only gave the retail fund investors the freedom to trade when they wanted, but also charged the same low fees the institutions paid to buy and sell large baskets of stock. Finally, it's a tale of how Wall Street ignored the product because it didn't pay enough to sell it. In spite of that, the ETF became one of the market's hottest products because it benefited the small investor.

Four months after the crash, the Securities and Exchange Commission (SEC) issued a report analyzing the market's fall. The SEC euphemistically called the crash "The October 1987 Market Break." In the February 1988 report, the SEC raised the question: What would have happened if there was a market-basket instrument that could have absorbed the shock to the individual securities underlying the Standard & Poor's 500 Index (S&P 500)? The SEC added that if an exchange did propose a market-basket instrument based on the S&P 500, it would receive a quick approval.

Nathan Most, the senior vice president for new product development at the American Stock Exchange (Amex), viewed this as an invitation to design a market-basket security. Over the previous decade, Most had been creating products for the Amex to trade. During most of the 1980s, the Amex had been losing market share in equities to heavy competition. Most's team focused on creating customized securities called *derivatives*, especially options. Futures and options are derivatives because their value is based on the value of an underlying asset without actually owning that asset. Futures are a promise to buy or sell a specific commodity or security at a specific price on a predetermined date. Options are the right to buy or sell an investment at a certain date for a preset price. These products sliced and diced the underlying assets, and repackaged them in a way that changed the investment's risk-and-return profile. In the end, it was a way of transferring the underlying risk elsewhere. There were some successes, but many ideas ran afoul of the regulators and were short-lived. But now the regulators at the SEC were requesting new market baskets; it seemed like a gift to the Amex.

"We began work on it the next day," said Steven Bloom.[3]

At the time, Bloom was the Amex's vice president of new product development and Most's right-hand man. With a Harvard Ph.D. in economics, Bloom came to the Amex in 1985 to learn from Most. He was only 26 years old. By 1992 *Worth* magazine named Bloom one of Wall Street's rocket scientists, a group of bright young derivative makers who fed investment banks a steady diet of synthetic securities to trade. It didn't hurt that he worked for a man whom *Worth* called one of Wall Street's original financial wizards.[4]

A Short History of the Amex

Originally called the Curb Exchange, the American Stock Exchange began as an outdoor market around the same time as the New York Stock Exchange (NYSE). The NYSE traces its beginning to the signing of the Buttonwood Agreement in May 1792. Underneath a buttonwood tree on Wall Street, 24 prominent brokers and firms agreed to trade securities for a commission, giving preference to one another over other brokers. The five securities traded were three government bonds and two bank stocks.

Historian Stuart Bruchey describes how the meeting "organized a broker's guild, whose major function was to exclude nonmembers and maintain rates while minimizing competition."[5] With the price of membership too high for most small dealers, "the exchange was virtually restricted to the wealthy members of the city's financial establishment."[6]

The Buttonwood Agreement brokers soon moved indoors to a local coffeehouse. By 1817, the group became the New York Stock & Exchange Board, also known as the Big Board, a forerunner of the New York Stock Exchange. Meanwhile, the brokers who couldn't afford to join the Big Board, for financial or other reasons, continued to trade in the open air just down the street. They became known as the curbstone brokers, because they traded at the "Curb" market.

With high standards for listing and trading, and an emphasis on respectability, the conservative NYSE shied away from new industries. Thus, the Curb earned its niche by functioning as the "proving ground for new securities."[7] Many of the stocks that proved themselves eventually graduated to the NYSE. Therefore, the Curb needed to constantly replenish its listings.

As the market for everything not traded on the Big Board, the Curb became known as the place for small and midsized companies and for entrepreneurial innovation. With the NYSE's narrow view of what constituted a respectable industry, the Curb by the late 1800s was the main market for the most exciting companies in the United States. Most of the mining and petroleum companies in America started trading on the Curb. So did a growing group of manufacturers, who would later become known as the industrials.

It wasn't until the founding of the New York Curb Market in 1911 that the curbstone group became an organized exchange. The Curb was no longer simply a place, but an actual organization with a constitution. Yet the traders still traded outdoors, in all kinds of weather, on the corner of Broad Street and Exchange Place. It was characterized as the "Broad Street Jungle" because telephone clerks hung out of the windows of the surrounding office buildings giving buy or sell hand signals to the brokers on the street. "To make it easier for a clerk to pick out his broker in the milling crowd below, each broker wore some distinctive article of clothing—a colorful jacket or an unusual hat," writes historian Stuart Bruchey.[8]

In 1921, the market finally moved inside to 113 Greenwich Street, five blocks away from the NYSE. By the end of the 1920s, the newly named New York Curb Exchange had become the second-largest exchange in the United States. The building expanded to 86 Trinity Place, its current address, in the 1930s. In 1953, the market changed its name to the American Stock Exchange.

But by 1987, the Amex was the nation's third-largest stock exchange—a distant third, too. It had lost a significant amount of market share to an electronic market, the National Association of Securities Dealers Automated Quotations system, better known as the NASDAQ. The NASDAQ was privately owned by the National Association of Securities Dealers, or NASD, a self-regulating organization responsible for the operation and regulation of the NASDAQ and over-the-counter markets.

The NASDAQ, which owns and operates the NASDAQ Stock Market, went public in 2002. It trades under the ticker NDAQ. In July 2007, NASD, which had created and continued to regulate the NASDAQ, and the New York Stock Exchange's regulation, enforcement, and arbitration operations merged to become the Financial Industry Regulatory Authority, or FINRA. When it commenced operations, FINRA was the largest nongovernmental regulatory organization for the U.S. securities industry.[9]

When Black Monday occurred, the NASDAQ was eating the Amex's lunch in terms of equity listings. It was beginning to make the Amex look irrelevant. The catalyst for the Amex's downturn was governmental. A decade earlier, Congress and the SEC began deregulating the securities industry to make it more competitive. This sparked a battle for company listings. The NASDAQ, an electronics version of the over-the-counter market, became the prime beneficiary.

The over-the-counter market refers to stocks that don't list on one of the exchanges. Stocks are typically "unlisted" because they don't meet an exchange's listing requirements. These stocks trade through a dealer network, in which people trade over the phone or by computer, rather than on a formal centralized exchange. While the NASDAQ is a dealer network with no physical trading floor, it is now considered a formal U.S. stock exchange. Nor does the NASDAQ trade over-the-counter stocks any longer. All the stocks that trade on the NASDAQ Stock Market are listed because they meet the NASDAQ's trading requirements.

Many of the small and innovative companies that in the past made up the Amex's bread and butter, were now flocking to the NASDAQ, especially companies in the newly developed personal computer and technology sectors.

At the end of 1973, the NASDAQ's second full year of operations, the Amex listed 1,292 companies. Ten years later the NASDAQ's volume surpassed the Amex's. According to NASDAQ, total share volume on the NASDAQ Stock Market in 1983 equaled 4.405 billion shares versus 2.081 billion shares on the Amex. The next year, the NASDAQ topped the Amex in the total number of listed companies.

By the end of 1984, 1,166 companies traded on the NASDAQ, while the Amex had just 792, a 39 percent decline from 1973. Fewer companies meant less revenue. Exchanges mostly make their money from listing fees and a percentage of the amount traded during the day. From $137.9 million in 1980, the Amex's average daily trading volume fell 22 percent to $107.2 million in 1985. Over the same time period, the NASDAQ's average trading volume surged 231 percent to $899.1 million.[10]

"The Amex's future is uncertain," the *Wall Street Journal* reported on July 2, 1985. The "coming months will help determine whether the Amex can survive as an independent institution."[11]

The Amex blamed the listing losses on companies it kicked off the exchange for failing to meet its listing standards as well as companies combining in the mergers-and-acquisition craze of the 1980s. While the number of new listings the Amex acquired stayed flat from year to year, the number of companies graduating to the NYSE grew, sorely highlighting the Amex's inability to attract new names.[12]

"There is doubt about the Amex's future as an independent exchange even within high circles at the Amex," the *Wall Street Journal* noted in the same article. It even quoted an anonymous member of the exchange's board of governors saying, "I think one has to wonder whether the Amex has the critical mass of product and support to continue going forward."[13] The idea of a merger with the New York Stock Exchange actually floated about, but the NYSE nixed that.

Years later, Richard Syron, then the Amex's chief executive officer, put this period in perspective. "The world changed in the late 1970s and early 1980s and we didn't change," he told the *Wall Street Journal* in March 1998. Once NASDAQ "started to grow and particularly developed this tie to the high-tech community, we had to think more carefully about why someone should come to the Amex." Syron acknowledged that in the early 1980s the Amex had dropped the ball competitively.[14]

Even during these down days, the Amex was always profitable. While it didn't have the sex appeal of the NASDAQ or the cache of the NYSE, it still had its reputation for innovation and new securities. Back when it started losing stock listings, the Amex jumped into the stock-option trading business. In 1975, its first year as an options market, the Amex traded 3.5 million options contracts. By the end of 1985, that number had soared to 48.6 million. This kept the Amex in the black, but in the early 1980s, profits alternated between up and down years.

After the Amex grabbed a significant amount of business from the main options market, the Chicago Board Options Exchange (CBOE), *Newsday* in 1986 called the thriving options unit the Amex's "crown jewel."[15] It was during this time that Nate Most invented a popular options contract called the Major Market Index. It tracked an index of blue-chip stocks similar to the Dow Jones Industrial Average.

"To say we were in dire straits would be an incorrect statement," said Joe Stefanelli, who worked in the exchange's options business at the time. Shortly after the launch of the first ETF, he became the Amex's executive vice president of derivative securities. "As far as the people involved in the options part of the business, we were doing extremely well. The Amex was profitable in those days. But, I can't say we were really growing as an exchange. Clearly, the ETFs put the Amex on the map. No question about that."[16]

During the two years before the 1987 crash, the stock market surged. The rising tide lifted all boats. The Amex saw listings rise by 39 percent in 1986 and 48 percent in 1987. But the year after the crash, equities resumed their downward trend. While the equities business declined, the options business blossomed and kept the exchange afloat.

Bloom acknowledged that even at its peak, the Amex "[was] number two as a stock market and number two as an options market. We were never number one."[17]

The Father of the ETF

Even in the mid-1970s, it wasn't hard to see the writing on the wall. As the number of equity listings declined, the Amex realized it needed new products to trade. With the success of the options business, the exchange decided to enter the commodities market. In 1977, it hired Nathan Most to be the director of Commodity Options Development.

Most's career took a circuitous path to the Amex. After studying physics at the University of California, Los Angeles (UCLA) in the 1930s, Most sold acoustic tiles in Asia. During World War II, he worked on submarine acoustics as a civilian scientist in the Navy, and joined the team that developed sonar. After the war he returned to the acoustic tile business before becoming an international commodities trader, first at Pacific Vegetable Oil from 1965 to 1970, and then with the American Import Company from 1970 to 1974. He helped found the Pacific Commodities Exchange in 1970 and was its president from 1974 to 1976. When the call came from the Amex in 1976, he was in Washington, D.C., working as the technical assistant to the chairman of the Commodities Futures Trading Commission. He was 62 years old.

At an age when most men would be retiring, Most began creating new products for the Amex. His first foray was the Amex Commodities Exchange. It lasted just two years. In 1983, he created the Major Market Index.

When the SEC's February 1988 report came out, Most was a spry 74-year-old. Drawing upon his commodities background, he brought a new mind-set to the equities world. Bloom recalls that Most asked the product development team, "Why can't we, in the security industry, create a warehouse receipt, which would be backed by the underlying stock in the index but trade like a share of stock itself?"[18]

The concept of the warehouse receipt is derived from the commodities world. Unlike stocks and bonds, which are simply paper backed by the word of the company and the investor's faith in that word, commodities are tangible objects, such as pork bellies, precious metals, or crude oil. They take up space. The entity that owns the physical commodity needs to store them somewhere, such as a warehouse.

A commodity contract represents a basket of one specific commodity. The typical transaction is that a commodities investor trades a commodity's futures contract for the promise to buy or sell the commodity at a certain price on a certain day in the future. Let's assume the futures contract is for 100 barrels of oil on June 21. The investor must close his futures position before it expires. Otherwise, he literally takes possession of all that oil. If this occurs, he has to pay transportation costs and storage costs in addition to the costs of selling the commodity. The warehouse receipt lists where the commodity is stored, how much the future is worth, and the day and price at which the contract expires.

Because options and futures change hands often, a lot of people can own one for a short period of time. It's understood that commodities traders trade warehouse receipts and not the underlying physical commodity.

"You store a commodity and you get a warehouse receipt and you can finance on that warehouse receipt," Most said in an interview years later. "You can sell it, do a lot of things with it. Because you don't want to be moving the merchandise back and forth all the time, so you keep it in place and you simply transfer the warehouse receipt."[19]

As a former commodity trader, Most was very familiar with the concept. He wondered why the market couldn't produce a warehouse receipt for a basket of stocks.

"We realized the best we could do in [stock] listings in those days was to list Volkswagen," said Bloom. "But, we could engineer Ferraris like the Spider. We realized that by engineering a new class of instruments for the Amex, we could repopularize the Amex with that new product."[20]

Bloom jokingly likened Most's query to President John F. Kennedy challenging the space industry to put a man on the moon by the end of the 1960s. Perhaps it was not that dramatic, but the development took nearly as long. It was six years before the exchange had identified and solved every hurdle the SEC came up with, including legal, operational, and marketing infrastructure.

Philly Strikes First

The Amex team was stunned when just one month after the SEC's February 1988 report, the Philadelphia Stock Exchange was the first to accept its invitation. Founded in 1790, two years before the NYSE, Philadelphia was the nation's oldest stock exchange. And, like the Amex, it had been losing business.

Over the previous four years, the Philadelphia Stock Exchange had been working on a single investment vehicle that could participate in overall stock market movements. In March 1988, it applied for approval to trade its new product, the Cash Index Participation contracts, or CIP shares. The CIPs were designed to allow investors to buy or sell an index of stocks in the same manner that they would buy or sell individual shares of stock. The CIPs, which held each stock in the same proportion as the index, were intended to last indefinitely and paid dividends from the underlying stocks in the index.

The first two CIPs tracked the S&P 500 and a portfolio similar to the Dow Jones Industrial Average. The Options Clearing Corp. was the issuer.

Meanwhile, back at the Amex, the launch of the CIPs immediately halted work on the warehouse receipt project, said Bloom. Nate Most had the entire product development team turn their focus to index participations.

Within two months the American Stock Exchange and the Chicago Board Options Exchange (CBOE) both filed similar products with the SEC. Like the CIPs, the Amex's Equity Index Participations (EIPs) were "designed to provide investors the opportunity to take a long-term position in an entire stock index with a single investment," said the Amex. The EIPs also received quarterly cash dividends.

The CBOE called its product Value of Index Participations (VIPs). These too were "designed to allow investors to participate in the performance of the portfolio of stock that make up the indexes," according to documents from that time. These were to benefit from lower transaction costs associated with cash-settled index options. Also designed not to expire, the VIPs give shareholders cash payments equal to a "proportionate share of any regular cash dividends," according the CBOE's statement.

On the face of it, all three sound very similar to an ETF. Actually, not only were they cheaper than mutual funds, but they would also have cost less than a comparable ETF because they didn't hold any physical shares. It was just the promise of the short position to pay the holder of the long position. On top of that, brokerage houses used the same commission schedules that they applied to options, cutting the cost to about 90 percent of what one would pay to trade a stock, wrote *BusinessWeek* in 1989.[21]

But a month later, June 1988, the Chicago Mercantile Exchange (CME), the largest futures exchange in the world, and the Chicago Board of Trade (CBOT), the world's oldest futures and options exchange, filed formal objections with the SEC. Index futures traded on their exchanges and they weren't pleased with the prospective competition. They argued that these new products weren't securities, but actually badly disguised stock-index futures that should be traded on their markets. As such, they felt the Commodity Futures Trading Commission (CFTC) should regulate the new products, not the SEC.*

By December 1988 everyone was piling on. The Investment Company Institute, the mutual fund industry's trade group, said index participation shares should be considered funds under the U.S. Investment Company Act of 1940 ('40 Act). The CFTC reiterated its position that these were futures and that it should regulate them. And the Philly Exchange asked the SEC for a 12 to 18 month monopoly in trading the CIPs because they were the first to present the idea.

---

*In July 2007, the 109-year-old Chicago Mercantile Exchange and the 159-year-old Chicago Board of Trade agreed to merge.

The SEC rejected the CFTC's argument. On March 14, 1989, it unanimously approved the controversial products. That same day, the two futures exchanges, the CME and the CBOT, sued the SEC in the U.S. Court of Appeals of Chicago.

On May 12, 1989, over the objections of the futures markets, the Philadelphia Stock Exchange and the American Stock Exchange each launched their index participation products. That first day, 42,595 contracts of the Amex EIPs traded, compared with just 545 contracts of the CIPs in Philadelphia. The Amex announced that the EIPs had the highest first-day volume for any new derivative securities product in the previous 20 years.[22] The VIPs were never launched.

Obviously annoyed that the CIPs weren't as popular as the EIPs, within a week the Philly Exchange filed a cease and desist letter, accusing the Amex of violating its copyright.

"They just photocopied our application," Nicholas Giordana, the president of the Philadelphia Stock Exchange later told *BusinessWeek*.[23]

Bloom acknowledged that the Amex used the Philly Exchange's product as the basis for the Amex's EIPs. But, he added that the Amex crew pushed the product one step forward with a substantial modification to the design: a physical delivery feature.[24] The CIPs only gave back cash, not stock; the Amex EIPs provided both. If an investor was long the EIPs and elected to close his position, he would receive the physical basket of stocks from the investor who held the short position. This delivery of a physical basket equal to a cash basket became the foundation for the ETF's creation unit.

Then, just as quickly as it started, it was all over.

On August 19, 1989, the U.S. Court of Appeals for the Seventh Circuit ruled that the SEC had overstepped its jurisdiction by calling the index participation products "shares" of stock. The court set aside the SEC's approval for the new financial instruments and said the CFTC should regulate them. However, none of the futures exchanges wanted to list the index participation shares. They already had stock-index futures.

Therefore, the stock exchanges had to stop trading them. Delisted that month, the index participation shares died an early death.

Calling the lawsuit "a turf battle between commodities and securities regulators," the *Financial Times* lamented that the products stopped trading, not because they were faulty or failed to satisfy investors' needs, but "in essence, the court banned trading because of an old border dispute between the SEC and the CFTC." Considering the court was in Chicago, many were not surprised by the outcome.

The index participants survived just three months. During their short run, they showed there was an appetite for such a product. It would be another four years before the Spider, the first true ETF, was launched.

Back to the Drawing Board

The day after the EIPs delisted, according to Steven Bloom, the Amex product development crew resumed work on the warehouse-receipt project. The Amex's EIPs had one major benefit over the Philly Exchange's CIPs. While the CIPS could only be redeemed in cash, the EIPS could be redeemed in either cash or physical delivery of the index's underlying stocks. With the enormous popularity of the EIPs over the CIPs, the Amex team realized the ability to receive the underlying shares was essential to the new product.

"We knew there had to be a basket that would take in the stock and track the index," said Bloom.[25]

Because they didn't hold physical shares, the EIPs were cheaper than the ETFs would end up being. No shares meant there was no need for either a custodian to hold the underlying securities, or a portfolio manager to ensure that the holdings tracked the index. Hence, no custodial or management fees were incurred.

EIPs were promises by the seller to pay the index performance to the buyers backed by deposits held in a clearinghouse. However, the Amex team decided to make the warehouse-receipt product *fully collateralized*. This meant that the receipts were backed by actual stocks, making them safer investments. It also enormously widened the net of potential investors by making them acceptable to an audience that could only invest in fully collateralized securities. Then the SEC told them it was more comfortable with the framework of a unit investment trust (UIT) than a mutual fund. (For a description of a UIT, see Chapter 3.)

Most and Bloom started shopping the idea around to Wall Street's custody banks. These banks provide the custody and processing of shares and cash, as well as short-term securities-lending services. Choosing the right company was essential. Much like a warehouse that held a commodity, the custodian was the warehouse that held the actual shares of stock in the fund. So, the ETF shares, or the warehouse-receipt, represented a quantity of stock held by the custodian. And because the unmanaged UIT structure was chosen, unlike a mutual fund, there was no asset manager. So, the custodian held a more prominent role in the ETF than in a mutual fund.

Four custodians expressed interest in the project: State Street, the Bank of New York, Bankers Trust, and Morgan Guarantee. The competition was steep. Wells Fargo had created the first index fund and was the industry leader. However, State Street's investment management arm, which would become State Street Global Advisors, ran some of the leading S&P 500 index funds in the country. Meanwhile, the Bank of New York was top notch in UITs.

The reason Wells Fargo was not in the running was wacky. It came down to money (of course, this is Wall Street). Money was the issue, not because Wells Fargo charged too much, but because the Amex thought it too expensive to do business with them. The Bank of New York, Bankers Trust, and Morgan Guarantee were all on Wall Street. State Street was in Boston. But Wells Fargo was in San Francisco. Bloom recalled that the simple but brutal reason Wells Fargo lost out was because the plane tickets to the West Coast were simply too expensive.

"We never went to Wells Fargo. We never contacted them because we recognized if we did end up working with them it would be expensive to go there," said Bloom. "It's not that the Amex couldn't afford it, but it wasn't a necessary expense. We were very prudent about how we spent the resources. We didn't feel the added expense to travel to California every time we wanted to meet with them was necessary."[26]

This is ironic, considering that Wells Fargo's index business was later bought by Barclays Global Investors (BGI). BGI's ETF family, the iShares, dominates the industry today. One wonders how different the industry would be today if Wells Fargo had launched the first ETF.

Most and Bloom first went to the Bank of New York. It wasn't far. The Bank of New York sits at the corner of Broadway and Wall Street, facing the Amex over the Trinity Church cemetery. They could have run a phone line straight over the cemetery from the exchange to the bank.

The men from the Amex told the people at Bank of New York that they were creating a listed product, a depositary receipt based on the Standard & Poor's 500 Index. The product team at Bank of New York took one look at it and said "It's a UIT." Bank of New York had a strong UIT business back then. By 2007, it controlled 98 percent of the market.

Bank of New York's UIT team took a look at it. They said "This isn't really a UIT. It lists on an exchange. It's more like a depositary receipt." They sent the product draft to its department for American Depositary Receipts (ADRs), foreign securities that trade in the United States. The ADR team determined that it wasn't a foreign stock; it was a domestic stock. They sent it to the mutual fund division, which said it wasn't a fund, but rather a UIT.

"The product was neither fish nor fowl," said Joseph Keenan, managing director at Bank of New York Mellon,* "These were all separate businesses and it created just enough confusion that we couldn't figure out the right home for the product. It took us a couple of weeks to get a hold on it, and by the time we did, State Street, who clearly understood what was required, got the mandate."[27]

Most and Bloom thought State Street would be the ideal company not only because it was a large index holder, but also because of the man running the index shop. Early in 1990, the two men from the Amex went

---

*The Bank of New York Co. and Mellon Financial Corp. merged in July 2007.

to Boston to meet Doug Holmes, the head of the U.S. passive equity department in what later became known as State Street Global Advisors. He immediately saw the product's potential and enthusiastically said he wanted in on the project.

"They wanted to have some experience at managing index funds," said Holmes, currently a Strategic Advisor at Rydex Funds. "As they talked I got very excited about the concept. I recognized it was more than just a portfolio management issue. It would have to include the rest of State Street in terms of administration, custody and the other services we had."[28] Holmes rounded up the folks from each department and introduced them to the men from the Amex.

Holmes completely understood the concept Most and Bloom wanted to achieve. Not only did he help design the product, but he contributed greatly to its success by championing the product throughout the bank.

Over the next three long years, State Street and the Amex had to make the SEC comfortable with the idea. Because it had never been done before, it was a long, drawn-out process with many hurdles to jump. A big reason it took so long was the decision to set up the ETF as a '40-Act investment company and not as a futures-like product. They wanted the ETF's share to trade on the stock exchange like shares of a closed-end fund. But they didn't like the idea of a limited number of shares. They wanted the ability to create and redeem an unlimited amount of shares in the manner of a mutual fund. But mutual fund shares don't trade on the exchange. In the end, the team filed for a variety of exemptions from the '40 Act in order to operate the ETF in this manner. They also needed relief from the Securities Exchange Act of 1934 (1934 Act) for various trading prohibitions, such as shorting fund shares.

During this time three other basket-of-securities products came out. Just months after the demise of the index participation shares, the NYSE answered the SEC's challenge with the Exchange Stock Portfolios (ESP). And it made sure the product was classified as a security, not a future. These baskets of all the stocks in the S&P 500 launched October 1989. Like the Amex, the NYSE realized the product needed to hold the actual stocks in the index. But Wall Street's securities firms gave it a poor reception.

While it sounds like an ETF, there was one humongous difference: the price. The smallest trade in an ESP was $5 million. Only nine ESP contracts, valued at $45 million, traded the first day.[29] By limiting the product to only the largest financial institutions, the NYSE starved it of the liquidity needed to trade. Trading never picked up, and two years later it was dead. The ESP's contribution to the ETF was the exemption from the "uptick rule." That rule mandates stocks must be at a price higher than the previous trade before they can be sold short. The ESP eliminated that restriction and could be sold short as the market moved lower.

March 1990 saw the launch of the Toronto 35 Index Participation Units, or TIPS, on the Toronto Stock Exchange (TSE). The TIPS tracked the Toronto Stock Exchange 35 Index, which held 35 of Canada's largest companies. It was soon followed by the Hundred Index Participation Units, or HIPS. This tracked the Toronto Stock Exchange 100 Index. Some people consider these the first true ETFs, and the Spider the first U.S. ETF. While the two products were popular among Canadian institutional investors, they weren't actively supported by the Toronto exchange. They never captured the imagination of individual investors and the industry didn't grow for many years. One important difference is that the TIPS and HIPS, investment trusts similar to the UIT, were responsible for buying and selling their underlying shares. So, they didn't have the "in-kind" transfer that became central to the ETF's success in the United States. The Spider advanced the product and cut its expenses by transferring that responsibility to an outside broker-dealer. In March 2000, the TIPS and HIPS merged into one product, the S&P/TSE 60 iUnits (i60) ETF, which is run by Barclays Global Investors.

The Super Trusts, also called Super Shares, came out in 1992. They, too, were baskets of securities based on the S&P 500. The Super Trusts moved one step closer to the ETF by getting the SEC to approve more exemptions from the '40 Act. But the Super Trusts had two big strikes against them. The first was that they were created by a risk-management firm called Leland, O'Brien & Rubenstein (LOR). In the years prior to the 1987 crash, this firm sold a product called portfolio insurance. It was supposed to protect investors in a market downturn by using a strategy called program trading. This strategy called for buy-and-sell trades, or stop-loss orders, to be entered into a computer. Should a stock fall below the sell order's price, the computer would automatically sell. Portfolio insurance didn't protect investors in the crash. It made things worse. It flooded the falling market with large numbers of sell orders. Many blamed Leland, O'Brien & Rubenstein for the size of the crash. So, when LOR called the Super Trusts a new portfolio protection product, investors were wary. In addition to the marketing hurdle, the product was extremely complicated to use, to such an extent that it's not even worth describing them.

It's not easy to get exemptions from the SEC. The Amex's new product needed even more exemptions than its predecessors, novel exemptions that had never been granted before. The exchange hired Sam Scott Miller, a partner at Orrick, Herrington & Sutcliffe, one of the nation's top securities law firms. Miller said that many at the firm told him it would be impossible to get the SEC to grant the exemptions, but he thought his request to be perfectly reasonable. So did Marianne Smythe, the SEC's top regulator of mutual funds and investment advisers at the time. Smythe, director of SEC's Investment Management division, understood what Miller wanted to do. However, the SEC's division of Corporation Finance concluded that the creation unit process made the broker-dealers into stock underwriters. And every time the SEC didn't like something, the Amex product group had to go back to the drawing board.

"The conclusion was not without logic," said Miller. "I was concerned and the Amex was concerned that the liability attached to being an under-writer would spook a lot of brokers from getting involved. We spent a lot of time negotiating the description of how a broker-dealer could break down a creation unit into Spider shares without being deemed an underwriter. There's one paragraph in the prospectus that cost half a million dollars in legal time."[30]

Working alongside Miller to get the exemptions were two young women lawyers: Terry Smith, and Kathleen Moriarty, who was later dubbed the SpiderWoman for super heroine effort. Miller said it was a simple concept that had to be shoehorned into a statute, the '40 Act, which had been created at a time when nothing like ETFs existed. He described the process as two steps forward, one step back.

"We were constantly seeing how far we could push things before the SEC got hung up on the details," said Holmes. "We knew it couldn't take forever to come out. So some of the decisions were to recognize that there was only so far you could go in a one-time leap from the existing products already out there."[31]

In order to make them cheaper than index funds, the project team brought in accounting teams to help design the most tax efficient product.

"Suppose it worked from the program trading side, but for whatever reason it didn't work well into the tax code," said Bob Tull, who would work in the Amex's ETF department from 2000 to 2005. "Then those securities would never have come out. Those two things together are what make them so important."[32]

The team realized they had entered head-to-head competition with the largest, most famous index fund in the world, the Vanguard 500 Index Fund, which also tracked the S&P 500. They knew that the ETF couldn't be more expensive. The Vanguard 500 was charging 0.2 percent at the time, and that became the goal for the first ETF's management fee.

Holmes said that when the SEC first decided the ETF should be a UIT, the project development team liked the idea. Unlike mutual funds, UITs don't need an asset manager or board of directors. Both would have made the ETF costlier, and they needed to cut every expense they could. An interesting attribute of the UIT structure is a limited lifetime. Although the ETF was originally designed to be closed and liquidated after 25 years, the product team amended the lifespan to 125 years.

The ETF had one big advantage over the Vanguard 500 and its pre-decessors: It had no minimum purchase requirement. Even the Vanguard fund required an initial investment of $3,000. Unfortunately, it had a big dis-advantage too. The ETF would sell through stockbrokers. Therefore every purchase incurred a commission. The Vanguard 500 was, and is, a no-load fund. Investors don't pay to invest in it and dividends are reinvested without cost. Still, when the development was done, State Street and the Amex felt confident they had created a magnificent product.

Along Came a Spider

When the traders entered the trading floor of the American Stock Exchange on Jan 29, 1993, a nine-foot inflatable spider dangled from the ceiling. Amid much fanfare, PDR Services, a wholly-owned subsidiary of the Amex, launched the Standard & Poor's Depositary Receipt (symbol: SPY). State Street Global Advisors was the trustee and custodian, a position that it holds today. The fund held all 500 stocks in the Standard & Poor's 500 Index in the exact same weighting. With the initials SPDR, it acquired the nickname Spider, often spelled Spyder as a play on its ticker symbol.

The launch was underwhelming. Opening at one-tenth the value of the S&P 500's January 28 close, or $43.87, it gained seven cents, or 0.1 percent, to $43.94. More than one million shares traded hands that day.

The Amex and State Street were ecstatic with the reception. For years they had battled critics who said no one would invest in the SPDR. They felt vindicated for their enthusiasm and confidence that the product could successfully compete with mutual funds. But in the year that followed, the declining volume disappointed them.

The next trading day, the SPDR climbed to $44.25, but volume dropped to 480,500 shares. On the third day of trading, volume fell to 201,300 shares. By February 11, volume had sunk as low as 19,500 shares for the whole day.

The volume fell so low that just three months after the launch the Amex considered delisting it. In spite of all the time and resources expended on it, it had hardly any assets under management.

"Few people realized that the product almost died in the birthing process," said Bloom. "The May 1989 launch of the index participations was much more successful than the launch of the SPDR."[33]

According to Bloom, in April 1993, Amex officials created a swat team of Bloom and Jay Baker, vice president of marketing. Their mission was to design a marketing plan to save the product from being liquidated. After identifying every benefit the product offered and what it added to the investing space, they implemented a marketing plan that remains to this day the script for how ETFs are sold. For the rest of the year, Bloom and Baker went to the major financial institutions and wire houses to persuade them to promote the new product.

"The equity desks didn't want to trade it because it wasn't a stock," said Bloom. "The mutual funds didn't want to sell it because it had no load. And the options desks didn't want to handle it, because it wasn't an option. It was a square peg in a round hole. We literally had to go around and ask the major wire houses how they would handle the market for this new class of security."[34]

"And several big wire houses said 'We won't trade them because it won't make us any money without a sales load.' They had no incentive to sell these things," recalled Moriarty. "But eventually people went to the online discount brokers and started buying shares themselves. That was when the big brokers started to really sell them. I love the SPDRs because people on Wall Street always say nothing is ever bought, it's all sold. But that's not true. The SPDRs were bought."[35]

At the end of 1993, the SPDR had a half-billion dollars in assets under management. It was an incredible achievement. They had entered head-to-head competition with the largest index fund in the world in a year the benchmark index rose only 7 percent.

While the SPDR was useful to day traders and other retail investors, they made up only about 15 percent of the trading volume. But institutional investors quickly saw its potential. The SPDR became the cash management tool of choice for many large investors. The sell-side investment banks used it in their trading activity as a hedging vehicle. Soon portfolio managers, including many mutual funds, used the SPDR to maintain full exposure to the market and avoid cash drag.

Typically mutual funds managers hold a little cash in the portfolio. This way the fund can quickly pay shareholders who want to redeem their funds without selling part of the funds' holdings, which upsets the portfolio's composition and incurs taxable capital gains for the fund. But holding cash creates a drag on returns. If the market rallies, the stocks in the portfolio rise in value—but not the cash. It remains the same value, dragging down the portfolio's return. However, now a fund manager could, at the beginning of the day, put cash into the SPDR, catch the market's move, then sell before the market's close. And he would still have cash to pay the shareholder sales clocked that day. Yet, without a big advertising budget, the Amex and State Street had a difficult time entering the consciousness of the small, retail investor.

"Even five years later, they were still describing SPDRs as a new investment vehicle you might not have heard of," said Holmes.[36]

The Birth of an Industry

The S&P 500 index was the cream of the crop of market indexes, so the project development team felt confident that an ETF tracking that benchmark would become popular. And while Most, Bloom, and Holmes anticipated more ETF products, they never imagined the size of the industry that would sprout from their one fund.

It had very much been a team effort. Many people at both the Amex and State Street worked hard to bring it off. Because all three team leaders had been integral in designing the product, they realized no one person could truly take credit for the concept. When they made the effort to patent the idea, Most, Bloom, and Holmes were all credited as inventors. They hired outside counsel to examine the product's patent ability. However, all the lawyers advised them that the idea was not patentable. At the time, it wasn't possible to patent a business process.

"Amex was going to file with the three co-inventors of the SPDR, but we decided not to pursue it," said Bloom. "We tried to get the methodology patented, but we were told it couldn't be patented. As it turns out, we believe there have been such significant advances in the intellectual property industry that if the SPDR had been introduced in 2007 instead of 1993, we would have been able to patent it."[37]

While the legal advice was bad for the financial fortunes of Amex and the three men, the decision essentially immortalized them in the financial industry's history. By 1995, Most had retired and Bloom had moved elsewhere in the Amex. The ETF then took on a life of its own. Essentially, every ETF is a direct offshoot of the original SPDR. While new entrants into the industry have tweaked the product a little, the original design of Most, Bloom, and Holmes remains the foundation for every ETF. By not being able to patent the design, it was easy to copy. Essentially, it was an open invitation for firms to create more ETFs.

The pattern was similar to what happened in the personal computer industry. When personal computers hit the market in the late 1970s, they were intimidating and expensive for the average businessman or individual. Then International Business Machines IBM, the largest computer maker in the world, produced a PC. Instead of keeping the information proprietary, IBM decided to not charge a royalty to access the design of its personal computer. By opening up the architecture it made it easier for software companies to create new applications, giving more people a reason to buy the computers. The idea was hugely successful and ignited the enormous growth of the personal computer industry. Now almost every employee of every business has a computer, as do most of the households in America.

While IBM's design became the widely accepted model for the personal computer, in the end it proved a poor decision for IBM's bottom line. By making the design accessible, competitors could copy it and make similar computers for less money. Eventually, IBM found the personal computer business unprofitable and sold it off.

Similar to the way that IBM's decision not to charge for its design sparked the computer industry's growth, the fact that new ETF issuers don't have to pay a royalty to use the SPDR design removed one potential road-block from the industry's phenomenal growth. If they had patented the SPDR and charged a royalty, it could have restricted entry into the industry by adding one more expense to a product sold as a low-cost alternative to index funds. That competitive hurdle would probably have prevented the ETF industry from getting as big as it is today. With the product design free, the barrier of entry to new sponsors was low, which in turn led to more ETFs.

Ironically, a company named Mopex, run by two young traders, did file for a patent on the "open-end mutual-fund securitization process" in 1995. By that time, business processes were being patented and Mopex received its patent three years later. Mopex then demanded that the Amex and other firms actively involved with the SPDR pay it a royalty. The small company asked for a fee on volume that could have earned it $20 million annually.

"After the SPDR had been up and trading, these two guys came to Nate Most and asked how the whole thing worked," said Moriarty, currently one of the leading ETF lawyers in the country. "Then they filed for a patent. Ultimately, they got it because in those days patent officers weren't used to dealing with financial processes and products. So, the officers didn't look at the prior art and the financial markets when deciding to give Mopex the patent. Mopex sued everyone who was involved in the SPDR and said, in essence, 'We'll be happy to give you a license for a $1 million.' Nineteen of the 20 firms involved paid them, but the Amex, which had every reason to sue, did, and won. The whole thing was so ridiculous."[38]

Because the SPDR had been trading long before the patent came out, Gary Gastineau, who ran the Amex product development group after Nate Most left, called the action "merely an attempt to extort."[39] The two firms countersued each other in 2000. Three years later, a federal judge ruled that Mopex's patent was invalid based upon a patent Tull said he helped create for Morgan Stanley's Optimized Portfolios as Listed Securities.[40]

Better known as the OPALS, Morgan Stanley listed these ETF-like products in Luxembourg soon after the SPDR's launch. While only sold in Europe, the OPALS introduced the concept of optimization to the ETF. Instead of holding every single stock that made up the index, the OPALS constructed baskets of securities that closely tracked the target index, without totally replicating it. These would be the prototype for Morgan Stanley's first U.S. ETFs, the World Equity Benchmark shares.

Let's Do It Again

The Bank of New York had been very enthusiastic about the SPDR when Most and Bloom first brought it to them in 1990. But, unfortunately, it didn't have a visionary like Holmes on staff.

"We figured out our mistake and made a bid for the second ETF," said Keenan, the Bank of New York Mellon's head of U.S. fund services sales. The Amex realized it shouldn't become dependent on one trustee bank. It "decided it needed to mitigate its risk and work with another provider. We were essentially across the street from the Amex and had good relations with the exchange on other fronts, so they asked us."[41]

It took half the time for the SEC to work out the bugs in the second ETF. The MidCap SPDR (symbol: MDY) came out in 1995. It tracks the Standard & Poor's MidCap 400 Index, which calls itself the most widely used index for midsized companies. Launched in 1991, this index of 400 companies with a capitalization between $1 billion and $5.5 billion covers about 7 percent of the U.S. equities market.

On the MidCap SPDRs first day, volume was 55,800 shares. The next day only 3,000 shares traded. That's the way it went for the rest of the year: occasional big days but most trading under 10,000 shares a day. The lowest volume was only 600 shares traded all day.

What Tangled Webs We Weave

The SPDR was registered as a '40 Act investment company, but structured as a unit investment trust. It's lack of a board of directors and asset manager made it cheaper than a mutual fund, but its structure had more limitations than a mutual fund. The next group of ETFs would move the product a huge step forward by becoming the first ETFs created as open-end funds. The open-end fund offered a lot more ways for the fund and the people running it to make money. These ETFs were much closer to mutual funds than the SPDRs. And because it was a new kind of investment company, it took nearly three years for these open-end funds to come to the market.

In a mutual fund, you can reinvest all the dividends given off by the securities and buy more fund shares. That's not allowed in a UIT; dividends cannot be used to purchase anything, not even a Treasury bond. The dividends spun off by a UIT can't earn interest or be reinvested to buy more shares. Though not a large amount, the dividend cash instead sits idle, a drag on performance on top of fees. Another thing a UIT can't do is lend out shares. A mutual fund can lend out up to 30 percent of its portfolio and charge borrowers a fee. This is a great way to lower the costs shareholders pay to the fund. But the SPDR and the MidCap SPDR can't do that because they are UITs.

Another advantage open-end funds had over UITs was an asset manager. When the UIT was created, it bought the exact same portfolio as the index—no futures, no derivatives. But open-end funds aren't as strict. With an open-end index fund, the asset manager didn't need to replicate the index perfectly, and could overlook small stocks that would jump in price if a fund bought a lot of shares. He could use some futures and options instead to capture that return. And, probably the biggest factor in the industry's growth, being the asset manager gave sponsors a way to make money off the funds.

The first open-end ETFs were also the first international ETFs. In March 1996, Morgan Stanley launched 17 World Equity Benchmark shares, or WEBS, on the Amex (get it? SPDRs and WEBS). And they did work well together. WEBS now gave an investor or portfolio manager a way to get worldwide exposure in ETFs. The SPDRs covered most of the U.S. market, while the WEBS gave indexed exposure across many countries.

Each WEB tracked a different country. Together the 17 WEBS approximated 90 percent of the 21 countries tracked by the MSCI EAFE (Morgan Stanley Capital International Europe, Australasia, Far East), which was then, and remains today, the most widely followed international index in the United States. The index just so happened to be owned by Morgan Stanley, too. But instead of buying the nearly 2,000 stocks in the index from 21 different markets, a U.S. investor could now buy shares in just 17 domestic securities to get nearly the same exposure and performance. It also gave retail investors foreign equity exposure that could be priced during the U.S. trading day. Previously, this had been the privilege of only institutional investors.

"It was revolutionary," said Tull, who ran the team creating the WEBS for Morgan Stanley.[42]

About a week later the CountryBaskets hit the market. Sponsored by the U.S. arm of Deutsche Bank, these were the first ETFs launched on the New York Stock Exchange. Unlike today, when stocks can be traded on many exchanges, at that time listings were proprietary. If you listed on an exchange, you traded on that exchange—and trading meant volume. You had to pay an annual listing fee. So, any listing that went to another exchange meant more volume and money for that exchange and less for yours. Remember, the Amex invented the ETF to increase listings, volume, and revenues. Now the NYSE was muscling in on its monopoly.

The WEBS and CountryBaskets, which had travailed the SEC's regulatory hurdles together, were a big advance for the industry. Not only were they the first international ETFs for U.S. investors, but they were the first to allow the lending of shares and reinvestment of dividends. The SPDR couldn't do that—and still can't.

"We started before them with the initial filing," said Joseph LaCorte, at the time a Deutsche Bank managing director on the project. "And we got the okay at the same time. The WEBS went to the Amex, but we listed on the NYSE, which had no experience trading ETFs, so we took an extra week to come to the market to make sure the operations worked."[43]

It proved to be a fateful decision. After a month, the WEBS had left the CountryBaskets in the dust. Its trading volume was 13 times greater than Deutsche Bank's product.[44]

The WEBS set the precedent for what would become a major theme in the ETF business. First to market was very important. Unlike mutual funds, there was little reason for two ETFs to track the same index or sector. With a week's head start and a bigger marketing campaign, WEBS grabbed the front-runner status and never let go.[45]

Granted, the CountryBaskets had a few strikes against them from the beginning. There were only nine compared to the 17 WEBS. While the WEBs tracked the well-known MSCI indexes, the CountryBaskets tracked the more obscure Financial Times/Standard & Poor's Actuaries World Indices index for each country. Also, the WEBS targeted retail investors by selling in units of $1,000, while CountryBaskets focused on institutional traders and charged $5,000.[46]

With investors moving toward the more liquid investment, trading volume begets more trading volume. Even though by January 1997, Country-Baskets had $240 million in assets under management, compared with the WEBS $250 million, exactly a year later Deutsche Bank pulled the plug. Liquidated in March 1997, they would forever after be derisively called the "CountryCaskets."

"Deutsche Bank didn't want to be in ETF business," said Tull, who jumped to Deutsche Bank in time to close down the CountryBaskets. "At the end of day, the Germans decided they didn't want these shares around. They liked active management and they thought it was a slur on the company to have index-based products."[47]

"It challenged their actively managed funds from a pricing point of view," said LaCorte. "Every dollar was converted at a lower margin."[48]

Actually, Morgan Stanley didn't want to be in the ETF business either.

That's because the sponsor didn't make money from launching an ETF. When the Amex created its subsidiary to sponsor the SPDR, it didn't charge a fee because sponsors couldn't get paid under the '40 Act. Typically, sponsors were paid for other roles, such as fund adviser or distributor. But this didn't bother the Amex for several reasons. Simply, one less fee kept the expense ratio down. Also, that wasn't the Amex's objective. It didn't have the desire or wherewithal to run a fund. It planned on making money from listing and trading fees, so it wasn't concerned about taking a fee for bringing the issue to the market. That became part of the formula. The sponsor doesn't get paid. While that might be fine for an exchange, what incentive did an investment bank have for launching an ETF?

The incentive was an asset management fee. No doubt, the most important feature of the new open-end ETF was that it needed an asset manager. That gave the company running the fund a way to make money. By giving

Wall Street's investment banks a fee for running an ETF, they were also giving an incentive to establish one.

Morgan Stanley made some money on custodian services, stock loans, cash management, and trading the WEBs, and the ETFs helped promote its international indexes. But, it didn't make any money sponsoring the funds because it wasn't the asset manager. Meanwhile, Barclays Global Investors, which ran institutional index funds, had been hired as the asset manager. It made the money. A while after the CountryBaskets went defunct, Morgan Stanley sold the WEBS to Barclays and they eventually became the first iShares.

"I don't think Morgan Stanley believed the ETF space was going to be that big," said Tull.[49]

Building a Business

At the end of the SPDRs first year, it had $464 million in assets under management. This was respectable, but not an overwhelming success. The next year, the SPDR's assets actually fell by $40 million. But after the dip, total ETF assets under management doubled each year from 1995 to 2000. Of course, the SPDR held the lion's share. Even with the launch of 26 international ETFs in 1996, the WEBs and CountryBaskets comprised just 10 percent of the industry's assets. It wasn't until 1997, four years after the SPDR's launch, that the ETF began to really take off.

In 1995, the emergence of the Internet industry sent shock waves of growth throughout the entire U.S. economy. That lifted the S&P 500 index. By 1997, the rally that would become known as the dot-com bubble was in full swing. And with the major indexes setting record highs at a fairly steady pace, retail investors flocked to index funds.

The S&P 500 index posted gains of 34 percent in 1995, 20 percent in 1996, 31 percent in 1997, and 27 percent in 1998. With the index beating more than 80 percent of the active mutual fund managers, more retail investors bought into the philosophy of John Bogle, the creator of the first retail index mutual fund. The growth of index funds exploded. By the end of the decade, his Vanguard 500 would become the world's largest mutual fund.

For buy-and-hold investors, index funds were wonderful. But institutional investors didn't like having their money locked up all day. However, they soon figured out how to use the new ETF product and they loved it. Even though the industry didn't launch a single ETF in 1997, the industry's assets nearly tripled.

It was the right product at the right time. The ETF modernized the open-end '40 Act investment company by allowing index funds to be accessible throughout the market session with the ease of trading a single stock. And the product development team had built it right. The structure's brilliance lay in its ease of replication, not only with equities, but with other assets classes as well. More important, it paved the way for easily investing in asset classes such as commodities and currencies. Everyone knew how to buy and sell stocks.

Conceptually, creating a new ETF was as easy as (1) start an investment company, (2) license an index, and (3) let's go. Practically, however, the process was slow because the SEC needed to grant exemptions from the '40 Act for each product.

"We did a lot of things in the first round to get a lot of things right," said Holmes.[50]

With most of the heavy lifting on the ETF structure done with the launch of the SPDR, Bloom moved to another department at the Amex and Nate Most retired. Clifford Weber, the third man in the Amex's three-man product development team, took over the job of supporting the product. Weber led the charge to grow the number of ETF listings.

Shine On, You Crazy DIAmonds

DIAmonds were the Amex's new best friend. The most striking thing about the DIAmonds Trust was that throughout its history, Dow Jones, the owner of the Dow Jones Industrial Average, had refused to license its indexes. But as the market rallied and other index makers licensed out their indexes for funds, futures, and options, the publisher of the *Wall Street Journal* realized it was giving up an easy revenue stream. In 1997, the company agreed to license the Dow Jones Industrial Average for the first time in its 101 years.

The CBOE received a license for options based on the Dow, and the CBOT was granted one for futures. They launched in 1997. But the greatest enthusiasm was garnered by the new ETF. The Amex won the license and on January 20, 1998, PDR launched the DIAmond Trust as a UIT (symbol: DIA). It was an acronym for Dow (Jones) Industrial Average Model New Depositary Shares.

Wow!

Retail investors might have been unfamiliar with the S&P 500, but everyone knew the Dow Jones Industrial Average. It *was* the stock market. Shares were initially priced at $77. 81. On its first day, the DIAmonds rose $1. It was the third-most-heavily traded stock on the Amex, with volume of 1.7 million shares worth more than $135 million. It even topped the one million shares on the SPDR's first day. At the end of the first day the fund's holdings were $38 million. They jumped to $160 million by the end of the second day, announced the Amex.

Arachnophobia?

By now, the stock market had bifurcated into the new economy stocks and the old economy stocks. People wanted to invest in the growth sectors: technology, biotechnology, telecommunications, and the Internet. They wanted extra growth and they didn't want industrial stocks holding them down. Sector funds blossomed. The Select Sector SPDRs launched into that atmosphere.

State Street decided it didn't want to be simply the custodian and trustee for ETFs. It wanted to run some. On December 22, 1997, State Street Global Advisors launched the Select Sector SPDRs. Each one tracked the performance and dividend yield of a particular sector index.

The Select Sector SPDRs
- Originally Basic Industries, changed to Materials Select Sector SPDR Fund (symbol: XLB)
- Originally Consumer Services, now Health Care Select Sector SPDR Fund (symbol: XLV)
- Consumer Staples Select Sector SPDR Fund (symbol: XLP)
- Originally Cyclical/Transportation, now Consumer Discretionary Select Sector SPDR Fund (symbol: XLY)
- Energy Select Sector SPDR Fund (symbol: XLE)
- Financials Select Sector SPDR Fund (symbol: XLF)
- Industrials Select Sector SPDR Fund (symbol: XLI)
- Technology Select Sector SPDR Fund (symbol: XLK)
- Utilities Select Sector SPDR Fund (symbol: XLU)

The Select Sector SPDRs didn't hit the market as well as the DIAmonds. On the first day only two funds topped 100,000 shares: Consumer Staples, at 149,000, and Technology, which went from 290,700 shares the first day to more than two million shares two months later. The Industrial sector was so far out of favor that year that it traded only 600 shares.

Wedding Bells

The American Stock Exchange's struggle to remain an independent, viable business ended in 1998. The National Association of Securities Dealers (NASD), which owned the NASDAQ Stock Market, agreed to buy the Amex that March. The minor-league electronic market that started just 27 years earlier had become the big show and left the 87-year-old Amex struggling to compete.

Apart from a few banner years during the bubble leading to the 1987 crash, the Amex's stock business had been in steady decline. While the Amex was down, it wasn't out. Its options business thrived during the 1990s. But as Richard Syron, the American Stock Exchange's chief executive officer, explained to the *Wall Street Journal* in September 1997, "The options business is more profitable for the Amex's member firms, [but] the stock business is more profitable for the exchange itself."[51] Of the Amex's 661 full members, a third traded only options.

Caught between the NASDAQ's army of high-tech companies and the blue chips of the NYSE, the venerable Curb had been kicked out to the curbside. As can be seen in Table 2.1, by the end of 1997, the NASDAQ listed 5,487 companies, and the NYSE 3,047, versus 771 on the Amex. That year, the NASDAQ posted revenues of $634.4 million, compared to the Amex's paltry $197.9 million. But it was the trading volume that solidified the Amex's status as the poor relation. Compared to the NASDAQ's average daily volume of 646 million shares, the Amex traded an embarrassing 24 million. This is even more mortifying when it is considered that the growing ETF business made up a large part of this volume and that the SPDR was the most actively traded issue on the exchange. The Amex's market share fell to between 2 percent and 3 percent of all the shares traded in the stock market, down from 4 percent in the mid-1980s.

For both the NASDAQ and the Amex, the merger was a way to regain momentum after scandals in the early 1990s. On the NASDAQ, some traders had been caught conspiring to rig prices. Meanwhile, the Amex had created a second-tier market with listing standards so lax that it accepted a company run by a convicted criminal.

TABLE 2.1   Comparing the NASDAQ, Amex, and NYSE in 1997

	NASDAQ	Amex	NYSE
Year founded	1971	1911	1792
No. of listed companies	5,487	771	3,047
Number of IPOs	475	22	279
Market capitalization of all companies	$1.835 trillion	$162.2 billion	$11.8 trillion
Average daily stock volume	648 million shares	24 million shares	527 million shares
Total volume for year	163.9 billion shares	6.2 billion shares	N/A
Revenue	$634.4 million	$197.9 million	$638.7 million
Net Income	$36.1 million	N/A	$86.1 million

Source: NASDAQ, NYSE Euronext

By November, the second- and third-largest stock exchanges in the country combined to take on the NYSE. Called the "market of markets," the NASDAQ-Amex Market Group was created as a subsidiary of the NASD with both the Amex and NASDAQ operating as separate markets under the subsidiary's umbrella.

While the Select Sector SPDRs were the first ETFs listed after the merger, they became lost in the excitement over the new technology ETF.

The Biggest ETF Launch

At the start of 1999, the ETF industry consisted of 29 index-tracking stocks with a total of $15.6 billion in assets under management. Despite the initial excitement of the DIAmonds, the lion's shares of those assets were concentrated in one fund, the SPDR. It took an index that captured the retail investor's imagination, one that tracked the outrageous rally in the technology sector, to push ETFs into the American consciousness.

The stock market had split into two markets: the new and old economy. With the exception of the late 1990s additions—Microsoft, Intel, and Hewlett Packard—the old economy included every stock in the Dow Jones Industrial Average, and much of the S&P 500: industrials, manufacturing, basic materials, and retail. The new economy was anything and everything that involved technology: computer hardware, computer software, telecommunications, fiber optics, biotechnology, and, of course, the Internet.

Like competing teams, the two markets were nicknamed the bricks and the clicks. The bricks, short for bricks-and-mortar, were so named because they needed a physical building to do business. Meanwhile, the clicks, named for the sound of a computer mouse, were any company that did business on a computer. One look at the major stock indexes and it appeared as if the bricks and mortar holding up the buildings of the old economy were literally weighing down the indexes.

The rising tide did lift all boats. But the differing rallies between the bricks and the clicks were striking. From Jan. 1, 1995, about the beginning of the dot-com bubble, to March 10, 1999, the day the NASDAQ 100 Index Tracking Stock launched, the Dow Jones Industrial Average more than doubled, but the NASDAQ Stock Market Composite Index more than tripled, rocketing 220 percent. The S&P 500 Index, which was a mix of old and new economy stocks, or as some preferred to see it, the real economy, fell in the middle nearly tripling.

For four years, the raging bull market rocketed at full speed and the NASDAQ was the vehicle—a vehicle driven by investors drunk on unrealistic expectations for Internet and other technology companies.

Yet, even though the NASDAQ composite was mentioned with the Dow and the S&P 500 on the stock market reports every night, the people at the NASDAQ-Amex Market Group strived to reinforce its relevance as a brand to individual investors. While the NASDAQ composite soared, there was no financial instrument to capture that market's move. The S&P 500 and now the Dow were cashing in on licensed products. But the NASDAQ, which called itself "The market for the next 100 years," had nothing. Rydex Securities offered a mutual fund that tracked the NASDAQ 100 index, but it was called the Rydex OTC Fund. Its steep $25,000 minimum initial investment made it clear that the small investor was not the fund's focus market. Well, there was a NASDAQ 100 future . . . but they wanted a NASDAQ-branded financial instrument that would appeal to retail investors.

Into this environment, the NASDAQ 100 ETF launched.

John Jacobs, the leading strategy planner for the NASDAQ, saw the successful institutional and retail business built on the SPDR and decided in 1997 that the NASDAQ should go with an ETF, too. Jacobs hired Steven Bloom, who had worked on the SPDR from Day One, as a consultant on the project. In 1998, *BusinessWeek* reported that 95 of its 100 Hot Growth Companies traded on the NASDAQ. These were the stocks that the small retail investors wanted. Jacobs decided to base the ETF on the NASDAQ 100 Index, a subindex of the NASDAQ composite, which held the stocks everyone heard about in the financial press.

The NASDAQ 100 Index holds the 100 largest nonfinancial companies in the NASDAQ Stock Market Composite Index. More than half the index was technology stocks. In 1998, the NASDAQ 100 had soared 85 percent, up from 21 percent the previous year, while S&P 500 rose only 27 percent—not just a third of the NASDAQ's rally, but down from its own 31 percent gain in 1997. And while that was what the people wanted, it was problematic.

The first problem was that the top five companies, Microsoft, Intel, Cisco Systems, MCI WorldCom, and Dell Computer, represented about two-thirds of the entire weight of the index. That prevented it from becoming a Regulated Investment Company, or RIC compliant, in the eyes of the Internal Revenue Service. Basically, the NASDAQ 100 Index wasn't diversified enough to support an investment company. Not being RIC compliant meant the fund couldn't pass along the responsibility to pay taxes on capital gains, dividends, or interest payments to its shareholders. To be RIC compliant, the index couldn't have any one stock comprising a weight in excess of 25 percent. Nor could the aggregate total of all companies with weights greater than 5 percent be more than 50 percent. With Microsoft's weight greater than 25 percent and the five largest together totaling more than 60 percent of the index's weight, this wouldn't do.

In a move of fancy financial engineering, Jacobs and Bloom rearranged the index even as a product, the NASDAQ 100 futures, already traded on it.

Typically an index is arranged before any products trade on it, so this was possibly the first time that was ever done. They created an algorithm, a small computer program that fixes a recurring problem, to create a new modified market-cap weighted index, shifting the weight from the top companies to distribute it proportionately across the rest of the portfolio. When it was done, the five stocks comprised about 40 percent of the index's market weight. It had taken the SPDR five years to come to the market. Six years later, the process had been shortened to two. Like the Amex, which had sponsored the SPDR, Midcap SPDR and the DIAmonds, NASDAQ wanted to sponsor the new ETF. And because the SPDR was the most successful ETF, the NASDAQ made the new ETF a UIT with no management fee. Ironically, the NASDAQ liked the way the SPDR traded so much, that it listed the new tracking stock on the American Stock Exchange. Now that they were part of the same company, it seemed a no-brainer.

The idea behind "The Market of Markets," as the NASDAQ-Amex Market Group called itself, was to combine the best features of the floor-based Amex and the electronic screen-based NASDAQ.

But also that had been part of the deal. The membership of the American Stock Exchange had huge power in deciding whether the merger would occur. The membership had said they wouldn't approve the deal unless the NASD agreed to preserve the economic model of the Amex floor exchange. This meant keeping ETFs, options and certain stocks on the floor. NASDAQ executives said the NASD made a conscious decision to reposition the Amex as an ETF market, while allowing the NASDAQ to maintain its status quo.

"It was purely to get the Amex membership to come along," said Jacobs, who by 2007 was the chief executive of NASDAQ Global Funds. "So, the NASD made the NASDAQ the equity marketplace and the Amex the ETF market."[52]

But the Amex also had an advantage in how it supported ETFs. Especially since the Amex had something the NASDAQ didn't have—specialists. This group of elite traders and firms traded only on the floors of the NYSE or the Amex, but not in the electronic market.

So called because they specialized in specific stocks, the specialists were analogous to market makers on the NASDAQ because they literally made the market in a stock. If no one else would make a trade in a particular stock, the specialists and market makers had an obligation to commit capital to make the market. Unlike company shares, which are launched in a finite amount in an initial public offering (IPO), ETF shares are created by authorized participants, such as specialists. In order to have shares to trade when the ETF went public, the specialist provided the initial funding, known as seed capital. This would be millions of dollars committed to a brand-new issue. The specialist would enter the market and buy shares in all the stocks and exchange them for an equal amount of shares in the ETF ahead of the launch. This ensured there were a sufficient number of shares to trade when the ETF hit the market.

In return, for providing the seed capital, the specialist became the only firm selling shares in the ETF. They didn't have to compete for trades because the order flow came to them. This gave the specialists the economic incentive to provide the seed capital and other support needed by a fledgling ETF. Because the market structure of the specialist system gave the specialists a monopoly in trading, they had an unfair advantage over the market makers in garnering the listings. The Amex still fought for new equity listings with the NASDAQ, but the NASDAQ was so hot and sexy that the Amex just couldn't compete in that arena. However, with the specialists, the Amex continued to be the preferred market of ETF sponsors. In 2005, the SEC passed Regulation National Market System, or Reg NMS, which eliminated the specialists' monopoly.

As a way to decipher which market a stock traded on, every stock trading on the NASDAQ was required to have four or five letters in their ticker symbols. Meanwhile stocks on the NYSE and the Amex could have ticker symbols of one, two or three letters. Since the new ETF would trade on the Amex, the NASDAQ-Amex Market Group wanted to give it the ticker symbol "Q", the last letter of NASDAQ. A single-letter ticker is a highly prized status symbol on Wall Street. It's a trophy for being one of the bluest of the blue chips. Companies that traded under one-letter tickers included AT&T (T), Ford Motor (F), Citigroup (C) and Kellogg (K). As for the ones that were unused, the NYSE had reserved them for future use.

The NASDAQ-Amex hoped that because "Q" was added to NASDAQ tickers when those companies went bankrupt, that the NYSE wouldn't want such a tainted symbol. But the NYSE said the Amex broke a decades-old agreement. In order to prevent the duplication of stock symbols, each exchange was required to notify the others before assigning a ticker. The NYSE had reserved the ticker and still wanted it. The Big Board threatened to sue the Amex. At the last minute, the Amex decided to use the ticker symbol (QQQ).

On March 10, 1999, the NASDAQ Stock Market launched the NASDAQ 100 Index Tracking Stock on the American Stock Exchange. Bank of New York was the trustee and custodian. In honor of its ticker symbol, the NASDAQ 100 Index Tracking Stock immediately received the nicknames "the QQQ", "the Triple Q," and "the Qubes," a bastardization of the "Qs." Options on the Qubes launched the same day.

The Qubes listing transferred to the NASDAQ Stock Market from the Amex in November 2004. Because, stocks on the NASDAQ need a minimum of four letters in their ticker symbol, the ETF's ticker changed from QQQ to QQQQ. In October 2006, NASDAQ sold the NASDAQ 100 Index Tracking Stock and the BLDRs family of ETFs to PowerShares. However, because many people knew the stock as the "Triple Q," PowerShares renamed the ETF the PowerShares QQQ. The Triple Q was the biggest, most exciting, and most successful ETF launch ever. On its first day, it traded 2.6 million shares, 53 percent more than the record set by the DIAmonds. In fact, it surpassed the DIAmonds first-day total of 1.7 million shares in just two hours. Within two weeks it had traded 30 million shares.

By the end of the year, they had more than $6 billion in assets, almost half the entire industry the previous year, while the industry doubled to $33.8 billion. After trading just 12 months, the Qubes had more than $12 billion in assets.

Ironically, exactly one year to the day, the dot-com bubble burst. On March 10, 2000, the NASDAQ peaked. Over the course of the year, the NASDAQ composite had doubled and the NASDAQ 100 index had surged 125 percent. Comparatively, the Dow only rose another 20 percent to its high before the bubble popped, while the S&P 500 gained just 19 percent (see Table 2.2).

The Qubes' stellar rise signaled to Wall Street that exchange-traded funds were not just a one-hit wonder. It showed potential sponsors there was a market for these products if the index was right.

The birth of the Qubes also epitomized the synergies to be derived from the marriage of the incubator of technology powerhouses with the home of the SPDR. But the Market of Markets never fully integrated. Two years later cracks began to show in the unhappy marriage. Six years after merging it was over. The NASD had spun off both the NASDAQ and the Amex.

All in the Family

Ironically, as late as early 2000, these financial instruments were still not known as ETFs, and barely known as exchange-traded funds. Small investors didn't consider them funds. They considered each one a unique stock. People called them the SPDR, the DIAmonds, or the Qubes as if they were individual companies, which, strictly speaking, they were. Few

TABLE 2.2 NASDAQ Indexes Double after QQQ Launch

	January 1, 1995	QQQ Launch (March 10, 1999)	Record High in 2000
NASDAQ Comp.	751.96	2406.00	5048.62
NASDAQ 100		2038.51	4587.16
DJIA	3834.44	9772.84	11722.98
S&P 500	459.27	1286.84	1527.46

people grouped them together as a single product category. If they did have a generic name, they were called index tracking stocks, index shares, or portfolio depositary receipts.

iShares changed all that.

Barclays Global Investors (BGI), the sponsor of the iShares product line, was the first to envision an entire family of products that would allow investors to build a truly diversified portfolio using only ETFs. At the same time, it would help Barclays capture part of the high-profit margin retail equity business.

In 1995, British investment bank Barclays bought the institutional money-management business of Wells Fargo Nikko Investment Advisors, a joint venture of Wells Fargo and Nikko Securities. Since creating the first index fund (see Chapter 4, "Index Fund-amentals"), Wells Fargo Nikko had become the world's largest manager of institutional assets using quantitative investment techniques. "Quantitative strategies are highly disciplined investments including index funds that attempt to match the performance of selected securities-market indexes."[53] In short, Wells Fargo Nikko managed $180 billion worth of institutional index funds.

Wells Fargo Nikko was Barclays' entrance into the U.S. market. The Wells Fargo unit merged with Barclays asset management group and was renamed Barclays Global Investors (BGI). With $256 billion in combined client funds, it was the world's third-largest money manager. Only Japan's Nippon Life, with $360 billion, and the $320 billion overseen by Fidelity Investments, the world's largest mutual fund company at the time, were bigger.[54]

BGI entered the ETF business the next year with Morgan Stanley's launch of the WEBS. Since BGI had the reputation for running index funds, Morgan Stanley, the WEBS' custodian, gave BGI the position of financial advisor. Essentially, BGI ran the fund. As mentioned earlier, this was possible because the WEBS were open-end funds instead of unit investment trusts. In addition to stocks, they can hold futures, options, and other derivatives to approximate performance of the index.

Since the Wells Fargo days, BGI had been a pure institutional shop. It created index funds for pension funds, endowments, and other large organizations. But business was slowing, and mutual-fund companies, such as Fidelity, began entering the market. While BGI was a subadvisor to some mutual funds, it had no real business with retail investors. Lee Kranefuss, the head of BGI's corporate strategy at the time, was looking for growth opportunities, especially ways to manage money for small investors. Managing money for institutions was an extremely low-margin business, but managers for the retail market charged high-margin fees.

Typically, Barclays would have two options: either buy an existing fund company or build one from scratch. Then the WEBS fell into BGI's lap. In their four years, the WEBS hadn't gained much traction among individual investors, raising only $2 billion among the 17 funds. Disenchanted with results, Morgan Stanley sold the funds to BGI.

Kranefuss realized this was an asset-management market with no real leader. There were a lot of single-product plays, but no one company offered a way to run a diversified investment strategy off these vehicles. The Select Sector SPDRs were an initial attempt, but even seven years after the SPDR, neither State Street nor Bank of New York focused a lot of energy on their ETF businesses.

In addition, the mutual fund industry essentially ignored ETFs. Like investors, most thought of ETFs as stocks not funds. Some companies did realize ETFs were new potential competition, but they shied away for fear that any ETFs they launched would cannibalize their existing funds business. Also, most traditional mutual funds focused on active management, not indexing.

With only 30 ETFs in existence at the start of 2000, BGI's ownership of the 17 WEBS made it the default market leader. Now running BGI's iShares business with the WEBS as the foundation, Kranefuss saw the opportunity to create a retail fund business for BGI. He also saw the chance to create the ETF marketplace, an opportunity Wall Street was just walking by.

"A lot of the work that Lee did in developing the strategy was just answering the question 'If we see a real opportunity, why don't the others see it?'" said J. Parsons, iShares' head of sales and Kranefuss's right hand man at the time. "We couldn't decide if we saw what they were missing or they didn't see it because it didn't exist."[55]

And the hard part, the ETFs based on international indexes, had already been done with the WEBS. As the only provider of international ETFs in 2000, BGI focused its attention on capturing a broad selection of asset allocations in the U.S. equity market. Because of its indexing background, BGI quickly grabbed all the major indexes, even the S&P 500. And following the WEBS playbook, BGI decided to launch the funds in groups, instead of the single offerings typical of its competitors.

The iShares had an auspicious beginning. They launched May 19, 2000 on the Amex, just two months after the dot-com bubble popped. On the first day, BGI rebranded the WEBS as iShares and launched four new funds.

1. iShares S&P 500 Fund, tracks the S&P 500 (symbol: IVV)
2. iShares Russell 1000 Fund, which tracks the Russell 1000, another index of large stock funds (symbol: IWB)
3. iShares Dow Jones U.S. Internet Fund (fund closed when index closed)
4. iShares Dow Jones U.S. Technology Sector Fund (symbol: IYW)

On their first day of trading, the four gathered $799.3 million in assets, with the S&P 500 fund getting nearly half. Overall, it was the best first day showing for a group launch. By the second day, they had more than a $1 billion.

The following week, BGI launched

- iShares Dow Jones U.S. Financial Sector Index Fund (symbol: IYF)
- iShares Dow Jones U.S. Telecommunications Sector Index Fund (symbol: IYZ)
- iShares Russell 1000 Growth Index Fund (symbol: IWF)
- iShares Russell 1000 Value Index Fund (symbol: IWD)
- iShares Russell 2000 Index Fund (symbol: IWM)
- iShares Russell 3000 Index Fund (symbol: IWV)
- IShares S&P 500 Growth Index Fund (symbol: IVW)
- iShares S&P 500 Value Index Fund (symbol: IVE)
- iShares S&P MidCap 400 Index Fund (symbol: IJH)
- iShares S&P SmallCap 600 Index Fund (symbol: IJR)

Since BGI didn't have a mutual fund business to cannibalize, it put all its efforts behind the iShares marketing campaign. It hired 30 salespeople and made a big, loud splash with a reportedly $12 million ad campaign, which the Amex paid for in exchange for more iShares listings. Later, the *Wall Street Journal* quoted Kranefuss saying that the way to get the funds in the hands of retail investors was "education, education, education." He built a large marketing team and sent them off to do "missionary work."[56]

"You had to overspend in the first few years to educate retail investors," said J. Parsons. "We had to give them the knowledge that let them know they could use these investments in their portfolio. We gave people something new to think about."[57]

It was a huge, risky bet during an uncertain time. The market was entering a two-year decline and index funds suffered along with actively managed funds. But over the next three years, BGI continued to meet and educate investment advisors, launch new funds, and spend on advertising. For the first three years, 70 percent of the business came from institutional investors. By 2004, 80 percent of money flowing into the funds came from retail investors, said BGI.

iShares were big step for BGI, but a giant leap for the ETF industry. With 55 ETFs under the iShares banner at the end of 2000, BGI became the undisputed market leader and has held onto the title ever since. The iShares also more than doubled in a single year the number of ETFs, sparking the industry's astronomical growth.

iShares success was the confluence of many factors. With the broad indexes consistently beating most actively traded mutual funds, index funds grew extremely popular. Then, in the wake of the dot-com bubble, investors saw their investments fall precipitously. They grew disenchanted with their trading skills and that of their stockbrokers. They decided they needed help, but not from that crowd. This led to the growth of a new class of broker:

Called certified financial planners (CFPs), these people had a fiduciary responsibility to the investors. They weren't just salesmen pushing the latest hot product. They tried to create fully diversified portfolios based on risk tolerance. The investors who were not totally discouraged with the stock market began to hire CFPs. Because mutual funds, especially technology funds, had been the vehicle many people were riding when they lost their money, small investors were gun-shy about going back into funds. Here was an audience of investors looking for something that didn't have the bitter taste of the market decline. CFPs were typically compensated with a percentage of assets instead of by the transaction, and the low-cost, flexible ETFs perfectly fit their and their clients' needs. The advisors began to heed Barclays's enormous marketing campaign.

"We sold as many SPDR shares as we did iShares because we were teaching people how to use these products," said J. Parsons. He said that at the end of 2000 the entire iShares family held about $7 billion in assets. It grew to $17 billion the following year.[58]

In the end, the bet paid off. At the end of 2006, iShares remained the market leader with a 60 percent market share and $251 billion in assets under management. Even with 270 new ETFs launched the next year, iShares still finished 2007 holding $328.7 billion, or 53 percent of the U.S. market. Not only was it the ETF market leader, it was now the fifth largest mutual fund company overall.

The First Assault

The ETF industry's growth had opened up the jealous eyes of the New York Stock Exchange. In late 2000, after years of trying, it finally broke open the Amex's monopoly as the only exchange to list ETFs. It worked with BGI to launch the first ETF on the NYSE since the demise of the CountryCaskets three years earlier. The iShares S&P Global 100 Index Fund (symbol: IOO) launched on December 8, 2000.

Launching the Global 100 Index Fund was highly symbolic, but not very important. No, the real challenge to the Amex's supremacy in the market was the NYSE decision to trade ETFs that listed on the Amex. Up until that point, neither the NYSE nor the Amex traded securities listed on the other's exchange. The regional exchanges—the Philadelphia, Chicago, and Pacific exchanges—did this often, as they listed few stocks. The majors could as well. They had "unlisted trading privileges," (UTP) which allowed them to trade each other's securities. But the NYSE and the Amex had too much pride to do this.

While the Amex hadn't necessarily given up on equities, equities had essentially quit the Amex. By 2000, the Amex's stocks listing had fallen to about 600, while the NYSE listed about 2,800 companies and the NASDAQ listed about 4,100. ETFs made up about 60 percent of the Amex's volume and the NYSE wanted some of that. It sparked a war in which the Amex now had to compete for listings of its own invention.

"We were always competing for ETF listings before they UTP'd our listings," said Cliff Weber, executive vice president of the Amex. "They just weren't successful."[59]

On July 31, 2001, the NYSE initiated the unlisted trading of the three most active exchange traded funds, the Qubes, the SPDR, and the DIAmonds.

If You Can't Beat 'Em, Join 'Em

The reluctance of most of the mutual fund industry to embrace ETFs was understandable. They weren't crazy about low-cost index funds to begin with. They loved actively managed funds and the high fees they could charge. But where was the king of index funds, The Vanguard Group?

John Bogle, the founder of Vanguard, had started the retail index fund industry 25 years earlier with the launch of Vanguard 500 Index. While Vanguard had some actively managed funds, 20 years later it was known as the premier shop for retail index funds. As the market reached is pinnacle, index funds hit the height of their popularity. When the S&P 500 hit its record high in 2000, the Vanguard 500, the index fund called Bogle's Folly and scoffed at as un-American in 1976, had became the largest mutual fund in the world.

ETFs seemed a perfect product line for Vanguard to expand into. Even Bogle seemed to like them. He worried that they would encourage investors to do more trading instead of long-term investing, but he called them "brilliantly designed investments"[60] and said that investing in these financial instruments was a "perfectly intelligent thing to do."[61]

In fact, Vanguard had been eyeing the marketplace and filed to get exemptive relief from the SEC to create a class of ETFs based on existing Vanguard funds. The only problem was that Vanguard didn't let Standard & Poor's, the owner of the S&P 500 index, know what it was doing.

The SEC approved the plans in May 2000 and Vanguard registered to sell five ETFs: the 500 Index Fund, the Total Stock Market Index Fund, the Growth Index Fund, the Value Index Fund, and the Small-Cap Index Fund.

Mutual funds companies can have many different classes of shares for the same fund. Some classes have loads, while some for 401(k) plans or fund supermarkets don't. Vanguard's big advancement to the industry was to create a family of ETFs that were a class of shares based on already existing mutual funds. And because some of these were offshoots of funds already licensed by Standard & Poor's, Vanguard didn't think it owed S&P any more in licensing fees.

Before the ETF was a sparkle in Vanguard's eye, S&P was already miffed at the fund company. When the Vanguard 500 Index Fund started out, S&P agreed to license its benchmark index in perpetuity for just $50,000 annually. This was fine while the index was small and shunned by Wall Street. But in 2000, when the index fund earned $187 million in fees from investors, S&P felt it should receive more. Vanguard said no, and there wasn't much S&P could do.

Furious at the brazen attempt to deny them any bounty from these new ETFs, Standard & Poor's sued Vanguard. S&P said the existing licensing agreement with Vanguard didn't include the rights to use their benchmarks for a class of ETFs. Not only that, but S&P had already given Barclays exclusive rights to use the S&P 500 index brand name. The case went to court and Vanguard lost. It couldn't enter into a licensing agreement to launch an S&P 500 ETF based on the Vanguard 500.

It took another year before Vanguard launched its first ETF. Vanguard introduced on the Amex in May 2001 the first member of the Vanguard Index Participation Equity Receipt family, then known as the VIPERs. The Vanguard Total Stock Market Index Fund (symbol: VTI) tracks the MSCI US Broad Market Index, which represents 99.5 percent of the total market capitalization of the U.S. stock market. It would be another seven months before the second VIPER, the Vanguard Extended Market ETF (symbol: VXF) came out. The Extended Market ETF follows the S&P Completion Index, which contains all the stocks in the U.S. market except those included in the S&P 500 Index. It's primarily an index of small and medium-sized companies.

By this time Bogle had retired from Vanguard, but remained a vocal proponent for index funds. He began to view ETFs as the territory of speculators and not long-term investors. His feelings about the ability to trade an index instead of a buy-and-hold strategy were succinctly captured in this quote: "An ETF is like handing an arsonist a match."[62]

Even though Bogle became critical, his old firm realized ETFs would be a growth driver for the business. Later, Vanguard realized it wasn't capitalizing on its best asset, one of the most recognized and trusted names in the fund industry. In order to avoid confusion and to alert investors that these ETFs came from the premier house for index funds, the company dropped the VIPERs name in 2006 and rebranded the series the "Vanguard ETFs."

Builders and Bonds

IShares in 2002 became the first company to launch ETFs based on fixed-income securities.

- iShares Lehman 1–3 Year Treasury Bond Fund (symbol: SHY)
- iShares Lehman 7–10 Year Treasury Bond Fund (symbol: IEF)

- iShares Lehman 20+ Year Treasury Bond Fund (symbol: TLT)
- iShares iBoxx $ Investment Grade Corporate Bond Fund (symbol: LQD)

The much more significant development was the NASDAQ Stock Market jumping into the fray by listing its first ETFs. Even though both it and the Amex were still owned by the NASD, and the NASDAQ had said the Amex was the place for ETFs in the NASDAQ-Amex Market Group, it later decided this was a market it needed to be in and started competing for listings. Needless to say, this didn't do much for the already strained relations between the two stock markets.

Meanwhile, Bank of New York was going through some reassessments of its own. As custodian and trustee of the second ETF, the Bank of New York had been there from almost the beginning. But, as the industry was evolving a lot of new players were making a lot more money with ETFs. BNY wanted to cash in on the new revenue streams, too. It addition to UITs, Bank of New York was a leading bank for American depositary receipts (ADRs) of foreign companies. ADRs are a way to buy shares in an foreign company. Representing stock that physically remains in a foreign country, ADRs trade like equities on the U.S. stock market. Bank of New York had created some ADR indexes as a way of promoting its brand.

The bank offered them to the NYSE, but the exchange wasn't sure it wanted to sponsor the product. Meanwhile, the Amex decided it definitely didn't want it. So, the Bank of New York went to the NASDAQ, which was also feeling left out of the party. Unlike most ETFs, which were created to fill an unmet need in the market, the BLDRS were created to fill the needs of the Bank of New York and the NASDAQ Stock Market. The Bank of New York wanted the revenue stream that came from licensing its indexes, and the NASDAQ wanted to list its first ETFs.

Launched in November 2002, the Baskets of Listed Depositary Receipts, dubbed BLDRS and pronounced "builders," were touted as a new way to play foreign markets. This family of four funds tracked indexes composed strictly of ADRs. The BLDRS also included the first emerging-market ETF.

- BLDRS Asia 50 ADR Index Fund (symbol: ADRA)
- BLDRS Developed Markets 100 ADR Index Fund (symbol: ADRD)
- BLDRS Emerging Market 50 ADR Index Fund (symbol: ADRE)
- BLDRS Europe 100 ADR Index Fund (symbol: ADRU)

But the BLDRS had problems right out of the gate. On the first day, the buyers weren't there and the spreads, or the difference between the buy and sell offers, was too wide to provide the proper liquidity. While the markets eventually improved, the BLDRS never caught on with retail investors and in 2006, NASDAQ sold the BLDRS family to PowerShares in the same deal in which it sold the Triple Q.

Free Again

The merger of the NASDAQ Stock Market and the Amex failed to live up to expectations. The culture clash between the floor-based traders and the electronic market makers was too much to overcome. Four years after the merger, in 2002, the NASDAQ's average daily trading volume in equities had more than doubled to 1.75 billion shares, while the Amex's stock volumes had doubled to just 62 million shares, or less than $1/_{32}$ the NASDAQ's total (see Table 2.3).

Nate Most passed away on Dec. 3, 2004. He was 90 years old. In the 11 years since the SPDR launched, he had seen the ETF grow from a niche product, used primarily by institutional investors, to a product with great exposure to the retail investors. In the process, it became one of the biggest selling products on Wall Street. Meanwhile, the Amex, which had created the ETF as a way to offset its inability to compete for equity listings with the NYSE and NASDAQ, now saw its in-house invention falling under the same intense competition for listings.

On March 19, 2004, the members of the American Stock Exchange bought the Amex back from the NASD. The financial terms of the deal weren't disclosed. Six years after the merger, the exchange was on its own again, and the world was a different place. However, because of its expertise in the ETF space, it remained the dominant market for ETFs, poised to take advantage of the incredible changes that would take place over the next three years.

TABLE 2.3 Average Daily Volume (in millions of shares)

	NASDAQ	Amex	NYSE
1997	648	24	527
1998	802	29	674
1999	1,072	33	809
2000	1,757	53	1,042
2001	1,900	66	1,240
2002	1,753	62	1,441
2003	1,687	69	1,398
2004	1,808	69	1,457
2005	1,799	66	1,602
2006	2,021	71	2,350
2007	2,166	46	2,119

Source: NASDAQ, NYSE Euronext

CHAPTER 3

The Evolution of the ETF

L ike mutual funds, ETFs are investment companies. According to the Securities and Exchange Commission (SEC), an investment company is:

> ... a company (corporation, business trust, partnership, or limited liability company) that issues shares and is primarily engaged in the business of investing in securities. An investment company invests the money it receives from investors on a collective basis, and each investor shares in the profits and losses in proportion to the investor's interest in the investment company. The performance of the investment company will be based on (but it won't be identical to) the performance of the securities and other assets that the investment company owns.[1]

Typically, investment companies are diversified portfolios comprised of a variety of assets. The appeal of the investment company is that it's an easy way for an individual investor to own a highly diversified portfolio at a fraction of the cost of purchasing each individual stock outright. Considering that the cost of building a diversified portfolio may be prohibitive for an individual investor who doesn't have much capital, the benefit of joining an investment company is immediate. A large group of investors pooling their money together creates much more buying power than any one individual could muster on his own.

An individual investor with $1,000 doesn't have enough money to create a truly diversified portfolio. He might be able to buy one share of many securities. Or he might buy a lot of shares from a few securities.

But if 1,000 small investors come together and each contributes $1,000, the investment company now has a $1 million to invest. This combined buying power allows the investment company to buy many securities in large quantities.

All investment companies in the United States are registered under the *Investment Company Act of 1940,* one of the seven laws that govern the *securities industry.* Investment companies register with the SEC, but are established under state law, usually in Delaware, Maryland, or Massachusetts. The registration lists the investment objectives, fees, risks, and other important details. It's the basis for the fund's prospectus and statement of additional information.

Better known as the 1940 Act, or '40 Act, the Investment Company Act of 1940 regulates the organization of investment companies, such as ETFs and mutual funds. Investment companies differ from *private funds* because their shares are offered to the investing public. Most private funds, such as *institutional* or *hedge funds,* restrict who can become a shareholder. They require huge minimum investments, typically more than $1 million. But if you can come up with the small minimum needed to invest, typically $1,000, you can own shares in any investment company.

In any fund, there are inherent conflicts of interest between the investors and the people running the fund. The more fees the fund managers charge, the less money the investors receive. In an effort to minimize conflicts of interest, the '40 Act focuses on disclosure. Its purpose is to ensure that the investing public receives information about the fund, such as its costs and investment objectives, as well its structure and operations. The '40 Act requires every investment company to issue a *prospectus* describing its financial condition and investment policies when investors initially buy fund shares, and subsequently on a regular basis.

> *It is important to remember that the Act does not permit the SEC to directly supervise the investment decisions or activities of these companies or judge the merits of their investments.[2]*

Investment companies as a group are the largest investors in the U.S. stock market. At the end of 2007, investment companies held 27 percent of all the outstanding stock from U.S. companies.[3]

This chapter will lay the foundation for the theme of this book, which is that investment companies are the best investment vehicles for individuals, and that ETFs offer individual investors the best return on their money. You will learn how to lower portfolio risk through diversification and how investment companies can offer diversification at a lower price than most other investments. You will learn about the different kinds of investment companies and the benefits of each. After that, it will focus on the most popular investment company, the mutual fund, and describe the different types. At this point, you will see how mutual funds and ETFs are very similar. Then this chapter will detail how the two products are created and how they operate, in order to show that ETFs are better investment vehicles than mutual funds.

The Importance of a Broadly Diversified Portfolio

Diversification is essentially a fancy word for "don't put all your eggs in one basket." It's important because it protects investors against risk. "Risk is the measurable possibility of losing or not gaining value. Risk is different from uncertainty, because uncertainty can't be measured."[4] By spreading risk over a group of investments, a significant loss in one investment won't destroy the entire portfolio. From the other angle, it means that if you spread your money around to different investments—at any given time—some will be doing well.

Any investment portfolio with a heavy weighting in one particular investment runs the risk of a dramatic loss should this one investment perform poorly. For example, many people hold a large amount of their retirement savings in their company's stock, either through stock options, or stock held in their *401(k) plans*. Should the company experience problems, sending the stock lower, this lack of diversification will have a severe negative effect on their savings.

The most famous example of this is Enron, the company that committed one of the biggest accounting frauds in American history. From the late 1990s through 2001, the executives at Enron, a U.S. utility and energy-trading company, used deceitful accounting practices to inflate the company's revenues and profits until it was the seventh-largest company in the nation. With the company's stock soaring, Enron's employees loaded up their 401(k) retirement plans with shares of Enron stock. Employees of many corporations buy shares in the company they work for. It makes sense considering the intimate view they have of the company's inner workings. But the Enron employees were unwitting accomplices in the fraud.

The fraud needed the stock to stay above a certain price or the entire scheme would unravel. Enron executives encouraged lower-level employees to put their retirement money into the stock in order to prop up the share price. Even as the scandal began to unfold, the executives continued to assure employees that all was well and that they shouldn't pull their money out of Enron's stock. After the fraud was discovered, the share price fell from an all-time high of $90 to 26 cents. The company soon filed for Chapter 11 bankruptcy protection and was forced to let go many of its employees. Talk about putting all your eggs in one basket! Not only did the employees lose their jobs, but they lost their life savings, too. Because they hadn't diversified, they had no money coming in and no money to fall back on.

Diversification lessens the portfolio's ups and downs, better known as its *volatility*. A diversified portfolio combines investments that are not highly *correlated*. Correlation means the extent to which the actions of one investment influence the actions of another investment. Investments with a low correlation won't all move in the same direction at the same time. While the portfolio won't surge as high when one investment posts astronomical gains, on the other hand, should one investment plunge in value, the portfolio's overall decline will be smaller. The investor gives up some upside to temper potential losses. For instance, a typical diversification strategy is to own both stocks and bonds. That's because typically stocks and bonds move in opposite directions. Bonds prices usually rise when stock prices fall.

However, an individual investor's ability to create a diversified portfolio on his own is constrained by the amount of funds he can invest.

Let's look at the portfolio of a hypothetical investor, Phil Mapockets. Phil has $10,000 to invest. He wants to build a diversified portfolio. He decides to allocate 80 percent of his money to stocks and 20 percent to bonds. It's a bit aggressive putting so much into stocks, but he decides he will diversify by buying stocks from different sectors, *large-capitalization* stocks, *small-capitalization* stocks and foreign stocks. According to Investopedia, companies worth more than $10 billion are considered to have a large market capitalization, or large-cap; these are the largest companies in the world. Companies worth between $2 billion and $10 billion are called mid-cap stocks, for middle market capitalization. Companies with less than $2 billion but more than $300 million are considered small-cap companies. Companies worth less than $300 million are considered *micro-cap* companies.

Phil buys two U.S. Treasury bonds at $1,000 each. With the remaining $8,000 he buys stocks. Typically, people buy stocks in units called *round lots*. Round lots normally equal 100 shares, or multiples of 100. Anything less than a round lot is called an odd lot and the brokerage fees are higher. Phil buys Company A, a large-cap company, at $35 a share. One hundred shares would cost $3,500, before commissions. His small-cap company, Company B, sells for $20 a share, so one lot costs $2,000. And Company C, the foreign stock, trades at $25 a share, for an investment of $2,500. While it would be true to say that Phil's portfolio is diversified among four components, the risk is still confined to a small group. With only four investments, a large loss in any one would have a significant impact on the portfolio (see Table 3.1).

Phil can say he's diversified into the small-stock sector, but he's placed all his bets on that sector in one stock. Small stocks in general may be having a great year, but what if Company B experiences manufacturing problems? Even though this may be a great year for investing in "small stocks" and the sector may surge 20 percent, because Company B has problems, its stock price may post a 25 percent decline. Thus, even though "diversified," this portfolio experiences a large loss in its small-stock component, because it consists of only one stock.

TABLE 3.1   Phil Mapocket's Portfolio

Investment	Cost	Percentage of Portfolio
Company A Large-Cap	$3,500	35%
Company B Small-Cap	$2,000	20%
Company C Foreign Stocks	$2,500	25%
Bonds	$2,000	20%
Total	$10,000	100%

For that same $10,000, Phil could purchase four mutual funds or ETFs: a bond fund and three stock funds. Each stock fund would cover a different slice of the market: a large-cap fund, a small-cap fund, and a fund of foreign stocks. If each stock fund contained shares from 100 companies, Phil effectively could spread the portfolio's risk over 300 companies instead of just three. The bond fund also diversifies into many different individual bonds.

The Appeal of Investment Companies

For most individual investors, picking stocks is a complicated, intimidating chore. Researching balance sheets, cash flows, and industry competition is a lot of work. Few investors have the time, interest, or skill to manage a portfolio on their own. And for those who have the interest, few have the money to build and maintain a truly well diversified portfolio.

Mutual funds are the most popular investment companies. They offer simplicity: They are easy to buy and sell. They don't require large up-front investments, and they allow the purchase of fractional shares. In short, they require very little work from investors. They come with a professional port-folio manager or team of managers, also known as an investment adviser or fund manager. The fund manager does the research and decides which securities to buy and sell. Funds also take care of all the work behind the scenes: keeping track of shareholders' accounts, paying out dividends, and sending out portfolio statements. In addition, funds will reinvest dividends back into the fund at no cost and allow for redemptions over the telephone.

Thus, the ability to easily buy a diversified portfolio with a small investment has made investment companies, mutual funds in particular, the primary savings and investment vehicles for most Americans. According to the Investment Company Institute, the industry's trade organization, registered investment companies—mutual funds, exchange-traded funds, closed-end funds and unit investment trusts—managed a record of nearly $13 trillion worth of assets by year-end 2008, "compared with less than $200 billion under management before 1980."[5]

With 88 million individuals and 44 percent of all U.S. households, about 51 million, owning mutual funds, these products make up the largest segment of the investment company industry.[6] Funds in investment companies account for 23 percent of all U.S. household portfolios, up from 8 percent in 1990 and less than 3 percent in 1980.[7]

Currently, there are more than 8,000 mutual funds with about 21,000 different share classes. Mutual funds alone accounted for $12.021 trillion, or 92 percent, of the total assets under management in investment companies. At the end of 2007, ETFs held $608 billion, closed-end funds had around $315 billion in assets, and unit investment trusts just $53 billion.[8]

Types of Investment Companies

Investment companies come in three flavors:

1. Management companies, which are either open-end companies (also called mutual funds) or closed-end companies (also called closed-end funds)
2. Unit investment trusts
3. Face-amount certificate companies

They must all register with the SEC. Face-amount certificate companies primarily issue debt securities. Typically, retail investors are only exposed to open-end funds, closed-end funds, and unit investment trusts. These three are covered in the following section.

Open-end Investment Companies

The defining characteristic of the *open-end investment company,* or *mutual fund,* is that there are no restrictions on the amount of shares it can issue, or when it can issue them. Hence, the open end. Investors buy shares directly from the fund itself, or through a broker, but not on a secondary market such as a stock exchange. Another important feature is that these shares are redeemable. When the investor wants to sell the shares, he sells them back to the fund for cash. The fund creates and sells new shares as long as there is demand. When demand drops, so does supply. The fund buys back shares and removes them from circulation.

The price that the fund's shares are bought and sold at is called the *net asset value (NAV).* The NAV is calculated once a day, after the stock market's 4 P.M. close. This ensures that the price doesn't fluctuate.

To arrive at the NAV, a fund multiplies the number of shares it owns of each security by the security's closing price that day. After the fund determines how much each security is worth, it adds them all up to get the total asset value. The fund then subtracts its total liabilities to get the net asset value. If the fund has $25 million in assets and $7 million in liabilities, the net asset value is $18 million. This number is then divided by the number of fund shares outstanding. If the fund has sold 900,000 shares, each share is worth $20; that is the NAV. Because the prices of the individual securities change every day, so does the NAV.

Closed-end Investment Companies

As one would guess, a *closed-end investment company* is the opposite of an open-end investment company. While they aren't mutual funds, they are often called closed-end funds. Unlike the open-end fund, which can create an endless supply of fund shares, the closed-end fund issues a fixed number of shares in an initial public offering, much like shares of a public company. Also, investors don't buy shares directly from the fund. Instead the shares trade on the secondary market—such as the New York Stock Exchange—like a common stock. This means the price of the fund's shares is determined by market demand, not the NAV. The closed-end fund's shares still have a net asset value, but because the shares are bought and sold on the exchange, they typically trade at a significant premium or discount to the NAV.

Because they trade on the exchange, shares of closed-end funds can't be redeemed. This means the fund isn't required to buy the shares back from investors. However, some closed-end funds will buy back shares at regular intervals. Not surprisingly, these are called interval funds.

Another big difference between open and closed-end funds is that closed funds can invest more of their assets in "illiquid" securities. The SEC considers a security "illiquid" if it can't be sold within seven days at approximately the price the fund used to determine the NAV. Thus, funds that invest in markets with more illiquid securities tend to be formed as closed-end funds.

Unit Investment Trusts

Unit investment trusts, better known as UITs, resemble open-end funds more than closed-end funds, but they are not managed.

This means that the trusts hold a fixed basket of securities, usually stocks or bonds. The portfolio isn't actively traded, rather it stays the same, or changes very little, for the life of the trust. Unlike actively traded mutual funds, which buy and sell securities all day long, investors buying a

UIT know exactly what they are buying for the length of their investment. And unlike both open and closed funds, the UIT does not have a board of directors, corporate officers, or an investment advisor managing the trust's portfolio. Without managerial direction, UITs miss out on some of the advantages of managed funds. Index funds with managers can reinvest dividends and take advantage of futures and options to tweak performance, without holding every single stock in the index. Index portfolios structured as UITs must strictly follow the target index and pay out dividends to investors.

Some unit investment trusts create a fixed number of shares, or "units," in a one-time public offering, like closed-end funds. Others issue their units continuously, like open-end funds. In either case, a UIT sponsor may, but is not required to, maintain a secondary market in the units, which allows investors to buy units from or sell units to the sponsors.

In either case, units of a UIT are redeemable, which means investors can sell them back to the UIT at the NAV, like the shares of an open-end fund. Yet, unlike the open- and closed-end funds, the UIT is created with a termination date, when the trust will close and be dissolved. These termination dates can be decades in the future. For example, UITs that hold bonds typically align the termination date with the date the bond investments mature. When the termination date arrives, the trust is dissolved. The securities that remain in the portfolio are sold and the proceeds are distributed to the trust's investors.

While ETFs and closed-end funds may seem similar, ETFs are never structured as closed-end funds. ETFs are either open-end funds or unit investment trusts. The first ETF, the Standard & Poor's Depositary Receipt (symbol: SPY) was formed as a UIT.

Types of Mutual Funds

The three most popular mutual funds are stock funds, bond funds, and money-market funds. Within these categories are a plethora of choices, each with its own investment objective. And just because stock funds may seek the same investment objective—say, beating the returns of the S&P 500 index by holding large-capitalization stocks—they all operate under different strategies, which opens them up to different risks, volatility, and expenses.

Stock Funds

Stock funds hold a basket of stocks. They come in a variety of investing styles, seeking a specific goal or allocation. Some funds hold only the stocks of large companies, others hold the stocks of only small companies, while others hold both. You can buy stock funds that focus on a narrow sector of the market, such as Internet or biotechnology companies, or you can buy funds that follow a particular strategy. Two popular strategies are growth and value. Growth funds buy fast growing, but highly risky, stocks, while value funds buy beaten-down stocks that look cheap compared to their intrinsic value. There are international funds that invest all around the world and there are funds that invest only in the market of one specific country.

Bond Funds

Bond funds come in many different investing styles too, but they all hold fixed-income securities. Some bond funds hold only U.S. Treasury bonds, some hold bonds from local municipalities, while others hold corporate bonds, from low risk to very risky. Funds holding bonds from foreign countries are also available.

Morningstar, a well-respected fund research company based in Chicago, tracks 31 categories of stock funds, including international funds, 30 categories of bond funds, including international, and seven categories of balanced funds, which hold portfolios containing both stocks and bonds.

Balanced Funds

Balanced funds are mutual funds that mix asset classes, typically holding both stocks and bonds in one fund. Balanced funds are a one-stop-shopping product for investors who don't want to spend much time managing their investments. The concept is simple. By holding both stocks and bonds, the manager of the balanced fund tries to create a well-diversified portfolio in a single package. Instead of having to pick a fund of large stocks, another for small stocks and another for bonds, investors pick one manager who takes care of everything for them.

Risk is a very big factor in the balanced fund. Fund managers are expected to get the highest rate of return possible while using a low-risk strategy. Lower risk typically means smaller returns. During stock market rallies, balanced funds underperform the market. On the other hand, when the stock market falls, balanced funds typically outperform the broader market.

Money Market Funds

Money market funds are required by law to invest in low-risk securities. Their objective is to earn a dividend approximating short-term interest rates while keeping their NAV at a steady $1.00 a share. In essence, this preserves an investor's principal. By investing in short-term, low-risk debt instruments such as government securities, certificates of deposit, commercial paper, and others, money market funds provide liquid vehicles that pay a dividend, but are much less risky than stock or bond funds. However, money market funds are not federally insured (as is the case with money market accounts at a bank). While extremely rare, investors can lose money in money market mutual funds.

Funds of Funds

These are mutual funds that build a portfolio out of other mutual funds instead of individual stocks or bonds. These are typically not good investments. In addition to paying the expense ratio for the mutual fund of funds, investors typically also have to pay the expense ratios of each mutual fund in the portfolio. On top of this, if the fund manager picks poor performing funds for the fund of funds, the investor holds them until the manager decides to sell. If the investor holds the funds individually as part of a portfolio, he or she can sell them whenever they want.

Running a Mutual Fund

Mutual funds are created and set up by fund sponsors. But, like every other public company, it is the investors, or shareholders, who actually own the fund. Like any other type of operating company, mutual funds have a board of directors who are elected to govern the fund and protect the shareholder's assets.

When a person wants to invest in a mutual fund, he or she opens an account with the fund company. He calls up either the fund or his broker, and says how much money he wants to invest.

Along with the money for buying shares, the investor needs to submit his name, address, social security number, and any other pertinent information. Should he want to buy a fund from another fund company, he would need to open up a separate account at that company. If he wanted to buy a third fund from a third company, he would have to go through the process all over again.

The investor needs to order his shares between 9:30 A.M. ET and 4 P.M. ET, the hours when the U.S. stock market is open. However, the NAV isn't calculated until after the market closes. This means the investor doesn't know at what price he's buying the shares, and prevents him from knowing exactly how many shares he's bought. The next day he can go online and find out exactly how many shares he bought and at what price. Later that month, he receives a paper statement in the mail noting the NAV and the number of shares bought. It will also tell him the price of his investment at the beginning of the month, and the value at the end of the month. This allows the investor to see if he's making a profit or taking a loss. Investors can also elect to receive this information in an online version.

Between the initial telephone call and the paper statement that arrives in the mail, a lot of actors will participate in an involved process to make sure the investor receives what he paid for and that his investment is safe. Some of these actors are people and some are corporate entities, but each one charges a fee to perform its function. While one can question whether each step of the process is necessary, this is the way the fund industry is set up. The industry has determined this to be the most efficient use of resources. All these fees add up to create a sizeable *expense ratio*, or percentage of assets that the investor pays to the fund advisor to manage the fund. However, the ETF, because it's structured differently than a mutual fund, avoids many of these fees. And that goes a long way to explaining why the ETF expense ratio is so much lower than that of a similar mutual fund.

Some fees are high for the function that is performed, but most are reasonable and necessary. Because of the many different steps required to run a mutual fund, even the most efficient fund finds it difficult to lower its expense ratio to match that of an ETF. The difference is so great because of the circuitous route your money takes to buy the mutual fund shares.

As soon as the fund receives the investor's money, it sends it to the fund's administrator, which typically performs many functions, including that of transfer agent. The administrator is a company that provides many services that funds need to deliver and that shareholders expect. The transfer agent keeps track of the individual accounts of every shareholder in the fund. It keeps track of the shareholder's transaction history. It calculates each shareholder's balance and tax basis. It distributes dividends and capital gains to the shareholders, as well as sending them information for their federal taxes at the end of the year. Transfer agents prepare and mail to shareholders statements detailing their accounts and balances on a quarterly basis.

Typically, transfer agents also run the fund's customer service department. Usually these are call centers that respond to shareholder questions or execute the purchase or sale of shares. These can facilitate wire transfers of money or money transfers between funds in the same family. So, the first cost the fund pays is to the transfer agent. In this example, the transfer agent records the amount of money the investor deposits into the fund. Then, the transfer agent sends the money to the fund's custodian. While the transfer agent can be part of the fund company, a separate custodian is required by the '40 Act. The custodian is a trust bank charged with the responsibility of holding both the fund's money and the stock certificates for all the shares the fund owns. Typically, the custodian is a member of the Federal Reserve

Bank. The money now sits in a special account with the fund's name on it. The second expense comes from the custodian.

Next the fund manager needs to buy securities to put in the fund; otherwise it will suffer a cash drag. Cash drag results from holding cash. Buying stocks or bonds gives your money the opportunity to appreciate in value. Funds don't pay interest. While some put the cash in money-market accounts to earn a little interest, most of the cash not invested just sits there, not earning anything. So, that's one day your money could have been earning, but wasn't.

Granted, investing in securities comes with the risk of losing money, so one could say, "At least I'm not losing principal." If that's your goal, though, you should put the cash into a money-market fund or a savings account. People invest in funds because they want to be invested in the market. If the fund doesn't invest the cash quickly, it drags down the fund's potential return. Regardless, some funds do keep a little cash on hand to pay investors who want to redeem fund shares. This spares the fund the hassle of selling securities, which incur capital gains.

In this example, let's assume the fund tracks an index of 1,000 different companies. In order to approximate the index's movement, the fund adviser needs to take the new cash he's received that day and buy shares in all 1,000 companies during that day's market session in the same weighting as the index. The fund manager calls up his stockbroker. The stockbroker is similar to one you might hire for your personal portfolio, but this broker deals exclusively with institutions. He is accustomed to buying large bundles of shares, sometimes millions, at a moment's notice. The fund will pay the broker a commission for his work.

The fund manager then tells the custodian bank how much money to pay the stockbroker and how many shares to receive in return. When the fund sells stock, the custodian sends the shares to the broker and receives the money from the sales. In short, the custodian settles the trade. In the old days, the custodian would hold the actual paper certificates in a vault on Wall Street in New York City. Each day the custodian's errand boys would run the certificates to and from the stock exchange to settle the trades. Nowadays, it's all done electronically. The custodian still serves the same function, which is taking the risk of holding the stock.

Why doesn't the fund simply take care of this transaction itself? Before the '40 Act was written, fund managers did hold the money and stock shares for the fund. But many of these managers didn't perform in the best interests of the fund's shareholders. Often the fund managers treated the fund's money as their own and used it for their personal benefit. Also, many fund managers were part of investment banks. The banks would often sell to the funds the shares they couldn't sell on the market. Thus, the shareholders were stuck with stocks that were not good investments. The

'40 Act was written to address these abuses, and one of the provisions is that custodians must hold the fund's shares and money.

The fund also doesn't want to spend the money on the infrastructure needed to maintain these huge systems. It's not an efficient use of the fund's money. Nor does the fund want to be a member bank of the Federal Reserve. Because the fund doesn't want to deal with the nuts and bolts of making everything work, it outsources these jobs. The fund would rather invest in people and research, because the fund manager wants to spend his time strategizing which securities to buy.

At the end of the day the custodian, which holds all the shares the fund owns, needs to determine the NAV for the fund. It then tells the transfer agent, who figures out how many shares your investment bought that day. It will then send the shareholder a statement confirming the transaction. Printing and mailing costs are part of the transfer agent's fee. It next tells the fund how many shares to create.

Other costs incurred by the mutual fund include administration, accounting, and compliance services. In order to run a mutual fund, the manager needs to pay a transfer agent, a custodian, a brokerage, an accounting firm, a compliance firm, possibly a separate administrator, and, of course, the manager needs to pay himself. On top of this is a separate fee called the 12b-1 which is part of the expense ratio, but broken out to highlight its size. This is a fee to pay for marketing and distributing the fund. Together, these usually add up to more than 1 percent and sometimes as much as 4 percent of fund assets. These costs will be described in further detail in Chapter 6, "The Better Mousetrap."

The Creation of an ETF

Registered as investment companies under the 1940 Act, ETFs are hybrids of open-end and closed-end funds. They are like closed-end funds in that their shares are listed and traded in the secondary market on a stock exchange. But they are not closed-end funds because they issue redeemable securities continuously and as many as needed to fill demand. In this way they are like mutual funds and UITs. However, because only large investors can redeem their shares, and due to their hybrid structure, ETFs need to act in ways the '40 Act does not allow. All ETFs must apply to the SEC for regulatory relief from certain rules contained in the '40 Act.

Typical ETF requests for relief from 1940 Act rules include the following:

- The request to allow individual shares to trade on a stock exchange at prices other than NA.
- The ability to redeem its shares at the NAV only in creation units.

- An exemption from prospectus delivery requirement in connection with secondary market trading activity. Prospectus delivery relief is conditioned upon the requirement that a "product description" summarizing the key features of the ETF is delivered to investors purchasing such ETFs as part of the primary listing rules.
- The ability to redeem creation units in excess of the statutory seven-calendar-day requirement. This is only for certain international funds.
- A "fund of funds" structure.
- The option to let certain affiliated parties deal with each other if the structure of the ETF and its relationship with its participants necessitate such relief.[9]

ETFs also require relief from various restrictions in the Securities Exchange Act of 1934, also known as the 1934 Act:

- The ability to permit broker-dealers and others to bid for, purchase, redeem or engage in other secondary market transactions for ETF shares and their underlying portfolio securities during a distribution or tender offer.
- Permit ETFs to redeem their shares in creation units during their continuous offering of such shares.[10]

After the ETF receives relief under these acts from the SEC, it needs to list on a stock exchange: the New York Stock Exchange, the American Stock Exchange, or the NASDAQ Stock Market. ETFs can trade on all exchanges, but the primary exchange where it lists provides product support, liquidity, and cross-listing arrangements.

The actual creation of the ETF starts when an institutional investor known as an authorized participant purchases all the securities contained in the index the ETF plans to track. The authorized participant, or AP, is typically a broker-dealer or specialist on the exchange. The AP is given the authorization to create and redeem the ETF's shares. ETF shares are created in lots of 50,000 shares and called "creation units." The AP buys a basket that holds typically 50,000 of all the securities in the index and deposits this portfolio with the ETF's custodian. In exchange, the ETF gives the AP an institutional block of 50,000 fund shares.

Because the ETF is an open-end fund, the AP can create more shares whenever demand outweighs supply. All the AP does is buy all the stocks in the index, in the requisite number, and exchanges them for the same amount of ETF shares. This barter is called an *in-kind trade* because they are trading the same kind of goods—stock shares for ETF shares. This barter does not create a taxable event as a cash sale would, so the ETF doesn't incur capital gains or losses.

On the flip side, when supply outweighs demand, the authorized participant can redeem shares. It gives the ETF back its fund shares and in return receives a basket with the same amount of individual securities. This *creation and redemption process* is one of the main differences between an ETF and a mutual fund.

At the end of the day, after the market closes, the NAV for the ETF is calculated. Just like a mutual fund, a full accounting is made of the assets and expenses, and the end result is the net asset value. This is important because the creation and redemption occur at the end of the day. The NAV is the price at which the authorized participant creates and redeems shares.

Mutual funds may have the ability to make "in-kind" trades, but they rarely do so. When mutual fund shares are created or redeemed, this usually creates a taxable event for the fund's shareholders, which they must file on their income tax forms. The ETF's avoidance of capital gains and losses is the key to its tax efficiency.

After creating the ETF shares, the AP may hold them, but typically, it sells them into the public, secondary market, better known as the stock exchange. Investors don't send a check to the ETF. Instead, they buy and sell the shares like equities, through a broker. The shares are not priced on the NAV. Rather, price is based on supply and demand, just like a stock.

Unlike mutual fund investors, retail investors in ETFs don't participate in the creation and redemption process. Because of the ETF's structure, individual investors don't redeem their shares. They trade them like any other stock on the secondary market. Only the authorized participants, who create the shares, are allowed to redeem them.

The ability to be bought and sold at a price other than the NAV is essential to the ETF. Mutual funds are created to be bought and sold at the NAV. However, the ETF is specifically designed to be bought and sold at secondary-market prices that differ from the NAV. Some people think the ETF's market price is the NAV calculated for that instant. They think that today's powerful computers capture the price for each stock in the index at that second and calculate the NAV for that moment in time. It doesn't work that way: While today's computers can compute the cost of the ETF's portfolio of stocks at any point in time, that isn't necessarily the price you get in the market. The ETF's price is a transactional number determined by demand for the shares at that moment.

However, because the ETF is transparent (which means investors can see all the investments the ETF holds), investors and authorized participants (APs) have a reasonable expectation of what the ETF's value should be at any given point in time. Because traders, brokerages and investment banks have the capability to figure out what the NAV should be at any second, they calculate a theoretical price at which the ETF should trade. This theoretical price becomes the basis for the price at which they are willing to buy or sell the shares. They meet in the marketplace and that is where the price is discovered. Because ETF creation units are officially priced at the NAV after the market closes, the market price is a theoretical approximation of the underlying value in the ETF.

"There is a theoretical value you can come up with and in a traditional stock you don't have that, just supply and demand," says Scott Ebner, senior vice president of the ETF Marketplace at the American Stock Exchange. "In this particular product, you know what the stocks are and what it costs to buy them. You can then buy them and give them to the trust in exchange for the shares. That makes it easy for the secondary market price to stay in line with the theoretical value of the fund, but doesn't guarantee that it will happen. The price doesn't come from a machine putting out quotes. You don't buy a synthetic instrument, instead you trade at what price people are willing to trade."[11]

Thus, ETF shares can trade at a premium or a discount to the true NAV. This creates arbitrage opportunities where APs can make a lot of money. "Arbitrage is a financial transaction involving the simultaneous purchase in one market and sale in a different market with a profitable price or yield differential. True arbitrage positions are completely hedged—that is, the performance of both sides of the transaction is guaranteed at the time the position is assumed—and are thus without a risk of loss."[12] People who arbitrage are called arbitrageurs or arbs.

The arbitrage is what keeps the ETF's share price in line with the NAV. While the ETF shares should trade at the NAV, increased investor demand causes the shares' price to rise. They then trade at a premium to the NAV. Since APs have the ability to create the underlying basket of individual securities very quickly, they buy the stocks and exchange them for ETF shares. Because it's an in-kind trade, shares for shares, no money changes hands.

For example, the NAV, or the value of the underlying basket of securities making up the Spa MarketGrader 40 ETF (symbol: SFV) is $20 a share, but investor demand pushes the share price up to $21. The arb typically buys 50,000 shares of each stock in the basket and trades them for 50,000 ETF shares. In this example, the creation unit would cost $1 million ($20 × 50,000 shares). The arb then sells the ETF shares on the open market for $21 each, or $1,050,000 ($21 × 50,000) for a quick $50,000 profit.

The same thing happens on the flip side. When the ETF's share price falls below the NAV, say to $19, the AP buys ETF shares on the open market at the lower price and returns them to the fund in exchange for the $20 basket of securities. The AP then sells the individual stocks for a profit on the secondary market.

But, every 15 seconds, an indicative value is determined to give a guide as to what is happening in the index. So, the arbitrage possibilities are neither very large nor available for a long period of time.

The ETF investor's brokerage firm takes on a lot of the responsibilities and services that the mutual fund performs, especially the transfer agent's services. The ETF doesn't keep track of its shareholders, and therefore doesn't need to keep track of shareholder accounts and all the work that entails. The ETF doesn't record how much money the shareholder invests, doesn't determine how many shares the investor owns, and thus, doesn't need to spend the money required to print and mail out shareholder account statements.

Much like buying shares of a stock, the investor's broker takes the money to buy the ETF shares. The broker purchases the shares and records how many the shareholder owns. The brokerage firm keeps track of the investor's account and is responsible for printing and mailing account statements.

Not providing all these services is a major reason why the expense ratios of ETFs are so much cheaper than a comparable mutual fund. And the ETF avoids these costs because its structure is completely different from the mutual fund.

While ETF investors pay a commission when buying and selling shares, considering how many transfer-agent tasks the brokerage takes on, one can almost make a direct cost comparison. Is it worth more to pay the broker only when you buy and sell, or pay the transfer agent an annual percentage of assets? It depends on the size of the commission compared to the size of your investment.

Summary

Investing is a complicated, intimidating, and expensive process for most individual investors. Most don't have the time, interest, or skill to do their own investments.

Investment companies are the best investment vehicles for individual investors. Investment companies make investing simple. They offer investors the opportunity to own a diversified portfolio with minimal investment and minimal work. ETFs and mutual funds are both investment companies.

Diversification is good because it lowers portfolio risk. It does this by investing in a diverse group of assets that don't move in sync with one another. This means a loss in one investment will not destroy the entire portfolio. Diversification also lessens a portfolio's volatility, so that it experiences less-drastic ups and downs.

Mutual funds are the most popular type of investment company. They have provided a great way for individual investors to gain exposure to the financial markets for nearly 70 years. But ETFs, in general, are an improvement on the old formula. The mutual fund's structure increases the costs necessary to operate. ETFs provide a similar investing opportunity at a lower cost and with faster execution.

Chapter 6, "The Better Mousetrap," will take many of the concepts outlined in this chapter and look at the nuts and bolts in both the mutual fund and ETF structures. It will delve deeper into the details of every cost involved and demonstrate how the ETF is a more efficient investment vehicle.

Since ETFs are index funds, the next chapter will explain the strategy of index investing. It will examine the benefits of passive versus actively managed mutual funds and how the low cost structure of the ETF provides a higher-value vehicle for passive investing than the index mutual fund.

CHAPTER 4

Index Fund-amentals

I t's all well and good to say an ETF is an index fund that trades on a stock exchange, but unless you know what an index is and why it's important, and what an index fund is, that description isn't very helpful. So, first things first: indexes will be described and discussed in this chapter.

Indexes measure the direction and health of a financial market. Most indexes track stocks or bonds, some follow commodities, and some follow other financial instruments. Indexes can be very broad; some track the entire stock market. Others are extremely narrow and follow a particular segment of the financial markets. For instance, one index measures only steel company stocks.

An index fund is an investment company whose objective is to earn the same return as a particular market index minus costs. The classic index fund is comprised of all the components of an index, in the exact same *weighting*. Sometimes this isn't possible, so the index fund creates an extremely close approximation. The key benefits of following this strategy are transparency and low cost.

Mutual funds follow one of two management styles, *actively managed* and *passively managed*. In addition to management style, all mutual funds have an *investing style*. This is outlined in the fund's prospectus. Examples of investing styles include building a portfolio around small stocks, or international stocks, or biotechnology stocks or growth stocks. But management style is the first decision an investor needs to make.

Actively managed funds are portfolios run by managers who actively trade stocks. An actively managed mutual fund can hold any security the manager chooses, as long as the portfolio follows the investing style. The active fund manager's job is to create a portfolio that will outperform the index for the fund's particular investing style or sector of the market. Passive management, predictably, is the opposite of active management. Instead of actively buying and selling stocks throughout the year, passive managers pick a portfolio and then basically leave it alone. The most famous form of passive management is the index fund. On average, in a single year, only a quarter of all actively managed portfolios, both mutual funds and private funds, beat the index.

Since ETFs are index funds at heart, understanding what makes a good index is essential to understanding what kind of investment vehicle you're investing it. From there, the chapter will compare the benefits of passive investing over actively managed funds. Indexing is now a large part of the financial landscape. Surprisingly, it wasn't always this way. Indexing as an investment style was a radical departure from the way Wall Street operated 40 years ago. In order to put indexing in perspective, there will be a short history to explain how indexing came about and why it's so important. Finally, the chapter will end with a list of the nation's largest and most influential index makers.

Why an Index?

One good way to understand indexes is to listen to an expert. Steven Schoenfeld, the founder of IndexUniverse.com, an online resource for index investing, developed some of the first emerging-market index products while at the World Bank. Later, during his six years as a managing director at Barclays Global Investors, he was responsible for the global ETFs at BGI's market leading iShares family. Currently, Schoenfeld is chief investment officer for Northern Trust Global Investments, in the global quantitative management group, which encompasses more than $280 billion in index, enhanced-index, and quantitative strategies. Schoenfeld's team brought Northern Trust's first ETFs the Northern Exchange Traded Shares, or NETs, to the market in the first half of 2008. These track foreign benchmark indexes. In his book *Active Index Investing*, Schoenfeld delineates four uses for benchmark indexes:

1. Gauge market and investor sentiment
2. Asset allocation and research
3. Performance measurement
4. Basis for investment vehicles[1]

The following sections go into each of these in detail.

Gauging the Market's Temperature

Ideally, the index gives investors a benchmark standard that provides a link to the past, a measurement of market sentiment and a way to track price movements. It shows where the market has been, what people think about the market today, and for some investors, it offers a view into the market's direction tomorrow. A broad index should reflect investors' views about the world at large, not only the individual stocks in the index. Like a thermometer, a good index takes the temperature of a particular financial community in relation to government policy, international conflicts, and the current state of and expected future of the economy. All benchmarks are indexes. Not all indexes are benchmarks.

Researching and Fine-Tuning Asset Allocations

If you think of an index as a portfolio holding a particular asset class, say large companies or short-term government bonds, this portfolio should be the best representation of the diverse kinds of securities available in that asset class or market segment. An index of energy stocks should hold a wide variety of stocks related to this sector of the market: oil companies, natural gas companies, drilling companies, providers of drilling equipment, and refiners. In this way the index captures what is going on throughout the industry. Then the index can be used to measure the risk and performance of this asset class or sector compared to other asset classes or sectors. This is very helpful in determining asset allocation strategies.

Some investors might be satisfied to buy an index fund based on an index that tracks the entire stock market. The big advantage to buying such a fund is that investors would get all the diversification offered by the market in one package and pay only one fee. But what if an investor wants to break up his stock portfolio into more precise allocations? If he buys a fund to track large stocks, another to track small stocks, and another to track mid-sized stocks, he can make more precise investment decisions.

For example, say the whole stock market index is up 5 percent. However, indexes that track smaller segments of the market give the investor a better idea of what parts of the market are doing well and which are not. If the asset manager sees that an index of small stocks is up 10 percent, while an index of large stocks is down 5 percent, he can fine-tune his asset allocations to pinpoint his investment strategy. If he thinks stocks that are down are cheap, he might sell some small stocks to buy more large stocks. If he feels that stocks that are doing well should keep on rising, he will sell large stocks to buy more small stocks.

The index also provides a research tool. This is especially true for one form of stock analysis called Technical Analysis. Technical analysts, also called technicians, chart indexes and compare them to trend lines, such as a 50-day moving average. Technical analysts believe that by comparing today's price movement to the past, the index reveals long-term patterns that can help investors find buy or sell signals.

Measuring Performance

You can build a portfolio in a vacuum, but without some measurement of how the broader market is doing, how do you know if you're doing well?

The index tells you. If the index rises, an indication of a healthy market, but your portfolio's value falls, it's time to make a change. But the example doesn't need to be so extreme. For example, your portfolio rose 10 percent last year. That's a respectable rate of return for one year. But, if the broader market index rose 20 percent last year, you realize that you have missed out on significant potential gains.

In particular, the index provides a benchmark against which active portfolio managers and investors can measure their skill at stock or bond picking. In a quick comparison, you can determine whether the active manager is adding any value for the fee you're paying him or her. If the portfolio created by the individual investor or the active manager doesn't beat the index's return, then the individual would have done better by just tracking the index instead of doing all that stock trading.

Creating Basis for Low-Cost Investment Vehicles

The index fund is a mutual fund comprised of all the components of an index, in the exact same weighting, or an extremely close approximation.

By following the strategy already designed by the index company, the portfolio should be both transparent and low cost. *Transparency* allows an investor to see everything in the portfolio. Most indexes publish the securities that make up the index, so an investor can easily see what should be in the index fund. And because the components of the index rarely change, the costs of running an index fund are very low. The index fund's goal is to match the index's rate of return, minus its low costs. The difference between the *rates of return* for the index and the index fund is called the *tracking error*. In a good index fund, the tracking error is very small, mere hundredths of a percentage point.

Fund Management Options

In Chapter 3, we learned that a mutual fund is an investment company. Investment companies pool money from many investors to buy financial securities such as stocks, bonds and short-term money-market instruments. Mutual funds can follow many different investment strategies and styles. But, in terms of management, funds fall into only two categories: actively managed and passively managed.

Actively Managed Funds

Actively managed funds are portfolios run by managers who actively trade stocks. As previously mentioned, most individual investors don't have the time, inclination, or skill to do the work necessary to make money in the market. By buying an actively managed fund, an investor essentially hires a specific portfolio manager to invest for him. An actively managed mutual fund can hold any stock the manager chooses, so long as the portfolio follows the investing style outlined in the fund's prospectus. The portfolio manager researches stocks, buys some that he thinks will rise in value and sells those that he thinks have reached their "full" valuation. If successful, the fund and its shareholders pocket healthy profits. In short, the fund manager's job is to create a portfolio that will outperform the index for the fund's particular investing style, or sector of the market. As long as the portfolio follows the chosen strategy, the fund can hold whatever stocks, bonds, futures, or options the manager thinks will perform best, and in whatever weightings he chooses. At the end of the year, funds compare their annual returns to the relevant index. For instance, large-capitalization stock funds typically compare themselves against the S&P 500 Index. An actively managed fund is considered successful if it beat the benchmark that year.

Beating an index isn't easy. A benchmark index reflects the collective wisdom of every investor buying or selling a particular type of security. As the sum total of all information available to investors, it's very hard to find an advantage to achieve a higher return than the index. So, anyone who beats the index must be smarter than every other investor. And these other investors include Wall Street investment banks and brokerages, large pension funds, hedge funds, other mutual funds, ETFs, analysts, researchers, and individuals who manage their own money for a living. Everyone has access to the same information, legally at least. So, it's not easy to get an edge on the competition. In order to beat the market, portfolio managers need to buy riskier investments with the potential for outsized returns.

Risk is defined as the measurable chance you take of making or losing money on an investment. The greater the risk, the more you stand to gain or lose. In the effort to beat the index, the manager could overweight the portfolio with a small group of stocks or sectors, making the fund less diversified than the benchmark. If the fund manager chooses right and his choices do very well, he will beat the index. Of course, if he chooses wrong, his portfolio will trail the index.

In this attempt to beat the market, the active-fund manager frequently buys and sells securities. This is called turnover. It's not uncommon to see a fund's turnover equal 100 percent. That means at the end of the year the entire portfolio is different from the one held at the beginning of the year.

No doubt, the active portfolio manager does a lot of work managing the fund's investments. In addition to performing research, he needs to watch the market, his stocks, economic indicators and other variables to decide the right composition of the fund and the proper time to buy and sell. But investors pay a high fee for this service. Actively managed funds charge anywhere from 1 percent to 5 percent of total assets each year. But if the fund manager doesn't beat the index, the investor is right to ask, "What am I paying him for? What value is he adding?" In this case, not much.

Passively Managed Funds

Passive management, of course, is the opposite of active management. Instead of actively buying and selling stocks throughout the year, passive management picks a portfolio and leaves it alone. The most famous form of passive management is the index fund.

On average, in a single year, only a quarter of all actively traded mutual funds and portfolio managers beat the index. For instance, the S&P 500 Index is a stock market benchmark that tracks the largest companies in the market. Market capitalization is a way to measure a company's size. All the companies in this index are large-capitalization companies, which S&P classifies as worth more than $5 billion. According to Standard & Poor's, for the five years ending March 30, 2007, the S&P 500 beat 72 percent of all large-cap funds. The S&P MidCap 400, which tracks companies with market capitalizations between $1.5 billion and $5.5 billion, outperformed 77 percent of all mid-cap funds. And the S&P SmallCap 600, which tracks companies valued under $2 billion, outperformed 78 percent of the small-cap funds.

Considering how few funds beat the index on a consistent basis, many people think that getting the index's return isn't such a bad deal. When you look at the index and see that it rose 10 percent last year, it feels good to know your investments kept pace with the broader market instead of lagging behind it. Of course, in a year when the index declines, the index fund does, too.

To provide a consistent barometer for the market they track, indexes need to be stable. They don't change their component stocks, or stock weightings, very often. Indexes do change when companies merge, go out of business or fail to meet index requirements, but for the most part there's little turnover. With very little movement in the index, once an index fund is created and all the necessary stocks have been bought, the fund pretty much takes care of itself.

Because the index fund's strategy is to simply follow the index, its portfolio manager makes few, if any, investment decisions. He essentially takes the cash invested in the fund and buys more of the same stocks, or sells stocks when investors redeem their shares. Now that's passive management. Some indexes are hard to replicate because some components are very small and illiquid. In these cases a fund manager may not own every stock, or may buy index futures to capture the movement of these stocks. But for the most part, index fund managers don't need to research or make investment decisions, Because of this, the manager can't reasonably demand a large fee. Therefore, passive management leads to low management fees. This is one of the biggest selling points for index funds.

The lack of turnover creates another advantage: fewer taxes. Every time the actively managed fund sells a stock it creates a tax event, which results in a capital gain or loss. More sales mean more capital gains. And, as we learned in Chapter 2, the tax liability in a mutual fund is passed along to its shareholders. Therefore, actively managed funds create a larger tax liability than index funds.

"Wall Street critics refer to index-fund investing as 'guaranteed mediocrity,'" wrote Burton Malkiel in his classic investing book, *A Random Walk Down Wall Street*. "But experience shows conclusively that index fund buyers are likely to obtain results exceeding those of the typical fund managers, whose large advisory fees and substantial portfolio turnover tends to reduce investment yields."[2]

See Table 4.1 for a summary of how index funds stack up against actively managed funds.

Chapter 5, "Fee Bitten," will provide a detailed explanation of how fund management fees can erode an investor's returns.

A Few Words About Risk

An important point to remember is that the structure and the management style of the product do not determine the fund's level of risk. Actively managed funds are not inherently riskier than passively managed funds.

TABLE 4.1   Actively versus Passively Managed Funds

	Actively Managed	Index Funds (Passively Managed)
Broad diversification	Maybe	Yes
Good for index funds	No	Yes
Guarantee to give rate of return very close to benchmark index	No	Yes
Low management fees	No	Yes
Low stock turnover	Possible, but unlikely	Yes
Low transaction fees	No	Yes
Tax efficient	No	Yes
Transparent	No	Yes
Risk level is known	No	Yes
Potential to beat index	Yes	Very small

Mutual funds do not automatically have more or less risk than ETFs. The amount of risk in the fund is determined entirely by the risk factor of the underlying securities.

An index mutual fund following the S&P 500 Index, such as the Vanguard 500, and an ETF tracking the same index, such as the SPDR, have identical risk profiles. They hold the exact same securities in the exact same weightings.

It's easy to see how the actively managed Fidelity Select Biotechnology mutual fund (symbol: FBIOX) is much riskier than the SPDR, an ETF based on an index. However, an ETF tracking a biotechnology sector index, such as the iShares Nasdaq Biotechnology Index Fund (symbol: IBB), would be much riskier than an actively managed mutual fund holding U.S. Treasury bonds.

Remember, the risk comes from the assets the fund holds, not the fund's structure.

The Rise of the Index Funds

In 1965, Paul Samuelson, a renowned economist and professor at the Massachusetts Institute of Technology, wrote a paper evaluating the information inherent in stock prices. One of Samuelson's influences was Louis Bachelier, who conceived the Random Walk Theory. As a French doctoral student in 1900, Bachelier wrote "The Theory of Speculation," in which he declared that "There is no useful information contained in the historical price movements of securities."[3] This is another way of saying that past performance has no bearing on future returns. Samuelson proved the theory, then expanded it in a paper called "Properly Anticipated Prices Fluctuate Randomly."

In the paper Samuelson concluded that "the intrinsic value of stocks is nothing but their market price at the moment."[4] Essentially, fluctuations in stock prices occur because buyers and sellers disagree over the stock's inherent value. At any point in time when both sides agree on a price, equilibrium is reached and a trade is made. In 1970, Samuelson became the first American to win the Nobel Prize for Economics.

Also in 1965, Eugene Fama, as a doctoral candidate at the University of Chicago, wrote a Ph.D. thesis advancing this argument. He concluded that stock prices fully reflect all the known and available information about that security at any given moment in time. He called this the "Efficient Market Hypothesis."

This is contrary to the thinking of most investors who buy securities based on the analysis of stock fundamentals, such as the price-to-earnings, or p/e, ratio. Fundamental Analysis holds that a stock's inherent value can be determined by looking at its financial statements or forming expectations of what the fundamentals will be in the future. Fundamental analysts look for an edge—a piece of information that will show that the stock should trade at a different price. If the analysts believe the stock is currently undervalued and worth more than its current price, they buy it. When the analysts believe the security has reached its true value, or is even overvalued, they sell it.

Of course, stock prices rise. What's the point of buying an investment unless you think the price will rise and you will make a profit? But the Efficient Market Hypothesis states that there's no way for an investor to know which stocks will rise or fall. It holds that all past and current information available about a stock and its performance is already incorporated into its price. Thus, the market is efficient because all the known information is already priced into a stock. If that's the case, then there's nothing to give an investor a clue as to a stock's future direction. Fama concluded that a stock's price movements were random and unpredictable because prices changed with the appearance of unexpected news. At any moment in time, when a trade occurs, that is what the buyers and sellers agreed is the best estimate of the stock's value. This thesis led to Fama's appointment as a professor of finance at the University of Chicago, where he continues to teach.

> An "efficient" market is defined as a market where there are large numbers of rational, profit-maximizers actively competing, with each trying to predict future market values of individual securities, and where important current information is almost freely available to all participants. In an efficient market, competition among the many intelligent participants leads to a situation where, at any point in time, actual prices of individual securities already reflect the effects of information based both on events that have already occurred and on events which, as of now, the market expects to take place in the future. In other words, in an efficient market at any point in time the actual price of a security will be a good estimate of its intrinsic value.[5]

Together, these two theories gave a sucker punch to active managers who think they can outperform the market. The Random Walk Theory says that because stock prices don't follow patterns, a stock's past performance can't predict its future movement. Then the Efficient Market Theory claims that markets are efficient and stock prices reflect all the available information, making them fully valued all the time. The combined theories indicate that people who pick stocks can't beat the market over the long term. Active investors who outperform the market do so because of luck, not skill.

Because they attacked the basic foundation of the investing business, these ideas were slow to gain acceptance on Wall Street. Five years later, at

Wells Fargo Bank, John McQuown, William Fouse, and James Vertin developed the first commercial product to track an index. It started when Charles Shwayder, a business school student at the University of Chicago, became enamored with the theories underlying index investing. McQuown, meanwhile, had learned about these theories by attending seminars for business people at the University of Chicago.[6] Shwayder convinced his father, who happened to run the Samsonite luggage company,[7] to let McQuown's crew create an index product for the company's pension fund. With $6 million from Samsonite, on July 1, 1971, Wells Fargo launched the first index fund.[8] The fund consisted of an equal weighting of all the stocks listed on the New York Stock Exchange, about 1,500. Constant rebalancing and excessive transaction costs turned the running of the fund into a "nightmare," according to Fouse.[9]

Two years later, Wells Fargo tried again. This time it decided to track the S&P 500 in a market-cap weighted closed-end fund for institutional investors. Also in 1973, another of Fama's students, Rex Sinquefield, launched "the first publicly marketed index fund" at the American National Bank of Chicago. This, too, was for institutional investors. But individual investors weren't left behind for long.

That same year, Princeton economist Burton Malkiel introduced the masses to the Efficient Market Hypothesis with his landmark book *A Random Walk down Wall Street*. He explained all the theories leading up to that point and concluded that it was a waste of time to pick stocks or invest in actively managed mutual funds. He called for the formation of an index fund for the small investor. The next year, in the article "Challenge to Judgment," Samuelson, now a Nobel Laureate, called on the financial industry to create a mutual fund to track the S&P 500 Index.[10]

In 1975, Charles Ellis called active management useless in his article "The Loser's Game." His research "showed 85 percent of active managers had failed to beat the S&P 500 index over the previous 10 years," because costs took 20 percent of the funds' returns.[11]

Soon, individual investors had that option. Dissatisfied with active management, John Bogle founded The Vanguard Group in 1975 to create a new way of investing. Vanguard launched the first index mutual fund for retail investors on May 1, 1976. Criticized by nearly everyone, the Index 500 Fund, which tracked the S&P 500, was called "Bogle's Folly."

It took quite a while for the idea to catch on. The second index fund didn't appear until nine years later. But by 2007, the renamed Vanguard 500 Index Fund (symbol: VFINX) was the largest mutual fund in the world, and Vanguard was the second largest U.S. mutual fund company. Currently 8 percent of the assets in the U.S. equity market are held in an index fund tracking the S&P 500.

The Big Index Companies

ETF providers and index providers are rarely the same organization. The ETF provider is concerned with managing and selling the fund. Creating and calculating an index takes a different skill set and uses other resources. The basic model for the index mutual fund is that the fund chooses an existing index and then pays the index provider a licensing fee to use it. ETFs basically follow this formula.

But the explosion of ETFs has created a need for many new indexes. Nearly every ETF tracks an index. Although there are many well-known benchmark indexes in the financial markets today, most, if not all, have been turned into ETFs already. ETF providers need new ideas, and hence new indexes in order to create new ETFs. This works well, because investors now seek more diverse asset allocations than simply large or small U.S. stocks and bonds.

This has sparked a cottage industry of new, small, index providers as well as giving a boost to the largest index providers. Now, instead of picking a benchmark or existing backlist index, many ETF providers are working together with index providers to create new indexes for innovative portfolio ideas, such as tracking stocks in foreign markets or obscure, under-the-radar U.S. industries.

This is a brief introduction to the most widely followed indexes, the companies that make them, and the ETFs that track them. All of these companies create and maintain many more indexes than mentioned here. At the end of each provider's description, a list of the ETFs that track the indexes mentioned is provided.

Dow Jones

The most famous index is the Dow Jones Industrial Average. It's owned by Dow Jones & Co., the publisher of the *Wall Street Journal*. Created in 1896, by Charles Henry Dow, the DJIA—also called The Dow Industrials, the Dow 30, or just the Dow—literally started out as a simple average. The prices of a group of stocks were added together, then divided by the total number of companies. This is called *price weighting*.

Much as in Dow's day, the component stocks of the Dow Jones Industrial Average are chosen by the editors of the *Wall Street Journal*. Currently comprised of 30 major U.S. industrial companies, it remains an average of the stock prices. However, instead of dividing the total price by 30, it's now divided by a factor that takes into consideration stock splits and new additions over the years.

The Dow is the stock market's premier index. When people say the market rose 100 points, they mean that the Dow rose 100 points. While the Dow is influential and an important link to the past, it focuses strictly on industrial companies, so it completely overlooks some important parts of the economy. Dow Jones creates many other indexes to track market sectors in both the United States and abroad.

At the opposite end of the spectrum from the 30-stock Dow Jones Industrial Average is the Dow Jones Wilshire 5000 Total Market Index. Created in 1974, the Wilshire 5000 measures the performance of all publicly traded U.S. stocks with available price data. Currently, that's a little less than 5,100 stocks. In 2004, Wilshire started working with Dow Jones to maintain and disseminate the Wilshire 5000 and its other indexes. While the Wilshire 5000 is considered the most comprehensive index for the U.S. equity market, it remains relatively obscure to the average investor.

Standard & Poor's

The age and history of the Dow Jones Industrial Average helps investors view the stock market's progression over the past 110 years. However, today most market participants consider the Standard & Poor's 500 Index to be the best gauge for measuring the performance of the U.S. equity market. Composed of 500 leading U.S. companies, the S&P 500 tracks about 75 percent of the U.S. equity market.[12] Chosen by a committee, these are not necessarily the 500 largest companies in the United States, but the ones that best represent the U.S. economy.

Unlike the Dow, which is an average, or price-weighted, index, the S&P 500 is a *market-cap weighted index*. That means each stock's weight in the index is proportionate to its market value. Market value, also known as *market capitalization*, is determined by multiplying all of a company's outstanding shares by its stock price. All the companies in this index are large-capitalization companies, which S&P classifies as a market value worth more than $5 billion.

For example, if Company A has 100 million outstanding shares and the stock trades at $55, the market capitalization is $5.5 billion. If a smaller company, Company B, can only sell ten million shares into the market, but it also sells for $55 a share, its market capitalization is only $550 million. Since Company A can sell 10 times as many shares as Company B, its market value is 10 times greater. If the total number of shares from all 30 companies on the Dow equaled 1 billion, in a market-cap weighting Company A would represent 10 percent of those shares, while Company B would represent just 1 percent. However, a price-weighted index such as the Dow would give them equal weight in the index because they have the same price. This gives the smaller company a greater impact than the larger one. Standard &

Poor's says that since creating the index on March 4, 1957, it is "widely regarded as the best single gauge of the U.S. equities market."[13] At the end of 2007, more than $1.53 trillion was directly invested in the index through index funds and ETFs. Both the largest index mutual fund, the Vanguard 500 Index Fund, and the largest ETF, the Standard and Poor's Depositary Receipts, or SPDR (symbol: SPY), track the index.

Russell

Founded as a brokerage in 1936 by Frank Russell, in the 1960s the firm began managing money managers instead of managing money. In 1984, the company decided it wanted its own tools to measure how the managers were performing. Researchers at the firm, now called Russell Investment Group, developed three indexes to act as objective benchmarks for measuring manager performance.[14]

They created the Russell 3000, comprised of the 3,000 largest U.S. companies by market cap. The Russell 3000 represents approximately 98 percent of the investable U.S. stock market. In order to measure the performance of small-cap funds, the Russell 3000 was broken in two. The Russell 1000 holds the 1,000 largest U.S. stocks by market cap and the Russell 2000 holds the 2,000 smallest stocks of the Russell 3000. With the large-cap market already widely tracked by the Dow Jones Industrial Average and S&P 500, the Russell 1000 didn't gain wide acceptance. However, at the time there was no broad measure for the universe of small-cap stocks. The Russell 2000 filled that void and is now considered the benchmark for the small-cap market.

MSCI Barra

When U.S. investors want to invest in an index of international stocks, they first think of MSCI. With more than 90 percent of the international equity assets in North America tracking MSCI indexes, the company is the leading benchmark provider of international equity indexes. Originally started in 1969 as Capital International Perspectives, it became MSCI (Morgan Stanley Capital International) in 1986, when Morgan Stanley bought a controlling interest in the index provider. In 2004, MSCI acquired Barra, a family of indexes that measure risk in the market.

The MSCI EAFE (Europe, Australasia, Far East) index is widely accepted as the premier broad U.S. index for tracking international equities.

FTSE International

FTSE is an independent company owned by the *Financial Times* newspaper and the London Stock Exchange. While FTSE has many international indexes, they are used primarily by investors outside the United States. The company's flagship index is the FTSE 100, which has been the benchmark for the London Stock Exchange since 1984. The company name is pronounced Footsie and the index is called the Footsie 100. The FTSE 100 comprises the 100 largest companies by market cap in the United Kingdom. It represents 81 percent of the U.K. market.[15]

FTSE is expanding its footprint in the U.S. equity market through a partnership with Research Affiliates. This investment management firm is a leading proponent of a new concept in indexing based on company fundamentals, or fundamentally weighted indexing. These indexes have the family name FTSE RAFI (pronounced "footsie rafi"). RAFI stands for Research Associates Fundamental Index. Fundamentally weighted indexes will be discussed in detail in Chapter 7, "The New Indexers."

FTSE also calculates a series of real estate indexes in a partnership with the National Association of Real Estate Investment Trusts (NAREIT). These indexes have been used as the basis for five iShares ETFs.

Indexes from the Stock Exchanges

The stock exchanges are where the stock market takes place. For the past decade, ETF listings have been a growth business for the exchanges. The exchanges provide services to support the products in terms of trade execution, marketing, and, of course, index creation. In addition to the corporate index providers, the stock exchanges have also seen the enormous revenue potential of index creation and licensing.

Having long used indexes to measure the performance of the stocks that trade on their own individual markets, and considering they have all the pricing data, they have a unique perspective on what makes a good index.

American Stock Exchange

The American Stock Exchange, or Amex, is the birthplace of the exchange-traded fund and the market with the most ETF listings. In-house developers devised the idea for the ETF in the early 1990s as a way to drum up trading volume. Together with State Street Global Advisors, it launched the first ETF, the SPDR, in 1993. The Amex Composite Index tracks the aggregate market value of the various products that trade on the exchange, such as closed-end funds, real estate investment trusts, and master limited partnerships as well as stocks and ETFs.

Because it tracks a varied group of asset classes, the Amex Composite isn't widely followed. However, as the premier exchange for ETFs, the Amex has either created or helped to create many of the indexes these ETFs are based upon. In 2003, the Amex created the 30 Intellidex (intelligent index) Indexes for PowerShares Capital Management. The main two indexes are the

Dynamic Market Intellidex Index and the Dynamic OTC (Over the Counter) Intellidex Index.

In early 2008, the NYSE Euronext, discussed below, agreed to acquire the Amex, its cross-town rival, for about $260 million. How this will affect the ETF industry in general and the Amex's index and ETF business, in particular, is discussed in Chapter 11.

NYSE Euronext

Founded in 1792, the New York Stock Exchange remains the premier U.S. stock market at the start of the twenty-first century.

In 1966, the NYSE created the Common Stock Index, later renamed the NYSE Composite Index, as a composite of all the common stocks listed on the exchange. For the next three decades, the NYSE Composite held most of the stocks listed in the United States. But in the 1990s, as the electronic NASDAQ Stock Market became the place for the hot technology sector, the NYSE Composite was no longer widely tracked.

Over the past decade, in order to keep up competitively, the NYSE has gone on a major growth spurt through acquisitions. In 2006 it merged with Archipelago Holdings, an electronic exchange, to create the NYSE Group. Archipelago became the NYSE Arca, a fully electronic stock exchange, analogous to the NASDAQ. With broader eligibility requirements and listing standards than the NYSE, the Arca provides a place where small and emerging companies can grow. This has also become the NYSE's main marketplace for ETFs.

The next year it merged with Euronext, the first cross-border stock exchange in the European Union. Currently it's the EU's second largest bourse, operating as a merged Amsterdam, Brussels, Lisbon, and Paris stock exchange. Then in 2008, it offered to buy the Amex.

In 2002, the NYSE created four proprietary indexes to be used for ETFs. The NYSE 100 tracks the 100 largest stocks on the New York Stock Exchange, covering 36 percent of the market cap on the exchange.

Originally a market-cap weighted index, the NYSE Composite Index was relaunched the following year as a float-adjusted cap weighting. Instead of multiplying the price by all the company's shares outstanding, many of which are held by insiders and don't trade, the relaunched index multiplied the price by just the actual number of shares that trade, also known as the float. Because traders can't buy shares held by insiders, the float-adjusted index is said to give a clearer picture of the company's market value that can be traded.

NASDAQ

The NASDAQ Stock Market, strictly speaking, isn't a stock exchange. A stock exchange is a physical building with a trading floor where human traders interact to trade securities. The NASDAQ, like the NYSE Arca, is an electronic stock market. This means all the trading occurs over computers. Because of its importance to the financial markets, even though it doesn't have a trading floor, the SEC now considers the NASDAQ a stock exchange.

A good index for tracking sectors of the economy completely ignored by the Dow is the NASDAQ 100. Considered the main index for the U.S. technology sector, the NASDAQ 100 tracks the 100 largest nonfinancial companies, domestic and international, on the NASDAQ Stock Market. The largest industry groups in the index are computer hardware, software, Internet, telecommunications, retail, and biotechnology. The ETF that tracks the NASDAQ 100 hit the market in 1999. It remains the largest ETF launch in history. Originally named the NASDAQ 100 Trust Shares ETF, it's better known as the Triple Q or the Qubes, because its original ticker symbol was QQQ. In 2006, NASDAQ sold its exchange-traded fund business to ETF sponsor Powershares Capital Management. Officially renamed the Powershares QQQ, the current ticker symbol is QQQQ because it now lists on the NASDAQ, which requires four letters in its tickers.

The NASDAQ Stock Market Composite Index tracks all the stocks on the NASDAQ Stock Market, the home for most of the nation's small and growth-oriented companies. This includes most the companies in the technology and biotechnology industries.

Actively Managed ETFs

Early in 2008, the SEC gave approval for the first actively managed ETFs. They were launched by Bear Stearns and PowerShares. At this time, the products were too new to do a proper comparison with ETFs based on indexes. At first glance they appear to lose some of the benefits that come from passively managed ETFs and take on the disadvantages of actively managed mutual funds. Their main advantage is they have lower expense ratios than the average actively managed mutual fund. These are still experimental products and it remains to be seen if there will be broad acceptance among investors. Most new ETFs continue to be index funds. This is discussed in more detail in Chapter 11.

Summary

An index is a tool for tracking the direction and health of a financial market. An index fund is an investment company whose objective is to earn the same return as a particular market index.

Mutual funds follow one of two management styles: actively managed and passively managed. Actively managed funds are portfolios run by managers who actively trade stocks in an effort to outperform the index for the fund's particular investing style. Passive investing managers pick a portfolio and do very little trading. Index funds are passively managed. Table 4.2 provides a list of the ETFs that track the benchmark indexes mentioned in this chapter.

ETFs are index funds, and as such offer the same benefits as index mutual funds:

- A broadly diversified portfolio for a very small investment.
- A guarantee that investors will earn the market's rate of return with very little effort.
- Very low management fees.
- Very low stock turnover, thus few transaction fees.
- Low turnover also means small capital-gains tax liability.
- The portfolios are transparent. All the stocks are known; thus it is easy to determine the risk level of the portfolio.

The big advantage that actively managed funds have over passively managed funds is the potential to beat the benchmark index. However, beating an index isn't easy, because the index reflects the sum total of all

TABLE 4.2   ETFs That Track the Indexes Listed in This Chapter

Index	ETF
Dow Jones Industrial Average	DIAmonds Trust Series (ticker symbol: DIA)
Dow Jones Wilshire 5000	SPDR DJ Wilshire Total Market ETF (TMW)
Standard & Poor's 500	SPDR (SPY)
	iShares S&P 500 Index (IVV)
Russell 1000	iShares Russell 1000 (IWB)
Russell 2000	iShares Russell 2000 (IWM)
Russell 3000	iShares Russell 3000 (IWV)
MSCI EAFE	IShares MSCI EAFE Index Fund (EFA)
FTSE 100	NETS FTSE 100 Index Fund (LDN)
FTSE RAFI 1000	PowerShares FTSE RAFI US 1000 Portfolio (PRF)
Indexes created by the AMEX	PowerShares Dynamic Market Portfolio (PWC)
	PowerShares Dynamic OTC Portfolio (PWO)
NYSE Composite	IShares NYSE Composite Index Fund (NYC)
NYSE 100 Index	IShares NYSE 100 Index Fund (NY)
NYSE Arca Tech 100	NYSE Arca Tech 100 ETF (NXT)
NASDAQ 100	Powershares QQQ (QQQQ)
NASDAQ Composite	Fidelity NASDAQ Composite Index Tracking Stock (ONEQ)

information available to investors. So, it's very difficult to find an edge to achieve a higher return than the index.

This quest to beat the market leads the active fund manager to trade more often, incurring more transaction costs, and to take on riskier investments, increasing the potential for large losses. For their work in trying to create market-beating returns, active fund managers charge higher fees than passive fund managers.

The question becomes, Are the potential market-beating returns of the actively managed mutual fund worth the extra cost and increased risk? With 70 percent to 80 percent of all active fund managers unable to beat their market index, there is a high potential to end up with a year-end return lower than the benchmark index. So the big advantages of the actively managed fund are hard to attain, while the benefits of the passively managed index fund are practically guaranteed.

Chapter 5, "Fee Bitten," will provide a detailed explanation of how fund management fees erode an investor's returns. This could prove our case that indexing is the preferred investment strategy for the individual investor.

Fee Bitten

One of the basic tenets of investing is "Don't pay more in fees than necessary." You can't control whether you'll make a profit or loss on any investment, but you *can* control what you pay to acquire and hold the investment.

Fees are fairly consistent, in the sense that they consistently eat into your profits (also known as your *return on investment*, or ROI). This is one area where investors should focus a lot of their attention. The concept is so obvious and simple you're probably staring at this page wondering if I take you for a dolt. But the sad fact is that many investors *never* consider fees when evaluating an investment.

Most financial advisers and mutual fund advertisements focus strictly on annual returns. Even articles by personal finance journalists can be guilty of this. The idea is that if a particular fund or stock earned a 15 percent profit last year, it has a good track record and a reputation for making money. Hence, it must be a good investment. Of course, the same advisers and marketers who promote the fund or stock will then add a phrase you've probably heard hundreds of times: Past returns are no guarantee for future performance.

The reason they say that is because the SEC makes them say it. Usually, they say it under their breath, or in small print, as if it were just a throw-away line. In fact, this is the most important piece of information they are telling you. Yesterday's great investment might be tomorrow's dud. That's because no one knows what will happen in the future. Yes, that's obvious too. Of course, no one knows the future. But Wall Street wants you to think that their products can be counted on as reliably as other products in your life.

Wall Street Produces Vintages

When you buy Coca-Cola, Heinz Ketchup, or a Hershey's chocolate bar, you expect the product to taste exactly the same as it did the last time you bought it and exactly the same as the first time you tasted it as a child. When you buy a prescription drug, you expect it to have the exact same affect on your body every single time. When you buy a specific laundry detergent, you expect your clothes to get just as clean as the last load. These businesses are built on the idea that they can give customers the exact same experience every time. Consumers rely on this consistency; it's a matter of trust. Companies achieve this by adhering to a specific formula and consistent use of the same ingredients under strict quality control.

However, Wall Street's products aren't like this. Investments are more analogous to the production of fine wine. In the wine industry, every year is a new vintage. And every vintage is a unique product that tastes different from the year before. If the Coca-Cola you bought yesterday tasted like cola, but the one you bought today tasted like root beer, you wouldn't know what to expect tomorrow and would be leery of buying the product again. Wine consumers, however, accept this inconsistency. It's part of the fun of drinking wine.

A winemaker may use the same type of grapes from the same plot of land every year, but no two vintages taste exactly the same, nor yield the same experience. Being an agricultural product, the wine is affected by factors outside the farmer or winemaker's control, most noticeably the weather. The only thing consistent is inconsistency. Every year the quality of the final product is a gamble. The Bordeaux region of France is famous for producing some of the finest wines in the world, but over the course of 20 years, two or three years will be exceptional, two or three years will be mediocre, and the rest will be in the range of high quality for which Bordeaux wines are known, but not amazing.

That's exactly the case with stocks, bonds, and funds. Every year, every investment is a gamble. You would be hard-pressed to find a mutual fund or stock that posted the same return on investment two years in a row. So many things can affect an investment: the economy, war, the price of oil, scandal, or simply poor management. But Wall Street doesn't want you to focus on this. Financial advisors and fund companies want you to look at the 15 percent return last year and say to yourself, "This fund is a winner, so I will buy this one over the one that fell 10 percent." But, in fact, last year's losers may be this year's winners, and vice versa.

While you can't predict how well your investment will do, you can control how much you pay for it. This is where index funds and ETFs shine. Currently, almost every ETF charges less than 1 percent in annual expense ratios. However, in November 2006, Claymore Securities broke the 1 percent barrier with two funds charging 1.6 percent: the Claymore Macroshares Oil Up Tradeable Share (UCR) and the Claymore Macroshares Oil Down Tradeable Shares (DCR). These are the exceptions to the rule,

Furthermore, these are not true ETFs, as will be explained in Chapter 8, "The ETFs That Aren't ETFs."

According to Morningstar, the average expense ratio for the entire universe of mutual funds is 1.31 percent a year. This includes all actively managed funds, many of which charge between 2 percent to 5 percent in annual expenses. Not including actively managed funds, the average expense ratio for index funds is 0.74 percent. But the average expense ratio for all ETFs is 0.44 percent.

Looking for Low Management Fees

Lower fees should be one of your top priorities in any investment product. Smaller fees equal more money in your pocket. Sometimes you need to pay more for a higher level of service, but not in index-based products. Let's be honest. Index funds are mostly a commodity business, so you should go for the cheapest one.

An index is a theoretical construct; it's just a number calculated from a mathematical equation composed of stock prices and their weightings. An index has a definitive value at any point in time, which is the total of that calculation. But, in the real world, holding a portfolio of those stocks entails costs.

According to Morningstar, the leading mutual fund research company, there are 42 index funds tracking the S&P 500 index. They should all have the same return minus the *expense ratio,* also called the *tracking error.* If the index rises 10 percent and the expense ratio is 0.5 percent, the shareholder's real return is 9.5 percent. The fund with the largest tracking error of 1.55 percent, the Rydex S&P 500 (symbol: RYSOX), would return a much worse 8.45 percent, while the one charging the smallest expense ratio, the TIAA-CREF Institutional S&P 500 Index (symbol: TISPX) at just 0.07 percent, returns the best result, 9.93 percent. And that's cheaper than the SPDR.

To see how deeply fees cut into returns, let's take another look at a fictional investor, Phil Mapockets. In this example, let's look at three funds with different expense ratios to see how they would affect Phil's returns.

The first is an ETF that charges 20 basis points, or 0.2 percent, just one fifth of one percent. One hundred basis points equal one percentage point. Financial insiders use the term because it's an easier way to describe percentages of less than one percent. Instead of saying 20 hundredths of a percent or zero point two percent, they say 20 basis points (also called bips, for short). One percentage point, and one percent, written as 1 percent, are not the same thing. For example, last year you paid your certified financial planner (CFP) 10 percent of your profits, and this year you agree to pay him 11 percent of your profits. It doesn't look like much more. It's just a

TABLE 5.1   How Fees Cut into Returns

Expense Ratio	0.2%	1%	5%
Principal	$10,000	$10,000	$10,000
10% return on investment (ROI)	$1,000	$1,000	$1,000
Gross assets after one year	$11,000	$11,000	$11,000
Annual expense	$22	$110	$550
Net balance	$10,978	$10,890	$10,450

one-percentage point increase. But in actuality, you've given the CFP a 10 percent raise. If you paid him $10 last year, you've given him $1 more this year. One dollar is 10 percent of ten dollars. The second fund is an index mutual fund that charges a fee of 1 percent of gross assets, or 100 basis points. It's not simply 80 basis points greater than the ETF, it's five times more expensive. The third fund is an actively managed mutual fund that charges 5 percent, or 500 basis points. It's only 4.8 percentage points more the ETF, but the cost increase over the ETF fee is 2,400 percent. In other words, Phil must pay 25 times more of his assets for someone to manage this fund. In Table 5.1, Phil invests $10,000 in a fund. In the first year, the fund earns a 10 percent return, or $1,000, for end-of-year gross assets of $11,000. But that's not what ends up in Phil's pocket, also known as the end-of-year balance. The fund company, which worked so hard to produce these profits for you, wants to be paid.

After the first year, on the gross balance of $11,000, the ETF charges Phil a management fee of $22. Phil ends up with a net balance of $10,978. The index mutual fund charges 1 percent in fees. Phil would pay $110, for a net balance of $10,890. And if Phil buys the actively managed fund charging a 5 percent fee, he forks over $550 to the fund management company. That's more than half the $1,000 profit and $528 more than the ETF, giving Phil a total of just $10,450.

While highly unlikely, for this example, Phil's investment earned 10 percent a second year in a row. In Table 5.2, the ETF profit would be

TABLE 5.2   How Fees Cut into Returns, Part II

Determining Results for End of Year 2	Phil's ETF	Phil's Index Fund	Phil's Actively Managed Fund
10% return after second year	$1,097.80	$1,089	$1,045
Gross assets	$12,075.80	$11,979	$11,495
Annual fee	$24.15	$119.79	$574.75
Net balance	$12,051.65	$11,859.21	$10,920.25

$1,097.80. At the end of year two, his gross assets would be $12,075.80. Subtract the 0.2 percent fee and the net balance is $12,051.65. The fund with the 1 percent fee earned $1,089 for a gross of $11,979. After paying the fund company its fee, this investor holds a net balance of $11,859.21, or $192.44 less than the ETF. And the 5 percent fund returns only $1,045, for a total of $11,495. After that fund company takes its cut, the investor is left with only $10,920.25.

By the end of the second year, the total in the 5 percent fund is $1,131.40 lower than the ETF fund. In fact, it's about $58 less than the ETF had at the end of first year. And if the initial investment was $100,000 instead of $10,000, that would be $11,314 less than the ETF. It's not chump change and the discrepancy continues to grow with each ensuing year.

Actively managed funds are graded on how well they do compared to the market benchmark for their investment objectives. Funds that invest in large-capitalization stocks typically compare themselves against the S&P 500. In this example, an actively managed fund beat the S&P 500 by three percentage points. That would be a successful year for the fund, but not necessarily for the investor.

Using our previous example, the S&P 500 index earned 10 percent last year. So $10,000 invested in an S&P 500 index fund would end up worth $11,000. But the actively managed fund earned 13 percent, or $1,300. That's 30 percent more than the $1,000 the index fund earned, for a gross balance of $11,300.

As we saw above, the index fund with a 1 percent annual expense ratio would take $110 from the principle, leaving a net balance of $10,890. The actively managed fund with the 5 percent expense ratio would take $565 in annual fees, leaving Phil with $10,735. So even though the fund beat the index, the large fees still left the investor with less than the index fund. Only when the actively managed fund earns 15 percent, or five percentage points more than the index, does Phil do better than the index fund. After the fund takes its 5 percent cut, Phil has $10,925 left. Therefore, the actively managed fund needed to earn 50 percent more than the index, or $500, for Phil to end up with $35 more than the index fund. The rest went to management fees. And even then, the actively managed fund earning 15 percent and charging 5 percent ended up with a net balance $53 lower than the ETF charging 0.02 percent on a 10 percent return.

As you can see in Table 5.3, the size of the expense ratio determines how much money the investor ends up with. And while a few index funds actually post better returns than their index, that's the exception. Remember, each and every mutual fund and ETF is a company—an investment company. They don't produce goods like Procter & Gamble, or provide retailing services like Wal-Mart Stores. They produce a return on your investment.

TABLE 5.3   Active Fund Beats Index Fund, but Both Lose to ETF

	ETF with 0.2% Expense Ratio Earns 10%	Index Fund with 1% Expense Ratio Earns 10%	Actively Managed Fund with 5% Expense Ratio Earns 13%	Actively Managed Fund with 5% Expense Ratio Earns 15%
Gross return after one year	$11,000	$11,000	$11,300	$11,500
Annual expense ratio	$22	$110	$565	$575
Net balance	$10,978	$10,890	$10,735	$10,925

A typical company makes *revenues* from the sale of its goods or services. The company subtracts the costs to produce those goods or services from the revenues, and what's left over is the *profit*.

Compared to other companies, a mutual fund's costs aren't large. But mutual funds don't have revenues, because what they produce are either profits or losses. So, all the costs come directly out of the profits. The inherent conflict of interest in the mutual fund structure is that the more the fund manager gets paid, the less the shareholder ends up with. If you cut costs, you can get a higher return on your investment. And that adds up over the years.

"In the fund industry you don't get what you pay for, you get precisely what you don't pay for," says John C. Bogle, founder of the Vanguard 500 Fund. "The more the managers take the less the investors make."[1]

Summary

Fees are the investor's enemy. They destroy returns. Lower fees should always be near the top of an investor's priority list in purchasing any investment product. Smaller fees equal more money in your pocket.

Because investors can't control whether they'll make a profit or loss on any investment, they need to manage what they pay to acquire and hold the investment. Don't pay any more in fees than necessary. In a head-to-head comparison of two similar funds, the one with the lowest expense ratio always ends up with the most money. This is usually the ETF. ETFs, on average, charge the lowest expense ratio, 0.44 percent, compared with the 0.74 percent average for index funds.

As you can see, the size of the expense ratio determines how much money the investor ends up with. And while a few index funds actually post better returns than their index, that's the exception.

In short, always go for the least expensive index fund and, whenever possible, go for the least expensive product. It will add up over the years.

The Better Mousetrap

How Can ETFs Charge So Little?

Whenever you read or hear about ETFs, people recite their benefits over mutual funds as if they were reciting a mantra: low costs, tax efficiency, transparency, and flexibility. But few people understand how this comes about. As Chapter 5 explained, your fund's returns can't be known ahead of time, but its costs can. And higher costs mean less money in your pocket.

From the investor's point of view, mutual funds are inefficient. Funds charge their shareholders for everything that goes on inside the fund, such as *transaction fees, distribution charges, and transfer-agent costs*. In addition, they pass along their capital gains tax bill on an annual basis. These costs decrease the shareholder's return on his investment. On top of that, many funds charge a sales load for allowing you the pleasure of investing with them.

Mutual funds charge a combination of transparent and not-so-transparent costs that add up. It's simply the way they are structured. Most, but not all, of these costs are necessary to the process. Most could be a little cheaper; some could be a lot cheaper. But it's nearly impossible to get rid of them altogether. ETFs have transparent and hidden fees as well—there are simply fewer of them, and they cost less.

This chapter will pull back the curtain and expose the many costs inherent in the mutual fund structure. It will unscrew the nuts and bolts of mutual funds and ETFs to examine their many moving pieces, and outline every cost that their shareholders pay. Most of these costs are created inside the fund, but a few come from outside the fund, and the investor must pay these as well, of course. This chapter also highlights the costs that the ETF structure avoids.

By breaking down the process of assembling the ETF's creation unit, it will be shown how ETFs create a more efficient and cost-effective way for investors to gain exposure to the market than by investing in mutual fund shares. Not that ETFs are cost free, but their efficiency cuts out a lot of the expenses that mutual funds incur. "When you compare mutual funds to ETFs, it's like lifting up the curtain on the backstage antics," says James Pacetti, the president of ETF International, an ETF consulting company. "In an ETF the broad costs are unbundled so everyone can see them, but in a mutual fund you can't discover the costs. They are hidden [behind] the curtain."[1]

This chapter will also closely examine the ETF's costs. While not hidden, these costs still need explaining. Nor are all ETFs cheaper than index funds. If an ETF and an index mutual fund track the same index and the mutual fund proves to be a cheaper investment, buy it: Cheaper is better. But, for the most part, ETFs are less expensive.

I will also outline *dollar-cost averaging,* an investment strategy that is the one key instance where index funds may be a preferred investment. Still, by the end, the case for why individual investors should make ETFs the principle investment vehicle in their portfolio will be very clear.

Transparent Costs of Mutual Funds

Transparent costs are the only ones the SEC requires mutual funds to report to shareholders. They are visible and usually easy to discern. The expense ratio is the fund manager's fee. Operating expenses are usually everything else: the custodian, the administrator, and the transfer agent. The 12b-1 fee is for marketing and advertising.

The Load

In the prospectus of every mutual fund is a section on fees. The first fee mentioned is the load. Most fees in a fund are not a set rate, but a percentage of either the investment or total assets. The load is essentially a commission to pay the stockbroker who sold it to you. It's the percentage of your investment that the broker or distributor takes as his fee to invest the rest of your money. The load is not part of the operating expense for running the fund.

There are three types of loads: front, back and constant. When a fund has multiple shares classes, Class A, B or C, each one has a different load structure. The front-end load is so called because you pay it at the front end of the investment, when you buy the shares. According to Morningstar, a mutual fund research firm, the average front-end load in 2007 was 4.81 percent, just shy of 5 percent. Typically, these are Class A shares.

For instance, you give your broker or a mutual fund distributor $10,000 to invest in a mutual fund with a 5 percent load. The broker or distributor would take $500 and invest the remaining $9,500 in the mutual fund.

Investing less money than you had intended results in the purchase of fewer shares. This adversely affects your future returns. If your investment earns 10 percent over the next 12 months, your returns are significantly affected by the immediate deduction of the load. If you had invested the entire $10,000, your profit at the end of a year would be $1,000. But, after paying the load, the profit is only $950.

Some funds are sold with what is known as a *back-end load*. Instead of taking a percentage when you put money into the fund, a percentage is taken when you sell your shares within a specified number of years. The cut is taken on the back end, hence the name. Each year the load gets smaller until it eventually vanishes, usually five to ten years after the initial investment. Class B shares usually charge back-end loads.

Class C shares typically have no load, but charge a higher expense ratio than the Class A or B shares.

The 12b-1 fee listed in the expense ratio is considered by some to be a hidden load. That will be discussed later in the chapter.

Most actively managed funds are sold with a load. Most of these funds are sold through stockbrokers, who are salesmen. These funds don't even want you to buy from them directly: They want you to buy through the broker. The load pays the broker for his efforts and gives an incentive to suggest a particular fund for your portfolio.

One way to stand out from the crowd is to market yourself as the low-cost alternative. Vanguard and T. Rowe Price are two fund firms that market themselves based on costs, but the marketing is pretty subtle. Another way to stand out from the crowd is to market yourself as earning great returns. Ironically, funds typically measure returns before fees, which gives a lopsided view of what the typical investor truly earns.

With more than 8,000 funds in the United States, funds are a large part of the financial markets. Many follow similar investment strategies and the majority of them will produce average returns. Most will return a performance in the range of their benchmark index. After deducting costs and fees, that amount will be less than the benchmark's return.

For these funds, the only way to stand out from the crowd is to have a salesman talk up the fund to prospective clients. These funds are rarely the low-cost choice. Once in a while, they are the fund with the best returns. While there are great fund managers that have consistent success, for the most part, brokers sell mediocre mutual funds. If you're sitting in the office of a stockbroker, distributor, or financial adviser who is pushing a certain mutual fund with a load, ask yourself, "If the fund was such a good investment, why would it need to give someone an incentive to sell it?"

Of course, investors go to brokers and financial advisers because they provide a service. They help people build investment portfolios. A good financial adviser will take the time to discuss your goals and your risk comfort level. Then he or she will do research to find appropriate funds and other assets to help you reach your goals.

Financial advisers get paid one of two ways for their professional expertise: by commission or by an annual percentage of your entire portfolio, usually between 0.5 percent and 2 percent, in the same way you pay an annual percentage of your fund assets to the fund manager. If you don't pay an annual fee, the load is the commission the financial advisor receives. And if your broker gets paid by the load, don't be surprised if he doesn't recommend ETFs for your portfolio. That's because the commission that brokers receive for buying ETFs is seldom as hefty as the load.

So, there is an inherent conflict of interest in working with a broker who makes his living off the load: the bigger the commission, the higher his salary, but the smaller your investment. Be cautious if he is trying to sell a fund paying him a 5 percent load rather than a similar one paying a 3 percent load. What if the fund with the 3 percent load is better for your investment goals? If the broker doesn't recommend the fund with the 3 percent load, you are likely to end up owning a poorly performing fund with a high entrance fee.

Investors often don't realize that most financial advisers are stockbrokers, and stockbrokers are not necessarily *fiduciaries*. Fiduciaries are required to look after the best interests of their clients over their own profit. Stockbrokers aren't obligated to look after your best interests. However, they are required to provide suitable recommendations for your financial status, objectives, and risk tolerance. As long as it's an appropriate investment, a stockbroker isn't obligated to give you the best investment in that category. A stockbroker who puts you into an S&P 500 index fund with a load is providing a suitable recommendation, but he or she is not looking out for your best interests, which would mean suggesting the lowest cost alternative.

THE ALTERNATIVE: NO-LOAD INDEX FUNDS   Mutual funds do offer a low cost alternative: the no-load fund. True to its name, the no-load fund has no load. Every single dollar of the $10,000 that you want to invest goes into the index fund; none of it is whisked away by a middleman. The reason for this is that you do all the work that the stockbroker does for the average investor. You do the research and you fill out the forms to purchase the fund. In essence you are paying yourself the broker's commission, which you invest.

Buying a no-load fund for yourself is a great way to appreciate what the broker does for investors who can't navigate the financial waters alone. It's also a good way to appreciate that it isn't that hard to do.

Most index funds and a small group of actively managed funds don't charge a load. No-load index funds are the most cost efficient mutual funds to buy because they have smaller operating costs. If there is one rule to investing in mutual funds, it is that you should try to avoid paying a load.

The Expense Ratio

In a mutual fund's prospectus, after the load disclosure is a section called "Annual Fund Operating Expenses." This is better known as the expense ratio. It's the percentage of assets paid to run the fund. Well, most of them. Many costs are included in the expense ratio, but typically only three are broken out: the management fee, the 12b-1 distribution fee, and other expenses. And, it's not that easy to find out what fees are contained in the "other expenses" category.

Mutual funds are created by a *fund sponsor,* also known as the *principle underwriter.* The large fund companies that you have heard of—Fidelity Investments, Vanguard, T. Rowe Price, Putnam, Oppenheimer, and American Funds—are all fund sponsors. They create large collections of funds called families. Often the fund sponsor provides the fund's investment advisor and administrator.

Creating the fund consists of registering the fund with the SEC, preparing the corporate documents, and filing it with individual states. The sponsor provides the *seed capital* needed to buy the initial portfolio. The '40 Act requires an initial investment of $100,000 in seed capital. Fidelity Investments and The Vanguard Group are two of the largest fund sponsors in the United States.

But funds are public companies owned by the investors, or shareholders, not the fund sponsors. Fund sponsors typically assemble the group of third-party entities needed to operate the mutual fund. The first group is the fund's board of directors. The board governs the overall operation of the fund, but doesn't deal with its day-to-day administration. The board is a fiduciary. A fiduciary looks out for the assets of an investor and acts in that person's best interests. The board negotiates contracts with all the entities that run the fund and makes sure the fund's costs are reasonable (see Figure 6.1).

The board itself is not a big expense. According to the Investment Company Institute, the mutual fund industry's trade group, "director compensation represents, on average, one-third of one basis point of fund complex

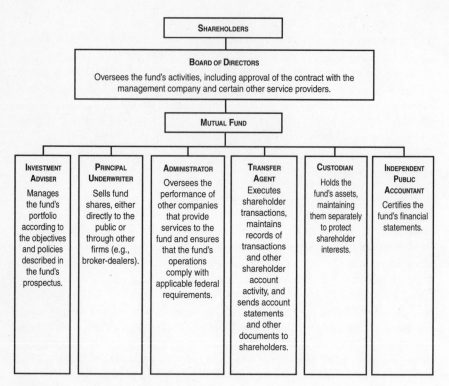

FIGURE 6.1   Structure of a Mutual Fund

Source: Investment Company Institute, *2007 Investment Company Fact Book*.
Copyright © by the Investment Company Institute (www.ici.org). Reprinted with
permission.

assets (0.000033). For example, a fund complex with $10 billion in assets
might pay $330,000 for all the directors of all the funds in the complex ($10
billion × 0.000033)."[2]

However, board members are typically affiliated with the mutual fund
company that sells the funds. So, they tend to be fairly liberal in how much
they will let the investment advisor charge to run the fund.

At least 40 percent of the board members must be independent of the
fund family. But investor advocates want board chairmen and 75 percent
of the board's members to be independent. They feel this will bring tighter
control to the fund's internal costs.

The board hires the investment adviser, also known as the portfolio
or fund manager, to manage the fund's assets. This is typically a team of
money managers that works for the fund sponsor. Every year, the board
evaluates and negotiates the fund management fee. This management fee is

broken out in the fund's prospectus as part of the expense ratio and is paid as a percentage of the fund's total assets.

In addition to paying the portfolio manager's salary, the management fee covers the cost of the investment manager's staff, research, technical equipment, computers, and travel expenses to send analysts to meet corporate management. It also pays for all the administrative and sales staff at the fund company.

Management fees can vary widely. The actively managed Federated Kaufmann Fund (symbol: KAUAX) charges a management fee of 1.43 percent out of an expense ratio of 2.18 percent. Meanwhile, the Fidelity Spartan 500 Index (symbol: FSMKX), an index fund tracking the S&P 500, has the lowest expense ratio of any mutual fund in the United States. It charges a management fee of 0.07 percent and a total expense ratio of 0.1 percent—only a tiny bit more than the SPDR. The average management fee is about 1.00%.

12b-1 Fees

Most mutual funds, including many no-load and index funds, charge a special marketing fee called a *12b-1 fee,* named after a section of the 1940 Act. The 12b-1 fee is broken out in the prospectus as part of the expense ratio. It can run as high as 0.25 percent in a front-end load fund and as high as 1 percent in a back-end load fund. Many investor-right advocates consider these expenses to be a disguised broker's commission.

One thing can be said for the front-end and back-end loads: They're upfront about what the fee will be, and it's a one-time charge. Essentially, you go to a broker, he or she helps you to buy a mutual fund, and you pay for the service.

This is not the case with the 12b-1 fee. While it is intended to pay for promotion and advertising, only 2 percent of the fees are used for that. The rest is paid to brokers for ongoing account servicing. Essentially, it's paid to the broker who sold you the fund on an annual basis, for as long as you own the fund, even if you never see him again. When they were created in 1980, the 12b-1 fee was the answer to a specific distribution problem. After the horrible stock market of the 1970s, the mutual fund industry was such in dire straits that Wall Street feared for its survival.[3]

Desperate to offset the cost of advertising and the printing and mailing of prospectuses and other sales literature, the industry convinced the Securities and Exchange Commission (SEC) to let them charge a percentage of investor assets for this specific purpose.[4] The implication was that investors would benefit because it would bring in more investors, and thus, more assets to the fund. The presumption was that the expense ratio would fall after spreading the fund's fixed costs over a larger group of shareholders.

But the fees didn't go away, and over time "instead of paying for distribution, [the fees quickly] became a substitute for front-end loads," said SEC Commissioner Christopher Cox in 2007. By charging a 12b-1 fee in the expense ratio, a fund could advertise itself as a no-load fund and still compensate brokers.[5]

Some fund industry members consider brokers part of the distribution process and claim this is simply another way of using the fees for their intended purpose. Some fund families use 12b-1 fees to cover the costs of being a member of a mutual fund supermarket. These supermarkets are centralized platforms where investors shop to access a wide variety of funds. The platforms charge the funds to participate in the supermarket.

In 2006, mutual funds collected $11 billion in 12b-1 fees. The SEC observed that the fees have moved away from their original purpose and accused some funds of using them to pay for administrative expenses. In 2007, the SEC began a formal review of how the fees are being used and whether to get rid of them.

With more than $12 trillion in assets at the end of 2007, the mutual fund industry is no longer at risk of going out business. As funds grow bigger, the 12b-1 fees harm investors in two specific ways. Like the management fee, the 12b-1 fee is a percentage of total assets. As a mutual fund acquires more assets, a percentage fee brings in more money to the broker. And if inflows rise the mutual fund gets bigger, so it doesn't need to spend on marketing. While managers like having a lot of assets in their funds, it can actually make it difficult for the fund to trade nimbly. This potentially lowers its total return.

Even worse, many mutual funds continue to charge 12b-1 fees even after they close to new investors and have no further need for promotion. ETFs do not charge 12-b1 fees: This cuts out a potential fee of 0.25 percent to 1 percent.

Operating Expenses

The final component of the expense ratio is operating expenses, an all-encompassing category for the many other costs needed to operate the fund. These include the administrator of the fund, the transfer agent, the custodian, and the accountant. This is a murky category, as these costs are not specifically delineated.

— **Administrator.** This entity is responsible for managing the day-to-day operation of the fund. This can be the investment advisor, another person from the fund sponsor, or a third party. The administrator can perform many functions, including transfer agent.

Custodian. After the fund's stockbroker buys the stocks for the fund's investment portfolio, he delivers them to the custodian who is responsible for holding the fund's assets in custody. The fund hires the custodian so the shareholders don't have to worry about the fund manager using the fund's assets for his personal use.

Transfer Agent. After the broker delivers the shares to the custodian, the custodian tells the transfer agent which shareholders invested money, how much, and how many shares they bought. The transfer agent is responsible for keeping track of each shareholder's account with the fund. It records how much money comes in and how many shares this buys. The transfer agent then sends out a statement describing the transaction. It also sends out quarterly statements telling investors how much they own. The transfer agent is also often the firm that provides the call-in center and phone representatives to talk to investors calling up the fund company to ask questions. The transfer agent can cost anywhere from 0.25 percent to 0.40 percent.

Accountant. Performs semi-annual audits of the funds holdings and assets and calculates the amount of capital gains taxes each shareholder must pay.

Index Provider. Index mutual funds and most ETFs don't create their own indexes. They track indexes made by companies that make indexes as part of their business. Many times these are publishers of financial news. Dow Jones, the company that owns the most famous index, publishes the *Wall Street Journal*. Standard & Poor's, which makes many indexes, also produces research for the financial industry and is a unit of the McGraw Hill publishing company. McGraw Hill also publishes *Business Week* magazine. These companies charge funds and ETFs a fee to name the fund after the index and track the index exactly.

Distributor. The distributor, or principle underwriter, is typically the fund sponsor. The principle underwriter signs a contract with the mutual fund to purchase its shares and then sells them to the public. Investors deal with the sponsor directly to buy and redeem shares. The distributor is also responsible for all marketing and advertising.

Taxes

Mutual funds are different from most companies because they distribute almost all their earnings to their shareholders each year. These come in the form of ordinary dividends and capital gains. By distributing the earnings, the fund pushes the responsibility of paying the fund's taxes onto the shareholder. This is called a "pass-through" because the taxes pass through the fund to the shareholders. The fund would pay taxes on any amount it retained. Funds and real estate investment trusts allowed to pass the taxes on to their shareholders are called Regulated Investment Companies (RIC).

DIVIDENDS   The dividends are regular equity dividends. This is a portion of a company's profit paid out to shareholders each quarter. If a fund holds a dividend-paying stock, it receives the dividend and then distributes it to the shareholders. This is taxed at the prevailing tax rate for dividends, which is 15 percent through 2010.

CAPITAL GAINS   Capital gains or losses come from the sale of any investment. When an investor purchases stock, bonds, futures, real estate, mutual fund shares, ETF shares, or any investment, he creates a taxable event. When he sells this investment, he creates another taxable event. If the investment sold at a price higher than the purchase price, he makes a profit, or a capital gain. If the investment is sold for less than the purchase price, the shareholder incurs a capital loss. Both are taxable events. Investors must pay taxes on capital gains. If the sale creates a capital loss, it can be written off against capital gains in other investments, or against ordinary income to lower the investor's total tax bill.

If the investment is sold less than a year after purchase, the capital gain is taxed as ordinary income. If the investor sells after holding the investment for more than year, the profit is taxed at a lower rate for long-term gains.

Like any other investor, when a mutual fund buys and sells shares it creates taxable events inside the fund. If it makes capital gains, taxes must be paid. Again the responsibility for taxes passes through the mutual fund to the investor. However, there is a big difference between the tax on the dividend and on the capital gains. The fund distributes the dividend to the shareholder. The shareholder can either receive the cash or reinvest the dividend in the fund. Either way, it's money he can spend. So, it seems reasonable that he would pay taxes on something tangible.

But shareholders never see the capital gains. They never leave the mutual fund. And while the mutual fund enjoys a capital gain, this doesn't necessarily increase the fund's share price. In fact, to add insult to injury, it's possible for the investor to have to pay capital gains even if the market is falling and the fund's share price is falling. This is because the stocks the mutual fund sells are trading at a higher price than when they were bought.

During the market crash of 2000, as fund share prices fell, many fund shareholders sold their shares. In order to redeem these fund shares from the shareholders, in other words give them back cash, the mutual funds needed to liquidate some stock in their portfolios, incurring capital gains. So, the investors that stayed in the funds got hit with a double whammy. The value of their investment declined, yet, they paid large capital gains taxes at the end of year because of portfolio stock sales.

While an actively traded mutual fund may buy and sell stocks constantly, creating what is known as turnover, typically index funds sell on only two occasions: when the composition of the index changes, or when shareholders want to redeem their shares.

While indexes are fairly consistent, they do rebalance occasionally. The Russell indexes—Russell 1000, 2000 and 3000—are reconstituted once a year, causing many stocks to move around the indexes. Some leave and new ones come in. If a stock is dropped from an index, index funds that follow the index must to sell the portfolio shares in that stock, incurring either capital gains or losses (more on this later).

However, the more common reason an index fund sells stock is when it needs to raise cash to pay shareholders who want to redeem their shares. To the buy-and-hold investor, an index fund's sale of its portfolio stock is particularly annoying. Many actively managed funds hold a small balance of cash in their portfolio to pay shareholders redeeming their shares back to the fund. Index funds have much less flexibility. They try to be fully invested at all times, because any amount that sits in cash will not grow with the rest of the portfolio. Holding cash would create cash drag, which causes the fund's performance to lag behind the performance of its index.

For instance, if the index fund is fully invested in stocks and I sell my shares, the fund may not have the cash to redeem me out. It needs to sell some stock to raise the money needed to buy my shares back from me. I leave with my money, but the fund incurs brokerage charges for the transactions. The remaining shareholders pay this cost. In addition, if the portfolio stock sale incurred a capital gain, I'm instigating a taxable event. However, I escape without paying it. Again, it's the fund's remaining shareholders that incur the capital gain and must pay taxes on it.

Hidden Costs of Mutual Funds

In addition to the transparent costs of owning a mutual fund, there are many hidden costs that affect the growth of your investment. Like the transparent costs, these hidden costs decrease the size of your principal, leaving you with less to invest.

You Don't Get Shares the Day You Open an Account

Before you even invest in a mutual fund, it's at a disadvantage to the ETF. Right off the bat, you get less value for your money.

For example, it's Monday and you think this is the first day of a stock market rally. You decide to buy shares in an S&P 500 index fund with the smallest expense ratio. In the old days you had to call up the fund company and have them send you an application. That could take a week to get to you. Nowadays, you or any retail investor can go to the mutual fund company's web site and create an account online.

Next, you mail a check to the fund. Because investors buy shares directly from the fund itself, they need to send money to the fund. Mailing the check and application can take from one to seven days to be delivered, depending on how far your letter needs to travel. You could use an overnight delivery system, but that's an additional cost.

Once the fund receives your check it can buy the shares for you.

In a best-case scenario, the fund may have your cash that Friday. If you were right and over those five trading sessions, the market tacks on a 5 percent gain, you've missed that entire move.

You could set up an electronic fund transfer to send cash from your bank directly to the mutual fund company. But this takes a few days to set up. After the process is set up, it is much quicker. But, even after it's set up, you may have to wait a day to buy the shares after the fund transfer.

Share Price May Rise by the Time You Buy

Actually, you could lose twice.

In addition to missing out on the market rally, now those shares cost more than when you decided to buy. So, you pay a higher price and get fewer shares, cutting out part of your potential profits. Instead of owning 50 shares in the mutual fund, maybe the money you sent in can now buy only 45 shares. The next time the fund increases a dollar, you make only $45 instead of $50. And if the price goes up $2 a share, you make $90 instead of $100.

Those are hidden costs because you don't see them. You don't necessarily keep track of how different the price is from the day you decided to buy to the day the shares were posted.

Once an investor owns a fund, he can buy shares via direct deposit, but that still leaves the investor at a disadvantage. If you have direct deposit, your bank delivers a set amount of money to the fund on a scheduled time period, like each week or each month. Scheduled deposits also have drawbacks. If the schedule buys shares on the first day of the month, that's not necessarily the best day for making a purchase for any number of reasons. A big one is *portfolio window dressing*. Window dressing is a way for managers to hide poor returns. Right before the quarter ends, managers sell poor performing stocks and buy some high-flying issues to make the funds look better than they really are for end-of-quarter statements. Therefore, you would be buying after they've pumped up the share price. The first day of the month could also be at the end of a rally and beginning of a downturn.

Shares Are Bought at the End of the Day

The only way to purchase a mutual fund's shares on the day you want to invest is to already own shares in the fund. Then, you can go to some financial institution and wire money to the fund. Yet, even this best-case scenario still falls short of the ETF.

While the fund gets your money during the trading session of the day you want to buy, mutual funds don't buy or sell their shares to investors until after the market's 4 P.M. close. The fund determines its net asset value (NAV) at the end of the day, after all the share prices have settled. This means that you, the investor, can't capture that day's market action.

So, if you wanted to buy into the fund because the market was rallying that morning, and the market climbed 1 percent that day, you don't earn that profit. You buy at the end of the day, after the rally ends. The NAV would reflect the highest prices of the day. Or, say the market falls 3 percent. If you decide to sell, and call the fund intraday, the NAV would reflect the stocks at their lowest price that day. You get the least amount for your shares.

ETF investors avoid these hidden costs because ETF shares are purchased through a stockbroker the same as shares of common stock. Not only are the shares bought the day they are ordered, but usually at a time and price very close to when you make the order. The cash comes out of the brokerage account and the shares are bought almost instantaneously. Like stocks, ETFs allow you to place *market orders, market on sell orders, stop loss orders* and *orders to buy.* These tell the broker the exact price you want to purchase or sell the shares. Mutual funds cannot offer this feature because their shares have to be bought and sold at the NAV. ETF investors also get their money faster than they do after selling mutual fund shares, because listed securities that trade on the stock exchange are allowed only three days to settle.

Transaction Fees

Every time a person buys shares in a mutual fund, the fund needs to buy more shares of stock for the portfolio. While actively managed funds have the option to buy as much or as little as they wish, every day that index funds get new cash they're required to buy more of the stocks in the index. Purchasing these shares costs money. Like any other investor, mutual funds buy shares through a stockbroker and pay a commission.

After the custodian receives your money from the fund, it sends the cash to the stockbroker who buys additional shares. In an S&P 500 index fund, the fund manager would need to purchase up to 500 individual stocks. The mutual fund could purchase each stock, do a program trade for the index, or buy futures. Whichever way, the mutual fund pays the broker a commission for the trade, then pays its custodian bank to receive the shares from the broker.

Every day that new money comes into the fund the manager needs to buy more of those same 500 stocks to keep the fund fully invested. The same happens when the manager sells: more commissions.

Brokerage commissions are not included in the Annual Fund Operating Expense. It's hard to imagine why, considering that the fund's main business is the buying and selling of securities. One would expect these commissions, which are a sizeable, necessary cost of running the fund—an outlay that affects the total return and is fundamental to operations—would be part of the expense ratio. But, for some reason, it's not.

Brokerage commissions are typically listed as a percentage of assets elsewhere in the prospectus. But it's a sneaky thing to do. You look at the expense ratio and conclude that's how much it costs to own the fund. But, it really costs more. And unless the investor realizes it's not part of the expense ratio and searches for it, he has a misconception of how much it costs to own this fund.

One study concluded that mutual fund managers were paying average annual brokerage commissions equal to 0.38 percent of a fund's assets, and average annual implicit trading costs of 0.58 percent.[6]

Meanwhile, a different study examined the trading costs, in terms of the bid-ask spread, of 1,706 funds in existence from 1995 to 2005. It discovered that the size of the stocks traded determined how much investor returns declined. Transactions in funds holding large-cap stocks curtailed returns by an average of 0.77 percent. Funds of small companies averaged costs of 2.85 percent.[7]

The Bid-Ask Spread

In addition to paying commissions, on every single stock trade, mutual funds, like all investors, pay the hidden *bid-ask spread*. The *bid* is the highest price a buyer offers to pay for the stock. The *ask* is the lowest price at which the seller is willing to sell. Typically it is written as two numbers, 20 to 20 $\frac{1}{4}$. The bid, $20, is the lower number, while the ask is the higher one, $20.25. The bid-ask spread is the difference.

These are two limit orders, not market orders. Chapter 9, "Putting The Trade in Exchange-Traded Funds," explains limit and market orders in more detail. This means that the buyer and seller have set their price and are waiting for the other person to meet their price. By placing a limit order, the buyer and seller risk losing a trade. Often, these orders are set by the specialists, the elite traders on the floor of the exchange, or the market makers on the electronic markets. Market makers are the brokers who provide liquidity by facilitating trades. All specialists are market makers, but the market makers on electronic exchanges are not "specialists."

When a person or fund needs to buy a specific stock immediately, the order comes in at the market price. They purchase the shares at the seller's higher price. If the seller needs to sell the stock immediately, he puts in a market order, which sells at the buyer's lower price.

Another way to look at it is from the market maker's point of view. For example, you want to sell shares of Intel. Using the example above, $20 is the bid. You would like to sell at a higher price, but $20 is all the market maker is willing to pay you for your shares. So, you sell at $20. Then another buyer comes into the market. The market maker turns around and sells the shares to that buyer for the asking price, $20.25. That's how the market maker captures the spread and makes his profit.

Because a mutual fund typically buys at the market price this works against the fund. Even worse, funds typically want to buy their shares near the end of the day. Because the NAV will be determined by the closing price of all the stocks in its portfolio, the fund doesn't want to buy early in the session and risk spending more than it sells the shares for at the end of the day. Funds often buy stock with what is called an "end of market" order. This type of order instructs the broker to buy the stock at the last trading price of the day. But this also telegraphs the fund's intention to buy and the quantity of the trade. It's not uncommon for brokers and traders to buy the necessary shares earlier in the session, then sell them to the fund at a price a few pennies higher, which also pushes up the fund's costs.

ETFs sometimes need to buy stocks on the market, and transaction fees are incurred when this happens—but it doesn't happen very often.

Soft Dollars

Many mutual funds work with their brokers in what is called a soft-dollar arrangement. This means the fund directs trades through a specific broker in return for research about stocks. Instead of charging the fund for research services and breaking out the cost, this broker typically charges a high, uncompetitive commission rate. This system is called soft dollars and it hurts investors by raising transaction costs. The fund isn't obligated to tell the investor how much it pays in commissions.

Table 6.1 includes a more thorough comparison of mutual funds and ETFs.

TABLE 6.1   Fee Comparison

Mutual Fund	Exchange Traded Fund
Possible load—percentage of investment	Stockbroker commission—fixed price
Management fee	Yes, if ETF is not a UIT
12b-1 fee	No
Custodian	Yes
Transfer agent	No
Administrator	Yes
Accountant	Yes
Index licensing fee	Yes
Tax on capital gains from inside fund	Rarely
Tax on capital gains from individual's shares	Yes
Distribution	No
Hidden costs in a mutual fund	
Profit lost between time the check is sent and the time the shares are bought	No
Profit lost in the future by purchasing fewer shares at a higher price	No
Mutual funds pay commissions to buy stocks for the portfolio and pay commissions to sell stocks in the portfolio.	Rarely
Mutual funds pay custodian banks to receive shares from broker, and give shares to broker to sell.	No
Transaction fees inside fund	No
Bid-Ask spread inside fund	ETFs don't pay bid-ask spread inside the fund; investors pay spread on secondary market.
Soft dollars	No

The Creation Unit: How They Make ETFs So Cheap

ETFs avoid many of these fees incurred by mutual funds because the fund usually doesn't buy or sell the stock held in its portfolio. This may sound strange: The fund holds stock but doesn't buy stock. That's the secret. By not buying stock, the ETF avoids all kinds of charges. Unlike the mutual fund, where the costs for adding or removing shares are paid by the shareholders that didn't do anything besides stay invested, the ETF pushes these costs out. It puts the burden on the people or firms causing the trades. It does this through a unique device called the *Creation Unit*. The Creation Unit is the basket of ETF shares that Nate Most, Steven Bloom, and Doug Holmes invented for the SPDR. It's Most's warehouse receipt concept in action.

As investors, we should look at all fees as a problem that hurts our investment returns. Investment advisors, portfolio managers, and others have the right to charge what they want for their services, but as my grandmother used to say, "The money's better in your pocket than theirs."

The Creation Unit, both intentionally and accidentally, solves a lot of those problems, erasing fees in the process.

Just because the ETF doesn't buy shares of stock, that doesn't mean it doesn't *own* stock. It does. It holds all the stocks in the index. So, how does an ETF acquire its stock? It acquires the shares through a fairly simple barter with a firm called an *authorized participant* (AP). The AP can be an investment bank, a specialist firm, a broker-dealer or another market participant. It just has to be a member of the Depository Trust & Clearing Corporation, which is the clearinghouse and depositary organization responsible for settling stock trades (see Figure 6.2).

Once a firm signs a participation agreement with the ETF's agent, also called the trustee, it becomes an Authorized Participant. Typically, it's a specialist or a broker-dealer, because only APs can create new ETF shares to sell on the market. Because specialists and brokers sell shares to institutional and retail investors, they have the greatest need to create shares. For small ETFs, often there is only one AP, while a larger liquid ETF, such as the SPDR, would have many APs.

Like the mutual fund, our example ETF will follow the S&P 500. We could purchase the iShares S&P 500 Index Fund (Symbol: IVV), but for our example we'll use the SPDR (Symbol: SPY).

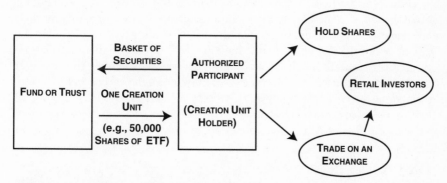

FIGURE 6.2   Creation of an Exchange-Traded Fund

Source: Investment Company Institute, *2007 Investment Company Fact Book,* Copyright © by the Investment Company Institute (www.ici.org). Reprinted with permission.

When an AP wants to buy new shares of the ETF, it gathers a basket of some or all the securities contained in the index, in the amounts specified by the fund.

The process starts with the AP informing the ETF's trustee that it wants more shares. To make it worth everyone's while, the ETF sells shares only in lots that can range in size between 25,000 to 600,000 shares. The trustee informs the AP what stocks are in the index. Because the SPDR is a unit investment trust (UIT), the ETF trustee tells the AP to purchase the exact 500 stocks in the index. If the AP wants to buy 100,000 SPDR shares, the firm needs to acquire a basket of underlying stocks in the proper quantity to deposit with the ETF in exchange for the necessary number of ETF shares in the creation unit. If the S&P 500 dropped a component stock and added a new one, the composition of the basket of shares needed to exchange for a creation unit would change.

Transparency Is a Direct Result of the Creation Unit

The Creation Unit is where the ETF's famed transparency comes from. Because the AP needs to know the exact composition of the fund's portfolio in order to purchase the basket of stocks to exchange for a creation unit, investors can always see what securities the ETF holds. This is a radical change from an actively managed mutual fund.

Because managers of active mutual funds try to beat other mutual funds as well as the market indexes, they do their best to keep their portfolio holdings and strategies a secret. They don't want other managers to steal their ideas. Even the managers of index mutual funds give themselves a lot of leeway on how much of the index they need to buy and what other securities can be held. So, index fund managers don't like to disclose their holdings, either. The SEC requires all mutual funds to release a list of their holdings at the end of every fiscal quarter. But the filing doesn't come out the day after the quarter ends. Funds have 60 days to release this information. By that time, the fund's portfolio could change dramatically. The manager could have sold off every stock he owned two months earlier, yet investors have no way of knowing this. However, in an ETF there isn't a lot of leeway on what the manager can do. The portfolio needs to be constrained; otherwise it wouldn't get SEC approval.

There's No Cash Drag

When people buy mutual funds they really don't know what is in it. They have an idea from the SEC filings, but they can't be sure the fund is holding 100 percent stock or if it's holding about 90 percent in stock and the remaining 10 percent in cash to meet investor's redemption demands. The uninvested money sits there, not earning interest, or very little interest. This is called cash drag because the uninvested cash drags down the fund's performance. One caveat: the ETFs that are UITs, the SPDR, the DIAmonds, and the Qubes actually have a little cash drag. Because UITs can't reinvest dividends, the dividends sit as cash until they can be distributed to the shareholders.

Style Drift Drifts Away

In addition, mutual funds sometimes experience something called *style drift*. Style drift occurs when a manager of a particular investing style, be it Large-Cap Growth stocks, Small-Cap Value, or the Health-Care sector finds his investment area out of style. So, he starts investing in stocks outside the advertised style. For instance, if the large-cap fund started buying mid-caps, or the health-care fund started buying Internet stocks, the fund's style would be drifting away from its stated purpose. According to a study by the Association of Investment Management, as many as 40 percent of the actively managed funds don't follow their advertised style. But because funds only need to disclose their holdings four times a year, investors can never really know whether the fund holds what it says it should hold.

Always Diversified

Another problem with mutual funds is that you may find your portfolio is much less diversified than you expected. Sometimes when you buy many funds to get different kinds of exposure, you could be doubling up on some areas without realizing it. Say you bought a NASDAQ 100 index fund, an actively managed technology fund, and an actively managed large-cap growth fund. While they give the impression of diversification, there would be significant overlap in these portfolios. Microsoft, Intel, and Google are just three of the stocks that would be in all three funds.

However, the portfolio of an ETF is very predictable. No guesswork is needed. This makes the job of investing much easier for both the investor and investment advisor. You can be sure you're getting what you pay for. The ETF offers purity in investing than one can't guarantee with the mutual fund.

If you buy the SPDR, the fund will be fully invested with the exact same 500 stocks as the index. No style drift. It can't get much purer than that. It has to be what it says it will be because the AP needs to replicate it for the creation unit. It doesn't matter what you buy. If you want a narrower focus, say a small-cap value fund, you can look at the iShares Russell 2000 Value Index Fund (IWN) and still see exactly what you're getting. Or, if you want something very specialized such as gold mining stocks, the Market Vectors Gold Miners ETF (GDX) will tell you the name and weighting of each of the 37 stocks in the fund.

So Long, Transaction Costs

The creation unit is the secret behind the ETFs success. By creating a way for the ETF to hold stocks without buying stocks, it doesn't have to pay brokerage commissions or any other transaction costs—that's a major area of cost savings. The buying and selling costs, the brokerage costs, and the transfer agency costs associated with buying the portfolio stocks and transferring them to the ETF are all borne by the AP. The AP even pays the fund's custodian a fee to receive the shares into the fund and another to deliver the shares out of the fund. That's because the AP, not the fund, is responsible for gathering the stocks for the creation unit and for taking them back upon redemption.

As always, there is an exception. All ETFs permit partial cash payments from the AP in certain circumstances, such as when the AP is restricted from purchasing a stock in the index. In this situation, the ETF would take the money and buy the shares itself. So ETFs do, from time to time, buy a limited number of shares. But this is rare and the total transaction costs would be minimal.

Still, most of, and usually all of, the frictional costs of converting cash into securities or securities into cash falls on the AP, while in the mutual fund these costs fall on the individual investor.

This is a big deal.

As mentioned before, the transaction costs in a mutual fund can be sizeable. Brokerage commissions and other transaction costs on average cost 0.38 percent of the fund's assets.

More to the point, because the AP instigates the transaction, it *should* be the one to pay. If the AP sees market demand for more ETF shares, it wants more to sell because it hopes to make a profit. And if demand dries up, the AP wants to lower its supply.

When ETF shares are redeemed, the reverse happens. If a lot of people are selling SPDR shares, the AP will be flooded with inventory. The AP can return, or redeem, the shares with the ETF. Instead of receiving cash for the ETF shares, the AP usually takes delivery in a physical basket of equities from the fund's portfolio. It can then sell these stocks or not.

This feature, the physical delivery of a collateralized basket of securities underlying the index, was the one thing that the SPDR builders salvaged from the Amex's Equity Index Participations (EIPs). It was the feature that made the EIPs more popular than the Philadelphia Stock Exchange's

Cash Index Participations (CIPs). It now serves as the foundation for the ETF's creation unit.

The Kindest Trade of All

After the AP creates a basket containing the index's component stocks, it deposits these securities with the ETF's custodian bank. In return, the ETF trustee gives the AP the matching number of ETF shares. The creation unit size for the SPDRs is 50,000 shares. The ETF shares are the warehouse receipts that Nate Most conceived: They're even called receipts. The SPDR's real name is Standard & Poor's Depositary Receipts.

Just as a warehouse receipt is returned to the warehouse in exchange for the physical commodity, the ETF shares function like depositary receipts for the actual shares deposited (warehoused) in the custodian's vault. Because the AP receives the ETF shares for the basket of stocks, not cash, it means they are swapping the same kind of thing, shares for shares. This is called an "in-kind" trade. An unexpected, but happy, circumstance of this in-kind trade was that it allows the ETF to avoid taxable capital gains. This unexpected benefit of the creation unit became the basis for the ETF's much noted tax efficiency.

The Internal Revenue Service (IRS) says that a transaction exchanging something for cash triggers a taxable event. But another rule under the U.S. tax code says that anyone who deposits shares and gets the same thing back in kind when asked for, has not created a taxable transaction. So, when the AP decides to redeem the SPDR shares, it receives the appropriate number of the fund's portfolio securities priced at the NAV for that day. Cash doesn't change hands at all. Just shares exchanged for shares. No taxable event has occurred. The taxable event that occurs when the AP sells the shares on the open market for cash belongs to the AP, not the ETF.

That's a far cry from a mutual fund, which incurs a capital gain or loss on every sale of stock in the portfolio.

Remember that earlier in the chapter I sold my shares in the index fund? The fund didn't have enough cash to pay me, so it had to sell shares from its portfolio to cash me out. I avoided the capital gain I instigated, but now the remaining shareholders must declare it on their tax forms. And if the market is falling and a slew of shareholders run for the exits, because there are fewer investors in the fund, each remaining shareholder gets a larger slice of the tax liability.

In contrast, when the AP gets the shares from the ETF, it isn't a sale, it's merely a trade of equals. In that deal there is no market impact cost. The AP then sells the ETF shares on the open market, where they are bought and sold between investors. These investors will all incur capital gains from their personal investment decisions. However, since ETF shares aren't bought directly from the fund, what goes on inside the fund has no tax implications for the individual investors.

Once again, because the ETF doesn't buy or sell the underlying shares in the index, it avoids a significant cost paid by mutual fund shareholders. If you are currently a mutual fund shareholder and want to know how much you're paying in capital gains tax, just take a look at your last tax filing.

"Under the tax code, the IRS can only tax on the difference of the two values on a cash basis and that is huge," says Bob Tull, who worked in the American Stock Exchange's product development department around the turn of the century. "Most people don't have this knowledge of the tax laws in relation to the barter regulations. This knowledge of how the commodity market, receipts and bartering were affected by the tax laws hadn't been considered by the equities world. But Nate Most understood it. He came from the commodities world."[8]

Tull suggests that if ETFs had worked from the program trading side but didn't work well with the tax code, then the product would never have come out. It was the combination of the low costs and the tax efficiency that made ETFs a big deal.

No Transfer Agent Fees

Nor do ETFs pay transfer agency costs. That's because through a weird machination, as far as the ETF is concerned, it only has one shareholder. The Depository Trust Company (DTC). The DTC is the central depository for holding stocks. The DTC is a subsidiary of the Depository Trust & Clearing Corporation, or DTCC. The DTCC and its subsidiaries, are the central depository and clearinghouse for settling nearly all trades for equities, corporate and municipal bonds, government and mortgage-backed securities and over-the-counter derivatives. The DTCC is also a leading processor of mutual funds, linking the funds with their distribution networks.

In the old days, before computers, when a stock was traded, an actual physical certificate was transferred to the buyer from the seller. But in the 1960s, so much paper needed to be moved that the stock market would close down for a period every week just to settle the trades.

Today, most people never see a stock certificate. Almost all stock is kept at the DTC's central depository and never leaves there. The DTC runs what is called a book-entry system in which everything is done via computer transactions. Instead of moving physical certificates between brokerages, the book-entry system moves electronic credits from one account to another. All in all it's a lot of electronic paper pushing.

Another unit of the DTCC, the National Securities Clearing Corporation (NSCC), is the central counter party computer that correlates, settles, and keeps track of all the stock trades on the exchange every day by using these electronic transactions. One of the NSCC's purposes is to guarantee that the trade is settled. Sellers are contractually obligated to deliver stock in three days. But, if the seller goes out of business, the NSCC will step in to complete the trade on the original terms. The NSCC is the clearing agent where the creation and redemption take place.

According to Investopedia, the "DTCC's function is to integrate the NSCC and DTC, streamlining their clearing and depository transactions in attempts to reduce costs and increase capital efficiency." If you own shares in a brokerage account, the broker doesn't actually hold the paper stock certificates. Instead, it's a computer file filled with electronic credits denoting the stocks you own. Moreover, the DTCC doesn't deal with individuals. It does business only with brokerage houses, banks, mutual funds, and other financial services institutions.

Say you have a brokerage account at Merrill Lynch. You want to buy 100 shares of Intel. A trader at Merrill goes to the stock exchange and buys 100 shares for you. The exchange then notifies the DTCC that Merrill bought 100 shares and at what price. If nine other investors buy 100 shares of Intel, the DTCC credits Merrill with 1,000 shares of Intel on its books. The DTCC doesn't know who the individual shareholders are, or how much each one owns, it only knows that Merrill is the shareholder of record and the total number of shares in Merrill's account. The broker is responsible for making sure the proper numbers of shares go into the right investor accounts.

When you buy a financial instrument through a broker, the money is electronically transferred to the seller. The shares are electronically removed from the seller's account, then an electronic credit transfers the shares into your account. This data entry credits the client with the appropriate number of shares, bonds, futures, or whatever. No paper certificates ever change hands, only electronic notations moving over fiber optic cables.

Institutions that trade through the system are called NSCC and/or DTC participants. DTC participants who are authorized to trade a particular ETF are authorized participants, or APs. When the AP assembles a creation unit for an ETF, the appropriate number of shares of each individual stock is electronically transferred to the DTC. The DTC electronically deducts them from the AP's account and credits the ETF's custodian. The ETF then credits the DTC's depositary with 50,000 ETF shares for the brokerage. This goes into what is called an omnibus account. As far as the ETF is concerned, the DTC is its only shareholder.

When it's time for the ETF to send proxy statements to its true shareholders, all the DTC participants notify the DTC how many proxies they need. The DTC then tells the ETF. The ETF delivers them all to the DTC, which allocates them to the DTC participants in the proper amounts.

Since investors don't buy ETF shares from the fund, and the DTCC is the shareholder of record, the ETF doesn't know who its shareholders are. There is no one place where all the investors of the ETF are listed. This works to the advantage of the ETF because there's no need for a transfer agent. The ETF doesn't need to keep track of how much money its shareholders invest, nor how many shares they own. The ETF also doesn't need to send out confirmation statements for each purchase, nor quarterly statements tracking their accounts. It doesn't need to worry about lost certificates. The ETF doesn't handle paper ever. It's all in the computer. Because the ETF doesn't need a transfer agent, it eliminates one of the larger expenses in an index fund. This can be anywhere from 0.15 percent to 0.4 percent of the index fund's expense ratio.

"The industry has told us that without DTCC involvement in the creation and redemption process, the proliferation of ETFs would not have occurred," said Hank Belusa, the DTCC's vice president of product management for equities.[9]

Don't Pity the AP

The creation unit pushes transaction costs and capital gains off the plate of the ETF shareholder and out of the ETF onto the AP's lap. But don't pity the AP for having to pay these expenses. First, large brokerage firms and other institutions have many more ways to offset capital gains than an individual investor. Second, brokerage firms don't pay commissions. They're the brokers. They pay only the bid-ask spread to the specialists, the elite traders on the floor of the exchange. And the specialists? They pay nothing.

"Ah-ha," you say. You're thinking that the spread is the specialist's commission, and that, in fact, the broker does pay a commission. You're right. But he doesn't pay brokerage commissions.

Nor does the AP necessarily need to go the market to get the shares. Broker-dealers often hold an inventory of stock, ready to sell to their own investors. If the broker pulls the shares from his house inventory, he doesn't pay any transaction costs. Or if the broker's clients want to sell shares, the broker can buy them directly from the client without going to the market. In this case, the broker also has no transaction costs or bid-ask spread. And he gets the commission from the client. Sweet.

By whatever means the AP collects the basket of shares necessary for an ETF creation units, the firm takes on the risk of another potential cost. While investors buy ETF shares at market prices during trading hours, AP's don't. They buy ETF shares like you buy mutual fund shares. Just like mutual funds, the ETF's NAV is only determined after the market's 4 P.M. close. Like the fund, the ETF needs to take a full accounting of the assets of the trust and the expenses.

The fluctuating prices the ETF shares trade at during the day is essentially an arbitrage on what the end of day NAV will be. Still, the AP doesn't suffer badly or garner much in capital. With thousands, if not millions, of trades a year, it can balance most of its gains and losses, to avoid capital gains taxes.

So What Costs *Do* ETFs Have?

Of course, ETFs have fees and expenses. It costs money to run a portfolio.

ETFs Charge Expense Ratios

When people say ETFs are cheaper than mutual funds, they're usually referring to the expense ratio being smaller than a comparable mutual fund. All the fees and expenses the ETF pays are expenses that mutual funds also pay. There are just fewer of them. ETFs pay the index company a licensing fee to use the name and calculations of the index company. ETFs that are unit investment trusts don't pay an investment manager, but open-end ETFs do. Still, because these are passively managed, not actively traded, funds, the management fee is small. UITs pay a trustee to run the fund. Open-end ETFs also pay a board of directors. The custodian receives a fee to hold the ETFs assets, both the shares of stock underlying the index and the ETF shares. Accountants charge for the audits.

Of course, sponsors don't get a fee. Because the American Stock Exchange didn't charge a fee to bring the first ETF to the market—it didn't want to run the fund, it wanted to get fees from increased trading volume—it set a precedent in which the sponsor received very little if anything.

These five main components make up the ETF expense ratio:

1. Index licensing fee
2. Trustee for UITs or fund manager for open-end funds
3. Board of directors for open-end funds
4. Custodian
5. Accountants

In addition to all the costs the fund incurs, the ETF investor has costs outside the running of the fund. The following sections outline these costs.

ETF Investors Pay Capital Gains on Their Own Terms

ETFs are more tax efficient than index funds because ETFs typically don't have capital gains to pass through to their ultimate investors, due to the in-kind creation and redemption mechanism. That doesn't mean ETF investors completely avoid taxes. ETFs may experience capital gains or losses when they have to sell portfolio securities for index rebalancing (see next section). But that's an uncommon occurrence. Most investors only have to worry about paying a capital gains tax on whatever profit occurs from selling their own ETF shares. There's no escaping taxes. But ETF investors incur taxes on *their* time schedule, not the fund's.

Instead of buying shares directly from the mutual fund, an ETF investor buy shares in a personal brokerage account. You earn capital gains in ETFs the same way you would if you were buying shares of company stock. Like any other taxable investment you might own, you can sell the ETF shares when it best suits your tax strategy.

The ETF investor can buy and sell his shares in one day or buy-and-hold for decades. He can sell his shares as part of a variety of tax strategies to lower his taxes. First, he can hold it longer than one year, to make sure he gets the lower long-term capital gains tax rate. Or he can also sell his ETF shares to offset gains or losses elsewhere in the portfolio. ETF shares can also be used for most of the tax strategies available to stocks. But whenever he sells, this decision affects no other shareholders in the fund.

A mutual fund shareholder also pays capital gains tax, but again it's the individual investor's taxable income, not the fund's. While the investor who sells his mutual fund shares escapes without paying a capital gains tax, that was only on the transactions made by the mutual fund itself. The capital gains from the fund's transactions are passed onto the individual shareholders in the fund, not the shareholder selling. But as always, the individual investor's own transactions cause taxable events in his own account.

ETFs are also a plus for registered investment advisors (RIAs). Not only do RIAs make sure their customers have the right diversification and return on their portfolios, but they also pay attention to their clients tax strategies.

After all is said and done, ETF investors typically pay a capital gains tax just once, while mutual fund investors pay it almost annually.

Exception to the Rule

There is one situation where ETFs could potentially pass through capital gains to shareholders before they sell their shares. As mentioned earlier in the chapter, index funds sell on only two occasions: when shareholders want to redeem their shares and when the composition of the index changes. Because individual ETF shareholders don't redeem their shares back to the fund, but sell them to other investors on the secondary market, ETF portfolio shares typically are not sold but exchanged for ETF creation units with APs. Because investors who are redeeming their shares don't affect the other shareholders in the ETF, the potential problem lies with index composition changes.

The managers of benchmark indexes want these indexes to experience minimal change, but mergers, spin-offs, and the inability to meet index standards are all reasons why a company may be dropped from an index. In addition, some of the more creative indexes rebalance often. But once a company is dropped, every index fund tracking the index needs to sell all their shares in that stock. So, just like a mutual fund, an ETF needs to sell shares in the portfolio.

The in-kind trade softens the blow. Capital gains are determined by subtracting the purchase price of an investment from its sale price. If the purchase price was $1,000 and the sales price was $2,000, the capital gains would be $1,000. If it's a short-term gain, the gain would be taxed as ordinary income, which could be around 35 percent, depending on your annual income. In this case that would create a tax bill of $350. If the shares went up only $100 to $1,100, the capital gain tax bit would be just $35.

However, unlike index funds, ETFs have the ability to make the gain smaller. It does this by raising the overall cost-basis of the stock underlying the fund. Whenever an AP buys ETF shares, he deposits an equal amount of stock with the ETF. If the price of the stock is rising every day, then the stock deposited today has a higher cost-basis than the stock deposited yesterday. This means the ETF holds a lot of the same stock with many different purchase prices.

When the AP redeems ETF shares, the fund returns a basket of its portfolio stocks to the AP. The stock the ETF returns to the AP are the shares with the lowest cost basis, usually the oldest shares, which would have created the largest capital gain if the shares needed to be sold at a later date. So, every time shares are redeemed, the ETF removes the cheapest stock, which has the affect of raising its average cost-basis.

This is the opposite of an index fund. When index funds sell stock, they usually sell the most recent additions, which typically have the highest cost-basis. By raising the cost basis of the shares inside the ETF, the ETF continually lowers the potential capital gains hit should the stock be dropped from the index. Meanwhile, mutual funds, by selling the most recent shares, continually lower the cost basis, increasing the potential for large capital gains if there is a big sell-off in the fund.

In its long history, the SPDR has never paid out a short-term gain distribution and has paid out only one single long-term capital gains distribution. This distribution of only nine cents a shares was attributed to a mistake in the management of the fund. Even though the potential is there, it rarely becomes an issue. That's because the astute managers of the ETFs that track classic benchmark indexes work hard to offset all their gains inside the fund.

Many of the new indexes created specifically for ETFs rebalance their portfolios often, some even on a monthly basis. Increasing the frequency of rebalancing causes more stocks to fall out of the indexes. This higher turnover has the potential to create a steady stream of pass-through capital gains. Still, even most of these ETFs have successfully managed to avoid capital gains inside the fund.

The Brokerage Commission

Proponents of index mutual funds will say, "Sure, the mutual fund has transaction costs and the spread inside the fund, but it doesn't cost the investor anything to buy shares in the no-load index fund."

For the most part that's true. Most index mutual funds are no-load funds. Obviously, the no-load fund has no load or commission. Because ETFs are bought and sold on a stock exchange, all transactions need to go through a stockbroker. And stockbrokers charge commissions. Investors pay a commission on every purchase or sale of ETF shares. This commission can be negligible or sizeable depending on the amount being invested. For instance, say you trade through a discount broker that charges $10 per trade.

If you invested $10,000, that $10 would be only 0.1 percent of the total investment, a tenth of one percent. That's miniscule. However, if you invested $100, that $10 commission would turn out to be a 10 percent load. That would seriously cut into your profits. And if you did dollar cost averaging, the fees could quickly add up to make the ETF more expensive than the index mutual fund. Dollar cost averaging will be discussed further on in the chapter.

One can make the case that the broker commission has taken the place of the transfer agent fee in the mutual fund. For the ETF investor, the brokerage takes on many of the duties performed by the transfer agent. The brokerage records the money you invest into your account. It makes the trade, then sends out a confirmation. At the end of the quarter, the brokerage sends out a portfolio statement listing all your investments and their value.

On a $10,000 investment, a $10 commission is 0.1 percent, or one tenth of one percent, or ten basis points. A $20 commission would be 0.2 percent. Compare that with the average transfer agent fee of between 0.25 percent and 0.4 percent. Here the transfer fee is twice as large as the commission and it's charged annually. Of course, it depends on the size of the investment. A $10 commission on a $1,000 investment would be 1 percent, or potentially four times larger than the transfer fee.

Bid-Ask Spread

While the AP pays the bid-ask spread when purchasing the underlying stocks to be deposited in the ETF, every time an ETF investor goes to the stock market to purchase or sell his ETF shares, he will pay both the brokerage commission and the bid-ask spread. While the bid-ask spread isn't factored into fees from your broker, it is an added cost in that you pay a higher price for the ETF shares.

But mutual fund investors shouldn't get all high and mighty. While fund investors don't pay the spread, the fund itself does every day when it goes to the market to buy more stock. Like the other transaction costs, this isn't factored into the mutual fund's expense ratio. Still, it's a real cost. Now, consider that there is a spread for each stock the mutual fund needs to buy every day. Multiply the spreads by all 1,000 stocks and that adds up.

Dividends

Both the mutual fund and ETF have to distribute 90 percent of income from dividends on annual basis. With both investments, you pay dividend taxes at whatever is the going tax rate. Here again, the advantage goes to the mutual fund. The fund can reinvest dividends at no cost to the investors.

Most ETFs don't take care of that. There is no automatic reinvestment. You have to do that yourself. Typically, you have to pay a broker commission again to reinvest dividends and other gains.

Why Would I Ever Buy a Mutual Fund?

Well, sometimes you have no choice.

DCPs Limit Your Options

Most *defined contribution plans* (DCPs) offer only mutual funds. DCPs are retirement-savings accounts that are typically funded by contributions from both an employee and employer. These are named by their section of the federal tax code. The 401(k) is for employees in the public sector. Educational and charitable organization use the 403(b) plan, while state and municipal government workers use the 457 plan. This is not to be confused with defined benefit plans, which are classic pension plans fully funded and managed by corporations for their employees.

The great benefit of defined contribution plans is that they allow you to save money on a tax-deferred basis. Typically money is taken out of your paycheck before federal income taxes are deducted. This helps lower the total of your annual taxable wages for income tax purposes. Then money in the account grows tax-free until you take distributions.

Almost all defined contribution plans offer a limited selection of mutual funds to invest in. Currently, there are very few options available to use

ETFs in defined contribution plans. In this case, you would have to invest in mutual funds.

The Index Fund's Ace in the Hole

There is one investing strategy in which the no-load index fund can shine brighter than the ETF. It's called dollar cost averaging. Dollar cost averaging offers you the opportunity to not commit all your capital at one price.

Dollar cost averaging is the strategy of investing on a regular schedule, such as once a week or once a month, to lower the average cost of your shares. The strategy forces you to buy continuously, even when the market is falling. If the market drops, then the NAV for the fund's shares would decline too. By forcing you to buy when the market falls, you actually purchase more shares at a lower price. This lowers an investor's average price for the shares.

Of course, the opposite happens when the market is rising. The investor purchases fewer shares at a higher price. But it's not hard to motivate investors to buy when the market is rising. It's harder to convince them to buy when it's falling. The discipline not only lowers the investor's average cost structure, but forces them to acquire stocks at low prices when it feels counterintuitive to do so.

Possibly the biggest benefit of all mutual funds is the fractional share/low minimum combo. The ability to purchase fractional shares means you can invest even if you don't have enough to buy a whole share. You can buy just part of one. This gives an investor the opportunity to buy an asset with a small minimum investment.

Not everyone has a sizeable amount of money to place on one large trade. You might not have $5,200 sitting in a bank. But, you might be able to squeeze out $100 from your paycheck every week to raise $5,200 in a year. You could wait a year for it to build up in a savings account, earning low interest, or you can buy fractional shares in a no-load index fund. Each week, the money would be immediately put to work in the market.

If you invest $100 in a no-load index fund whose share price is $75, you can buy $1\frac{1}{3}$ (1.33) fund shares. Not so with the ETF. ETF shares must be bought in whole numbers. If you invest $100 in an ETF whose share price is $75, you get one share and $25 sits in cash. That money doesn't go into the market until you gather another $50 to buy a second share. In dollar cost averaging without fractional shares, the money would sit in cash for two weeks before the third deposit makes enough to buy another share.

The cost savings depends on the size of the investment. If you're investing thousands of dollars at a time, the ETF commission is negligible. In another example, the stock costs $52. A purchase of 100 shares of a

$52 stock would take an investment of $5,200. A $10 commission would be just 0.19 percent of your total investment.

Yet, the cost of dollar cost averaging with an ETF can be significant. It can essentially wipe out the strategy's benefits. If you invest with a discount broker, paying $10 for each trade seems like a great deal. However if you put $100 a week into an ETF through a discount broker charging $10 a trade, the costs would be outrageous. While you would invest $5,200 in the market over the course of a year, it would cost $520 in commissions, essentially a 10 percent load. By investing a little weekly, the ETF's low-cost benefit was erased. Dollar cost averaging increased the amount of broker commissions for an investment of $5,200 by 51 fold, from 0.19 percent to 10 percent.

No commission, fractional share purchases, and the ability to maximize dollar cost averaging are three advantages that no-load index mutual funds have over ETFs. So, if you're investing a small amount on a regular basis, dollar cost averaging in no-load index mutual fund may be a better way to go.

In that situation, a no-load index fund has the potential to be a less costly investment than a similar schedule of investing in an ETF, especially if the mutual fund's expense ratio is lower or equal to the ETF. You do, however, give up the tax efficiency, transparency, and flexibility to trade when the market is open.

ETF COMMISSION VERSUS LOADED INDEX FUNDS   If an investor buys a no-load index fund directly from the fund company, he won't pay any commission. However, the mutual fund's dollar-cost-average advantage decreases significantly the further away the investor moves from the no-load index fund model.

According to the Investment Company Institute, about 82 percent of all mutual fund investors buy their funds through stockbrokers or registered investment advisors (RIAs); that includes index funds. As explained previously, these professionals expect to be paid for their service.

Fee-based advisors may sell you a no-load index fund, but you will pay between 0.5 percent and 2 percent a year for the service. Non-fee-based advisers typically receive the load for helping you invest in a mutual fund, so they are unlikely to sell you a no-load fund. As mentioned earlier, stockbrokers don't need to act as a fiduciary. They need to make suitable recommendations, but don't necessarily have to offer what is in your best interests.

So, while these RIAs may put you in an index fund, that index fund may, in fact, charge a load. Then, on top of that, the expense ratios for the index funds sold through brokers are much higher than no-load index funds—usually around 1 percent of assets.

Because the load is a commission, if you dollar cost average in index funds with loads and higher expense ratios, the advantage is severely diminished with a small investment of $100 a week, and eventually disappears as the investment gets bigger and the ETF commission becomes a smaller percentage of the total. Don't forget that shareholders in index mutual funds still pay capital gains taxes an annual basis.

For instance, if you put $100 into an ETF every week with a $10 commission, that's a 10 percent load. But if you put $500 into an ETF every week, that $10 is just a 2 percent load. On the flipside, if you put $500 into an index mutual fund with a 2 percent front-end load, you're even. Then you're back to comparing the funds on their expense ratios. Nine times out of 10, the ETF will be lower priced. So, the ETF wins again.

You would have to run the numbers with how much you're paying in broker commissions, but an ETF commission should be a fixed cost that gets smaller with a larger investment, while the load is a percentage of the investment, which increases with the size of the deposit.

In terms of commissions, the world is moving away from the model of the commission-based stockbroker to the fee-based registered investment advisor (RIA). This is more accommodating to the individual investor.

Many RIAs don't charge a commission per trade, but charge an annual asset-based fee. Not only does the commission for each trade disappear, but this also ties the RIA's interests with yours. By taking a percentage of your assets, the RIA makes more money when your assets rise, and he loses money every time your assets fall. In this case, where the RIA takes a percentage of your assets, no matter whether it's a mutual fund or an ETF, you'll be paying the same service fee. Typically, that fee is around 1 percent annually. Only in rare occasions should an investor agree to an annual fee greater than 1 percent.

In addition, the RIA can manage the ETF commission costs for his investors. If he has 100 investors and all buy shares of the same ETF, the RIA can make the purchase with one trade at a discount broker, then divvy up the shares to his individual clients, much like the way the mutual fund's transfer agent works. This brings the cost down to just pennies.

Some People Like to Gamble

Despite the evidence that an indexing strategy beats an actively managed strategy about 75 percent of the time, some people still want to invest in actively managed index funds.

Why? In short, people want to beat the market. They're not happy with the idea of just making the "mediocre" returns of the market. Some people think they're smarter than the market and some people get enjoyment out of the challenge. It's definitely true that there are hot money managers who can outperform the index. Everyone would love to have a hot manager working for him or her. There are even a few that have done it on a consistent basis. Finding that hot manager is a goal for some people. But eventually, all streaks come to an end.

Summary

This chapter essentially concludes the main argument of the book, the case for investing in ETFs versus mutual funds. Chapter 4 explained that at its heart, this is an argument of indexing versus active management. If you buy into the philosophy that indexing is the preferred strategy for investing, then it's an argument of structure. Chapter 3 shows that because both are investing companies, at this point, costs, efficiencies, and portfolio holdings become the main issues. Chapter 5 showed how your fund's returns cannot be known ahead of time, but its costs can, concluding that you should focus on cutting costs. Higher costs mean less money in your pocket. The investor's objective is to get the best investment for the least amount of money.

Chapter 6 was the evidence. In closing this section, ETFs are much more efficient vehicles for retail investors to gain exposure to the market than mutual funds. There are two reasons for this. ETFs allow you to purchase your investment immediately and cost less to buy and maintain. Mutual funds, on the other hand, are not immediate and can cost at lot.

By delving into the nuts and bolts of the ETF's structure to see how the creation unit is built, we now understand how it produces the leaner structure leading to the ETF's key benefits: low costs, tax efficiency, transparency, and flexibility. At the same time, pulling back the curtain on the mutual fund exposes transparent and hidden costs detrimental to shareholder returns. In comparison, ETFs are fairer to investors by not making them pay the taxes and transaction costs that occur from actions taken by other investors. Instead, most of the costs are pushed out of the ETF onto the authorized participant, an entity responsible for creating and redeeming shares.

The rest of the book looks at the innovations in both index structure and ETF structure that have created more diverse investing opportunities than had been previously available to the small, retail investor. After that it gets down to the business of creating your own portfolio.

Finally, portfolio merit depends on the strategy and holdings of the fund. Because it's hard to be sure what the index mutual fund is holding, despite the fact that it is tracking the index, the ETF is the preferred choice because of its transparency.

CHAPTER 7

The New Indexers

The ETF hit adolescence a little early.

Ten years after its birth, as it found wider acceptance in the marketplace, the ETF's second phase began. Just like an adolescent, ETFs experienced a phenomenal growth spurt. From the end of 2003 through 2006, the number of funds tripled to 359, according to the Investment Company Institute (ICI), with assets under management surging nearly as much: 180 percent. The ICI is the trade association for the mutual fund, closed-end fund, UIT, and ETF industries. In 2007 alone, the ICI said the industry nearly doubled, adding 270 new funds, a 75 percent increase, for a total of 629 funds.[1] Including exchange-traded products not regulated by the '40 Act, there were 657, according to Lipper, a fund research firm. And not unlike a typical teenager, most of the companies that sprouted during this second wave were creative, original, wacky, loud, blindly courageous, and given to calling their elders out-of-touch.

During the ETF's first decade, the product and its issuers were like children. They were learning to walk, get a feel for how the product worked, and trying to see where it fit into the world. During the 1990s, the industry took baby steps toward each major index. It started with the king, the S&P 500. It took two years before it built the second ETF, the S&P MidCap 400. Two more years to bring the Dow Jones Industrial Average into the fold, then it was another two years before the NASDAQ-100 Index joined the party. At that pace, the five giants of indexing—Dow Jones, S&P, NAS-DAQ, Russell, and MSCI—had enough name brand indexes to satisfy the industry's needs.

After the first ten years, there were only five ETF issuers, the founding fathers of the ETF industry. State Street Global Advisors, which with the Amex created the SPDR, sold its ETFs under two brands, SPDRs/Select Sector SPDRs and StreetTracks. Bank of New York ran the MidCap SPDRs and BLDRs. Barclay's Global Investors (BGI) produced the iShares. The Vanguard Group created the VIPERS and Merrill Lynch had the HOLDRs. And the HOLDRs weren't true ETFs, as will be explained in Chapter 8.

iShares launched its first ETFs in 2000, a total of 38. Another 19 hit the market in 2001. That was on top of the 17 original WEBS, which became the first iShares. With 74 ETFs, it controlled 73 percent of the market. With a limited number of indexes truly accepted as benchmarks in the U.S. stock market, iShares made a brazen land-grab for everything it could find in the cupboards at Dow Jones, S&P, and Russell. Barclays Global Investors (BGI) intended its iShares family to be all-inclusive. So, after it went through the first tier, it launched a significant amount of funds with second-tier indexes. It chopped the big indexes into sectors and styles—growth and value, and, finally, obscure indexes. The idea was that an investor would never need to look to another issuer for any important ETF: iShares could offer its own copy.

Amidst this flurry of launches, iShares launched its own version of the SPDR, the iShares S&P 500 Index Fund (symbol: IVV). The iShares S&P 500 Fund soon became the first victim of what is known as the *first-mover advantage*. Essentially, the first ETF to track a particular index gets a big head start in the market. It receives all the attention and all the investible dollars interested in this kind of investing strategy, until a similar ETF shows up. More investors mean more trading, which means greater liquidity. Greater liquidity means smaller bid-ask spreads, usually just pennies, which cuts down on one hidden cost that eats into returns.

Near the end of 2007, the SPDR, the original S&P 500 ETF, had $76.0 billion in assets under management. Meanwhile, the iShares S&P 500 Index Fund, which came out seven years later, had $19.4 billion, just one-fourth the size. One can say the SPDR had a seven-year head start, but the same thing happened with gold. This time the StreetTracks Gold Shares (symbol: GLD) launched just two months ahead of the iShares Comex Gold Trust (symbol: IAU). Regardless, by the end of 2007, the StreetTracks Gold Shares had $15.2 billion in assets under management, while the iShares Comex Gold Trust had only $1.4 billion.

Mutual funds have an easier time with this. There can be a lot of actively managed large-cap funds. They are judged on profits. The one with the highest returns on investment receives the most new assets. Even index funds have an easier time, because they have distribution networks. Some brokers and investment advisors receive a load to sell index funds in certain fund families, rather than the best one. Also, employees locked into 401(k) plans can only pick from the selection offered by their employer. So, index funds in 401(k) plans have a captive audience from which to gain assets. But ETFs don't have these kinds of distribution networks; therefore, being the first to the market is a huge deal.

The ETF companies of the second wave realized they couldn't merely replicate what had gone before, because they would never attract enough assets to compete. They knew they had to come up with original ideas to attract many investors. And that's what they did. They revolutionized the index space by breaking open the classic recipe that formed the foundation for most of the market's benchmarks.

They became the New Indexers.

The original benchmark indexes, such as the S&P 500, the NASDAQ-100, and the Dow Jones industrials, were created as market barometers. They were designed to measure the health of the overall market, not as investment vehicles. With the exception of the equal-weighted DJIA, most benchmarks chose their component stocks by their size in the market, by a measurement called market-capitalization. Market-cap measures a stock's value in the market. Market-cap is derived by multiplying the number of shares outstanding by the price of a single share. The total is the stock's market value. The higher the value, the "bigger" the company. After choosing the stock by market-cap, the index is weighted by market-cap. This means, the larger a stock's market-cap, the larger its weighting in the index. The larger its weighting in the index, the more influence this one stock has over the index's movement.

The new indexers pushed the indexes, pulled them, chopped them up, and poured a sauce of quantitative analysis on top in order to create a bubbling stew best described as an active index. They aren't actively managed funds, but rather indexes that change their underlying portfolios more often than the benchmark. The new indexes are rebalanced on a regular schedule, usually every fiscal quarter, but some are monthly.

The new indexes continued to be rules-based, transparent portfolios. But instead of just picking stocks by size, they added an extra factor, quantitative analysis. And instead of weighting their indexes by market-cap, many created new weightings to give smaller stocks greater significance in the index. Quantitative analysis didn't measure a stock by its size, but rather valued it based on its investing merits. By throwing certain variables in, the index maker could value certain fundamental attributes more important than stock price, attributes such as earnings momentum or cash flow. The index maker then screens the possible universe of stocks, and the ones with the top score go into the index.

Most important was their philosophy. Unlike the traditional index fund, which seeks to match the index, minus the expense ratio, these indexes had the mandate to beat the market.

If iShares brought the ETF to the masses by creating an identifiable brand name and then marketing it heavily, the new indexers expanded the concept of the index. As the ETF industry grew, it pushed out the boundaries of where it could play.

Missed Opportunity

In an ironic twist of fate, the ETF's second wave began around a conference table at a mutual fund company that never produced even one exchange-traded fund. In 2000, the architect of this index revolution, Bruce Bond, suggested to his boss at Nuveen Investments that the company should enter the still nascent ETF industry.

The Nuveen organization had a history of innovation. Founded as an underwriting specialist and trader in 1898, the Chicago-based firm helped create the U.S. municipal bond market in the early twentieth century. Some of those bonds helped fund the urban development of its hometown. In 1961, Nuveen began using *unit investment trusts* (UIT) as a way to sell muni bonds to institutions. From the high inflation-high tax era of the 1980s to the early 1990s, Nuveen helped popularize the UIT by being the first to offer tax-free municipal bond UITs to retail investors. The fund company also sold closed-end funds.

But by 1997, Nuveen was no longer the UIT market leader. It had fallen behind, especially in the area of equity UITs, to Van Kampen Investments and its cross-town rival, First Trust Portfolios, another leading UIT/closed-end fund shop. At the time, Bond was working at First Trust with a high school friend, Dave Hooten, and a college buddy, Ben Fulton. Bond and Hooten were top sales managers at First Trust, and Fulton was a senior vice president in product development.

"We told Nuveen we could bring them back to the number-one spot," said Bond. "So, they hired us to do that for them."[2]

All three men left First Trust the same day in 1998 to turn around Nuveen's equity UIT department. Bond was the head of sales; Hooten was head of national accounts; and Fulton head of the new products department. In their first year at Nuveen, Bond said they increased the business to $4.2 billion in assets under management from just $700 million the year before. Soon they ran the entire structured products division, along with Bill Adams and Bob Kuppenheimer. This put them in charge of UITs, closed-end funds, and anything else that was "structured," such as ETFs.

Considering that all the major ETFs during the 90s were structured as UITs, the structured products team convinced Nuveen it needed to get into ETFs. It seemed a natural. Nuveen had already called its closed-end funds "exchange-traded funds" long before the ETF became popular.

Fulton suggested they bring in a friend of his from the American Stock Exchange, Gary Gastineau, to get the effort started. Gastineau was already a big name in the ETF world. After Nate Most, the father of the ETF, retired from the Amex in 1995, Gastineau became the Amex's head of product development. During his tenure he oversaw the launch of the WEBS, the first ETFs to track foreign markets, the DIAmonds, the Select Sector SPDRs, and the Qubes. But he was itching to create his own ETFs. Gastineau's March 2000 arrival led to Nuveen's announcement that it would enter the ETF market.

iShares had just launched its first series of ETFs. Bond said that as soon as Gastineau arrived, he realized that ETFs would be a great opportunity.

The first big step in creating an ETF is filing a request with the SEC to receive exemptions from the 1940 Act. In October 2000, Gastineau helped Nuveen file its exemption request for the first ETFs to hold bonds and "an index of fast-growing, mostly small-capitalization stocks," according to the *Wall Street Journal*.[3] Simultaneously, iShares was also working on bond ETFs. Nuveen, however, was on track to be the first to the market with a fixed-income product.

Soon, a philosophical rift developed in the offices of Nuveen's structured products department. This rift would become a basic theme of the ETF's second phase. Would these products create alpha or just beta?

Alpha measures a mutual fund's excess return compared to the return of the benchmark index, relative to the extra risk it took. Beta measures how a portfolio's volatility, or systematic risk, compares to the rest of the market. Beta tells the investor how the portfolio will respond to the market's moves.

"A beta of 1 indicates that the security's price will move with the market," according to Investopedia. "A beta of less than 1 means that the security will be less volatile than the market. A beta of greater than 1 indicates that the security's price will be more volatile than the market. For example, if a stock's beta is 1.2, it's theoretically 20 percent more volatile than the market."[4]

Beta meant tracking a standard benchmark index very closely. But, the alpha contingent wanted indexes that were more strategy based and designed to beat the indexes.

The debates inside Nuveen resembled the Miller Lite beer commercials. Gastineau led the side that was "less filling," the beta side. He wanted to create building-block ETFs at the lowest prices for institutional investors, hedge funds, and fund asset mangers to use in asset allocations. Seeking the first-mover advantage, he pushed to launch the bond ETFs first. But the plan was they would only charge an annual fee of 0.15 percent. For Nuveen, which was used to expense ratios in the 1 percent range, this was truly less filling. Nuveen also proved to be less-than-thrilled to enter into a new product category charging razor-thin profit margins.

"They didn't believe me at first that the fees would be low," said Gastineau. "They assumed BGI was making a lot of money. But, even though iShares had a large amount of assets under management, its fees were so low the company still wasn't profitable." Gastineau said that at the time a lot of investment banks considered buying BGI, but after taking one look at the profit margins, they said "we don't want anything to do with this business."[5]

While Gastineau was pushing bonds, Bond, ironically, was pushing stocks. Bond was the guy saying it "tastes great." He felt Nuveen couldn't compete with the beta indexes already established, but should go after mutual funds. He pushed for new index funds that would "use algorithms to pick stocks in an effort to seek better returns than the stock market." Bond thought they could charge as much as 0.6 percent of assets. It would have been the highest domestic ETF expense ratio up until then.

"I respect Gary and his points, but I thought he was wrong," said Bond. "It was a case [in which] you have someone you respect, but you can't agree. But he wasn't that far off. He believed if you build it and it's cheap, they will come. Those were the days when if you had the right idea and priced it low, it would be huge."[6]

There was also a third group at Nuveen. This team didn't like ETFs and feared they would cannibalize the company's existing mutual fund business, or that there was no money to be made because of the low fees. They ended up winning the battle. But they lost the war.

The low prices were a serious issue. According to Hooten, Nuveen's Chief Executive Tim Schwertfeger and President John Amboian were very leery of the ETFs. They worried that it would require billions of dollars worth of sales to break even with the very small expense ratios. They also worried the cheap ETFs would cannibalize its products with higher annual fees. Hooten also believes that the philosophical differences inside the ETF group factored in Nuveen's decision to abandon the project.

Nuveen and BGI's iShares were neck-and-neck in the race to get the first exemptions for Treasury-based ETFs. At the time, it was reported that Nuveen was worried about the immediate competition from iShares. It shouldn't have been. As the Gold Shares showed, even a two-month advantage could lock in the leadership position. Had Nuveen decided to issue the first bond ETFs it might have solidified the first-mover advantage for not only a specific index, but an entire asset class.

While all this was going on, Nuveen underwent a reorganization. Realizing it couldn't do everything well, the firm decided to focus on what it excelled at: asset management, hedge funds, and closed-end funds. Nuveen had recently bought a private fund firm for a large premium. The thinking inside Nuveen was that it was better at growing an existing company with value, even if bought at a premium, than to incubate a start up, such as the ETF business. Nuveen also decided to get out of the UIT business.

Hooten saw the writing on the wall. He and Fulton left Nuveen on Sept. 1, 2001 to found Claymore Securities as a UIT and closed-end fund firm and focus on commission-based products, just like Nuveen. It would be five years before Claymore launched its first five ETFs.

They didn't ask Bond to join them. He was shocked.

Bond had been friends with Hooten since high school in Wheaton, Ill., just outside of Chicago. Hooten was the best man at Bond's wedding, and Bond was in Hooten's wedding. But the fights over the ETFs spilled into their friendship, so Hooten left Bond at Nuveen. It created bad blood between the two. But Hooten wanted to run his own firm and understood there can only be one boss. The fights made Hooten realize he couldn't work for his old friend. He also understood Bond wouldn't be happy playing second fiddle to him. He made the break.

As everyone expected, Nuveen received the exemptions first. And in a fateful move, it decided not to produce the ETFs. It shut down the UIT and the ETF departments in 2002.

"Nuveen made an executive decision to focus on areas of the market where they were the strongest," said Bond. "And that didn't include ETFs because they didn't have any yet. For them it was the right decision and they have been very successful."[7]

"I truly believe if Nuveen had gone into ETFs then, it would be bigger than Barclays Global Investors in terms of ETFs and assets," said Hooten. "They left a massive opportunity behind. They could have been a leader in that space. People at Barclays later told me the biggest fear they had was Nuveen entering the space."[8]

While BGI was bigger, it was a foreign bank focused on institutions. Meanwhile, Nuveen was a North American retail firm. It already had a powerful brand and a great reputation among retail investors. With a huge distribution network into brokerages, wire houses and independent channels, most investment advisors were already familiar with the firm.

Gastineau and Bond went to Nuveen and offered to buy the SEC exemptions. Gastineau walked away with the fixed-income exemptions and left Nuveen. Bond stayed another year to shut down the UIT department and tried to convince Nuveen to change its mind about ETFs. When he saw that wasn't going to happen, he bought Nuveen's ETF business, which included the SEC exemptions for the equity funds, and left to start his own company.

It's easy to look with shock and pity at Nuveen's lack of vision in deciding to not get into the ETF business. But for an individual or a company, success comes from an honest assessment of strengths and weaknesses. Nuveen realized it was better at growing a business, and this proved to be a good decision. The firm is a leader in both the closed-end fund and separately managed account businesses.

Still, the idea of how much money Nuveen left on the table by not jumping in before the gold rush is staggering, especially considering the incredible concentration of talent on its payroll. At the end of 2001, just a few months before Nuveen called it quits on ETFs, there were 493 closed-end funds with $141.2 billion in assets under management, according to the ICI. Comparatively, 2001 ended with 102 ETFs and $82.99 billion in assets under management. By the end of 2007, the number of closed-end funds had jumped 35 percent to 668, with assets more than doubling to $314.94 billion. Meanwhile, the ETF industry had increased five-fold, to 629 ETFs with assets of $608.42 billion.[9]

Unfair Fight

Gastineau took the exemptions for the fixed-income ETFs and started his own firm, ETF Advisors, with Rosenkranz Asset Managers. While he had the exemptions before iShares, Gastineau didn't have the infrastructure to create and support the funds, like Nuveen, nor the distribution sales force. He had to build the company from scratch. Without the support of a large financial company, Gastineau's start-up firm took much longer to come to the market than Nuveen would have. Gastineau lost the "first mover" advantage. In July 2002, iShares released the first four fixed-income ETFs:

1. The iShares Lehman 1 to 3 Year Treasury Bond Fund (symbol: SHY). This fund follows the Lehman Brothers 1 to 3 Year US Treasury Index, which tracks the price and yield of the U.S. Treasury market's short-term sector, before fees and expenses.
2. iShares Lehman 7 to 10 Year Treasury Bond Fund (symbol: IEF) tracks Lehman's index for the intermediate-term sector of the U.S. Treasury market.
3. iShares Lehman 20+ Year Treasury Bond Fund (symbol: TLT) follows Lehman's index of the same name, which tracks the long-term sector of the U.S. Treasury market.
4. The iShares iBoxx $ Investment Grade Corporate Bond Fund (symbol: LQD) was originally issued as the GS $InvesTop Corporate Bond Fund. It seeks to replicate the performance of the corporate bond market as defined by the iBoxx $ Liquid Investment Grade Index.

A year later iShares launched the Lehman Aggregate Bond Fund (symbol: AGG) to track the total U.S. investment grade bond market and the iShares Lehman U.S. Treasury Inflation Protected Securities Bond Fund (symbol: TIP). The Treasury Inflation Protected, or TIP, fund tracks the inflation-protected sector of the U.S. Treasury market, as defined by the Lehman Brothers U.S. Treasury TIPS Index.

All the iShares bond funds charge an annual expense ratio of 0.15 percent of assets, the price Gastineau wanted for Nuveen's bond ETFs. The TIPs charge a bit more, 0.2 percent yearly.

The bond ETFs were a hit. Within two weeks, they acquired more than $3 billion in assets.[10]

Bond ETFs are '40 Act products, the same as equity ETFs. Except for taxes, the benefits are exactly the same: lower costs than a bond index mutual fund, transparency, and flexibility to trade on the exchange during the trading session. However, bond ETFs don't have the tax efficiency of stock ETFs. Bonds pay out interest quarterly during the life of the bond. This income is typically distributed to the shareholders and taxed at their regular tax rate.

Wall Street's machinations to make money from your investments remind me of the Wizard of Oz at the end of the movie. As Dorothy stands in a large room in front of a terrifying floating image of the wizard, a man stands hidden behind a curtain at the far end of the room. As the floating head yells, "Don't look behind the curtain," Dorothy's dog pulls the curtain away to reveal the real wizard, a much less impressive figure. The bond ETF, like Toto, tore away part of the curtain hiding Wall Street's secrets.

Unlike stocks, bonds don't trade on a central market. They trade between brokers over phone lines. So, investors can never be sure that they received the best price for their bond. But with the bond ETFs, prices needed to be transparent to make the creation units. The fixed-income ETFs brought transparent pricing information to the bond market, a radical improvement for investors.

Four months later, November 2002, ETF Advisors launched the four Fixed-Income Treasury Receipts. They were called the FITRs, pronounced "fighters." Six months after that, in May 2003, they closed. Much like Deutsche Bank's decision to discontinue the CountryBaskets (or CountryCaskets), because they couldn't overcome being the second issue in their investment space, ETF Advisors decided to liquidate its funds. Together, the four FITR ETFs had raised only $75 million in assets under management.[11]

In fact, iShares' first-mover status in bonds was so strong, it was five years before a bond ETF from another company hit the market. Gastineau went back to the drawing board. His new firm, Managed ETFs, is working to launch "actively managed" ETFs. More on this in Chapter 11.

BONY Builds a BLDR

At the end of 2002, the Bank of New York launched its one and only family of ETFs, the Baskets of Listed Depositary Receipts. Better known as the BLDRS, they're pronounced "builders." These were also the first ETFs to list on the NASDAQ Stock Market. This family of four funds tracked indexes composed strictly of the American depositary receipts (ADRs) of foreign companies. ADRs are receipts for securities that physically remain in a foreign country. The BLDRs never garnered a big following. The exception was the BLDRS Emerging Markets 50 ADR Index (symbol: ADRE). As the first-mover into the emerging markets space, it proved to be the most popular of the bunch, garnering close to $1 billion in assets under management. (For more on BLDRS, see Chapter 2.)

The Name Is Bond

Bruce Bond left Nuveen in August 2002 with three assets: the equity exemptions allowing him to sell ETFs; the name he had created for the business, PowerShares; and the domain name on the Internet. Ranga Nathan, a Nuveen colleague who understood the operational side of the business, and John Southard, one of Bond's First Trust colleagues, joined him to become founding partners in PowerShares Capital Management.

Known to be a whiz at building quantitative investment models, Southard was working as a senior equity analyst at Charles Schwab. At Schwab, Southard helped develop an innovative system for ranking thousands of stocks based on fundamental data. He also had developed quantitative models for First Trust Portfolios. Southard became PowerShares's director of research and portfolio manager.

Bond wanted Southard to develop research that would allow for this next generation index to be built—an index that would consistently beat the S&P 500 and the NASDAQ-100. These classic indexes are based on market-capitalization weighting, a way to measure a stock's value in the market. Their goal was to create an index methodology that would continually evaluate the market to identify the securities with the greatest investing merit. They developed research for a new type of index, one with "stock-picking intelligence." This index would pick component stocks by quantitative measures, which are less capricious than share prices; something that would offer broad market exposure with a disciplined selection process. Their methodology incorporated 25 different factors that fell into four categories: fundamentals, valuation, timeliness, and risk. All the factors were combined to produce one score. The highest scoring stocks landed in the index. "We understood ETFs only replicated indexes," said Bond. "To add value we needed an intelligent index to create an ETF that sought to provide outperformance."[12]

They called their new indexes the Intellidexes, a combination of "intelligent" and "index."

Running low on money, Bond took the idea to First Trust, his old firm. First Trust chief executive James Bowen offered to buy the PowerShares business and let Bond run it. Bond answered "No." He knew he had to own the idea to do it right. PowerShares then took the idea to Standard & Poor's and Dow Jones. The young firm offered the index giants the rights to the indexes research if they let PowerShares own the funds. The index firms declined.

There was no money coming in and the partners were spending their retirement savings. It began to get very hot in the kitchen. Nathan was putting children through college. He decided he couldn't afford the risk of the business failing, and sold his stock back to Bond. After only four months, he left the firm.

Bond and Southard then took the idea to the American Stock Exchange. There they received a warm welcome from Bob Tull. Tull knew a good idea when he saw it. He had been on the team that created Morgan Stanley's WEBS and OPALs. Then he joined Deutsche Bank in time to help close the CountryBaskets. He now worked on the Amex's product development team and brought the idea to his boss, Cliff Weber, the Amex's head of ETF marketplace.

Weber was devoted to the ETF concept. He had been in the industry from the beginning. Nate Most hired Weber as the third man on the SPDR team when he, Steve Bloom, and State Street were still figuring out how to make the fund work. Coming out of University of Pennsylvania with a master's degree in systems engineering, Weber programmed the computers during the SPDR's early days, making sure everything worked. Within two years, Most had retired, Bloom had moved on, and the Amex's Gastineau era began. Weber stayed on as a key member of the ETF team.

Ten years after the SPDR launched, Weber finally became the ETF chief. By this time, ETFs had become such a huge piece of the Amex's revenues that the job title was changed from head of product development to head of the ETF marketplace. Now that he was in charge, he went looking for a way to grow the number of tradable funds.

Weber turned the PowerShares team over to his own young computer whiz, Scott Ebner. Ebner took PowerShares raw material and fashioned it into a fully functioning index. It was a win-win for everyone. The Amex secured an exclusive global license agreement to develop indexes under the Intellidex brand, while PowerShares held the exclusive rights to develop funds using these indexes.

"The Intellidexes opened up the ETF's second wave of products," said Weber. "It started the movement from the pure-passive benchmark ETFs to the strategy- and theme-based investing products."[13]

Of course, it wasn't all smooth sailing.

Radically changing the indexes from basic market-cap weighted benchmarks to the Intellidexes, with its quantitative approach and quarterly rebalancings, didn't sit well with the Securities and Exchange Commission. The SEC ruled that the original exemption orders didn't apply to the new indexes. PowerShares couldn't use the Nuveen exemptive relief it had purchased. Instead, it was forced to reapply to the SEC. The SEC liked the new idea and PowerShares received the exemption relief after just two months, the shortest amount of time the SEC has ever taken to grant these regulatory approvals.

Four weeks before the FITRs closed, PowerShares launched its first two ETFs:

1. The Dynamic Market Portfolio (symbol: PWC)
2. The Dynamic OTC Portfolio (symbol: PWO)

They were built to beat the S&P 500 and the NASDAQ-100 Indexes. They charged the 0.6 percent Bond wanted at Nuveen. It was among the highest fees for domestic equities in ETF Land at that time. The quantitative methodology claimed to offer more protection on the downside, while keeping pace with the benchmarks on the upside. By picking stocks with "merit," not momentum, PowerShares expected the portfolio to cut down on its volatility and offer protection during a market correction.

It appears to be a good strategy. From their launch on May 1, 2003, through Dec. 31, 2007, the Dynamic Market Portfolio posted a total return of 92.1 percent, the Dynamic OTC Portfolio had climbed 84.5 percent, and the S&P 500 had gained just 60.3 percent.

It would be another 18 months before PowerShares released another ETF.

Rydex Rides In

PowerShares was not the first new indexer. Rydex Investments was. Rydex issued its first ETF, the Rydex S&P Equal Weight ETF (symbol: RSP), exactly one week before PowerShares first two ETFs hit the market.

Rydex had been in the mutual fund business a decade before it launched its first ETF. The Rockville, Maryland, firm's first mutual fund was an innovative index fund that introduced the concept of leverage. Launched in 1993, the Nova fund tries to earn 150 percent of the S&P 500's daily return. So, if the S&P 500 index rises 1 percent, the fund gains 1.5 percent. Rydex also launched the first inverse index fund, the Ursa fund, which tries to capture the negative return of the market's daily movement. If the S&P 500 falls 1 percent, the Ursa fund gains 1 percent. These can be leveraged too, to create double the negative return.

In 1994, five years before the Qubes, Rydex became the first to launch a mutual fund based on the NASDAQ-100. It peaked at $4 billion in assets under management. Even a year after the Qubes were launched, it still held $3.4 billion.

After iShares broke open the ETF market, Rydex began researching the marketplace to determine if it should get involved. In the 1990s, before Rydex launched the NASDAQ-100 mutual fund, it had run an index fund based on the NASDAQ Composite Index. After it decided to enter the ETF business, it hoped its history of licensing NASDAQ indexes would help it to get the rights to an ETF based on the NASDAQ Composite. That was awarded to Fidelity Investments, one of the largest mutual fund firms in the world. The Fidelity NASDAQ Composite Index Tracking Stock (symbol: ONEQ) is the only ETF to come out of Fidelity.

After losing the Composite, Rydex approached Standard & Poor's. Since iShares had made growth and value ETFs from S&P's major benchmarks, Rydex suggested using the S&P 500, but with an equal weighting instead of a market-cap weighting. Thus, Rydex launched the first ETF with an alternative weighting.

The difference with the market-cap weighted index is pretty radical. In the S&P 500, the largest stocks represent a larger percentage of the index. For instance, the top 10 stocks in the index represent about 20 percent of the index's weighting. This means the bigger companies have a greater affect on the index's movement. At the end of 2007, ExxonMobile had a market value of $513 billion, giving it a weighting of 3.8 percent.

But in an equally weighted index, each of the 500 stocks represents only 0.2 percent of the index. Equal weighting boosts the impact of the index's smaller stocks, while diminishing the effect from the giant companies. Yet, equal weighting is difficult in a mutual fund. In a market-cap weighted index, a stock's weighting changes with its price. But in an equal-weighted index, price moves disrupt the weightings. The portfolio needs to be rebalanced on a regular basis, which can create huge transaction costs. The ETF is rebalanced on a quarterly basis, and the in-kind trade makes it easy to move stocks in and out of the index to maintain the proper weighting.

Rydex and PowerShares are both new indexers, but they approached indexes differently. Rydex based its ETF strategy on the weighting of the index. PowerShares made stock selection its main criteria. These would become the two parallel strategies open to the new indexers. Index weighting broke down into three categories, market-cap (or some modification of market-cap), fixed-weight (such as equally-weighted), and fundamentally weighted. Stock selection would fall into passive, quantitative or screened (such as thematic indexes).[14] Most of the time, an ETF would break away from the classic index model by following one path. But sometimes, it would differentiate itself by both selection and weighting.

Rydex and PowerShares both realized they needed to offer something new, but they weren't selling the same idea. So, while Rydex beat

PowerShares to the market, there was no first-mover advantage because they were completely different strategies. Rydex also took a different strategy on the entire product line. It wanted to see if the concept worked and took its time learning the business. It would be another two years before Rydex launched its second ETF, the Rydex Russell Top 50 (symbol: XLG). Rydex rarely gets credit for recognizing early on the potential of the ETF market. Aside from Vanguard, which realized ETFs were a direct assault on its index fund business, Rydex was only the second company focused solely on mutual funds to enter the field. Part of the reason is that Rydex has a small presence in the market. The company has been methodical about launching products. It launched equal-weighted ETFs for all the S&P sector indexes. And it wasn't until late 2007 that it finally won approval for its first six leveraged and inverse ETFs.

Another reason Rydex rarely gets credit is because PowerShares' impact was so much greater. While Rydex launched the first ETF with an alternative weighting, PowerShares reworked the concept of what it means to be an index. The Intellidex ETFs are much more innovative products and were a bigger risk to bring to the market. Rydex also ceded its leadership position by taking so long to come out with its second ETF. More important, Power-Shares was the first firm to prove a company could build a business out of ETFs and nothing else. ETF Advisors, producer of the FITRs, may have been the first independent upstart to enter the business, but PowerShares was the first independent upstart to survive. It had no mutual fund business to fall back on. If its ETFs failed it would die. Rydex did make a name for itself in the ETF industry by issuing the CurrencyShares, the only exchange-traded products to track the foreign exchange market by holding a single currency. These are explained in detail in Chapter 8, "The ETFs that Aren't ETFs."

Vanguard Makes a Splash

Vanguard was not exactly a big presence in the ETF market when Rydex entered.

In 2001, it launched two Vanguard Index Participation Equity Receipts, known as the VIPERs. Then its ETF strategy went dormant for the next two years. In January 2004, it finally made a big commitment to the market with the launch of 14 sector ETFs. Nine months later it launched four more. These track sector indexes from MSCI and have some of the lowest expense ratios in the industry.

As previously noted, most of the new VIPERs were just a class of shares from already existing mutual funds. This means that all the assets from the mutual fund and the ETF are pooled together. This has the effect of giving the mutual fund shareholders better tax efficiency. The older stocks in the fund that would create the largest capital gain distributions are pushed out through the ETF's in-kind process. Then the newer shares brought into the ETF are sold through the mutual fund.

Critics say this helps the fund shareholders at the expense of the ETF shareholders. Should the mutual fund pay out a capital gains distribution triggered by redemptions, it wouldn't affect only the mutual fund shareholders. The ETF shareholders would also receive part of the distribution and have to pay taxes on it. Vanguard says ETF shareholders benefit, because any capital losses in the mutual fund would offset future gains, which helps both classes of investors. The VIPERs name was changed to Vanguard ETFs in 2006.

For the most part, the tax efficiency question is an academic debate. Vanguard is extremely adept at minimizing capital gains, to the point of eliminating them for most ETFs.

For most investors, Vanguard should be one of the first places, if not *the* first, to look for basic market tracking ETFs, especially the Total Stock Market ETF (symbol: VTI) and Total Bond Market ETF (symbol: BND). It is almost always the lowest cost provider. Total Stock has an expense ratio of 0.07 percent, while Total Bond charges 0.11 percent. Most of its ETFs charge less than 0.2 percent, while the sector funds charge 0.22 percent. One downside is that Vanguard doesn't track the most well-known indexes, such as those from S&P, Dow Jones, or Russell. Its ETFs track the MSCI indexes from Morgan Stanley, although it doesn't track MSCI's benchmark, the EAFE (Europe, Australasia, Far East).

The sector ETFs launched in January 2004 are:

- Vanguard Consumer Discretionary ETF (symbol: VCR)
- Vanguard Consumer Staples ETF (symbol: VDC)
- Vanguard Financials ETF (symbol: VFH)
- Vanguard Growth ETF (symbol: VUG)
- Vanguard Health Care ETF (symbol: VHT)
- Vanguard Information Technology ETF (symbol: VGT)
- Vanguard Large Cap ETF (symbol: VV)
- Vanguard Materials ETF (symbol: VAW)
- Vanguard Mid Cap ETF (symbol: VO)
- Vanguard Small Cap ETF (symbol: VB)
- Vanguard Small Cap Growth ETF (symbol: VBK)
- Vanguard Small Cap Value ETF (symbol: VBR)
- Vanguard Utilities ETF (symbol: VPU)
- Vanguard Value ETF (Symbol: VTV)

There's Power in Them There Shares

PowerShares didn't have the luxury of a mutual fund company paying its salaries while it decided if the ETF project would work. PowerShares had no money coming in.

It was tough to build a brand new company on an investment vehicle with which few people were familiar. Bond said the first two years were very dark days. He didn't take a salary and the partners had their salaries cut in half. After the initial funding ran out, Bond had everyone commit more money to guarantee their share of the business. Everyone leveraged their homes and Southard even raided his kids' accounts.

"As you can imagine, it was very hard. Everybody and their brothers were betting against us, including Claymore, First Trust, and Nuveen," said Bond. "No one knew what PowerShares was or what an ETF was. They knew the QQQ and the SPDR, but they didn't know those were ETFs. And they couldn't understand how an index could be intelligent."[15] Things were so dire, Bond even visited Hooten's new firm, Claymore Securities, to discuss hiring Claymore to distribute PowerShares products. He decided against it because he felt the firm knew only how to sell products with loads.

Claymore wanted to get into the ETF business, but it didn't want to go through the long, drawn-out process of acquiring SEC exemptions, or building an infrastructure from scratch. Hooten wanted to skip over that and enter ETF Land by buying an existing business.

By this time, Hooten and Fulton had suffered a falling out over the vision and focus of Claymore. Fulton quit and began consulting on product development with PowerShares, First Trust, and others. He eventually joined PowerShares as head of product development in January 2005.

One thing Bond did know was marketing. Fittingly, he had begun his career selling and marketing bonds to wealthy investors. After 18 months of heavy marketing, explanations, and introductions to many registered investment advisors around Wall Street and the rest of the country, PowerShares launched its second set of Intellidex ETFs:

- PowerShares Golden Dragon Halter USX China Portfolio (symbol: PGJ) tracks the Halter USX China Index. This index is comprised of U.S.-listed securities, which derive the majority of their revenues from the People's Republic of China. Most of the stocks are ADRs of Chinese companies.
- PowerShares High Yield Equity Dividend Achievers Portfolio (symbol: PEY). This fund seeks to deliver high dividend income and capital appreciation by tracking the Mergent Dividend Achievers 50 Index. Comprised of the 50 highest yielding companies with at least 10 years of consecutive annual dividend increases, it's rebalanced quarterly and reconstituted annually.

By December 2004, PowerShares had built enough excitement that the products were a hit. The head of steam was so large that in 2005 it launched 32 ETFs, with 25 of them using the Intellidex strategy. With another 35 launched in 2006, it would become second only to Barclays in the number of ETFs issued. Elsewhere in ETF Land, the other major development in 2004 was the launch of the first exchange-traded vehicle based on a commodity: State Street's StreetTracks Gold Shares came out in November 2004. See Chapter 8 for details.

Mutual Fund Scandal Helps ETFs

In the 18 months between PowerShares' first and second launches, the mutual fund industry dropped a big present in the ETF industry's lap: a huge scandal. In September 2003, New York State Attorney General Eliot Spitzer shocked Wall Street by announcing he had been investigating fraud in the mutual fund industry. He accused the funds of breaking their own rules by allowing market timing and violating the law by allowing late-day trading.

Market timers are similar to the day traders of the mutual fund world, rapidly trading in and out of mutual funds, sometimes within 24 hours. The market timers' strategy was to try to buy shares on days the funds' prices went up and sell on the days they fell. Day traders do this in the stock market, but they pay a commission on every trade. The market timers traded for free. They bought no load funds. The way some foreign funds were priced, in particular, provided low risk profit opportunities to market timers.

While the market timers make commission-free profits, their trades hurt the returns of buy-and-hold investors. As explained in Chapter 6, the people who buy and sell shares in mutual funds don't bear the costs of their actions. The buy-and-hold shareholders do. The traders generate both transaction costs and capital gains, which are later taxed. In addition, market timers trading huge amounts of money limit the fund manager's flexibility. In order to pay the timers when they sell, the manager may need to hold a large amount of cash, which may create cash drag. This cuts the fund's performance. At the time, *Fortune* magazine said "timing costs long-term mutual fund shareholders as much as $4 billion a year."[16]

While not illegal, the fund companies explicitly forbade market timing with blunt language in their prospectuses. It also went against the image the industry sold to retail customers. Fund companies said their managers weren't the typical Wall Street sharks. Rather, they were honest, reliable people running stable, long-term portfolios to help small investors capture a piece of the market. The scandal showed that market timing was allowed, but only for a select few, usually hedge funds. Unlike mutual funds or ETFs, hedge funds aren't regulated by the SEC. They can use strategies and hold assets not allowed in a '40 Act investment company. They also don't have to report their holdings, so it's extremely difficult to know what these funds hold.

In what would become the biggest scandal in the industry's history, Spitzer's investigation proved that not only did the fund companies allow market timing, but some even catered to the market timers by giving proprietary information about fund holdings. Essentially, the fund companies sold out their long-term shareholders to boost their own profits.

Before the stock market's Internet bubble popped, mutual funds launched a steady stream of technology-related funds to capture investor interest in this sector of the market. In 1999, 50 new technology funds hit the market. The next year saw the launch of 113 more tech funds. After the bull market crashed in 2000, unsophisticated small investors blamed the funds for ruining their nest eggs by hyping and selling extremely risky and speculative investments. Whatever shares they had left they sold. Over the next few years, the combination of falling stock prices and investors bailing out, sent assets under management plummeting at many fund companies. Because fund companies charge fees as a percentage of assets, fewer assets mean smaller revenues. They need to attract new money and make it grow. Desperate for assets, the fund companies exempted the hedge funds from the short-term redemption fees charged to discourage market timers. The market timers, in return, left large amounts of "sticky assets" in the funds. These separate accounts sat in a fund generating management fees.

It wasn't just market timing that gave the hedge funds an advantage over the retail investor. They also took advantage of late-day trading. And this was flat-out illegal. Remember, one of the big advantages ETFs have over mutual funds is that fund shareholders need to make their sale or purchase order during the trading day, before the market's close. But the actual trade occurs after the market closes, the 4 P.M. net asset value. Late trading is similar to inside trading in that one investor acts on material information before it becomes available to the rest of the market.

For instance, if after 4 P.M. Monday a big company announces a huge profit, the news would affect the market on Tuesday. Fund shareholders wouldn't be able to act on the news until Tuesday's market session. They would only get the price at Tuesday's close, after the market had already moved higher.

The late traders and market timers would see the profit news late Monday, but instead of having to wait until the next day, the fund company would let them get the fund's net asset value as of 4 P.M. Monday. By buying the shares at Monday's price instead of Tuesday's, the market timer captured the gains related to the news during Tuesday's session, while the long-term shareholders couldn't. Some trades "were submitted between 6 P.M. and 9 P.M.—and still got the 4 P.M. price!"[17]

Spitzer called it "betting on a horse race after the horses have crossed the finish line."[18]

The entire industry came under investigation by the New York State attorney general's office, other state regulators, the Justice Department, and the SEC. The scandal tarnished the reputations of some the industry's largest players, including Pimco, Janus, Invesco, Strong Capital, Putnam, MFS, Franklin Templeton, PBHG, Alliance, Bank of America, Bank One, and CIBC.

Fortune reported at the time that of the 88 largest fund companies, half admitted to allowing market timing—and 25 percent allowed late trading. Most of the fund companies involved had to pay hundreds of millions of dollars in fines. Chief executive officers and other top executives were fired and some faced criminal charges.

"Every time we turn over a rock in the mutual fund business," Spitzer famously declared at the time, "we find vermin crawling beneath it." Working with the SEC, his office negotiated four mammoth settlements totaling more than $1.65 billion.[19]

Even though many fund companies did nothing wrong, the credibility and reputation of the mutual fund industry was in tatters. Not only did the funds charge high fees as a normal course of business, but when given the chance many would actively screw over their own customers. This provided a perfect opening for the ETF to fill. The individual investor who had been burned by the fund industry needed a safe place to invest. Already, investors had become interested in ETFs because of their lower fees. But now the ETFs had a new selling point. The investments of ETF shareholders couldn't be affected by market timers or late-day traders. Here was one more reason to leave funds behind and jump into ETFs.

In fact, ETFs are perfect instruments for market timers. They can jump in and out as often as they want in order to capture the strategy and it doesn't affect the ETF's other shareholders. Of course, the market-timers' returns received a significant boost from trading in no-load mutual funds, because they had no transaction costs. Market-timers using ETFs have to pay a commission the same as everyone else, which can amount to a significant expense.

PowerShares Becomes a Powerhouse . . . and Other Important Developments of 2005

At the end of 2004, PowerShares had four ETFs with $280 million in assets. Over the next twelve months it would become a powerhouse, issuing 32 new ETFs for a total of 36, and holding $3.5 billion in assets. In merely two and a half years, out of nothing, and as the only company without the backing of a larger institution behind it, PowerShares became the ETF company with the second largest number of funds. Only BGI's iShares had more. In terms of assets under management, it was the fourth largest, behind iShares, State Street, and Vanguard.

According to the ICI, during 2005 the ETF industry added 52 new funds, a 34 percent year-over-year increase, for a total of 204 funds. Assets under management grew 32 percent from 2004, to $300 billion.

The other big developments occurred so late in the year that their effect was only really felt in 2006.

- Rydex issued the first currency-based exchange-traded vehicle, the CurrencyShares Euro Trust (symbol: FXE). The Euro Trust holds actual euros and is a bet against the U.S. dollar. Its value rises when the currency advances against the dollar. (See Chapter 8.)
- In addition to its many Intellidex ETFs, PowerShares also launched the first fundamentally-weighted ETF, the PowerShares FTSE RAFI US 1000 (symbol: PRF). (More on this later.)
- First Trust, the UIT shop that Bond, Hooten, and Fulton left for Nuveen, launched its first ETF, the First Trust Dow Jones Select Micro-Cap (symbol: FDM). This ETF tracks microcap companies, which have market-caps typically less than $500 million.

The Buy-Out

For the most part, mutual fund companies continued to view ETFs much like Nuveen had: they didn't have a dedicated distribution network and they charged very low fees. Mutual fund companies love their fees, otherwise, there wouldn't be so many of them: the load, the large expense ratio, and the 12b-1 fee. Thus, most mutual fund companies are focused on high-fee active management, not indexing. Whether it was low fees or fear of cannibalizing their other products, most fund companies ignored the growth opportunity, leaving the field wide open for small firms with an index and a dream.

However, one big fund company noticed.

Amvescap is one of the world's largest publicly-traded mutual fund managers in terms of market-cap. On January 23, 2006, it bought Power-Shares, the only independent ETF firm, for $100 million. And if PowerShares met management fee benchmarks over the next five years, there was the potential for another $630 million in contingent payments.

Bruce Bond had done it.

He proved that an independent firm with the sole purpose of selling only ETFs, and with no connection to an existing Wall Street company, could be built from scratch and make the mutual fund industry stand up and take notice. Not just that, but he and his partners became multimillionaires virtually overnight. And PowerShares was still pretty small. It had $3.5 billion in assets under management, compared with iShares' approximately $193 billion at the time.

Amvescap, an Anglo-American fund management firm that sold funds under the brand names Invesco and AIM, had come through a very bad year. U.S. regulators had named its Invesco funds as one of the biggest players in the mutual fund scandal. In September 2004, Amvescap agreed to settle charges with a $450 million payment. Over the next 15 months Amvescap suffered huge fund outflows as clients, disgusted with the scandal and sick of the funds' poor performance, withdrew their money. Amvescap would change its name to Invesco in May 2007.

It was a big deal for Amvescap, but it was a huge deal for the ETF industry. Not only did Amvescap become the second-largest ETF company in terms of funds, the purchase immediately announced that the ETF industry was the real deal, and that it needed to be taken seriously by the mutual fund industry. On top of that, by giving PowerShares access to its huge institutional and retail distribution capabilities, Amvescap, in essence, announced that iShares better watch its back. There was now a serious challenger for the ETF throne.

Opening the Floodgates

Amvescap's purchase of PowerShares was huge.

"AIM's acquisition of PowerShares opened up a lot of people's eyes to the potential of the marketplace," said Cliff Weber, the Amex's ETF marketplace chief during this time. "And that led the more recent entrants into the market."[20]

The new firms entering the ETF marketplace in 2006 brought innovations not only in indexing, but also in product structure and asset class. This was the year of the exchange-traded vehicle (ETV), products that look like ETFs, but are not funds. With the commodity and currency markets surging, the gold ETVs and the Euro Trust proved there was a market for alternative products tracking assets besides stocks and bonds.

February 2006 saw the launch of the first ETV based on an index made up entirely of commodities, not stocks nor bonds. The PowerShares DB Commodity Index Tracking Fund (symbol: DBC) holds futures contracts on six of the most heavily traded and important physical commodities in the world—crude oil, heating oil, gold, aluminum, corn, and wheat.

DB (Deutsche Bank) Commodity Services launched it alone. Power-Shares' name was added when it partnered with Deutsche Bank to become the fund distributor. DB remains the manager for all of PowerShares' commodity products.

The union came about after college friends Ben Fulton and Kevin Rich both left Claymore Securities in 2003. After a stint consulting on ETF product development, Fulton joined PowerShares. Meanwhile, Rich joined Deutsche Bank's commodities group, which was working to create ETFs based on their proprietary commodities indexes. They decided to partner once Rich convinced his superiors that this was a way to re-enter the market after the CountryBaskets debacle eight years earlier. Over the next year, the PowerShares/DB partnership would launch seven more commodity index ETVs and three currency-based ETVs.

Upstart firm Victoria Bay Asset Management launched U.S. Oil (symbol: USO), the first ETV to track the price of oil. Rydex launched a family of six CurrencyShares to join its Euro Trust. Barclay's also began tracking commodities and currencies with a different structure, the exchange-traded notes. (These products are explained in Chapter 8.)

By 2006, iShares, State Street Global Advisors, Vanguard, and Power-Shares had expanded their lines with ETFs tracking global stocks, individual sectors of the market, and funds following style biases, such as growth and value, for all the major indexes.

In 2006, the ICI reported 155 new ETFs were launched, a 76 percent increase over 2005, for a total of 359. Assets under management grew 40 percent to $422.55 billion. For a good overview of the growth of the ETF industry from the SPDR's launch in 1993, see Tables 7.1 and 7.2.

Once again, in order to stand out, the new ETF firms needed to innovate.

For the '40 Act ETFs, the two strategic themes of index creation—selection and weighting—took on greater significance. The stock selection proponents began creating more narrowly focused, niche indexes. On the weighting side, a new formula weighting stocks based on their fundamental features—such as sales and profits—proved to be as incendiary as if they had thrown Molotov cocktails through the windows of Standard & Poor's.

The three firms that came to personify the niche indexes were Claymore Securities, Van Eck's Market Vectors, and ProShares. The niche indexes are basically sector or style indexes taken to an extreme.

Market Vectors

Founded in 1955, Van Eck said that it was one of the first U.S. money managers to offer investors diversification through global investing. In 1968, the New York company introduced the nation's first gold mutual fund, Van Eck International Gold. So it was fitting that Van Eck Global would launch the first ETF to focus strictly on gold mining stocks. Van Eck's first ETF, the Market Vectors–Gold Miners hit the market in May 2006, just as gold hit a

TABLE 7.1   Number of ETFs, 1993–2006

		Investment Objective					Legal Structure	
Year	Total	Broad-Based Domestic Equity	Sector/Industry Domestic Equity	Global International Equity	Bond	Hybrid	Registered	Non-Registered
1993	1	1	-	-	-	-	1	-
1994	1	1	-	-	-	-	1	-
1995	2	2	-	-	-	-	2	-
1996	28	2	-	26	-	-	28	-
1997	19	2	-	17	-	-	19	-
1998	29	3	9	17	-	-	29	-
1999	30	4	9	17	-	-	30	-
2000	80	29	26	25	-	-	80	-
2001	102	34	34	34	-	-	102	-
2002	113	34	32	39	8	-	113	-
2003	119	39	33	41	6	-	119	-
2004	152	60	43	43	6	-	151	1
2005	204	81	68	49	6	-	201	3
2006	359	133	135	85	6	-	343	16
2007	629	197	219	159	49	5	601	28

Source: Investment Company Institute, *2008 Investment Company Fact Book.* Copyright © by the Investment Company Institute (www.ici.org). Reprinted with permission.

26-year high of $719.80 on the New York Mercantile Exchange. The ETF tracks the Amex Gold Miners Index, a collection of 35 international mining companies. It immediately received the nickname "GoldieStox."

Investing in gold bullion or the StreetTracks and iShares gold ETVs eliminates the company and stock market risk from the equation. This gives investors a return that matches the price of gold. However, traditionally, gold-mining stocks offer earnings and operating leverage. Even if the price of gold doesn't move, if the company does well the stocks can rise. And when gold's value does increase, gold-mining stocks typically return two to four times more than the price increase in the actual metal. Of course, the leverage also increases losses on the down side.

Because it's a '40 Act ETF holding stocks, not futures or the actual commodity, it also gets greater tax efficiency than the ETVs. The Market Vectors family contains only nine equity ETFs right now:

1. Market Vectors–Gold Miners ETF (symbol: GDX)
2. Market Vectors–Agribusiness ETF (symbol: MOO)
3. Market Vectors–Coal ETF (symbol: KOL)

TABLE 7.2   Net Assets of ETFs, 1993–2006

		Investment Objective					Legal Structure	
Year	Total	Broad-Based Domestic Equity	Sector/ Industry Domestic Equity	Global International Equity	Bond	Hybrid	Registered	Non-Registered
1993	$464	$464	-	-	-	-	$464	-
1994	424	424	-	-	-	-	424	-
1995	1,052	1,052	-	-	-	-	1,052	-
1996	2,411	2,159	-	$252	-	-	2,411	-
1997	6,707	6,200	-	506	-	-	6,707	-
1998	15,568	14,058	$484	1,026	-	-	15,568	-
1999	33,873	29,374	2,507	1,992	-	-	33,873	-
2000	65,585	60,529	3,015	2,041	-	-	65,585	-
2001	82,993	74,752	5,224	3,016	-	-	82,993	-
2002	102,143	86,985	5,919	5,324	$3,915	-	102,143	-
2003	150,983	120,430	11,901	13,984	4,667	-	150,983	-
2004	227,540	163,730	21,650	33,644	8,516	-	226,205	$1,335
2005	300,820	186,832	33,774	65,210	15,004	-	296,022	4,798
2006	422,550	232,487	58,355	111,194	20,514	-	407,850	14,699
2007	608,422	300,930	93,023	179,702	34,648	$119	579,517	28,906

Source: Investment Company Institute, *2008 Investment Company Fact Book.* Copyright © by the Investment Company Institute (www.ici.org). Reprinted with permission.

4. Market Vectors–Environmental Services ETF (symbol: EVX)
5. Market Vectors–Gaming ETF (symbol: BJK)
6. Market Vectors–Global Alternative Energy ETF (symbol: GEX)
7. Market Vectors–Nuclear Energy ETF (symbol: NLR)
8. Market Vectors–Russia ETF (symbol: RSX)
9. Market Vectors–Steel ETF (symbol: SLX)

Each one is a very specific niche market, most with a commodity focus.

Claymore Securities

After PowerShares' huge success, it became clear that Claymore Securities couldn't buy its way into ETF Land. It decided to build its own operation. Even though it had been the first to spring from Nuveen, it was five years before Claymore launched its first ETFs, and these were in Canada. In September 2006, after building a $14 billion asset base in closed-end funds, unit investment trusts, and other managed portfolios, the Lisle, Illinois, firm entered the U.S. market. While the firm has launched a few that track more classic market areas, Claymore has made a reputation for high concept ETFs. They include:

- Claymore/Sabrient Insider ETF (symbol: NFO) tracks an index that focuses on legal purchases by company insiders and analyst upgrades.
- Claymore/Sabrient Stealth ETF (symbol: STH) holds 150 stocks that are expected to outperform based on the academically observed "neglected stock effect." These stocks are not followed by Wall Street analysts but post superior returns.
- Claymore/Zacks Yield Hog (symbol: CVY) invests in preferred stocks, master limited partnerships, unincorporated energy companies, and closed-end funds to create a income stream higher than the typical dividend-based ETF.
- Claymore/BNY BRIC ETF (symbol: EEB) focus solely on the economies of Brazil, Russia, India, and China.
- Claymore S&P Global Water Index (symbol: CGW) tracks companies in water-related business, both utilities and infrastructure, and equipment and materials.

ProShares

On June 21, ProShares entered the ETF market by launching eight innovative exchange-traded funds. Four were the first ETFs to provide short exposure to market indexes. The other four were the first to magnify the returns of the benchmark indexes.

ProShares carried on the tradition of its parent company, the ProFunds Group, a small mutual fund firm that sells leveraged and inverse mutual funds. The firm was founded in 1997 by William Seale, commissioner of the Commodities Futures Trading Commission from 1983 to 1988, and Michael Sapir, previously a senior vice president at Rydex Investments, the firm which invented these concepts. ProFunds was the first company to offer leverage and short funds in one package. These funds would give you two times the index's negative return.

While Rydex produced the first leveraged and inverse mutual funds in 1994, ProShares launched the first ETFs to follow these strategies. It hadn't been easy. ProFunds saw the ETF's potential as early at 1999, when it filed its first registration for ETFs with the SEC. The firm waited seven years to receive approval from the SEC.

The short ETFs return the inverse of the index's performance. For instance if the NASDAQ-100 Index fell 1 percent during the day, the ProShares Short QQQ ETF (symbol: PSQ) would post a 1 percent gain. The beauty of these ETFs is they let investors short an index, while at the same time being long.

The first short ETFs were:

- Short QQQ ProShares (symbol: PSQ) seeks to return the opposite of the NASDAQ-100 Index.
- Short S&P500 ProShares (symbol: SH) returns the inverse of the S&P 500 Index.
- Short MidCap400 ProShares (symbol: MYY) earns the S&P MidCap 400 Index's negative return.
- Short Dow30 ProShares (symbol: DOG) gives investors the inverse performance of the Dow Jones Industrial Average.

That same day the firm also launched the first ultra, or leveraged, ETFs. These ETFs use leverage to return double the performance of the index they track, before fees and expenses. Magnifying the market's return is a good way to post a decent return in a year the market isn't moving much. Of course, a leveraged instrument that offers you twice the potential profit on the way up, also offers the risk of posting losses twice as wide on the way down.

These are the first leveraged ETFs:

- Ultra QQQ ProShares (symbol: QLD) seeks to return double the daily performance of the NASDAQ-100 Index.
- Ultra S&P500 ProShares (symbol: SSO) doubles the S&P 500 Index.
- Ultra MidCap400 ProShares (symbol: MVV) returns twice the S&P Mid-Cap 400 Index.
- Ultra Dow30SM ProShares (symbol: DDM) gives two times the performance of the Dow Jones Industrial Average.

All the short and ultra ETFs seek to return either the inverse return or double the actual return on a daily basis, not over the long term.

While the ETFs track benchmark indexes, ProShares gave small investors access to powerful strategies that had previously been the domain of well-financed, sophisticated traders and institutions. They also provided new, easy ways for investors to hedge risk. The short ETFs offer investors a much less risky way to make money in a down market. And investors are not required to set up margin accounts. The fund charges a 0.95 percent expense ratio, which is one of the more expensive in ETF Land. However, it takes on more risk to generate these returns. (For a detailed explanation of construction, tax requirements, and trading and strategic benefits of ProShares short and ultra ETFs, see Chapter 9.)

The Fundamentalists

The indexing world is not what one would call a hotbed of controversy. The portfolio managers are not hotshots looking for, and then jumping on, the market's next gravy train. Rather, they are the sensible, sober people who judge which companies are the best representatives of their industries. They aren't supposed to care if the companies go up or down. They care that the stocks picked for the index are representative.

The Intellidexes raised the hackles of the index community because they didn't just track the market, they were built to select companies that could beat the market. Still, that was nothing compared to the uproar when one man came out and called the market-cap weighted index a flawed measuring tool.

Rob Arnott doesn't look like a revolutionary. He looks like an investment banker: short hair, gray suit, and white shirt. The most radical thing about him is his goatee. The next most radical thing is a sensibility that gave him a reputation as one of the most provocative financial analysts.

Arnott is the chairman of Research Affiliates, a research-intensive asset-management firm based in Pasadena, California. Well-known as a financial thinker, Arnott has published more than 100 articles in the *Financial Analysts Journal, Journal of Portfolio Management*, the *Harvard Business Review,* and other respected journals. In one of those articles, Arnott launched the grenade that would expose the main structural flaw of the market-cap weighted index.

Arnott literally wrote the book on fundamental indexing. In the March 2005 issue of the *Financial Analysts Journal*, he and two associates published a paper called "Fundamental Indexation."[21]

As explained earlier in this chapter, market-capitalization measures a company's total stock market valuation by multiplying its share price by its total outstanding shares. This is the foundation for the S&P 500 and most other market benchmarks. This value determines the stock's proportional weight in the index. This criteria gives big companies with higher stock prices a greater weighting in the market than big companies with lower stock prices or small companies with high stock prices. A $1 move in a stock with a 3 percent weighting will move the index a lot more than a $1 move in a stock with a 0.1 percent weighting.

In short, Arnott argued that price is not the best way to measure a stock's value. The theory behind fundamental indexing is that market-cap-weighted indexes were overweighted with overpriced stocks.

If a stock is overvalued to its "true fair value," it will have a greater weighting in the index than it should have. Meanwhile, a stock undervalued to its true fair value will have a smaller weighting than it should have. But this is exactly the opposite of what investors want. They want to be overweight undervalued stocks, because, for those stocks to approach their true fair value, they have to rise in price. Not so with the overvalued stocks. To get to their true value, they need to fall in price. More to the point, Arnott demonstrated that using metrics other than cap-weighting outperformed the S&P 500 over a 43-year span by an average of more than two percentage points.

In the church of market-capitalization, this was blasphemy.

"Indexes should be cap-weighted because the market itself is cap-weighted," said David Blitzer, managing director and chairman for the Standard & Poor's index committee. "The people behind fundamental indexes claim that they can beat the market, and essentially they are saying they are smarter than the market. But it's not a free ride. The further you move away from cap-weighting, the more risk you take on."[22]

"I've never seen an idea gain so much traction as early as this one has," Arnott said. "But it's hitting a nerve because it addresses a concern people have had for not just years, but decades. Ever since the S&P 500 launched in 1957, people have expressed concerns that it's inherently designed to overweight the overvalued and underweight the undervalued, even though we can't know which stocks are overvalued."[23]

"Fundamental Index seeks to mirror the composition of the economy, rather than the composition of the stock market," said Arnott. "It seeks to weight companies according to their footprints in the economy, which can be measured. It breaks the link cap-weighting has between the errors in the price and the weight in the portfolio. With cap-weighting, they are intrinsic links. If we weight companies by their scale in the economy, the errors still exist, but aren't linked to their weight anymore."[24]

In short, fundamental indexing is weighting companies by their size in the economy. Arnott uses four fundamental metrics—revenues, profits, book value and gross dividends—to determine how large a company is as a percentage of the economy in each of these measurements, then averages them.

Not only did Arnott think his index could beat the market, but he realized he had a marketable investment strategy. But he had no desire to run an ETF company. He realized an index was just as marketable a product as an actual fund. Like the Intellidexes, he had a unique investing strategy that could be used in ETFs, but could also be licensed to mutual funds and other investing houses. He trademarked the name Fundamental Index, has a patent pending on the concept, and created the Research Affiliates Fundamental Index, or RAFI, based on the four fundamental metrics. No one else was doing it, so there was no reason he couldn't build an index shop around a family of indexes based on this concept. Research Affiliates partnered with indexing company FTSE, which manages, disseminates and runs the actual day-to-day calculations for the index series named FTSE

RAFI, and pronounced "footsie rafi." Pimco was the first to embrace the idea in the mutual fund world in an enhanced index. Later the Charles Schwab firm created passive indexes to follow FTSE RAFI for its mutual funds. It wasn't surprising that the FTSE RAFI would attract the attention of PowerShares. This was during Power Share's initial surge. Bruce Bond was already the bad boy of the index community. His Intellidex-based ETFs had a fundamental component to them, but they were equally weighted. So when Arnott came along and declared the days of market-capitalization were over, Bond knew he had found a kindred spirit. PowerShares approached Arnott and they decided to make ETFs together.

The first FTSE RAFI ETF, the PowerShares FTSE RAFI U.S. 1000 Portfolio came out in December 2005, but fundamental indexing was really a 2006 story.

The PowerShares FTSE RAFI U.S. 1000 Portfolio (symbol: PRF) tracks the top 1,000 companies screened by the FTSE RAFI. Much like the Intellidex can be adapted for many segments of the market, so too, can the FTSE RAFI. PowerShares has launched a whole family of FTSE RAFI ETFs for investors who want to make a diversified portfolio based solely on fundamental indexing. So, far fundamental indexing is winning. Since the inception of the FTSE RAFI 1000, it has consistently beat both the S&P 500 and the Russell 1000 by at least two percentage points and sometimes as much as five percentage points.

Here is a sampling of the FTSE RAFI ETFs:

- PowerShares FTSE RAFI Asia Pacific ex-Japan Portfolio (symbol: PAF)
- PowerShares FTSE RAFI Developed Markets ex-U.S. Portfolio (symbol: PXF)
- PowerShares FTSE RAFI Emerging Markets Portfolio (symbol: PXH)
- PowerShares FTSE RAFI US 1500 Small-Mid Portfolio (symbol: PRFZ)
- PowerShares FTSE RAFI Energy Sector Portfolio (symbol: PRFE)

In September 2006, PowerShares launched 10 FTSE RAFI ETFs tracking U.S. market sectors and in 2007 launched nine FTSE RAFI funds to track the international markets. But before any of these funds were launched, FTSE RAFI would face it biggest challenge. It wasn't from the market-cap community, but from another upstart firm that had independently discovered the beauty of the fundamentally weighted index.

WisdomTree

For six months, the FTSE RAFI 1000 stood as the lone renegade fighting the cause of the fundamental indexing. While Arnott was a lonely figure fighting the indexing establishment, he enjoyed having the stage to himself.

He had come to preach the gospel of fundamental indexing to the masses, and he owned the entire concept. He had filed for patents on any index based on fundamental metrics.

Then in June, a challenger arose to steal Arnott's thunder. WisdomTree Investments hit the ETF stage with a big splash. On June 16, 2006, WisdomTree launched 20 ETFs on the New York Stock Exchange based on its own fundamentally weighted indexes. It was the largest single-day launch of ETFs ever seen on the New York Stock Exchange and it was heralded by a huge flashy marketing campaign all over the media. In one fell swoop, WisdomTree simultaneously became the leading provider of fundamentally-weighted ETFs, with the most on the market, and the largest independent ETF shop overall

WisdomTree is the baby of Jonathan Steinberg, the son of financier Saul Steinberg. His story is possibly the most round-about path to ETF Land.

In the 1990s, during the stock market's technology bubble, Steinberg ran a small media company called Individual Investor Group. In 1988, Steinberg bought a penny-stock tip sheet that he turned into *Individual Investor* magazine, a research-driven publication that used quantitative screens to pick stocks. According to Registered Rep magazine "*Individual Investor* magazine had, at its peak in the mid-1990s, a half-a-million paid subscribers."[25] It also ran a hedge fund called WisdomTree. In 1998, the company created a small-cap index called America's Fastest Growing Companies, which was calculated by the Amex. During this time, Steinberg got caught up in the ETF situation at Nuveen Investments. In early 2000, Nuveen licensed the index to use as the basis for an ETF. But, this was canceled along with the projects that would later turn into the FITRs and PowerShares.

After the dot-com bubble popped, business publications saw newsstand sales plummet and advertising dollars dry up. By July 2001, *Individual Investor* magazine ceased publication. Steinberg closed the WisdomTree hedge fund, sold the magazine's subscription list, took the money, and turned the company into an index shop called Index Development Partners with his director of research, Luciano Siracusano.

They realized that the only way they could compete in the index business was to create something different. They decided to change the index weighting and created a family of dividend-weighted stock indexes that later became the WisdomTree indexes.

A company's weighting was determined by the contribution the actual cash dollar value of its dividends made to the index's total dividend stream. In testing, it proved to give a better return than the comparable cap-weighted indexes with less volatility, said Siracusano.

But in 2002, there wasn't a lot of money floating around to finance a new index development company. Steinberg and Siracusano decided that the only way they could commercialize their indexes was to do it themselves.

They decided to turn the company into an asset management firm, using the old WisdomTree name. Up until this point, index companies and ETF companies had been separate entities. But WisdomTree became the first index builder to create and issue funds based on its own indexes.

Cash was tight. Trying to get startup money during a disastrous bear market wasn't easy. They knocked on a lot of doors and a lot of people said "no." Much like Bruce Bond at PowerShares, Steinberg called it a "very difficult and very dark period."[26]

Then in late 2003, his fortunes began to turn. A friend introduced him to legendary hedge fund manager Michael Steinhart. Steinhart was intrigued by the idea, but it took another seven months for Steinberg to convince him to even consider becoming an investor.

"He had two tests," said Siracusano. "To get an outside authority to validate the research and, two that we attracted an established venture capital firm to provide oversight to the company."[27]

They went to Philadelphia to show their research to Jeremy Siegel, a finance professor at the University of Pennsylvania's Wharton School. A well-respected commentator on Wall Street, Siegel had also grown disenchanted with market-cap weightings after the bubble burst. Coincidentally, he had begun his own independent research for a book on how dividend-yielding stocks compared to the broader S&P 500. Siegel was supposed to give his opinion to Steinhart, telling him that WisdomTree's work was consistent with his own research. But Siegel was so impressed with WisdomTree's methodology and research that he wanted to join the firm.

"Dividend indexes are less volatile and particularly resistant to bear markets," Siegel said. "They sell off less than cap-weighted indexes in a bear market and just about keep up in a bull market."[28]

When Steinberg and Siracusano went back to Steinhart's office in New York, Steinhart introduced them to his newest hire, a recently graduated MBA from one of the country's best business schools. The newly minted MBA was there to debate the merits of the WisdomTree proposition.

"All the very big people around [Steinhart] were telling him not to do this, that we were wrong," said Siracusano. "I had to debate and rebut this MBA to convince him we were right and everyone else was wrong."[29]

In a conference call with Siegel, Siracusano said the professor told Steinhart, "I've never joined a company in this capacity, but I would join this company."[30] And he did, as director and senior advisor.

"WisdomTree's commitment to develop products designed to generate alpha is very much in line with my own investment philosophy," Steinhart told Registered Rep magazine, adding he was drawn to the product's discount cost structure.[31]

Steinhart introduced them to RRE Ventures, the private equity firm of James D. Robinson III, a former chief executive and chairman of American

Express. Over two rounds of financing, Steinhart raised $16.5 million. With most of it from his own pocket, he became the company's largest stockholder and chairman of the board. Then they hired Bruce Lavine, who helped create Barclay's ETF business, to become president and chief operating officer.

The June 2006 launch of the New York asset manager's first 20 ETFs was big. While PowerShares FTSE RAFI U.S. 1000 Portfolio was the first, it was on the market all by its lonesome. WisdomTree's huge one-day launch instantly made it the leading issuer with the most fundamentally weighted index/ETFs and the first ETF provider to track international small-cap stocks.

The festivities started with a slew of newspaper and television ads featuring Steinhart and Siegel endorsing the ETFs, and a few appearances on CNBC, the nation's largest business news channel. Of course, it didn't hurt that Siegel was a regular commentator on CNBC, or that Steinberg's wife was Maria Bartiromo, the channel's most popular anchor, better known as the "Money Honey."

But the highlight was an opinion piece Siegel wrote for the *Wall Street Journal* in favor of fundamentally weighted indexing. While Arnott's theory was known on Wall Street, it was Siegel's piece in the *Wall Street Journal* that concisely explained the concept of fundamentally weighted indexing to the masses.

"The philosophical foundation of market-cap indexes is the 'efficient-market hypothesis,' which assumes that the price of each stock at every point in time represents the best, unbiased estimate of the true underlying value of the firm," wrote Siegel. "But a new paradigm claims that the prices of securities are not always the best estimate of the true underlying value."[32]

"Siegel said stock prices often move on factors unrelated to fundamentals, or market 'noise,' such as speculators, momentum traders, insider buying, or enthusiastic investors chasing returns by piling into stocks that have already rallied strongly. Such factors could make a stock overpriced to its fair value, which would effectively overweight it in the index. Meanwhile stocks underpriced to their fair value would be underweighted in the index."[33]

WisdomTree called this a structural flaw in cap-weighted indexes.

Much like Arnott, Siegel said the passive nature of index investing would allocate new money to overvalued stocks and less to undervalued stocks. Because this ran counter to common-sense investing, Siegel argued that indexing based on fundamentals was a better approach.

Siegel's claim that a stock's price doesn't always reflect its true fundamental value was a bold attack on the efficient-market hypothesis, the theory behind indexing.

This didn't sit well with two of the leading proponents of indexing, Princeton University professor and author of *A Random Walk Down Wall*

Street Burton Malkiel, and John Bogle, founder of the Vanguard Group and the first index fund. Together they published a sharp rebuttal in the *Wall Street Journal*. They "argued that fundamental indices experience more portfolio turnover than typical index funds, incurring higher transaction costs and capital gains. And finally, they dismissed the outperformance of fundamental indexing over the previous five years compared with market-cap weighted indexes to fundamental's propensity to give greater weighting to value stocks and companies with smaller capitalizations. It just so happens that those two sectors have been in favor over the past five years."[34]

Following is a selection of ETFs from WisdomTree's first-day launch:

- WisdomTree Total Dividend Fund (symbol: DTD)
- WisdomTree High-Yielding Equity Fund (symbol: DHS)
- WisdomTree LargeCap Dividend Fund (symbol: DLN)
- WisdomTree MidCap Dividend Fund (symbol: DON)
- WisdomTree SmallCap Dividend Fund (symbol: DES)
- WisdomTree DIEFA Fund (symbol: DWM)
- WisdomTree International SmallCap Dividend Fund (symbol: DLS)
- WisdomTree International Dividend Top 100 Fund (symbol: DOO)
- WisdomTree Europe Total Dividend Fund (symbol: DEB)
- WisdomTree Japan Total Dividend Fund (symbol: DXJ)

Fundamentally Weighted Indexes

Arnott's FTSE RAFI is based on four fundamental metrics: revenue, book value, free cash flow, and gross dividends. According to "Fundamental Indexation," the article that started it all, Arnott ranked all companies by each metric, then selected the 1,000 largest by each metric. Each of these 1,000 largest was included in the index at its relative metric weight to create the fundamental index for that metric.

The measures of company size used are as follows:

- Book value (Book)
- Trailing five-year average cash flow (Cash Flow)
- Trailing five-year average gross sales (Sales)
- Trailing five-year average gross dividends (Dividends)

The four metrics on size were then equally weighted and put together in a composite index.[35]

Instead of using a formula of fundamental metrics like FTSE RAFI, WisdomTree based its entire family of indexes on dividend weightings. While not the first to issue dividend-based ETFs, WisdomTree was the first to make dividends the foundation for index weighting. Obviously, companies without dividends are excluded from these indexes. Since technology and biotechnology typically don't pay out dividends, this means these two sectors are under represented in dividend-weighted indexes. On the other hand, dividend indexes are overweight with mature sectors such as industrials, financials, consumer products and utilities. This lack of growth companies and overweighting of potentially value stocks removes a lot of the volatility seen in cap-weighted indexes.

WisdomTree arrives at its weighting structure by taking the dividends per share and multiplying them by common shares outstanding. This number is the aggregate dollar value of the dividend being paid to the shareholders. It's the actual dollar value of the dividend that matters. So, a small company with a large dividend has a greater weighting in the index than a large company with a small dividend.

For example, say General Electric pays $10 billion in dividends a year. Currently, all the companies in the U.S. pay approximately $270 billion in dividends to shareholders. So, GE's weighting would be 10 divided by 270, or nearly 4 percent.

So who's right? The market cappers or the fundamentalists? The jury is still out, but in Smartmoney.com, I wrote that "independent research, though, appears to back Arnott and the fundamental indexers. Robert Schwob, chief executive of Style Research, a research and consulting firm in London, said he initially found Arnott's claims 'unbelievable.' So, his firm constructed portfolios based on earnings, dividends, sales or book value going back five, 10 and 20 years across markets in the U.S., the United Kingdom, Europe, Southeast Asia, and Japan. The result? 'We found that over the length of the horizon, fundamental indexing did outperform on an average of 2% to 2.5% per annum,' said Schwob.' "[36]

The Feud

While FTSE RAFI and WisdomTree are both battling the indexing establishment to earn respect for the concept of fundamentally-weighted indexes, they are also battling each other for bragging rights.

At the end of 2007, WisdomTree had the most fundamentally-weighted ETFs. In September 2006, PowerShares launched 10 FTSE RAFI ETFs tracking U.S. market sectors, and in 2007 launched nine FTSE RAFI funds to track the international markets, but still WisdomTree has about double the amount of FTSE RAFI ETFs.

But it isn't enough to be the sector leader. WisdomTree doesn't like that Arnott is considered by many to be the "godfather" of fundamental indexation. WisdomTree counters that Arnott didn't come up with the idea of using fundamental variables to weight an index. Similar ideas had been used at investment banks such as Goldman Sachs for more than 20 years.

WisdomTree is also peeved that they don't get credit for being innovators. They say they were working on the same concept at the same time as Arnott.

Still, Arnott was the first one to publish the idea and explain the concept. In most circles, the first one to publish gets the credit. He got the term Fundamental Index turned into a trademark and he has patents pending on the use of the term and other fundamental variables. On top of that, the PowerShares FTSE RAFI 1000 was the first fundamentally weighted ETF to reach the market. Also, if the patents are awarded, WisdomTree may end up being guilty of patent infringement.

Still, in the end, both FTSE RAFI and WisdomTree have interesting ideas worth putting into a portfolio. One might want to split allocations between market-cap and fundamentally weighted. For instance, suppose you hold 30 percent of your portfolio in the SPDR currently. You get broad market exposure with a fundamental weighting with the FTSE RAFI 1000. So, instead of giving all 30 percent to the market-cap weighted SPDR, give it only 15 percent of the portfolio and possibly give the other 15 percent allocated to large-cap stocks to the FTSE RAFI 1000. That way you can cover your bases in case it's actually true that the fundamental indexes have the small-cap value bent they are accused of having.

Grow, Baby, Grow

If anything characterized the ETF industry in 2007, it would be more of the same. A few new independent firms joined the party, a few mutual fund companies got in on the action, and of course, more phenomenal growth occurred. Every single ETF company launched more ETFs. For the twelve months ended December 31, 2007, the industry grew 75 percent over 2006 to a total of 629 funds, according to the ICI. Including exchange-traded products not regulated by the '40 Act, there were 657 total, according to Lipper, a fund research firm.

With PowerShares now part of a huge mutual fund company, Wis-domTree took the mantle as the industry's top independent firm. Tiny Victoria Bay with the U.S. Oil Fund was the only other firm not aligned with a larger company. But before the first month of the new year was over, a New York firm called XShares soon became the independent with the second most funds.

XShares

XShares was started by Jeffrey Feldman, a former broker and owner of an asset management firm. Feldman said he had been teaching macroeconomics at a Rutgers University when he realized "There were no capital market tools for tracking the healthcare sector other than investing in the pharmaceutical giants. And this was an industry 25 times larger than agriculture."[37] Even though he had never created even a mutual fund before, Feldman decided to start making ETFs.

According the TheStreet.com, "XShares was born from the marriage of two companies: Ferghana Partners, a company that provided advice to life-sciences firms, and Wellspring BioCapital Partners, an investment firm offering products based on next-generation treatments, therapies and cures for diseases. Under the name Ferghana-Wellspring, the company filed as a corporate entity; then changed the name to Xshares" just before the first ETF launched.[38]

Feldman decided to break the healthcare industry into subsectors. Over the course of the year, Xshares released 19 ETFs in a fund family called HealthShares. Each fund focused on a very specific part of the health-care market, such as the HealthShares Cancer (symbol: HHK), HealthShares Cardiology (symbol: HRD) and HealthShares Dermatology & Wound Care (symbol: HRW). They are highly specialized niche products best used for hedging. For an industry overview, the HealthShares Composite Index (symbol: HHQ) captures all the subsectors in one fund.

The obvious appeal here is the U.S. population is getting older and will be spending more on healthcare in the near future. Still, these are high-risk ETFs. The risk comes from their narrow focus on small biotechnology and biopharmaceutical companies, many of which don't turn a profit. These companies can spend up to ten years navigating the drug approval process at the U.S. Food and Drug Administration. While the potential profits from bringing a new drug to the market are huge, any setback along the approval process can decimate a company's shares. Another risk, especially in the cancer drug sector, is that whenever one drug makes a big move closer to getting on the market, its rivals in the sector actually see their shares fall as their perceived value drops.

Yet, without a doubt, there will be big winners in these sectors. For people who are interested in these submarkets of the healthcare sector, the HealthShares Composite Fund provides a good overview as part of a small-cap or mid-cap asset allocation. All the HealthShares carry high expense ratios, between 0.75 percent and 0.95 percent.

But the long and difficult process of applying for exemption relief from the '40 Act gave Feldman an even better idea than the healthcare portfolios. Once the SEC gave a company exemption relief, future ETFs went through the process much quicker. He decided to leverage Xshares exemption relief to build a platform for creating ETFs. Other companies could piggyback on the Xshares filings to launch ETFs without going through the long, drawn-out process. Because the company would present the blank slate for others to write their ideas on, they called the company Xshares, with the X being the space holder for whatever another creator wanted to name his or her ETFs.

In September, Xshares created the seven Adelante Shares Real Estate ETFs for a firm called Adelante Shares. Then in October Xshares teamed up with the second-largest discount brokerage, TD Ameritrade, to launch the first target date ETFs, the TDAX Independence Funds.

Over the prior two years, target-date mutual funds had become one of the fastest growing segments of the retirement market. "Target-date funds offer investors with little time, inclination, or skill at managing their money a simple way to save for retirement. All you do is select the date you plan to retire and select the appropriate fund. As the target date approaches, each fund gradually rebalances from a fairly aggressive mix of U.S. and international stocks and bonds to a more conservative one."[39]

The date on the fund is the target date the investor expects to start pulling money out of the fund:

- TDAX Independence In-Target (symbol: TDX)
- TDAX Independence 2010 (symbol: TDD)
- TDAX Independence 2020 (symbol: TDH)
- TDAX Independence 2030 (symbol: TDN)
- TDAX Independence 2040 (symbol: TDV)

All have an expense ratio of 0.65 percent and are rebalanced quarterly.

The TDAX funds were innovators because the indexes are comprised of both stocks and bonds. This makes the TDAX the first hybrid ETFs because they hold both stocks and bonds in one fund.

Ameristock

One of the big themes for 2007 was the emergence of the bond ETF. After Gary Gastineau's FITRs closed shop in 2003, iShares six-bond ETFs were the only fixed-income ETFs for the next four years. But in 2007, a slew of bond funds hit the market. State Street Global Advisors and Vanguard each came out with a family of bond ETFs, with Vanguard's significantly cheaper than iShares. No small shakes there! Then iShares, State Street, and PowerShares each released the first municipal bond ETFs within two months of each other. Van Eck released its muni bond funds early in 2008.

Ironically, a group of bond ETFs very similar to the FITRs also launched. Tiny mutual fund firm Ameristock, the sister company to Victoria Bay, which launched the U.S. Oil ETF, entered the ETF market for the first time in July with a family of five fixed-income ETFs. They are based on the work of bond indexing giant Ron Ryan, who created the Lehman bond indexes. At his former firm, Ryan Labs, Ryan had developed the indexes that Gastineau used for the FITRs.

Classic bond funds such as the iShares Lehman 1 to 3 Year Treasury Bond ETF (symbol: SHY) track a group of securities with maturities ranging between one and three years. The Ameristock/Ryan ETFs focus is unlike other bond ETFs in that they track the index with just one or two Treasury securities. For instance, the Ameristock/Ryan 2-Year U.S. Treasury ETF (symbol: GKB) tracks an index with only one security: the most recently auctioned two-year Treasury note. The benchmark changes every time the old note rolls out and a new two-year note is auctioned off by the Treasury. The funds hold some other securities to offset the turnover every time a new bond hits the market.

- Ameristock/Ryan Treasury ETFs seek to match the price and yield performance of the Ryan Treasury indexes, which typically track the one benchmark bond in that time range. The funds hold at least 90 percent of their assets in U.S. Treasury securities and 10 percent in derivatives and other investments.
- Ameristock/Ryan 1-Year U.S. Treasury ETF (symbol: GKA), which tracks an index with a 66.7 percent weight on the most recently auctioned 6-month Treasury bill and 33.3 percent weight on the most recently auctioned 2-year Treasury note.
- Ameristock/Ryan 2-Year U.S. Treasury ETF (symbol: GKB) tracks the most recently auctioned 2-year Treasury note.
- Ameristock/Ryan 5-Year U.S. Treasury ETF (symbol: GKC), tracks the most recently auctioned 5-year Treasury note.
- Ameristock/Ryan 10-Year U.S. Treasury ETF (symbol: GKD), tracks the most recently auctioned 10-year Treasury note.
- Ameristock/Ryan 20-Year U.S. Treasury ETF (symbol: GKE), reflects an equal blend of the most recently auctioned 10- and 30-year Treasury notes.

SPA ETF

SPA ETF is the first foreign company to launch ETFs in the United States—that is, after Barclays. Founded in 2007, the British upstart is a sister company to London & Capital, a 21-year-old British money manager.

In October 2007, Spa launched six ETFs based on fundamental criteria. The funds track a series of indexes from MarketGrader, an index house in Coral Gables, Fla. The MarketGrader indexes aren't fundamentally weighted like the FTSE RAFI; they're equally weighted. MarketGrader lays a quantitative screen over the entire universe of U.S. stocks and grades each company on 24 fundamental factors. The score comes from the average of six indicators in each of four key areas—growth, value, profitability and cash flow. Then the top-graded companies land in an index.

The MarketGrader 40 is the flagship fund, based on an index that has been around since 2003. In this index, market cap has no bearing. The entire universe of stocks get filtered, and the 40 top-rated stocks make up the index, regardless of size. Typically, 50 percent of the stocks in the MarketGrader 40 are mid-caps, with large-cap and small-cap stocks each comprising about 25 percent.

Using the same filter, the MarketGrader 100 is a basket of the top 100 stocks and the MarketGrader 200 holds the top 200.

Ironically, three of the indexes have a market-cap component. The stocks are filtered after breaking the market into large-cap stocks, mid-caps, and small-caps. The 100 top-graded stocks in each group make it to their respective index.

When the ETFs launched, the MarketGrader 40 Index had outperformed the S&P 500 by 15.6 percentage points on an annualized basis since its inception in April 2003. The fundamental screen is supposed to help the ETFs outperform the benchmark. But the stock market took a downturn almost immediately after the launch. They have not been around long enough to accurately measure how well they do against the benchmark.

The expense ratio for all six ETFs is 0.85 percent, one of the highest rates in the industry. The indexes rebalance either quarterly or semi-annually. The six Spa ETFs are:

1. Spa MarketGrader 40 (symbol: SFV)
2. Spa MarketGrader 100 (symbol: SIH)
3. Spa MarketGrader 200 (symbol: SNB)
4. Spa MarketGrader Large-Cap 100 (symbol: SZG)
5. Spa MarketGrader Mid-Cap 100 (symbol: SVD)
6. Spa MarketGrader Small-Cap 100 (Symbol: SSK)

Ziegler Capital Management

Ziegler is an unusual ETF issuer. It came out with one fund in March and doesn't plan to issue any more.

NYSE Arca Tech 100 ETF (symbol: NXT) seeks to replicate the NYSE Arca Tech 100 Index, which consists of 100 companies from multiple technology-related industries. The index is 25 years old, and it used to be the Pacific Stock Exchange Technology Index. The Pacific Stock Exchange was bought by the former Archipelago Exchange, the first open, all-electronic stock exchange in the United States. This is a flagship index for the NYSE Arca, the electronic exchange that came from the merger of Archipelago and the New York Stock Exchange. The NYSE Arca is now the

NYSE's electronic stock exchange and currently trades about 40 percent of the volume from the ETF industry.

This price-weighted index competes with the Qubes, the ETF for the NASDAQ-100, which has a market-cap weighting. Because of this, the top ten holdings make up between 40 percent and 50 percent of the Qubes. However, the NYSE Arca is more diversified because its top ten components represent only about 24 percent of the index. The NYSE Arca 100 is expected to be less volatile than the Qubes. The expense ratio is 0.5 percent.

Ziegler is a small investment management company, with two actively managed mutual funds and seven index funds. One of the index funds tracks the NYSE Arca 100. Because of their relationship with the exchange, and the exchanges growing importance in the ETF industry, Ziegler launched the ETF.

"This is our only ETF. We want to go after the QQQ head-on," said Lisa Matza, director of sales and marketing at Ziegler Capital Management. "We want to begin with one product we truly believe in and be great in that one before expanding."[40]

Focus Shares

The last new company to debut in 2007 listed four offbeat ETFs in November, based on indexes of 20 to 30 stocks from the International Securities Exchange:

- FocusShares ISE Homebuilders Index Fund (symbol: SAW) tracks companies focused on the residential home construction and prefabricated housing market.
- FocusShares ISE SINdex Fund (symbol: PUF), holds companies involved in the casino, liquor, and cigarette industries.
- FocusShares ISE-CCM Homeland Security Index Fund (symbol: MYP) tracks companies that have contracted work with the Department of Homeland Security, such as bio-vaccine outfits.
- FocusShares ISE-REVERE Wal-Mart Supplier Index Fund (symbol: WSI) tracks companies that derive a large portion of their revenues from sales to Wal-Mart.

They are too new to evaluate.

Summary

One of the hallmarks of the ETF industry has been innovation.

For the industry's first 15 years, the SEC required all ETFs to track an index. While managers of actively managed mutual funds have the flexibility and spontaneity to build a fund as they choose, ETF fund managers didn't have that freedom. They needed to acquire an index based on rules determining what can and cannot go into the benchmark. Because most index funds are commodities—two index funds tracking the same index should give investors the same return—there was little reason to have two funds tracking the same index.

In addition, there was a phenomenon called the first-mover advantage. This advantage came about because the first fund to track an index garnered all the early attention and assets. So, by the time a similar index fund was launched, it was difficult to overcome the branding advantage already built by the prior ETF. Together, the first-moved advantage and the commodity-like nature of index funds provided little incentive for new firms to create ETFs on existing indexes.

Once the major fund sponsors in the ETF industry gobbled up most of the well-known benchmark indexes, there was little left over for small firms looking to enter the market. Altogether, these factors could potentially cause the industry's growth to stall.

But new and young companies saw opportunity in the ETF market. They also realized that to enter the industry they needed to come up with innovative ideas for new indexes, both in construction and security selection.

Upstart companies and small mutual fund firms, sensing the potential and possibilities in the ETF market, decided to create unique indexes that offered new investing options to investors. PowerShares, Research Affiliates, and WisdomTree are the leaders of this movement, which I call the New Indexers. They broke open the index structure to incorporate new ideas on building portfolios, while staying true to the index form.

Some used the classic market-capitalization index structure to create narrowly focused indexes following industry sectors, investment styles, and previously untracked niche markets, such as water and dermatology-drug companies. Others threw out the market-cap structure and based their index construction on variables other than price, most often the fundamental metrics used to measure a company's health. Some even found ways to make indexes based on other asset classes.

Altogether, this paradigm shift in the way indexes are built and used was the catalyst for the explosive growth the ETF industry experience between 2003 and 2007.

CHAPTER 8

The ETFs That Aren't ETFs

ETPs, ETVs, and ETNs

I f exchange-traded funds were merely a less expensive, more tax-efficient way to invest in stocks and bonds, they would be worthy of all the praise bestowed upon them. But they are so much more.

Exchange-traded funds have changed the face of investing for the individual investor. Little did the inventors of the ETF realize that when they applied the warehouse-receipt concept to stocks and funds that this would spark a revolution in the world of asset management. This revolution expanded the universe of investment options for small, retail, individual investors. The flexibility of the ETF structure broke down barriers across nontraditional asset classes such as commodities and currencies.

Commodities and *currencies* are considered good assets for diversifying a portfolio because they have little if any *correlation* to stocks and bonds. Correlation means the degree to which asset classes move independently of each other. So, these assets can move up when stocks move down.

Of course, it's worth noting that people didn't want to invest in commodities just because they were there. During the first decade of the twenty-first century, as ETFs gained a wider audience, there occurred simultaneously a huge bull market in commodities: gold, silver, oil, copper, uranium, water, and many agricultural products. Retail-investor demand to get into commodities was huge, but it was difficult. The most common way to trade commodities and currencies is through the *futures* and *options* market. Trading futures, however, is much more complicated than the straightforward way to invest in equities. By creating a familiar structure in which investors could invest in commodities and currencies just like stocks, these ETF-like products made investing in these assets easier to understand, cheaper to trade and essentially effortless.

These products opened up commodity and currency investing to a whole new audience. Institutional funds, pension funds, endowments,

401(k) plans, and individual retirement accounts often don't permit trading in currencies or commodities. But because these new ETF-products traded like ETFs and could be held like shares of funds, many of these institutions were suddenly allowed access to previously restricted assets, giving them greater opportunities to diversify.

This makes the ETF unique among all other products sold by Wall Street. Instead of merely creating a new asset class, the ETF structure opened up many asset classes to a new and easier way of investing. It's had the dual effect of bringing in investors who would never have ventured here in the past, as well as increasing the liquidity of the underlying markets.

It's an ironic development. The stock depository receipt based on the warehouse receipt from the commodities market has come full circle and had the unintended effect of opening up the commodities market to small investors. Prior to the introduction of the new ETF-like products, these assets classes had been nearly impossible for small investors to navigate by themselves and difficult to access even with the help of an investment advisor. When investors did manage to invest in these assets they were charged hefty commissions.

Strictly speaking, these new ETF-like products aren't funds at all. As registered investment companies, true ETFs can only hold securities. They're restricted from holding more than a very small amount of commodities or other kinds of assets. These new offerings are *exchange-traded products (ETPs)* or *exchange-traded vehicles (ETVs)*. The industry has not made a statement on which term it prefers, but I like to call them ETVs, because I like the word "vehicle." For the most part, exchange-traded vehicles share many characteristics with and behave a lot like exchange-traded investment companies. They cost little to own, trade on a stock exchange, and are flexible and transparent. But they are neither open-end funds nor unit investment trusts. In fact, they aren't even regulated by the Investment Company Act of 1940. These ETF-like products have different structures and many actually hold commodities and futures contracts. Some are regulated by the Commodity Futures Trading Commission, which oversees futures and options, and are not required to have a majority of the independent directors on their boards.

The first exchange-traded products, the *HOLDRs*, are very similar to ETFs in that they hold portfolios of stocks. But, they aren't funds either. They're trusts with different structures and tax implications.

Exchange-traded notes (ETN) are a completely different animal. They don't actually hold assets, but are unsecured debt purchased from an investment bank. As such, they have completely different characteristics from the other products. They offer better tax efficiency and less tracking error than true ETFs. However, in addition to regular market risk, they come with additional credit risk from the issuing bank.

The two major fund research companies, Morningstar and Lipper, both classify these ETF-like securities as ETFs. And most of the producers of these products also call them ETFs. But they're not ETFs. They are not the same family of products. They're related like first cousins, but they're not brothers and sisters to true ETFs. And just as you went to a different school from your cousins, and your respective parents fell into different tax brackets, such is the case with ETFs and ETVs. Currently, the industry has little desire to differentiate the products. According to a survey by Rydex Investments conducted during the summer of 2007, out of 500 mutual fund investors, 38 percent did not know what an ETF was and 53 percent didn't know the difference between an ETF and a mutual fund.

With the need to educate the investing public about ETFs, Wall Street isn't ready to confuse investors by throwing around a few more abbreviations. And as ETFs gain wider acceptance among investing professionals and retail investors, many on Wall Street want to jump on the bandwagon and be part of the party. So, to start throwing around the initials ETF, ETP, and ETV may create confusion that will cause investors to throw up their hands and say, "Forget it. I'll just buy mutual funds."

Investors should always approach Wall Street and its products with the philosophy of caveat emptor, which is Latin for "Let the buyer beware." However, I think Wall Street is doing ETVs a disservice by not immediately differentiating them. The hesitation to differentiate these products may come back to haunt the ETF industry when investors learn after the fact that these are not ETFs and don't all have the benefits touted for ETFs, especially in the area of tax efficiency. The possibility that investors could file lawsuits on the grounds of false advertising is not to be taken lightly. And such a situation could cast a black cloud over a group of products that in general have greatly benefited the small investors by opening up nontraditional asset classes at very affordable prices. Unlike regular ETFs, commodity and currency ETVs have been available only since 2004.

This chapter will examine the major ETVs on the market. It will explain the differences between these exchange-traded vehicles and '40 Act ETFs. Typically, the tax implications for an exchange-traded commodity product and an exchange-traded currency product are dramatically different from an ETF—and sometimes even from each other. Many don't have the tax efficiency for which ETFs are known. Regardless, they make investing in commodities and currencies much cheaper and much easier to grasp. And for most investors, that is enough of an improvement. I will also address how large a percentage of one's portfolio should be committed to these asset classes.

You've Got a HOLDR to Cry On

The first exchange-traded vehicles were the Holding Company Depository Receipts, or HOLDRs. Produced by brokerage giant Merrill Lynch, the HOLDRs are similar to ETFs in that they are transparent baskets of stocks. But they're not '40 Act companies; rather, they are *grantor trusts*, a nontaxable entity that corporations use to issue asset-backed securities.

Grantor trusts register their shares for public sale under the U.S. Securities Act of 1933, also known as the 1933 Act, or the "truth in securities" law. This is the first law to regulate the securities industry after the stock market crash of 1929.

The act has two basic objectives:

1. Require that investors receive financial and other significant information concerning securities being offered for sales.
2. Prohibit deceit, misrepresentations and other fraud in the sale of securities.[1]

In short, any company that wants to sell a security to the public must disclose important financial information to investors. Securities that are sold on an exchange are also registered under the Securities Exchange Act of 1934, also known as the '34 Act. Because there were so many important issues related to the sale of investment companies that weren't addressed in the 1933 Act, Congress wrote the 1940 Act. However, as explained earlier, investment companies are very specific entities. So, public shares of any kind of investment vehicle that fails to fall under the '40 Act's parameters are regulated by the 1933 Act.

The grantor trust concept is interesting because ownership of the underlying investment held by the trust passes through directly to the investor. In ETFs and mutual funds, shareholders don't own the stocks, but rather a pro-rata share of the entire portfolio. The grantor trust gathers and holds assets, but the shareholder actually owns a proportionate share of the underlying assets relative to the number of shares owned. Thus, in the HOLDRs, shareholders get the benefits of owning the actual stocks outright, such as retaining voting rights and receiving dividend distributions sent directly to them.

The difference between a fund and a grantor trust is analogous to the difference in apartment ownership. In a condominium, the person owns the actual apartment and can do with it as he pleases. In a co-operative apartment building, an investor doesn't actually own an apartment, but rather owns shares in the co-op that are represented as an apartment. The co-op apartment owner needs to work within the rules of the larger organization, while the condo owner has fewer restrictions.

While HOLDRs are baskets of stocks that issue shares that trade on an exchange, they're quite different from ETFs. First, they don't track financial indexes. They are just portfolios of stocks from a specific industry. They can only be bought in round lots of, or multiples of, 100 shares. They are depositary receipts for a specific basket of stocks, so once the portfolio is set it can't be changed. Because they are unable to add new companies to the original portfolio, if a company merges or goes out of business it isn't replaced. The portfolio just gets smaller. The HOLDRs were created from 1999 to 2001 with portfolios of about 20 stocks. They're like sector funds in that each one focuses on just one industry or area of the market. The HOLDRs are also like time capsules in that they capture the most important companies in these industries in the year they were created, not today. But if a lot of these portfolio companies cease to exist, the HOLDRs' inability to add new companies to the existing portfolio can create heavy concentrations in a small group of stocks. For instance, the B2B Internet HOLDR (symbol: BHH) only has two stocks left in the trust. And one stock makes up an outrageous 86 percent of the portfolio.

The big advantage to buying a HOLDR is the ability to invest in many stocks in a sector in one trade for one commission. The expense ratios also are pretty low. Then when you sell your shares back to the trust, you don't get cash back. Instead, you receive possession of the actual underlying stocks. So, selling HOLDRs shares themselves doesn't incur a capital gain.

The downside is, in order to get your cash you have to sell each stock received from the HOLDR in a separate transaction. This is when you get hit with capital gains, as well as incurring numerous commissions. While a few of the products have more than $1 billion in assets under management, the majority hold less than $100 million.

The HOLDRs don't have an expense ratio, or any percentage management fee. They charge an annual custodian fee of $8 for every round lot of 100 shares. If the average price for a HOLDR share is $100, then a round lot would be worth $10,000. In that case, the custodian fee equals 0.08 percent, about the same as the SPDR. The higher the share prices rises, the smaller the fee percentage, and vice versa.

Overall, there's no reason to own HOLDRs. They're not very popular, so they're not very liquid. ETFs are more tax efficient and their portfolios remain dynamic representations of the industries they cover. Here is a representative list of HOLDRs:

Biotech (symbol: BBH)
Broadband (symbol: BDH)
B2B Internet (symbol: BHH)
Europe 2001 (symbol: EKH)
Internet (symbol: HHH)

Internet Architecture (symbol: IAH)
Internet Infrastructure (symbol: IIH)
Market 2000 + (symbol: MKH)
Oil Service (symbol: OIH)
Pharmaceutical (symbol: PPH)
Regional Bank (symbol: RKH)
Retail (symbol: RTH)
Semiconductor (symbol: SMH)
Software (symbol: SWH)
Telecom (symbol: TTH)
Utilities (symbol: UTH)
Wireless (symbol: WMH)

Exchange-Traded Notes

Exchange-traded vehicles may be a generic catch-all phrase for any ETF-like product that isn't a '40 Act investment company, but exchange-traded notes (ETNs) are a specific category of structured products. ETNs are neither the first ETVs (those were the HOLDRs), nor the first to track commodities or currencies. However, because the ETN structure lends itself to both commodities and currencies, which will be examined in detail later in the chapter, it's worth explaining them first. That will make the comparisons easier as we go along.

Invented by Barclays Bank in 2006, the ETNs were created to make it easier for retail investors to invest in hard-to-access asset classes. Barclays Global Investors, a subsidiary of Barclays Bank, runs iShares, the largest family of ETFs. To differentiate the products, the ETNs received the family name iPaths. BGI has released commodity products under the iShares brand, but anything that doesn't contain equities or bonds misses out on some of the tax advantages of ETFs—especially commodities and currency. And stocks in emerging markets have high spreads and aren't necessarily liquid enough to be purchased in large amounts.

Barclays created the ETN to make it easier to invest in and maximize the returns of those hard-to-access instruments. It did this by eliminating the costs associated with holding commodities, currencies, and futures and revving up the tax structure to make it potentially the most tax efficient product in the exchange-traded product industry.

Like ETFs, ETNs trade on a stock exchange and track a benchmark index. If the index falls in value, so does the ETN. But that's where the similarities end. Funny thing though, the ETNs don't really own what they track. ETNs don't hold stock, bonds, or even futures contracts.

Unlike ETFs, ETNS are senior, unsecured debt issued by an investment bank. The principle isn't protected and there is no collateral backing it. ETNs are similar to *prepaid forward contracts*. According to the *Tax Adviser*, a publication of the American Institute of Certified Public Accountants: a prepaid forward contract is a structured investment instrument in which an entity, in this case the ETN issuer, sells shares to the investor for upfront cash payment. The ETN provider transfers to the investor a significant portion of its risk of loss and opportunity for gain. Investment banks have long offered structured instruments and notes like prepaid forward contracts to institutional clients.[2]

Once again, the ETF structure broke open an old investment vehicle to make it available to the individual investor, and at a lower cost with better liquidity.

The key difference between the ETF and ETN is that the ETN doesn't actually own anything. An ETF holds assets with real value. Each ETF's portfolio holds underlying shares of companies which will be worth whatever the stocks are worth on the day that the ETF's shares are redeemed. Also, the ETF could be liquidated by selling all the underlying shares and end up with a pile of cash.

ETN investors don't own shares of a portfolio of stock. It's essentially a bet on the index's direction guaranteed by an investment bank. The bank promises to pay at maturity the full value of the index, minus the management fee. That means investors might not get paid if the issuer goes belly up. This exposes the investor to credit risk.

Currently there are four ETN issuers. Three are investment banks— Barclays Bank, a unit of Barclays PLC, Bear Stearns, and Goldman Sachs. The fourth is a consortium called Elements ETNs. Deutsche Bank and Swedish Export Credit each issue products under the Elements banner, and Merrill Lynch and Nuveen Investments distribute them. All of these companies were considered good credit risks when they launched their ETNs. However, questions about their credit worthiness have recently been raised.

This risk is not to be taken lightly. In March 2008. the credit crisis roiling the financial markets led to a run on the bank at Bear Stearns. The ensuing liquidity crisis caused the investment bank to collapse. Fearing disastrous consequences for the entire U.S. financial market, the U.S. Federal Reserve Bank quickly engineered a plan in which rival bank, J.P. Morgan Chase agreed to buy Bear Stearns at the bargain basement price of $2 a share. What this means to the Bear Stearns ETN is unknown at this time. But the lesson is, there is real potential for an ETN investor to lose his or her entire investment if the issuing bank goes out of business. Investors need to do additional research to make sure the ETN issuer isn't having liquidity problems.

So, why take on the risk of unsecured debt backed only by the faith that the bank won't go bankrupt or be unable to pay back the principal? Because the benefits are sizeable:

- No tracking error
- Greater tax efficiency

Theoretically, an ETF should give you the exact return of the index it tracks, minus the expense ratio. But sometimes, the difference between the ETF and its index is larger than the expense ratio. This extra difference between the portfolio's return and the value of the index is called the *tracking error*.

Tracking error is a big problem for the commodity pools holding futures contracts. The rolling of the futures can cause the ETV's return to dramatically differentiate from the index or commodity it's tracking. But tracking error also affects ETFs. When an ETF can't hold all the components of an benchmark index, either because there are too many, causing huge transaction costs, or they are too illiquid, forcing the buyer to pay a high spread, it can cause a discrepancy between the portfolio and index. This differential can be significant.

The ETN issuer, however, promises to pay the full value of the index, no matter what, minus the expense ratio. This completely eliminates excess *tracking error*. To achieve this, the issuer uses futures, options, stock swaps, and other instruments to approximate the index's return. If the bank's strategy fails to match the index, it is on the hook for paying off the rest of the gains. Of course, the bank could make more money from these other investments than it returns to the ETN investors.

According to Morgan Stanley, the average tracking error among U.S. ETFs rose to 0.29 percent in 2006, from 0.18 percent in 2005.

The percentage of return lost to tracking error can add up. However, investors need to offset that against expense ratios. Because the ETNs take on the risk to equal the index's return, they are compensated more than the average ETF. All the Elements ETNs charge 0.75 percent. The iPath ETNs charge between 0.4 percent and 0.89 percent, with the average expense ratio being 0.75 percent.

In July 2007, Bear Stearns launched its first ETN, the BearLinx Alerian MLP Select Index (symbol: BSR). This ETN tracks an index of energy-related Master Limited Partnerships and charges 0.85 percent. Goldman Sachs launched its first ETN in August 2007. The GS Connect S&P GSCI Enhanced Commodity Total Return Strategy Index ETN (symbol: GSC) charges a whopping 1.25 percent expense ratio. There is no reason for an individual to own the Goldman Sachs ETN. Not even an aggressive, risk-loving investor. It follows an esoteric index that is hard to understand and its expense ratio is one of the largest in the ETF industry.

Greater Tax Efficiency

An even better reason to buy an ETN is because it might be the most tax efficient vehicle in the ETF universe. The iPaths definitely are. The other ETNs are too new to evaluate.

ETNs are not only much more tax efficient than the ETVs that hold commodities, they're better than ETFs as well. Unlike ETFs, the iPath ETNs make no distributions of dividends or income. This is a very big deal. Even regular ETFs can distribute quarterly dividends, on which taxes need to be paid annually, and which can be charged as ordinary income.

Because ETNs don't hold any portfolio securities, there are no distributions to make to their investors during their 30-year lifetime. However, the ETNs promise to pay the *total return* of the index it tracks. Total return of an index, which is considered the most accurate measure of actual performance, assumes that all dividends and distributions are reinvested in the index. Because the value of the ETN's shares are the total return of its index, the value of the dividends has been incorporated into the index's return.

Because the "dividends" are "reinvested" in the ETN, the shareholder doesn't pay taxes until he sells the shares. At that point they are taxed as long-term capital gains. If you hold the shares for more than a year, you pay a lower long-term capital gains tax of 15 percent for the entire investment.

This ability to significantly boost returns by escaping annual taxes on dividends is as close to magic as one gets on Wall Street. The one downside is that while the ETF investor gets to spend the dividends immediately, the ETN investor has to wait until he sells his shares.

This is also a very big advantage over the commodity ETVs. Commodity ETVs are typically commodity pools that hold futures and interest-bearing collateral. As the futures expire, they must be sold, creating either capital gains or losses that are distributed to the investors annually and subject to taxes. This is just like capital gains inside mutual funds. Even if you hold commodities more than a year, they still incur a higher tax rate than the rate for long-term capital gains.

There are two caveats.

1. Unlike the iPath products, the BearLinx Alerian MLP Select Index ETN does make an income distribution on which investors must pay annual taxes.
2. The tax efficiency isn't written in stone.

The Internal Revenue Service had yet to issue a final ruling on the tax structure of the ETNs. The IRS isn't crazy about products that help investors dodge taxes, so the fate of the ETN as the most tax-efficient product in the ETF universe remains uncertain. In December 2007, the IRS did make a ruling on ETNs that track currencies. Not surprisingly, it wasn't good for investors. This is described fully in the Currencies section.

Investors need to research this feature beyond the scope of this discussion. Talk to your tax adviser to be up to date on the ETN's tax status.

Commodity-Based ETVs

Commodities are raw materials—the stuff that companies use to make other things. For the most part these are natural resources, such as gold for jewelry or oil for gasoline, or agricultural products, such as wheat for bread, pork bellies for bacon, and concentrated orange juice for the cartons you find in your local supermarket.

Commodities are *fungible*, which means they're brandless, generic, moveable goods. One is usually as good as another. Since you should be getting the same quality product no matter where or from whom you buy it, the key factor in commodities is price. For many people, S&P 500 index funds are commodities. Since they should all produce the same return as the index, the expense ratio, or lowest price, should be the determining factor on which one you buy.

Companies use commodities, such as peanuts, milk, or eggs, in original formulas to make their unique branded products. A good example is ketchup. Tomatoes are the commodity and are typically not differentiated by quality. So, producers will buy any tomatoes from any producer if the price is right. However, once those tomatoes are turned into Ketchup by Heinz, Del Monte, or Hunts, consumers may be willing to pay a higher price for what they consider a better taste.

When the companies need more raw materials, they go to the cash or spot market, much as you would run to the supermarket for some late-day supplies for dinner. Or they can enter the futures market to guarantee their supply at a specific price in the future. That will be discussed later in the chapter.

I've Got a Golden Ticket

The first commodity-based ETV was the streetTracks Gold Shares (symbol: GLD). Sponsored by the World Gold Council and marketed by State Street Global Advisors (the trustee for the SPDR), it launched November 18, 2004, on the New York Stock Exchange. Each share represents one-tenth of an ounce of gold bullion as priced by the London Bullion Market Association (LBMA), the British gold industry's trade association. The iShares Comex Gold Trust (symbol: IAU), the second gold fund, launched January 25, 2005, on the American Stock Exchange. It tracks the price of gold on the New York Commodities Exchange, also known as the Comex.

Together, the two funds were a dramatic breakthrough for the ETF industry. Neither one holds stocks or bonds, nor do they track an index. Each holds hundreds of tons of real gold bricks.

Prior to the gold ETVs, buying gold was difficult for retail investors. They had the choice of buying gold coins or gold bricks. Brokers in these products charged steep commissions. Because these are physical commodities, upon taking possession, an investor would need to pay for storage and insurance. If the investor didn't want to take possession, he would invest in the futures and options markets.

Because the process and commissions are onerous, many investors used the shares of gold-mining companies as a proxy for the price of gold. By trading on the stock market, these investments were easier to buy and liquidate. But, gold-company stocks come with their own issues. Because you are first and foremost buying shares in a company, you place a layer of risk—stock market exposure—on top of the risk from exposure to the gold market.

All the problems that affect stocks can send your investment tumbling, even as the price of gold rises. Any issue that affects the broad stock market can potentially affect gold stocks. Basic company fundamentals such as revenues, earnings, rising costs, and poor management can also send a stock lower. In addition, because gold is mined and not produced in a factory, factors such as collapsing mines, empty mines, and adverse publicity caused by the deaths of miners need to be factored into the risk equation. On top of that, many gold-mining companies exist outside the United States. Political turbulence in a foreign land can send a gold stock plummeting while simultaneously lifting the precious metal's price.

The gold ETVs changed all that. Because the shares of these ETVs list on the stock exchange, average investors now have a hassle-free way to own the precious metal without opening a futures account or hoarding bars in a vault. The ETV structure allows them to buy it instantly at the spot price for a small commission.

Like an ETF, the objective of the ETV is to capture the return of underlying assets, in this case gold, minus expenses. It's hard to compare a stock fund to a commodity vehicle because the assets don't operate the same way. For instance, gold needs to be stored somewhere. This isn't an issue for stocks and bonds. They exist solely inside computers. While shareholders in the gold shares don't need to worry about it, much like any other purchaser of gold, both ETVs need to pay fees to store and insure the gold. This can get expensive and the fund may sell off gold to pay expenses. The shareholder's expense ratio on both funds is 0.4 percent and paid for in gold. When these ETVs came out, 0.4 percent was considered very high, but with time this has become the average expense ratio charged by an ETF.

The gold ETVs are not registered under the Investment Company Act of 1940, nor the Commodity Exchange Act (CEA). Thus, the gold ETVs are neither investment companies nor commodity pools that hold and trade futures contracts. Shareholders don't get the protections associated with either act. Like the HOLDRs, the gold ETVs are structured as grantor trusts.

Shareholders will be taxed as if they own the underlying gold, just like a gold coin. Under current law, gains on gold bullion held for more than one year are taxed like the sale of "collectibles," at a maximum rate of 28 percent, rather than the 15 percent rate applicable to most other long-term capital gains.

Like an ETF, the ETVs have *authorized participants* (AP) to gather the appropriate underlying assets and exchange them for a creation unit of ETV shares. Much as APs for stock funds need to be a member of the Depositary Trust company, the APs for the gold shares need to have accounts with a custodian bank that is a member of the LBMA. Obviously, these APs are the big players in the gold market. But also they need to be able to bring the ETV shares to the stock market for trading. Essentially, the gold trusts are issuers of securities that are sold through a brokerage account and are bought and sold like any other shares on the stock exchange.

"The AP has to be a participant in the gold market," says Kathleen Moriarty, a lawyer at Katten Muchin Rosenman, who helped create several exchange-traded vehicles since her work on the SPDR. "You have to make a representation that you are a certain type of person. You don't just show up at the Bank of England with some gold bars and say 'Hold this.' You need to have a gold account with one of the gold custodians, who will move the gold bars to your pigeon hole in the vault from someone else's pigeon hole."[3]

Like the ETF, the custodian holds the assets and moves them in and out of the ETV. There is no fund manager, only a trustee, the same as in a unit investment trust. The trustee is the fiduciary for the shareholders and has the responsibility to make sure everything works properly and that the custodian doesn't run off with the funds.

How Everything Still Turns to Gold

The allure of gold is that it's considered a hedge against inflation. In inflationary times, gold is said to "hold" its value, meaning gold is inflation proof.

Paper money is always at risk of *inflation*. Inflation is rising prices on goods and services. It's a response to *supply, demand,* and *liquidity*. When there's not enough corn to satisfy all consumers, from food producers using it for corn syrup, to individuals eating corn on the cob, to ranchers feeding it to cattle, to the makers of biofuels such as ethanol, the price of corn goes up. Thus, it costs more to make these sweetened products and to feed cattle. Prices then increase for steaks, hamburgers, and a multitude of processed foods. This leads to higher grocery bills and restaurant checks.

Rising prices erode a person's buying power. If hamburger meat cost $2 a pound last year and $3 a pound this year, you've lost a third of your buying power. The dollar's value has fallen. The same amount of money, $2, now buys only $2/3$ of a pound of meat. Presumably the same amount of gold will buy the same amount of hamburger. So, people buy gold to make sure their money holds its value.

When money flows like water the system is liquid. When people want to protect their money or fear they won't have enough to pay their bills, they hoard it. Pulling money out of the economy tightens the *money supply*, causing it to dry up and become illiquid. If people spend less, businesses sell less. They stop growing. If businesses sell less, workers get laid off, increasing unemployment. Which comes first is a matter of debate. But when both happen it often leads to *recession*, which is two consecutive quarters of a shrinking economy.

In short, in times of great uncertainty, people buy gold. Inflation and recession are just reasons for uncertainty. In a political crisis, a country's paper money may experience a steep decline in value, and even become worthless in times of war or invasion. After the destruction of the World Trade Center in 2001, the security of the United States became a big issue, highlighted by the wars in Iraq and Afghanistan. On top of that, Iran has hinted at building a nuclear bomb. Should the unthinkable happen, one of the few things that will still have value will be precious metals.

The last great rally in gold came at the end of the 1970s stagflation, a period of rampant unemployment and inflation. On January 21, 1980, the price for an ounce of gold hit an all-time intraday high of $875, and a closing high of $825. After the Reagan administration broke the spiraling rate of inflation, gold began a 20-year descent. It hit a low of $252.80 in July 1999, the height of the stock market's dot-com bubble, according to the LBMA.

After a little bounce, two years later, April 2001, gold still traded at $255.95. Since 2001, the U.S. dollar has been in a steady decline. Because gold is considered a safe haven investment, as the value of the dollar fell, people sought safety in yellow metal, causing its price to soar. By the end of 2007, the price of gold had more than tripled from its 2001 low, and was approaching its 1980 high. In early 2008, it surpassed $1,000.

Ironically, the gold ETVs were partly responsible for increasing demand for gold, both before and after their launch. In order to have shares to sell when the products hit the market, the authorized participants needed to acquire gold prior to the launch to exchange for creation units of the two ETVs. Gold market participants recognized this and hopped on the rally. Over the six-month run-up to the November 2004 launch of the StreetTracks Gold Trust, the price of gold surged 19 percent. But, within weeks of the trust's launch, demand dried up. From there it quickly fell 9 percent to a tight trading range. It was another nine months before it regained its early high of $456. But with the price of gold doubling from the end of 2005 to 2007, it appears that there had been a lot of pent-up demand for gold among retail investors that was finally satisfied once the gold shares were launched.

According to the LBMA, the price of an ounce of gold leaped 24 percent in 2006 and an additional 32 percent in 2007. With gold up more than 227 percent in six years, the easy money is gone. While there might be more profits to be gained from owning gold, investors need to be cautious, and realize the yellow metal has already passed its previous high.

Hi Yo Silver, Away!

The Gold ETVs were such a success that a silver one seemed like a logical step. Silver is another precious metal used as currency for thousands of years.

In April 2006, the iShares Silver Trust (symbol: SLV) debuted on the American Stock Exchange. Like the gold ETVs, the silver ETV is a grantor trust that holds actual silver in a vault. Whereas the gold ETVs equal the price of one-tenth of a gold ounce, the silver shares reflect the price of 10 ounces of silver. Silver's expense ratio is 0.5 percent.

Silver is a much more volatile commodity than gold. However, it has virtually no correlation to stocks or bonds. It does have a 0.66 correlation to the price of gold.

For most the first 70 years of the 20th century, silver traded for less than $2. During the economic crisis of the 1970s, the price of silver climbed into the $5 range as two oil magnates, brothers Nelson Bunker Hunt and Herbert Hunt, bought it up. In 1980, their attempt to corner the silver market sent the metal's price up to $50 an ounce. When traders realized that the Hunt's owned nearly a third of the market, they began to sell and short futures. The price of silver plummeted 50 percent in only one day, March 27, 1980, better known as Silver Thursday. The Hunts nearly lost their oil business.

From 1980 through 2004 silver bounced around between $4 and $6 an ounce. At the beginning of 2006, silver had climbed to around $9, according to the London Bullion Market Association. Much like the gold shares, the creation of the Silver Trust generated significant demand for the metal, so traders and speculators bought silver to capitalize on this, causing the precious metal's price to surge.

In order to launch with 150,000 shares, Barclays Global Investors, the trust's sponsor, needed to have 1.5 million ounces of silver on deposit. As the authorized participants built up inventory of silver ahead of the launch, this took much of the supply off the market. By the time the trust launched on April 28, 2006, the price of silver had surged an additional 42 percent to $12.55, according to the LBMA. After just three days of trading, the iShares Silver Trust held 32 million ounces.[4]

Two weeks later it culminated its biggest rally in a quarter century with a high of $14.95, according to the LBMA. Then demand fell. Silver share investors suffered as the metal's price tumbled 22 percent over the next 15 months.

People who don't want to deal with an ETV that holds the actual commodity and has to pay storage costs can invest in gold and silver through the futures market. In 2007, a PowerShares-Deutsche Bank partnership issued pure plays on the gold and silver markets with ETVs that track an index of futures contracts. The PowerShares DB Gold (symbol: DGL) is a pure play tracking an index of gold futures. Also a pure play is the PowerShares DB Silver Fund (symbol: DBS), which tracks an index of silver futures.

The Outlook for Silver and Gold

Obviously, after tripling in price over the past six years, the low-hanging fruit in terms of profits in precious metals is over. Investors shouldn't expect these kinds of returns in the future and should exercise caution when purchasing gold and silver ETVs.

However, there are strong fundamental reasons why precious metals will continue to rise in the near future. The falling U.S. dollar is a big reason. Strong economic growth in China, India and other Asian nations has increased the demand for silver and gold. Silver has more industrial uses than gold; jewelry, photography, dentistry, medical device, and electronics industries all use silver.[5]

Yet even as demand increases, supplies are tight. When both metals traded at multiyear lows during the 1990s, mining companies didn't invest enough in exploration. So, while demand in Asia is rising, there is not enough supply coming out of the ground to satisfy it. These are major reasons why the precious metals should continue to rise. However, just as a rising dollar will send precious metals lower, so too will an increase in supply, which occurs when mining companies bring more product to the market. Eventually, the supply will equal demand. At that time, prices will stop rising.

However, because commodities don't move with equities, they offer diversification to a portfolio. Many portfolio managers now recommend investors hold between 5 percent and 20 percent of all their assets in commodities. Be aware that 20 percent is a very aggressive amount to hold for your entire commodities portfolio.

Oil's Well Ends Not So Well

Just like gold, which began a years-long rally in 2001, oil spent most of the first decade of the early twenty-first century in a raging bull market. The spot price for West Texas Intermediate, the U.S. benchmark for crude oil also known as Texas Light Sweet, bottomed out at $10.82 a barrel on Dec. 10, 1998. By the end of 2007, the price hit $96.

There are quite a few fundamental reasons why the price of oil has surged over the past decade. Bigger cars and sports utility vehicles increased U.S. demand for oil. At the same time, the country's refinery infrastructure was running at capacity, with few if any new refineries expected to open in the coming decade. So, even if the supply entering the refineries is strong, the supply coming out is limited.

Much like gold and silver, the phenomenal economic growth in China and India over the past decade has increased demand for oil. In fact, the economies of many Asian countries are experiencing rapid growth, adding to total demand.

On top of that, there is the issue of international instability. The Iraq War did little to increase a stable flow of crude from the Middle East, but the U.S. military's needs increased demand for oil. Meanwhile, Iran, the world's number two producer of oil behind Saudi Arabia, has become a wild card in the market as it antagonizes the United States and the United Nations by pursuing a uranium enrichment program. Venezuela, the third-largest producer in the Organization of Petroleum Exporting Countries (OPEC), has also been striking a belligerent tone on the world stage. Overall, it creates a perfect recipe for higher crude prices. In fact, unstable political situations cause many commodities to rise by creating uncertainty about what affect it may have on the flow of supply.

In April 2006, when oil traded around $68, Victoria Bay Asset Management, an upstart firm with few connections to Wall Street, entered the ETF industry. It launched the United States Oil Fund (USO), the first exchange-traded vehicle to track the price of a barrel of oil. The expense ratio was 0.5 percent.

Like the precious metals ETVs, USO is a pure play on the oil market. The big difference is, that unlike the precious metals ETVs, U.S. Oil doesn't own the physical commodity. It tracks the price of oil through futures contracts. U.S. Oil's structure is different from the precious metals ETVs, which are grantor trusts. U.S. Oil is structured as a limited partnership called a commodity pool. The commodity pool is similar to a mutual fund in that it pools money from many investors to invest in a portfolio, usually futures contracts. Because commodity pools trade commodity futures, it needs to register with the National Futures Association and agree to be regulated by the Commodity Futures Trading Commission, or CFTC. In addition, because the ETV sells a security traded on an exchange, and issued in a public offering, it also registers its shares under the 1933 Act and is regulated by the SEC.

Unlike stocks, futures are not transferable. The owner of a futures contract can't assign it to another investor. So, the commodity pool's creation unit is not an in-kind trade like an ETF. The AP pays cash to the commodity pool for the value of the ETV's shares. Unlike the ETF, the commodity pool ETV must go into the market and buy its own futures contracts. This adds a commission, or transaction cost, not found in the traditional ETF. Recently the New York Mercantile Exchange ruled that although an AP cannot "transfer" the underlying futures to the commodity pool, they can sell them to the pool at the target price.

Futures and its brother, options, are derivative instruments because they don't really own an investment. "Futures are an obligation to buy or sell a commodity for an agreed upon price on a specific day in the future. Options give an investor the right, but not the obligation, to buy or sell something for a specific price on a specified day or period of time in the futures."[6]

Because they don't actually own assets, futures are bets on the direction the price of a commodity may move.[7] The futures market consists of two distinct classes of participants: hedgers and the speculators.

Futures are contracts tied to where traders think a commodity will trade weeks or months from now. The hedgers are businessmen and companies that use futures to reduce risk. Originally, futures contracts guaranteed that a seller would deliver a certain commodity at a specific time in the future. In return, he locks in the price he will receive when delivery is made.

Farmers sell futures to lock in a price for their wheat, corn, orange juice, or livestock to protect against falling prices from an oversupply. Meanwhile, a food processor using the commodity as a raw material, fearing the price will be higher when needed in the future, buys a future to guarantee the price he will pay, thus, keeping his costs fixed. For example, an oil refinery may buy a future from an oil company to guarantee shipments of crude at $90 a barrel. If the spot price jumps to $110 a barrel, the refiner is protected against having to pay the increase.

While many businesses use futures and options to smooth out unexpected price moves, many investors in futures and options are merely speculators. They have no intention of taking delivery of the actual product. They just try to make money off the price movement. Most futures contracts expire within a year, and can typically be bought for one month out, two months out, and so on.

Futures offer this protection because they offer *leverage*. "Leverage, in financial terms, means using a small amount of money to make an investment of much greater value."[8] People use leverage to buy cars and houses. Typically, a futures contract costs 10 percent of the spot price. Leverage makes a small move in the futures cause a big price change in the actual contract. This can cause huge gains or disastrous losses. Futures and options trading are not for the faint of heart. Opening up an account to trade futures and options, and the actual trading, is much more complex than trading stocks. Just like gold, many people who want to invest in oil avoid this process, instead buying stocks of oil companies. The Energy Select Sector

SPDR (symbol: XLE) is a good ETF for this strategy. But again, buying stocks as a proxy for a commodity opens the investor up to factors not tied directly to the price of crude oil. The internal workings of the companies and the dramatic fluctuations of the stock market can send the investment lower even as the commodity rises.

The NAV for the U.S. Oil Fund is determined by the performance of its portfolio holdings, a basket of futures contracts for light sweet crude oil, and other oil-related securities that trade on the New York Mercantile Exchange. One big advantage in buying a futures contract is that taking delivery of oil is a much bigger headache than gold or silver. This eliminates transportation, storage or insurance costs. They are priced into the contract.

But investors need to be clear that USO doesn't track the spot price of oil, the price you can buy it for today. The value of a share of the U.S. Oil fund won't equal the price of a barrel of crude. Instead, the share's value will be determined by its tracking the movement of the nearest month's futures contract, also called the *front month*. The price of the front month contract is usually close to the *spot price*. But, any factor that causes prices to rise could send the futures price much higher than the spot price of the same commodity. This created problems for the fund. Many investors don't understand this point and it has caused much disappointment as the price of USO hasn't moved in line with the spot. In fact, there have been huge discrepancies between the spot price of crude and shares of USO.

Investors need to be aware that comparing futures ETVs to equity ETFs is like comparing apples to oranges. For instance, to stay invested in equities one just buys stock and holds onto it. But futures expire. Futures contracts need to be rolled into the future. To stay invested, the fund needs to sell or swap the expiring contract and buy the next one. The returns come from the spot move.

"Futures contracts for delivery in a given month expire around the 20th of the preceding month. To prevent an actual delivery—the typical investor doesn't really want barrels of oil off-loaded in the driveway—traders sell the contracts before expiration, thus closing out the transaction. Every one of these adds another transaction cost."[9]

According to USO portfolio manager John Hyland, transaction fees can run as high as 0.15 percent of assets a year. That comes on top of a 0.50 percent annual fee paid to management for a total annual expense rate of 0.65 percent, an above average fee.

This need to swap contracts, closing out and buying new ones every month, creates what's called a "roll." Frequently, there's a difference between the trading price of the futures contract that makes delivery within the next month and the futures contract that expires and contemplates delivery in a later month.

*There are different terms for when a later month trades above or below
the current one. Take a crude contract in May. If the June contract
trades at a price below May, this is a condition called "backwardation."
Conversely, if the June contract trades at a higher price than the one in
May, this condition is called "contango."[10]*

Essentially, these are factors of demand. In backwardation, supply is
tight and demand is greater today than for delivery next month. Since everyone wants oil today, today's price is higher than the future's. In contango,
today's supply is fine, but future supply is in doubt. So, the demand for oil
in the future is greater than today's demand. And heavy contango can be an
indication that the market is considered oversupplied, making today's spot
price cheaper. In contango, the higher price of the month further out also
reflects the cost of storing the oil for a month.

So, in addition to the actual change in the price of oil, "backwardation
or contango have a real impact on the futures contract, hence, on the rate
of return of U.S. Oil."

For instance, "if a May future contract sold at $68.98 per barrel, while
the June contract sold for $70.35 per barrel, it experiences a contango of
$1.37 a barrel. A single contract is worth the price of a barrel of oil multiplied
by 1,000. So, with USO's initial $100 million investment, it would end May
with 1,450 contracts. But that same amount of money would only buy 1,420
contracts for June. Those fewer contracts will need to experience a higher
percentage gain to meet the same total rate of return. Contango eats into
returns. So, there's a risk that even though the price of oil is rising, the
contango could actually create a loss for the pool."[11]

While it's not an inherent structural flaw, investors need to be very
clear about what they are buying and how it compares to the other oil
ETVs. According to USO's 10-K filing with the SEC, during 2006 the price of
the ETV fell 23 percent, while the spot price of oil declined 11.2 percent.

Of course, in backwardation, the opposite occurs. If the price of the
futures contract further out is cheaper than the near month contract, the
same money will buy a greater number of contracts for the month further
out. This could potentially help returns.

Funny thing about this ETV: Although it tracks the futures contract, it
doesn't actually spend a lot to buy the contract. Futures investors don't pay
for the whole contract. A margin payment with a broker of around 8 percent
is all that is required to hold a futures contract. U.S. Oil takes the remaining
cash in the fund to purchase U.S. Treasury bills and cash equivalents, such
as money market funds. The fund hopes the additional yield will offset
the higher expenses and contango risk. But U.S. Oil doesn't buy more
contracts that the actual amount of cash. So, the vehicle is balanced, not
leveraged.

Taxes

Because U.S. Oil Fund invests the majority of its cash in 90-day Treasury bills it earns interest, or a yield. Unlike an ETF or mutual fund, the yield is not distributed to shareholders. It will be reinvested in the pool. Investors still must pay a tax on this, and it's taxed at their ordinary income rate.

Futures also generate a lot of taxes. Because futures need to be closed out monthly, the fund incurs a capital gain or loss every month depending on how the market moved. In addition, the pool is required to "mark-to-market" the contracts open at the end of the year. This means all open contracts will be treated as if they were sold on the last day of the year, even if they weren't.

All commodity gains in the fund are taxed the same as regular futures contracts. No matter how long the assets were held, these yearly capital gains are taxed as if 60 percent were long-term gains, currently a tax rate of 15 percent, and 40 percent were short-term gains, as much as 35 percent. Because it's structured as a limited partnership any capital losses inside the ETV may be used by the investor to offset his personal capital gains. This is a big advantage over a mutual fund, which keeps the capital losses inside the fund to cut internal capital gains.

Partnerships report taxes on a complicated and lengthy form known as a K-1 schedule. You should seek an accountant's advice on how to handle this.

The Intelligent Commodity ETVs

U.S. Oil had been created by guys with little experience with commodities. After its launch the ETV quickly fell into contango. This sucked money out of the pool. The ETV sharply diverted from the spot price of crude oil, which it had been expected to track.

DB found a way to eliminate some of the problems with U.S. Oil. Together with PowerShares it launched the PowerShares DB Oil Fund (symbol: DBO). Like U.S. Oil, DB Oil is a commodity pool that owns futures contracts for a single asset, West Texas Intermediate crude. But instead of tracking the spot price by way of next month's futures contract, it's based on an index—an intelligent index, like the kind PowerShares used with equities. It's a strategy that adds a quantitative twist that over time is expected to add more return.

Instead of simply buying the future for the next month, like USO, DB Oil's index looks at each of the next 13 months and calculates an implied yield. It determines the answer to the question If I sold the future for this particular month, what would my return be? and chooses the optimal contract to hold. In a contango market for the whole year, it chooses the least negative of the contango futures. Of course, the investor isn't always sure of exactly what future the ETV holds. The index says that when you're in a contango market, the best place to be is far out in the curve. This causes less erosion on the return. But in backwardation, you keep rolling from front month to front month.

Like U.S. Oil, the AP gives the ETV cash for the creation unit. The ETV must invest the cash in the futures itself. And because only a small amount of money is in futures, the rest earns interest in Treasury bills. The PowerShares commodity index ETVs are taxed the same as U.S. Oil. All commodity gains in the fund are taxed the same as regular futures contracts, 60 percent for long-term gains and 40 percent for short-term gains. Interest is taxed as ordinary income.

Oil should be a good way to diversify a portfolio because rising oil prices often lead to an economic slowdown. A slowing economy hurts corporate earnings, which sends stocks lower. In theory, U.S. Oil sounds wonderful. But in practice it failed to live up to investor expectations of closely tracking the spot price of oil, as well as the fund's expectations of tracking the futures price. U.S. Oil has since addressed most of these issues, and the ETV has become one of the best products for investors who want to track the price of oil. This will be discussed further later in this chapter.

In light of its bad contango experience with U.S. Oil, in December 2007, Victoria Bay launched U.S. 12 Month Oil Fund (symbol: USL). This commodity pool looks similar to DB Oil in that it's constructed to minimize the negative issues experienced by contango. Instead of holding only the forward month, the new ETV will hold an equal number of contracts from each of the 12 forward monthly contracts for light, sweet crude oil delivered to Cushing, Oklahoma. Over the 12 months contango and backwardation will be ironed out, creating a total return that more closely tracks the spot price of crude.

Victoria Bay also manages the U.S. Natural Gas Fund (symbol: UNG). This commodity pool is structured the same way as U.S. Oil, but tracks natural gas.

The Commodity Indexes

In keeping with the theme of index investing, instead of buying an ETV tracking a single asset, the best move for individual investors may be to buy an ETV that tracks an index. They give exposure to assets with little correlation to the stock market, but minimizes the risk by adding diversification.

About a year after the iShares Comex Gold hit the market and a couple of months before U.S. Oil, German investment bank Deutsche Bank created the index-based ETV, which holds a basket of commodities, instead of only one. In February 2006, the first and best known, the PowerShares DB Commodity Index Tracking Fund (symbol: DBC), launched on the Amex. The index ETV became the flagship for PowerShares commodity offerings,

a family of commodity ETVs managed by DB (Deutsche Bank) Commodity
Services and distributed by PowerShares.

The PowerShares DB Commodity Index Tracking Fund tracks the
Deutsche Bank Liquid Commodity Index–Optimum Yield Excess Return.
It's a rules-based index comprised of futures contracts for six of the most
heavily-traded, physical commodities in the world—crude oil, heating oil,
gold, aluminum, corn, and wheat. Table 8.1 shows the commodities and
their base weighting in the index.

The commodity index provided the platform from which Deutsche Bank
created its seven futures-based ETVs that track commodity sectors. The ETVs
have a special delineation for each commodity called the Optimum Yield
Index. By using an index, they have rules for weightings and balancing.

- The PowerShares DB Agriculture Fund (symbol: DBA) is comprised of
  futures in corn, soybeans, sugar, and wheat.
- The PowerShares DB Base Metals Fund (symbol: DBB) holds futures
  for aluminum, copper (grade A), and zinc.
- The PowerShares DB Energy Fund (symbol: DBE) tracks Brent crude
  oil, heating oil, light crude oil, natural gas, and gasoline.
- PowerShares DB Precious Metals Fund (symbol: DBP) holds a combination of gold and silver contracts.
- The PowerShares DB Oil (symbol: DBO) is an index of crude oil futures
  as explained in the previous section.
- The PowerShares DB Gold (symbol: DGL) is not an index. It is a pure
  play on gold by holding futures.
- The PowerShares DB Silver Fund (symbol: DBS) is also not an index,
  but a pure play on silver.

Noting Commodities

One of the reasons Barclays created the ETN was to track hard-to-follow
markets, primarily commodities and currencies. It must be reiterated that
index-tracking ETNs don't actually hold the assets in the index. As described
earlier in the chapter, iPath ETNs are unstructured debt securities issued

TABLE 8.1   Commodity Weightings for the Deutsche Bank
Liquid Commodity Index

Commodity	Weighting
Light Crude	35%
Heating Oil	20%
Aluminum	12.5%
Corn	11.25%
Wheat	11.25%
Gold	10%

by Barclay's Bank. They guarantee the return on the index, minus fees. While Barclay's may hold the futures or Treasury bills, shareholders don't own anything but a promise from Barclays to match the index. Because shareholders don't hold the actual physical commodity, they don't have to pay storage costs. And because they don't hold futures, investors don't have to worry about transaction costs from rolling the contracts.

The second exchange-traded product to track the oil market after U.S. Oil was the iPath S&P GSCI Crude Oil Total Return Index ETN (symbol: OIL). GSCI stands for Goldman Sachs Commodity Index. This exchange-traded note tracks the West Texas Intermediate crude oil futures contract plus the Treasury Bill rate of interest that could be earned on funds committed to the trading of the underlying contracts, according to iPath.

The iPath oil ETN also experiences contango and backwardation. It moves in near perfect alignment with U.S. Oil. In addition to no transaction costs, it also benefits from a better tax structure. The downsides—the shareholder takes on credit risk and the tax structure may be changed.

iPath ETNs also follow indexes that track the commodities markets. The iPath S&P GSCI Total Return Index ETN (symbol: GSP) has an energy weighting of around 70 percent. The other weightings include livestock, precious metals, industrial metals, and agriculture. The iPath Dow Jones–AIG Commodity Index Total Return (symbol: DJP) tracks a broad commodities index of the same name, which is composed of energy, livestock, precious metals, industrial metals, and agricultural products.

The subindexes offer the opportunity to invest in just one sector of the broader index:

- iPath Dow Jones-AIG Agriculture Total Return Sub-Index ETN (symbol: JJA) tracks soybeans, coffee, cotton, sugar, soybean oil, wheat, and corn.
- iPath Dow Jones-AIG Energy Total Return Sub-Index ETN (symbol: JJE) tracks crude oil, natural gas, heating oil, and gasoline.
- iPath Dow Jones-AIG Grains Total Return Sub-Index ETN (symbol: JJG) tracks soybeans, wheat, and corn.
- iPath Dow Jones-AIG Industrial Metals Total Return Sub-Index ETN (symbol: JJA) tracks copper, aluminum, nickel, and zinc.
- iPath Dow Jones-AIG Livestock Total Return Sub-Index ETN (symbol: COW) tracks live cattle and lean hogs.

The following three are not indexes, but track single commodities:

1. iPath Dow Jones-AIG Copper Total Return Sub-Index ETN (symbol: JJC) tracks the price of copper.
2. iPath Dow Jones-AIG Natural Gas Total Return Sub-Index ETN (symbol: GAZ) tracks natural gas.
3. iPath Dow Jones-AIG Nickel Total Return Sub-Index ETN (symbol: JJN) tracks the movements of nickel.

MacroMania

The third oil ETV came as a pair. The MacroShares Oil Up Tradeable Trust (symbol: UCR) and the MacroShares Oil Down Tradeable Trust (symbol: DCR) are unlike any other ETF or ETF-like product.

This brainchild of Yale economist Robert Shiller (best known for the book *Irrational Exuberance*, an examination of the late 1990s' technology bubble) and Allan Weiss is a much more complicated way to track the movement of the crude oil market than the other options. Entrepreneur Sam Masucci founded the firm MacoMarkets to bring this vision to the market. But, he needed someone to figure out how to make the whole thing work. That job went to Bob Tull, a man who had been at the scene of a lot of the industry's innovation. Tull had worked on Morgan Stanley's WEBS and OPALs, helped close Deutsche Bank's CountryBaskets and encouraged the American Stock Exchange to create the Intellidexes with PowerShares. "Shiller conceived of the structure initially as a way to create equitized markets based on housing prices—and that is one important way it could work," wrote the Web site IndexUniverse, which follows the indexing and ETF industries. "Theoretically, MACROs could be created tied to . . . anything. Possibilities mentioned include unemployment numbers, gross domestic product, the consumer price index, and more."[12]

"They must be issued in pairs of interlinked securities, both up and down. The best way to understand the dynamic is to imagine a seesaw. As created, when the price of crude oil rises by $1, the Up Trust is supposed to increase by $1, while the Down Trust falls $1."[13] The products have been compared with total return swaps, in which the two funds swap the appropriate Treasurys between each other to get the proper pricing.

Unlike U.S. Oil, MacroShares are not a commodity pool; they do not hold crude oil futures. The MacroShares are trusts that hold short-term Treasury notes and overnight repurchase agreements. The MacroShares seek to return the price performance of crude oil plus income. In order to receive a creation unit, the AP must deposit cash for the ETF shares. The biggest difference from any other ETF-like product is that the AP must buy an equal amount of Up and Down shares simultaneously. This increases the risk to the AP because most investors will be investing in just one direction, leaving the AP with the hedge side of the equation.

"As the front-month crude oil contract moves, the Macros will move proportionately," wrote IndexUniverse. "This income will be used first to cover expenses, and then to compensate the opposing MACRO if there are any changes in the value of the contract for the losing party. If the changes exceed the interest income, which is likely if interest rates fall below 1.6 percent, the value of the paying contract itself will fall. Any excess income will be distributed to shareholders each quarter."[14]

While U.S. Oil charges an expense ratio of 0.75 percent, each MacroShare charges an annual fee of 1.6 percent, making it the largest expense ratio of any ETF or ETF-like product. Although more expensive than U.S. Oil, the MacroShares have a big advantage over that fund—no roll, meaning no contango. Many investors in U.S. Oil were caught unaware of the contango, only to watch the price of the fund fall almost 25 percent even as the price of oil rose.

Because the MacroShares don't hold futures they have moved in closer alignment with the crude oil spot market. However, the MacroShares don't track the spot market either. The ETV wants to reflect the long-term view of the oil market, potentially going out as far as 20 years.

Even though the trust's net asset value (NAV) closely follows the spot price of oil, through some complicated formula, which incorporates the future direction of crude, the share price doesn't track the spot price. Instead, it can trade at a premium or discount to the NAV, much like a closed-end fund. If the Up Trust trades at a discount to the NAV, then the Down Trust trades at a premium, which can be huge. When the price of the Down Trust trades at the premium, it means more people expect the price to fall. This is seen as a clear sign for the direction of the market as the one trading at the premium is the one with the greater demand for its shares. One reason the shares of ETFs stay so close to their NAV is that arbitrageurs seeing small discrepancies compared with the prices of the underlying securities quickly buy shares. This drives the price back to the NAV. However, for the MacroShares, the large premium, discount, and difficulty in arbitraging away the difference has been a roadblock in gaining large investor acceptance. The average trading volume for the Up Trust was 12,000 shares a day near the end of 2007, while the Down Trust traded 36,000 daily, according to Yahoo Finance, creating a not very liquid asset. However, considering the MacroShares are Treasury instruments, they post a yield to offset the high expense ratio and they offer much greater tax efficiency than futures-based products.

The MacroShares are structured as grantor trusts. Because they hold Treasurys, they get the tax efficiency of the ETF's in-kind trade. However, the income from the Treasurys passes through to the shareholders. Because this is taxed as ordinary income, it offsets any benefit from zero capital gains. The structure of the AP, which needs to create both the Up Trust and Down Trust shares at the same time, has been responsible for some of the fund's problems. The lack of liquidity also adds to the huge premiums and discounts. While this may be considered a classic case of an academic ideal not working, if the volume increased the spreads might shrink.

With a complicated structure, extreme premiums and discounts, and little tax efficiency, who should consider the MacroShares? MacroMarkets says "the ability to make a long-term investment in oil is important to everyone who does not already have an exposure to oil." The main reason people should hold the Oil Up Trust is that it hedges their risk to a major asset class which is necessary for their cars, their houses, everyday plastic products, and sometimes their very jobs. The Oil Down Trust is good for people who want to short the oil market. Investors who might be interested include individuals, institutional investors, and funds with investing restrictions such as funds that don't allow short positions or the holding of commodities. That problem would be solved because the MacroShares hold Treasurys. The MacroShares Down Trust is a long position on essentially a short play, investors profit from a falling market without the risks of being a short seller.

"One controversial—if expected—tweak to the products is that they will terminate and settle if the price of crude oil moves dramatically. Specifically, if the reference price of crude falls to $9.00 or rises above $111.00 for three consecutive days, the MACROs will terminate on the next distribution date as the underlying assets of the losing trust will become unacceptably skimpy."[15]

In April 2008, this is exactly what happened. The NYMEX light sweet crude oil futures contract for June closed above $111 three days in a row, triggering the early termination for the securities. Surprisingly, the stopout didn't immediately end the securities. By early May, the NAV for the Down Trust had fallen to a penny a share. Ironically, as the closing date drew near, trading and creation of shares increased and liquidity improved. This was partly because it became an easier mathematical problem for traders to solve. On June 25, its last day of trading, the MacroShares had 38 million shares outstanding and trading volume of almost 64 million shares. MacroShares was expected to launch in July new oil MacroShares with a new benchmark price of $100 per barrel and a management fee of 0.95 percent, much lower than the original product. The ticker symbols are expected to be UOY for the new up oil trust and DOY for the down oil trust.

Oil Comparison

For a quick comparison of how the oil exchange-traded products did in 2007, take a look at Table 8.2, which measures the rate of return beginning

TABLE 8.2   Comparison of the Oil ETPs

Type of Product	Name of Product	Rate of Return Jan. 5, 2007 – Dec. 31, 2007
Commodity	West Texas Intermediate Crude Oil	70.46%
ETN	iPath S&P GSCI Crude Oil Total Return Index (OIL)	59.83%
ETV	US Oil (USO) [commodity pool]	58.39%
ETV	MacroShares Oil Up Tradeable Trust (UCR)	47.45%
ETV	DB Oil (DBO) [commodity pool]	43.02%
ETF	The Energy Select Sector SPDR (XLE)	41.90%

January 5, 2007, the day the PowerShares DB Oil Fund launched on the Amex. That day West Texas Intermediate Crude Oil closed at $56.29. On Dec. 31, 2007, it closed at $95.95, a 70 percent surge.

All the oil ETVs lagged the price of spot oil. But out of the bunch, the best performing product was the ETN with the ticker OIL. Because oil was in backwardation for part of the year, U.S. Oil overcame some of its issues, regained its mojo, and did nearly as well as the ETN. While the stock fund, the Energy Select Sector SPDR, performed worst at the end of the year, to be fair, up until the stock market's downturn in October, its operating leverage actually helped it outperform most of the others.

Miners and Shiners—Commodity ETFs

While this chapter is about exchange-traded products that aren't '40 Act companies, it's also about investing in commodities. So, this seems the best place to address ETFs that track commodities by investing in the stocks of companies in those industries.

Before the ETVs, ETPs, and ETNs, the only way for retail investors to track the commodity markets was to buy the commodity itself, enter the futures market, or buy the stock of companies in that industry as a proxy for the commodity itself. Investing in gold bullion or the streetTracks and iShares gold ETVs eliminates the company and stock market risk from the equation. This gives investors a return that matches the price of gold.

However, many investors still like to buy the shares of gold mining companies. While gold-mining stocks have all the negatives of stock market risk mentioned earlier, the flip side is that gold-mining shares offer earnings and operating leverage. Even if the price of gold doesn't move, if the company cut costs and posts better-than-expected earnings, the stock can rise. And when gold's value does increase, gold-mining stocks typically post returns two to four times greater than the move in the actual metal. Of course, the leverage also increases losses on the down side.

Van Eck came out with the MarketVectors Gold Miners ETF (symbol: GDX) in May 2006. Because it tracks the stocks of 35 gold mining companies, this is a true exchange-traded fund, not an ETV. Not all are U.S. companies, but they all trade on U.S. stock exchanges. The expense ratio is 0.55 percent.

Because it's a '40 Act ETF holding stocks, not futures or the actual commodity, it also achieves greater tax efficiency than the ETVs. In addition to the Gold Miners, the Market Vectors family offers ETFs that hold the shares of companies involved with commodities not yet offered by the ETVs and ETNs:

- Market Vectors-Coal ETF (symbol: KOL)
- Market Vectors-Agribusiness ETF (symbol: MOO)
- Market Vectors-Global Alternative Energy ETF (symbol: GEX)

- Market Vectors-Nuclear Energy ETF (symbol: NLR)
- Market Vectors-Steel ETF (symbol: SLX)

Market Vectors currently has a monopoly on coal, nuclear, and steel.

There are many ETFs that track the energy, basic materials, natural resources, and alternative energy markets. These are just a few options.

- Energy Select Sector SPDR Fund (symbol: XLE)
- iShares Dow Jones U.S. Energy Sector Index Fund (symbol: IYE)
- iShares Dow Jones U.S. Oil & Gas Exploration & Production Index Fund (symbol: IEO)
- PowerShares Dynamic Energy Sector Portfolio Fund (symbol: PXI)
- SPDRs S&P Oil & Gas Exploration & Production (symbol: XOP)
- Vanguard Energy ETF (symbol: VDE)

Three Clear Plays on Water Purification

In addition to the classic commodities of oil, precious metals, and agricultural goods, the value of water as a natural resource has increased tremendously over the past decade. This is an edited version of an article I wrote for TheStreet.com on July 24, 2007, which compares the ETFs that track the water market.

"Water, water everywhere, nor any drop to drink."

Samuel Taylor Coleridge's famous phrase describes life on the high seas 200 years ago. But it also applies to modern-day India and other places with regular shortages of water for drinking or agriculture. Even in the United States, a safe, reliable water supply is not a given. Many of the water-treatment plants built in the 1970s are nearing the last days of their usefulness just as contaminants in water that were unknown 30 years ago become more prevalent.

With water expected to be in much shorter supply within the next 50 years, one of the hottest commodity areas has been investing in the fresh water industry.

In 2007, three exchange-traded funds focused on the water industry hit the market, following on the success of the PowerShares Water Resources Portfolio (symbol: PHO) which launched in 2005. Water Resources holds only stocks that trade in the United States.

All the water ETFs focus on companies that provide potable water, water treatment, and other technologies and services related to water consumption. Their returns have been promising during their short lives.

The First Trust ISE Water Index Fund (symbol: FIW) tracks a portfolio of domestic stocks similar to that of Water Resources.

The Claymore S&P Global Water Index (symbol: CGW) allocates about two-thirds of its assets to foreign companies, holding stocks from

16 countries. At the time of its launch, 75 percent of the portfolio was held in just four countries: the United States, France (19.1 percent), the U.K. (14.0 percent), and Switzerland (8.1 percent). It tracks an S&P index of 50 stocks that ranks constituents according to their market capitalization as well as the percentage of revenue they derive from water.

Of the 18 non-U.S. markets represented in the PowerShares Global Water Portfolio ETF (symbol: PIO), Japan has the largest allocation at 11 percent. Nine of the other countries are in Western Europe, and after Canada a group of emerging markets such as Singapore, South Korea, Brazil, Malaysia, and Chile round out the list. The ETF tracks an index of 37 stocks that weights constituents more or less equally and is rebalanced quarterly.

PowerShares Global Water and Claymore S&P Global Water are both made up from six sectors: water utilities, which provide water to end users; water-treatment companies; infrastructure companies, which make pipes, pumps, and valves and build distribution systems for transporting water; analytical companies, which measure and monitor water conditions; resource-management companies, such as engineering and construction firms, which work with municipalities for the comprehensive management of water resources; and businesses that receive less than 50 percent of their revenue from water.

While there is some crossover between their individual holdings, Claymore focuses on bigger companies, with 35 percent of its portfolio in large-capitalization stocks, 53 percent in mid-caps, and 13 percent in small-caps. The ratio is almost the reverse for PowerShares, with 33 percent in small-caps, 55 percent in mid-caps and 13 percent in large-cap. The expenses of the two funds are not far apart, with PowerShares charging 0.75 percent of assets and Claymore charging 0.65 percent.

Money Makes the World Go 'Round

Trading foreign currencies is simply exchanging one country's currency for another. Currencies are bought on the spot market, called the Foreign Exchange or Forex market, or with futures contracts. It's the largest market in the world with between $2 trillion and $3 trillion traded a day.

It's also the world's most liquid market. Some call it a "perfect market" because it relies solely on supply and demand. No company profits, revenues, or costs to worry about, as in the stock market. No production or supply issues to worry about, as in the oil market. Unlike stocks and futures, there is no central marketplace. Trading occurs over the counter, via telephones and computers, around the clock, five days a week.

Currencies can be very volatile. The same factors that affect the price of gold affect a currency's value. While war and times of crisis can cause major moves in a currency, all manner of macroeconomic factors, such as trade deficits or interest rates, are also very influential.

Up until 1971, the value of the U.S. dollar was fixed to the price of gold. This was called the gold standard. An ounce of gold equaled $35. The currencies of the major economic powers were then fixed in relation to the dollar. But that year, the gold standard was abandoned. "Currencies now float in relation to each other, and their relative strength depends on supply and demand."[16]

The seven major currencies in the market are the U.S. dollar, euro, British pound, Japanese yen, Canadian dollar, Australian dollar, and Swiss franc, but every currency can be exchanged. Any individual, company, or country may participate in the market.

The euro is the currency of European Union, which includes 27 European countries. Over the past five years, the dollar has fallen nearly 40 percent against the euro. For most of 2007, the euro hit record highs against the falling dollar. The British pound hovered in the range of $2, a 26-year high. Reasons for the dollar's decline include an economic slowdown in the United States, a huge level of consumer borrowing, a large trade deficit, the Iraq War, and massive debt for the federal government, which causes the government to borrow money from other nations. The beginning of the subprime mortgage crisis also pressured the dollar. In this crisis, commercial banks and mortgage lenders began to experience a large number of defaults in mortgages sold to subprime borrowers. This situation spread to other investors as Wall Street investment banks had repackaged the mortgages as securities called asset-backed securities and collateralize debt obligations. When the underlying assets began to go sour, the trouble spread to everyone who owned a piece of this action. Investors might want exposure to currency because it is an attractive diversifying element in a portfolio. It has a very low correlation to equities, both domestic and international.

Money, That's What I Want

Currency ETVs come in two varieties: the kind that hold the actual foreign currency and those that track currencies through futures contracts. Again, the tax structures are different from ETFs and must be examined before buying the shares.

In December 2005, Rydex Investments introduced the first ETV tied to a currency, the CurrencyShares Euro Trust (symbol: FXE). In June 2006, Rydex launched additional currency based ETVs:

- CurrencyShares Australian Dollar Trust (symbol: FXA)
- CurrencyShares British Pound Sterling Trust (symbol: FXB)
- CurrencyShares Canadian Dollar Trust (symbol: FXC)

- CurrencyShares Japanese Yen Trust (symbol: FXY)
- CurrencyShares Mexican Peso Trust (symbol: FXM)
- CurrencyShares Swedish Krona Trust (symbol: FXS)
- CurrencyShares Swiss Franc Trust (symbol: FXF)

It filled out its offerings with the February 2007 launch of the Japanese Yen Trust (symbol: FXY).

Like the gold and silver shares, the currency shares are grantor trusts that hold the actual currency, not futures. Unlike ETFs, they don't have any diversification. They are pure plays. The ETVs give currency exposure to a single currency and allow the shareholder to participate in the movement of that currency relative to the dollar. In most of the CurrencyShares, each share is equal to 100 units of the underlying currency and mimics its spot price. The Yen Trust holds 10,000 yen per share, while the Peso Trust and the Krona Trust each hold 1,000 of their respective currency per share.

The currency shares each charge an expense ratio of 0.4 percent. But unlike gold and silver, which incur costs for storage and insurance, financial institutions will pay you to let them hold your money. So, the currency ETVs hold their currency in interest-bearing accounts in a depositary at J.P. Morgan, London. Just like a savings account at a bank, the depositary credits an overnight rate to the portfolio, which is distributed monthly in the form of income.

As with any other ETF-like structure, the AP needs to deposit the asset in order to receive a creation unit consisting of 50,000 shares. For instance, if the AP wants shares in the CurrencyShares Australian Dollar Trust, it needs to deposit $5 million Australian dollars. Remember, each share of FXA is worth 100 Australian dollars. The AP wires the money to J.P. Morgan in Melbourne, Australia. It tells the trustee, the Bank of New York Mellon, to release the shares to the Depositary Trust Company. The DTC releases the creation unit of 50,000 shares to the AP, which it then sells on the stock market. Again, the ETV doesn't pay for any of this to happen. The AP pays the fee to complete the transaction.

Like the gold and silver shares, the grantor trust is a pass-through vehicle. Therefore, the shareholders are treated as if they own the foreign currency directly. There is no in-kind process to pull taxes out of the trust. Because of this, the currency shares do not get the favorable tax treatment bestowed upon stocks and bonds. All the capital gains and interest distributions from the currency trusts are taxed as ordinary income.

If you think the U.S. dollar is going to fall, you could purchase currency ETVs. If the foreign currency goes up in value and the dollar falls, when you convert back into dollars, you will get more than you originally paid.

"If you've ever bought currency while traveling in a foreign country you know what it means to not get the best rates," remarked Michael Panzner, vice president of sales trading at British brokerage Collins Stewart, in Smart-Money.com. "In theory, ETFs can help you do it cheaper. And trading currencies [via ETFs] like shares in a brokerage account makes the process much less complicated. It's the same reason people buy ADRs [American depositary receipts] instead of stocks on foreign markets. It's easier."[17]

Some think currencies are simpler than equities. No balance sheets, earnings, or industry competition to deal with. You don't need to pour over financial statements to find out what is going on. They react mostly to macroeconomics. While it looks simple, currencies can be very volatile, hence potentially riskier than equities. A myriad of factors home or abroad can affect an economy, sparking a dramatic move in a particular currency. It is a zero-sum investment over time, but directional trends tend to last a long time.

In a SmartMoney.com article, I explained how the currency market works: "Most currency trading is conducted through large commercial banks such as Citigroup and Bank of America. Big institutional investors deal directly with a bank trading one currency for another. An individual investor could go to a bank but more likely would deal with a broker, who would take the opposite side of the transaction. However, setting up a currency trading account can be a logistical hassle. Investors need to open a nondollar-denominated account in a bank, then after purchasing the currency they need an interest-bearing account to stash it in. And while forex markets may be more liquid, they're also largely unregulated. That means there's very little transparency on the price at any moment leaving retail investors at a disadvantage. The lack of transparency means retail investors can't access the best prices, which typically go to institutional investors."[18]

In addition to avoiding the aggravation of setting up a futures account, the CurrencyShares, because they track the spot price of a currency, also provide greater price transparency. Everyone gets the same price. This is a huge benefit to the retail investor as it lowers the broker's spread. Also, unlike a currency account, you don't need a lot of money to take a position. You can buy only one share of the ETV.

Back to the Futures

PowerShares offers two ETVs that track the dollar:

1. PowerShares DB US Dollar Bullish Fund (symbol: UUP)
2. PowerShares DB US Dollar Bearish Fund (symbol: UDN)

The bullish dollar fund is based on the Deutsche Bank Long US Dollar Index Futures Index. It is a rules-based index composed solely of long U.S. dollar index futures contracts. It is designed to replicate the performance of being long the dollar against the following currencies: euro, Japanese yen, British pound, Canadian dollar, Swedish krona, and Swiss franc.

The bearish dollar fund is based on the Deutsche Bank Short US Dollar Index Futures Index. This index is comprised solely of short U.S. dollar index futures contracts. This is designed to replicate the performance of being short the dollar against the same currencies.

The PowerShares DB G10 Currency Harvest Fund (symbol: DBV) is based on the Deutsche Bank G10 Currency Future Harvest Index–Excess Return Index. The index is comprised of currency futures contracts on certain G10 currencies. It buys futures contracts on the three currencies associated with the highest interest rates on average, and sells futures on the three with the lowest yield.

The G10 currency universe from which the index selects currently includes U.S. dollars, euros, Japanese yen, Canadian dollars, Swiss francs, British pounds, Australian dollars, New Zealand dollars, Norwegian krone and Swedish krona. It's rebalanced on a quarterly basis.

The same tax rules that apply to the PowerShares commodity ETVs—60 percent long-term capital gains/40 percent short-term capital gains—apply here.

Currency Notes

Three currency exchange-traded notes are sold by iPath.

1. The iPath Eur/USD Exchange Rate ETN (symbol: ERO) tracks the exchange rate between the euro and the dollar.
2. The iPath GBP/USD Exchange Rate ETN (symbol: GBB) tracks the exchange rate between the British pound and the dollar.
3. The iPath JPY/USD Exchange Rate ETN (symbol: JYN) tracks the exchange rate between the Japanese yen and the dollar.

These have the same structure as the other ETNs mentioned earlier in the chapter; however they are taxed differently from other ETNs.

In December 2007, the IRS issued a ruling on ETNs that track currencies that wasn't good news for the ETNs or investors. Before the ruling, ETNs that tracked foreign currencies "were more tax efficient than holding currencies outright, or investing in Rydex's CurrencyShares. Like currencies, gains from the CurrencyShares were always taxed as ordinary income, no matter how long they were held."[19] Before the ruling, the sale of currency ETNs after more than a year resulted in paying the capital gains rate of 15 percent, instead of paying the tax as though it were ordinary income, which currently has a tax rate as high as 35 percent. For currency investors paying 35 percent, this was a huge benefit.

The IRS ruling concluded that ETNs that track foreign currencies must be considered debt for federal tax purposes. This completely eliminated the favorable tax treatment. Like other currency investments, currency ETNs are now taxed as ordinary income. While it looks like it levels the playing field, it actually puts the ETNs at a disadvantage.

The ETNs don't hold actual currency reserves the way that the Rydex CurrencyShares do. These currencies must sit in a bank somewhere, where they are invested in overnight notes earning income. So, in addition to capital gains, this interest is distributed to CurrencyShares shareholders, who then pay annual taxes on it. Because the ETNs don't hold currencies, they don't generate income. But much in the way that dividend distributions increase an index's total return, this implied currency interest is considered to be reinvested to boost the value of the currency ETNs. The IRS ruled that even though ETN shareholders didn't receive the income as a distribution, they still need to pay taxes on the implied "phantom" income. So, in an opposite situation from the dividends, holders of currency ETNs are paying taxes now on income they won't receive until they sell their shares at a later date.

The ruling only affects the three ETNs mentioned earlier.

Summary

In terms of the commodity asset allocation for your portfolio, most investment advisors suggest between 5 percent and 20 percent of the entire portfolio should be invested in these two together. Obviously, 20 percent is a very aggressive strategy. And individual investors shouldn't be putting more than 5 percent into any one commodity or currency product.

While the ability to trade commodities and currencies in an ETF-like format is a big step forward for the individual investor, it doesn't necessarily mean it's the best move for a well-diversified strategy. In short, is the *beta*—or risk inherent in the investment—too large for the *alpha*, or return above the benchmark index? Is the risk worth the chance for additional gains?

When is all said and done, the pure commodity and currency ETVs are speculative plays. Both can switch direction on a dime and make huge moves on unexpected macroeconomic news. In keeping with the ETF theme, instead of buying an ETV tracking a single asset, the best move for individual investors may be to buy an ETV that tracks an index. They give exposure to these assets, with little correlation to the stock market, but minimize the risk by adding diversification. While investing in commodities and currencies is a good way to diversify a portfolio, investors need to be aware that most commodities in the world have been in a bull market for

TABLE 8.3 Exchange Traded Vehicles (as of February 28, 2008)

Name	Ticker	Structure	Index or What It Tracks	Expense Ratio	Launch Date	Sector/Style
Biotech HOLDRs	BBH	Grantor Trust	No Index	$2.00 for each round lot per quarter	11/22/1999	Biotech
Broadband HOLDRs	BDH	Grantor Trust	No Index	$2.00 for each round lot per quarter	4/5/2000	Broadband
B2B Internet HOLDRs	BHH	Grantor Trust	No Index	$2.00 for each round lot per quarter	2/23/2000	Internet
Europe 2001 HOLDRs	EKH	Grantor Trust	No Index	$2.00 for each round lot per quarter	1/17/2001	ADRs of European companies
Internet HOLDRs	HHH	Grantor Trust	No Index	$2.00 for each round lot per quarter	9/22/1999	Internet
Internet Architecture HOLDRs	IAH	Grantor Trust	No Index	$2.00 for each round lot per quarter	2/24/2000	Internet
Internet Infrastructure HOLDRs	IIH	Grantor Trust	No Index	$2.00 for each round lot per quarter	2/24/2000	Internet
Market 2000 HOLDRs	MKH	Grantor Trust	No Index	$2.00 for each round lot per quarter	8/29/2000	Size: Large Cap
Oil Services HOLDRs	OIH	Grantor Trust	No Index	$2.00 for each round lot per quarter	2/6/2001	Energy
Pharmaceutical HOLDRs	PPH	Grantor Trust	No Index	$2.00 for each round lot per quarter	1/31/2000	Pharmaceutical
Regional Bank HOLDRs	RKH	Grantor Trust	No Index	$2.00 for each round lot per quarter	6/22/2000	Financial

(Continued)

TABLE 8.3 (Continued)

Name	Ticker	Structure	Index or What It Tracks	Expense Ratio	Launch Date	Sector/Style
Retail HOLDRs	RTH	Grantor Trust	No Index	$2.00 for each round lot per quarter	5/2/2001	Retail
Semiconductor HOLDRs	SMH	Grantor Trust	No Index	$2.00 for each round lot per quarter	5/4/2000	Technology
Software HOLDRs	SWH	Grantor Trust	No Index	$2.00 for each round lot per quarter	9/27/2000	Technology
Telecom HOLDRs	TTH	Grantor Trust	No Index	$2.00 for each round lot per quarter	1/31/2000	Telecom
Utilities HOLDRs	UTH	Grantor Trust	No Index	$2.00 for each round lot per quarter	6/22/2000	Utilities
Wireless HOLDRs	WMH	Grantor Trust	No Index	$2.00 for each round lot per quarter	10/31/2000	Telecom
ETNs						
BearLinx Alerian MLP Select Index ETN	BSR	ETN	Alerian MLP Select Index	0.85	7/20/2007	Master Limited Partnerships Sector
Claymore CEF Index–Linked GS Connect ETN	GCE	ETN	Claymore CEF Index	0.95	12/10/2007	Closed-end Funds
ELEMENTS "Dogs of the Dow"	DOD	ETN	DJ High Yield Select 10 Total Return Index	0.75	11/7/2007	Size: Large Cap
ELEMENTS MLCX Biofuels Index (Exchange Series)–Total Return	FUE	ETN	MLCX Biofuels Total Return Index	0.75	2/5/2008	Commodities

ELEMENTS MLCX Grains Index – Total Return	GRU	ETN	MLCX Grains Total Return Index	0.75	2/5/2008	Commodities
ELEMENTS Morningstar Wide Moat Focus Total Return Index	WMW	ETN	Morningstar Wide Moat Focus Total Return Index	0.75%	10/17/2007	Style - Value
ELEMENTS RICI–Agriculture	RJA	ETN	Rogers International Commodity Index Agriculture Total Return	0.75	10/17/2007	Commodities
ELEMENTS RICI–Energy	RJN	ETN	Rogers International Commodity Index Energy Total Return	0.75	10/17/2007	Commodities
ELEMENTS RICI–Metals	RJZ	ETN	Rogers International Commodity Index Metals Total Return	0.75	10/17/2007	Commodities
ELEMENTS RICI–Total Return	RJI	ETN	Rogers International Commodity Index Total Return	0.75	10/17/2007	Commodities
ELEMENTS Spectrum Large Cap U.S. Sector Momentum Index	EEH	ETN	Spectrum Large Cap U.S. Sector Momentum Index	0.75	8/1/2007	Size: Large Cap

(Continued)

TABLE 8.3 *(Continued)*

Name	Ticker	Structure	Index or What It Tracks	Expense Ratio	Launch Date	Sector/Style
ELEMENTS/Australian Dollar/U.S. Dollar Exchange Rate	ADE	ETN	DB AUD Overnight Index	0.40%	2/20/2008	Currency
ELEMENTS/British Pound/U.S. Dollar Exchange Rate	EGB	ETN	DB GBP Overnight Index	0.4	2/20/2008	Currency
ELEMENTS/Euro/U.S. Dollar Exchange Rate	ERE	ETN	DB EUR Overnight Index	0.4	2/20/2008	Currency
ELEMENTS/U.S. Dollar/Canadian Dollar Exchange Rate	CUD	ETN	DB CAD Overnight Index	0.4	2/20/2008	Currency
ELEMENTS/U.S. Dollar/Swiss Franc Exchange Rate	SZE	ETN	DB CHF Overnight Index	0.4	2/20/2008	Currency
GS Connect S&P GSCI Enhanced Commodity TR	GSC	ETN	S&P GSCI Enhanced Commodity Total Return Strategy Index	1.25	7/31/2007	Commodities
iPath CBOE S&P 500 BuyWrite Index ETN	BWV	ETN	CBOE S&P 500 BuyWrite Index	0.75	5/22/2007	Size: Large Cap
iPath DJ-AIG Agriculture Total Return Sub-Index ETN	JJA	ETN	Dow Jones-AIG Agriculture Total Return Sub-Index	0.75	10/23/2007	Commodities

Name	Symbol	Type	Index		Date	Category
iPath DJ-AIG Commodity Index Total Return ETN	DJP	ETN	Dow Jones-AIG Commodity Index Total Return	0.75	6/6/2006	Commodities
iPath DJ-AIG Copper Total Return Sub-Index ETN	JJC	ETN	Dow Jones-AIG Copper Total Return Sub-Index	0.75	10/23/2007	Commodities
iPath DJ-AIG Energy Total Return Sub-Index ETN	JJE	ETN	Dow Jones-AIG Energy Total Return Sub-Index	0.75	10/23/2007	Commodities
iPath DJ-AIG Grains Total Return Sub-Index ETN	JJG	ETN	Dow Jones-AIG Grains Total Return Sub-Index	0.75	10/23/2007	Commodities
iPath DJ-AIG Industrial Metals Total Return Sub-Index ETN	JJM	ETN	Dow Jones-AIG Industrial Metals Total Return Sub-Index	0.75	10/23/2007	Commodities
iPath DJ-AIG Livestock Total Return Sub-Index ETN	COW	ETN	Dow Jones-AIG Livestock Total Return Sub-Index	0.75	10/23/2007	Commodities
iPath DJ-AIG Natural Gas Total Return Sub-Index ETN	GAZ	ETN	Dow Jones-AIG Natural Gas Total Return Sub-Index	0.75	10/23/2007	Commodities

(Continued)

TABLE 8.3 (Continued)

Name	Ticker	Structure	Index or What It Tracks	Expense Ratio	Launch Date	Sector/Style
iPath DJ-AIG Nickel Total Return Sub-Index ETN	JJN	ETN	Dow Jones-AIG Nickel Total Return Sub-Index	0.75	10/23/2007	Commodities
iPath EUR/USD Exchange Rate ETN	ERO	ETN	Euro	0.4	5/8/2007	Currency
iPath GBP/USD Exchange Rate ETN	GBB	ETN	British Pound	0.4	5/8/2007	Currency
iPath JPY/USD Exchange Rate ETN	JYN	ETN	Japanese Yen	0.4	5/8/2007	Currency
iPath MSCI India Index ETN	INP	ETN	MSCI India Total Return Index	0.89	12/19/2006	Country stocks: India
iPath S&P GSCI Total Return Index ETN	GSP	ETN	S&P GSCI Total Return Index	0.75	6/6/2006	Commodities
iPath S&P GSCI Crude Oil Total Return Index ETN	OIL	ETN	S&P GSCI Crude Oil Total Return Index	0.75	8/15/2006	Commodities
Commodity ETVs						
streetTRACKS Gold Shares	GLD	Grantor Trust	Gold	0.4	11/18/2004	Physical Commodity
iShares COMEX Gold Trust	IAU	Grantor Trust	Gold	0.4	1/21/2005	Physical Commodity
iShares Silver Trust	SLV	Grantor Trust	Silver	0.5	4/21/2006	Physical Commodity

Name	Ticker	Type	Underlying Index	Ratio	Date	Category
MACROshares Oil Up Tradeable Shares	UCR	Trust	NYMEX Division Light Sweet Crude Oil Futures Contract	1.6	11/30/2006 Closing 6/25/2008	Commodity Futures
MACROshares Oil Down Tradeable Shares	DCR	Trust	NYMEX Division Light Sweet Crude Oil Futures Contract	1.6	11/30/2006 Closing 6/25/2008	Commodity Futures
PowerShares DB Agriculture Fund	DBA	Commodity Pool	Deutsche Bank Liquid Commodity Index Optimum Yield Agriculture Excess Return	0.91	1/5/2007	Commodity Futures
PowerShares DB Base Metals Fund	DBB	Commodity Pool	Deutsche Bank Liquid Commodity Index Optimum Yield Industrial Metals Excess Return	0.78	1/5/2007	Commodity Futures
PowerShares DB Commodity Index Fund	DBC	Commodity Pool	Deutsche Bank Liquid Commodity Index Optimum Yield Excess Return	0.83	2/3/2006	Commodity Futures

(Continued)

TABLE 8.3 *(Continued)*

Name	Ticker	Structure	Index or What It Tracks	Expense Ratio	Launch Date	Sector/Style
PowerShares DB Energy Fund	DBE	Commodity Pool	Deutsche Bank Liquid Commodity Index Optimum Yield Energy Excess Return	0.78	1/5/2007	Commodity Futures
PowerShares DB Gold Fund	DGL	Commodity Pool	Deutsche Bank Liquid Commodity Index Optimum Yield Gold Excess Return	0.54	1/5/2007	Commodity Futures
PowerShares DB Oil Fund	DBO	Commodity Pool	Deutsche Bank Liquid Commodity Index Optimum Yield Crude Oil Excess Return	0.54	1/5/2007	Commodity Futures
PowerShares DB Precious Metals Fund	DBP	Commodity Pool	Deutsche Bank Liquid Commodity Index Optimum Yield Precious Metals	0.79	1/5/2007	Commodity Futures

Name	Ticker	Structure	Index/Description	Expense	Inception	Category
PowerShares DB Silver Fund	DBS	Commodity Pool	Deutsche Bank Liquid Commodity Index Optimum Yield Silver Excess Return	0.54	1/5/2007	Commodity Futures
United States Gasoline Fund	UGA	Commodity Pool	Gasoline Futures	0.6	2/22/2008	Commodity Futures
United States Natural Gas Fund	UNG	Commodity Pool	Natural Gas Futures	0.6	4/18/2007	Commodity Futures
United States Oil Fund	USO	Commodity Pool	Oil Futures	0.5	4/10/2006	Commodity Futures
United States 12 Month Oil Fund	USL	Commodity Pool	Oil Futures	0.6	12/6/2007	Commodity Futures
Currency ETVs						
CurrencyShares Australian Dollar Trust	FXA	Grantor Trust	Australian Dollar	0.4	6/21/2006	Currency
CurrencyShares British Pound Sterling Trust	FXB	Grantor Trust	British Pound Sterling	0.4	6/21/2006	Currency
CurrencyShares Canadian Dollar Trust	FXC	Grantor Trust	Canadian Dollar	0.4	6/21/2006	Currency

(Continued)

TABLE 8.3 *(Continued)*

Name	Ticker	Structure	Index or What It Tracks	Expense Ratio	Launch Date	Sector/Style
CurrencyShares Euro Trust	FXE	Grantor Trust	Euro	0.4	12/8/2005	Currency
CurrencyShares Japan Yen Trust	FXY	Grantor Trust	Japanese Yen	0.4	2/12/2007	Currency
CurrencyShares Mexican Peso Trust	FXM	Grantor Trust	Mexican Peso	0.4	6/21/2006	Currency
CurrencyShares Swedish Krona Trust	FXS	Grantor Trust	Swedish Krona	0.4	6/21/2006	Currency
CurrencyShares Swiss Franc Trust	FXF	Grantor Trust	Swiss Franc	0.4	6/21/2006	Currency
PowerShares DB G10 Currency Harvest	DBV	Commodity Pool	Deutsche Bank G10 Currency Future Harvest Index	0.81	9/18/2006	Currency Futures
PowerShares DB US Dollar Index Bearish Fund	UDN	Commodity Pool	Deutsche Bank Short US Dollar Futures Index	0.55	2/20/2007	Currency Futures
PowerShares DB US Dollar Index Bullish Fund	UUP	Commodity Pool	Deutsche Bank Long US Dollar Futures Index	0.55	2/20/2007	Currency Futures

Source: ExchangeTradedFunds.com. Reprinted with permission.

most of the decade. In addition, the dollar has been in a six-year decline. The easy profits in both of these assets have already been captured. While both the commodity and currency markets could continue with their current trends for a while, both are entering uncharted territory. Investors should be extremely cautious. The odds have increased that either one or both will peak in the near future. Of course, because these ETVs can be shorted like ETFs, it's possible to make money in either direction.

In the end, when picking an ETV, in addition to the asset's risk, investors need to consider the tax issues and which ETV structure best suits their needs. See Table 8.3 for a list of available ETVs.

CHAPTER 9

Putting the "Trade" in Exchange-Traded Funds

As should be clear by now, the big innovation of ETFs over mutual funds is that you can trade them like stocks. You can do a stop-loss order or a limit order, and you can sell them short.

Why is trading so important? ETFs give investors the ability to trade a "single stock without the single-stock risk."[1] Trading allows you to make the trade when it's most advantageous to you. Trading offers continuous pricing and liquidity, which is the ability to buy or sell very quickly. If you need money fast, the ability to price and time your purchase or sale can mean the difference in millions of dollars.

Prior to ETFs, investors used futures for index funds to catch the market's move. Many investors like ETFs better than index futures because they offer four distinct advantages: smaller order sizes, no special accounts, no roll costs, and futures have tighter margin requirements.

Investors who couldn't fund futures accounts, or just didn't want to trade futures, were left with trading shares of index funds. As mentioned before, this harms both the trader of the fund shares and the fund's long-term investors. The trader can only buy or sell at the end of the day, with little control over the price he pays. Meanwhile, the long-term investor suffers because on every sale the fund must pay a broker commission and potentially incur capital gains taxes. Therefore, mutual fund investors also benefit from ETFs because they remove cost-producing traders.

Ironically, the mutual fund scandal of 2003 showed how the interests of fast traders harmed long-term shareholders. Some fund companies allowed favored investors to trade long after the market closed at the known end-of-day price. It was a flat-out violation of the rules. These favored investors looted the returns of the fund's long-term shareholders (see Chapter 7). While that was flagrant thievery, it did shine a light on legal day-trading in mutual funds, which also increased fees and lowered returns. ETFs give traders the forum to enact these strategies without affecting mutual fund shareholders, thus lowering their hidden costs.

At first glance, the ability to trade ETFs like stocks appears to have been invented for day traders. In a sense it was. Institutional investors were the first to accept ETFs as a new trading product and discover its many uses. The original ETF day trader was the institution looking for a way to maximize the returns on its cash management. The institution, which could be a pension fund, an endowment fund at a university, or any large corporation, takes cash not yet allocated for an investment and buys shares of a broad market ETF. The institutions typically buy in the morning and sell all their shares in the afternoon. They do this to put the cash to work while they evaluate longer-term investments. The cash catches the market's move, but avoids the risk of bad news coming out when the market is closed.

In light of that, giving investors the opportunity to trade in and out of the funds as often as they wish seems like a recipe for disaster. As John Bogle said in 2001, "An ETF is like handing an arsonist a match."[2]

But trading ETFs shouldn't be any different than trading stocks. As ETFs become more prevalent in the market place, institutions began using ETFs as the core holdings for their portfolios, as a way to get sector exposure, and as hedging instruments. Individual investors should follow the same pattern. If you follow a buy-and-hold strategy with your stocks, bonds, and mutual funds, you should follow the same philosophy with ETFs. Constant trading undermines many of the advantages offered by index funds in general and ETFs in particular.

Warren Buffett said, "For investors as a whole, returns decrease as motion increases."[3] But, unlike mutual funds, whenever you make a move in an ETF you will have to make a trade on the stock exchange. So, every single time you want to buy or sell shares in an ETF you will have to go through a broker, and experience transaction costs from the bid-ask spread to the broker's commission.

Trading costs are not to be taken lightly. Even if you trade with a discount broker, they can add up. *Market timing*, a strategy that tries to pick the best times to enter and exit the market is risky and seldom pays off. In a best-case scenario, if you make a profit going in and out of stocks, you will hold them for less than a year. Short-term gains incur a significant capital-gains tax penalty. All the gains will be taxed at the short-term rate, which is equal to the tax rate on your regular income. You also risk being out of the market when the big rally begins.

In light of all this, I think a *buy-and-hold strategy* is the best one to follow. It lowers costs and, as mentioned in Chapter 5, costs kill returns.

"In the fund industry you don't get what you pay for, you get precisely what you don't pay for," Bogle told me in an interview. "The more the managers take, the less the investors make."

"Investors' timing is always wrong," he said. "They get into gold after it goes up, not before. The money poured into technology funds in the late '90s. The returns for mutual funds were not so bad, but the returns of investors were horrible. Investors put a lot of money in when the market is high and little when it is low. Investors themselves pay a timing penalty and a selection penalty. The nice thing about the index fund is it takes that out of your hand. You own the market."[4]

I won't be examining day-trading strategies, nor explaining fundamental or technical analysis. If you want to day-trade stocks, buying and selling the same company in one day, or just trade a lot, I recommend that you buy an additional book that explains trading strategies, as well as stock analysis, in detail.

Still, the best way to take advantage of the ETF's low-cost benefits is to trade them yourself. This chapter is a short primer on trading for people who want to buy and sell their own shares, but not get into complicated trading strategies.

Discount Brokers

The first choice you need to make as an investor is whether to hire an investment adviser or handle your own portfolio. All investment advisers automatically add a layer of fees. And sometimes, it can be very hard to determine what value or service you're getting for your money. A good investment adviser will spend time talking to you, asking questions to determine what your investing goals are and your risk tolerance. He or she should provide advice on constructing an appropriate portfolio for your risk tolerance. They should also take care of all the buying and selling involved in the process.

Some people don't like the hassle or stress of actually trading in the stock market. However, in order to minimize costs, you need to trade for yourself. So, you need to learn the basics of trading. The easiest way for the small investor to trade is to open an account with an online, discount broker. Full-service brokers provide research and advice in addition to taking care of trades. However, they charge a fee higher than the discount brokers. If you don't need advice and can do your own research, the discount broker is the way to go.

Choosing a discount broker shouldn't be too hard. They are always offering incentives to join, such as free trades for a certain period of time or unique trading tools. You have to decide what you want from your discount broker. Do you want the cheapest commission, or is access to Wall Street research more important? Do you want the fastest trade, or do you like the proprietary features that help you screen and evaluate securities? Is a responsive call center important, or will you be strictly online? Some sites offer video lessons in how to trade.

When evaluating a discount broker, or any broker for that matter, the prime variables should be costs, balance requirements, products, services, and reputation.

These are the best rated discount brokers, in alphabetical order. I'm not recommending any one in particular. They all have good reputations:

- Charles Schwab—866-232-9890, http://www.schwab.com. No account service fees and low minimums. It also has one of the largest mutual fund supermarkets.
- E*Trade—800-ETRADE (387-2331) https://us.etrade.com. Cheap commissions, high interest money market accounts.
- Fidelity—800-FIDELITY, https://www.fidelity.com. Cheap commissions and access to all Fidelity mutual funds.
- FirsTrade—800-869-8800, http://www.firstrade.com. FirsTrade offers commissions for just $6.95.
- Muriel Siebert—800-872-0711, http://www.msiebert.com. Free independent research.
- Options Xpress—888-280-8020, http://www.optionsxpress.com. This firm gets high points from many financial publications. OptionsXpress offers a nice comparison with other discount brokers. http://www.optionsxpress.com/welcome/broker_comparison.aspx?sessionid=
- Scottrade—800-619-7283, http://www.scottrade.com. Very low commissions, real-time news from Dow Jones, access to independent research.
- SogoTrade—888-818-SOGO, http://www.sogotrade.com. Deepest discount commissions, trades cost between $1.50 and $3.
- TD Ameritrade—800-454-9272 http://www.tdameritrade.com. Free research and trading tools.
- TradeKing—877-495-5464, http://www.tradeking.com. Highly rated and very low commissions.
- Vanguard—800-992-8327, http://www.vanguard.com/us/accounttypes/brokerage. Access to all Vanguard mutual funds.
- Wells Fargo—866-243-0931, https://www.wellsfargo.com/investing/styles/independent/wt. If you keep $25,000 with Wells Fargo, they will give you 100 commission free trades.

The Actual Trade

In the early 1800s, when the NYSE existed in a coffeehouse on Wall Street, people would come in offering to sell some kind of security. They would then have to wait around until someone else offered to buy it. They would haggle over the price with one side having a clear advantage over the other in terms of who was more desperate to close a deal.

Today, a stock's price and trading volume are instantly available anywhere there is Internet access. To make a trade, you send your order over computer wires, where it matches up with another order, usually within seconds.

Market Order

The most straightforward, fastest, and easiest trade is the *market order*. You place an order to buy or sell shares of a particular stock or ETF immediately. There are no contingencies on the order and price is not an issue. You want shares and you want them now. The order will be filled at the best price available at that moment. You won't know what price you paid until the traded is completed. The most liquid stocks and ETFs will process the trade almost immediately at the price last quoted. However, orders of illiquid, thinly-traded stocks may require some time to be filled and the price might have a larger-than-normal bid-ask spread.

Limit Order

As you might guess, the *limit order* puts a limit on your order. With the limit order, you place an order to buy or sell shares at a specific price. A limit order is the opposite of the market order. In the market order price is not important, but speed is. In the limit order, speed isn't important, but the price is.

If you want to buy shares at a price lower than where the stock currently trades, you place a limit order. Limit orders not only let you specify the price, but they allow you to trade without having to watch the market all the time. You place the order, then go about your business. When the stock hits your price, the trade gets filled.

For instance, the stock is trading at $25.50. You expect it to fall and want to buy it at a cheaper price. You put in an order to buy 100 shares at $24. If the stock falls down to your limit price of $24, the trade will be filled and you will get the shares at the price you desired. Of course, there are two risks with a limit order. The first is that the stock may rally and never fall to your limit price. You order goes unfilled. Now the price to purchase the shares has increased above even the market price available when you placed the order. The other risk is that the stock may get bad news and plunge down to $20. Your limit order will probably get filled, but you will pay $24 for a stock now worth only $20.

The same thing works on the flip side. You can place a limit order to sell. Say you bought the shares at $24 and wanted to sell at $30. Put the limit order in to sell when the stock hits $30. However, if the stock rises to

$29 then falls, never reaching $30, your trade never closes. So, while you could have sold at $29 and taken a nice profit, because you used a limit order, you missed making the trade.

Stop-Loss Order

The *stop-loss order* is similar to the limit order in that you set a price limit for when to sell, but the strategy behind it is different. With the limit order you want to sell when the price increases by a certain amount. Basically, if you can't watch the market all day, but you want to sell at $30, you place the limit order. That way, no matter where you are, if the price gets to $30, you still make the sale, getting the desired profit.

With the stop-loss order, the investor doesn't really want to sell; he wants to protect the profit he already has. Say you buy 100 shares at $24. The stock rises to $30. You don't need to get out of the investment. It has momentum and you want to let it ride. Still, after watching it climb to $30, a 25 percent increase, you don't want lose the profit you've accumulated on paper.

So, you protect the profit by placing a floor under your shares. The price floor is the stop-loss order. You put in the order for less than the current price, for example, $29. This way, if the market takes a sudden downturn, dragging your stock with it, you don't have to give back the profit. Instead, you pocket it.

You made the stop for $1 lower because you want to give the ETF a little room to trade. Prices fluctuate all day, so if you really don't want to sell, you need to give the shares an appropriate trading range that allows them to fall, then rise, without closing you out of the trade. In order to avoid closing their position during the course of daily market movements, investors need to not place the stop-loss too close to the current price. So, by placing the stop-loss at $29, instead of $29.75, the investor potentially gives up an extra 75 cents per share, but also gives himself a 75-cent cushion for typical market volatility.

For instance, the stock falls to $29.50 before bouncing back to $31. The woman with a stop-loss at $29.75 would immediately have her position sold, closing out her transaction.

Meanwhile, the woman who put the stop-loss at $29 doesn't cash out because her price was low enough not to get triggered. She continues to own the stock and watch it climb to $31.

The Time Orders

In addition to price, with limit and stop-orders you need to tell the broker how long the order should last.

The *day order* is good for only that one day. If the trading session ends without the order being filled, it's automatically canceled. Traders use day orders so they don't have to keep track overnight or over weeks of what orders they have.

The other time order is *"good-'til-cancelled."* It's the opposite of the day order. Instead of expiring at the end of the day, it stays open until the order is filled.

We Like Short Shorts

One of the big advantages trading offers ETFs over mutual funds is the opportunity to sell short. *Selling short* allows an investor to sell shares before he or she actually owns them. This is a powerful tool if you fear the market is about to fall.

Every trade has two sides: a buyer and a seller. When the buyer makes a purchase he goes *long* the shares. He has the long view. Typically, one would have to buy something, such as a car or a concert ticket, before that person could sell it to someone else. But this is not the case in securities. The purchase doesn't always have to be the first transaction in a trade. You can sell first even before you own the security. The reason someone would sell first is that he or she thinks the market, the ETF, or one particular stock, will go down in the near future.

Before ETFs, if you felt the S&P 500 was going to take a tumble and you wanted to capitalize on this hunch, you couldn't short any mutual fund tracking the S&P 500. You would have to make a separate bet against each individual stock or invest in the futures market.

It's no secret that the way to make money is to buy low and sell high. But what if it's too late to buy low? The stock already had a nice rally. It's sitting at a *52-week high,* which is the highest price this stock has seen over the past year. You could buy now, but you wouldn't be buying low. Or, considering the stock is at a 52-week high, this seems like a good place to take a profit. You could sell the ETF today in anticipation of it dropping in price, then buy it back later at a cheaper price. Shorting allows you buy low after the stock has already rallied.

But how does one sell something they don't own? The buyer wants to walk away with his stock or bonds within the three days allowed to close the transaction. The seller needs to have shares to give in exchange for the money the buyer will pay him. The short seller goes to a broker and says he wants to borrow shares. The brokerage then lends shares from another investor—an individual or fund—or from the brokerage's own inventory. The short takes the shares and sells them on the open market. When the sale is complete, the shares' total amount is deposited into the short's account. Until the short returns the shares, he pays the lender interest for the loan. If the ETF pays out a dividend while the short position is in effect, the short must give that money to the lender.

Short sellers don't like to have open positions for a long time. The longer the short keeps the position open, the more interest he pays the lender. This cuts into the short's profit. The short closes the transaction by buying back the shares and returning them to the lender. If the ETF has fallen in price, the short makes a profit (see Table 9.1). The profit is the difference between the price the shares were initially sold for, $20, and the price for which the shares were later bought, $15. If the price goes up to $25, the short takes a loss.

Short selling is a very risky enterprise. When an investor purchases shares he has unlimited (long) upside potential and a limited loss potential. The maximum loss the long can incur is the price paid for the shares. If you buy a hundred shares of the PowerShares Dynamic Small Cap Growth Portfolio (symbol: PWT) for $20, for a total of $2,000. The most you can lose on this investment is $2,000.

The short seller takes the flip-side of the trade. The short seller gets the limited, or short, side of the profit potential and unlimited potential for losses. If the short sells the PowerShares Dynamic Small Cap Growth Portfolio to the long for $2,000, the most he can make is $2,000. That's if the share price falls all the way to $0. However, the sky's the limit for the potential losses. If the short sells 100 shares at $20, but instead of falling, the ETF rallies to $30, it will now take $3,000 for the short to buy back the shares needed to close out his position. The short needs to buy back the shares to give them back to the brokerage. However, this is more than the $2,000 he originally received for the shares. The short needs to pull an additional $1,000 out of his account to purchase the shares, leaving him with a $1,000 loss.

Short Squeeze

A *short squeeze* occurs when many people shorting a stock or ETF suddenly all want out. If the shares suddenly surge higher, the shorts rush to close out their positions. This creates heavy buying pressure, causing the stock to rally,

TABLE 9.1 Winning and Losing in Short Trades

100 Shares of ETF Borrowed from Broker	If Stock Price Drops	If Stock Price Rises
Initial Sale	$20 a share or $2,000	$20 a share or $2,000
Price When Shares Are Bought Later	$15 a share or $1,500	$25 a share or $2,500
Total	$500 profit	$500 loss

pushing the price even higher, exacerbating their losses. The higher prices lead more shorts to decide to close their positions, flooding the market with more buy orders, pushing the price up still higher. Think of it as a room filled with short sellers ready to buy stock to close their positions. Outside the door is the one investor selling the stock they need. The short/buyer needs to line up in front of the seller, and each purchase price is progressively higher. All the shorts wanting to be first in line rush the exit at the same time, then try to get out of the room by squeezing through the door. That's a short squeeze.

It's Not That Easy to Short

Betting on a market decline by shorting an ETF is much easier than trading futures or shorting an entire portfolio of stocks. "But the truth is, it's not as easy to sell an ETF short as the industry would have you believe."[5]

Because ETFs trade like equities, in theory, you should be able to short them as easily as stocks. In truth, the ability to sell short depends on the availability of shares to borrow. Some stocks are very easy to borrow. These would be the very liquid issues with heavy trading volume. But if it's an illiquid small-capitalization stock or an issue already heavily shorted, these can be hard to borrow.

But ETFs shouldn't have this problem. When someone shorts a stock, they have to find a broker or investors willing to lend them the shares. Sometimes this can be difficult because there is a fixed number of shares for each company. But people shouldn't have to search for ETF shares. They can create as many shares as needed. So, the authorized participants, who are usually brokers or specialists, can create new shares by assembling the component stocks. One caveat: the typical creation unit is 50,000 shares.

"So, getting the AP to create new shares to short shouldn't be a problem for institutional investors or hedge funds. The trade should be large enough so that the broker isn't left with many shares and allows him to charge a big commission. Also, the broker wants to keep the institution as a client, so he will make the institution happy. But if a small individual investors wants to short a much smaller number, say 1,000 shares, the specialist would be left holding the remaining 49,000 on its books."[6]

The idea of being long a large amount of shares in a down market isn't terribly appealing for the broker. In addition to exposing the broker to additional market risk, it also ties up a lot of capital. So, the smaller the transaction, the less likely it becomes that the broker will help you.

It should be very easy to find shares to borrow in the extremely liquid SPDR or the PowerShares QQQ (symbol: QQQQ). However, because "securities lending is one of the least automated activities in the securities industry, ETF investors may find it just as hard to borrow shares of small and illiquid ETFs as it is to borrow small and illiquid stocks."[7] This would apply to many of the newest ETFs, especially the ones tracking niche markets and with less than $100 million in assets under management.

If the broker doesn't have the shares in his inventory or one of his clients' accounts, it could be very difficult to borrow the shares you want to short. Sometimes, people don't want to lend out their shares, and sometimes the broker simply can't find anyone who has the shares. Small brokers won't have the access to shares that a large brokerage has, nor is a smaller broker willing to take on the additional credit risk. In addition, the broker incurs an administrative cost for lending the shares. So, if your trade won't cover the cost to get it done, the brokerage's stock loan department may just say it's hard to borrow, when in fact, it's costly to borrow. Brokers have no obligation to perform a transaction that loses money for the firm, so they don't have to find shares for you. If you want to short only 200 shares, it's much easier for the broker to simply tell you that he can't find what you want.

If you really want to short an ETF and the trade is turned down, don't give up. Be persistent. If you trade through a discount broker, calling the trade in to a broker on the phone could yield better results. If you work with a full service brokerage, ask to speak to another representative if your broker won't get it done.

Going Long to Go Short

In the end, it may be easier to buy ETFs that do the shorting for you. In much the same way that ETFs have made it easier for individuals to invest in commodities and currencies, ETFs also make it easier for individuals to short the market. ProFunds and Rydex Securities are the leading providers of mutual funds that return the inverse, or opposite, of the market. If the market goes down 2 percent, the fund will return 2 percent. In short, they short the market.

Both companies have offered inverse mutual funds for more than a decade. In 2006, ProFunds launched its family of short ETFs, the ProShares. By the time Rydex launched its first six leveraged and inverse ETFs in November 2007, ProShares had already launched nearly 60 ETFs, with 35 shorting the market.

ProShares' ETFs try to produce the inverse return of all the major benchmark indexes. It also offers a series called the "Ultra Shorts." These ETFs seek to return two times the inverse move. So, if the Dow Jones Industrial Average lost 1.5 percent in a single session, the UltraShort Dow 30 (symbol: DXD) would post a gain of 3 percent. Here are a few:

- Short QQQ (symbol: PSQ)
- UltraShort QQQ (symbol: QID)

- Short S&P 500 (symbol: SH)
- UltraShort S&P 500 (symbol: SDS)

Buying an inverse ETF as a way to short the benchmark indexes is a better play than actually shorting an ETF because:

- You avoid the risk of unlimited losses. Even though the ETF is shorting the market, you as the investor are going long because you are purchasing shares. The ability to short without taking on the risk of unlimited losses is quite amazing. As a long, you only take on the risk associated with the long side of the trade.
- There isn't any difficulty in buying or selling the ETF. It is a much easier process than borrowing shares.
- There isn't any interest to pay.
- You don't have to set up a margin account for shorting.

It's now easier to hedge a long position. According to Michael Sapir, CEO of ProShares, "This is shorting made easy."[8]

ProShares was also the first provider to issue ETFs that bet on declines in international markets:

- Short MSCI EAFE (symbol: EFZ) seeks to produce the inverse of the daily return of the Morgan Stanley Capital Investment Europe Australasia Far East index. This is the most widely followed U.S. benchmark for tracking international equities. Buying the EFZ is an easy way to bet on a world-wide decline in stocks.
- UltraShort MSCI EAFE (symbol: EFU) seeks to double the negative return of the index.
- Short MSCI Emerging Markets (symbol: EUM) and Ultrashort MSCI Emerging Markets (symbol: EEV) seek to return one or two times the inverse of the MSCI Emerging Markets index.
- UltraShort MSCI Japan (symbol: EWV) offers a way to double down on a bet against the Japanese market.

For people who feel that the Chinese stock market has entered a bubble state, the Ultrashort FTSE/Xinhua China 25 (symbol: FXP) provides a bet on the Chinese market's decline. It gives two times the FTSE/Xinhua China 25, which tracks the 25 largest companies by market-cap that operates in mainland China.

The inverse and double inverse ETFs don't short a basket of the component stocks; instead they use derivatives that don't have trading costs associated with shorting.

These derivatives include futures and swap agreements. The funds sell or short futures contracts to get short exposure. They also buy swap agreements, which are contracts between two parties to exchange a revenue stream. I pay you when the swap goes in a certain direction and you pay me when it goes in the opposite direction. In addition, the long side of the swap pays the short interest in exchange for getting the upside return on the fund. When the swap turns downward, the short receives the downside returns as well as the interest.

ProShares says the futures are more effective in getting a short position than actually shorting stocks that have uptick rules. The futures in the funds do roll over to keep a steady position. That means as the future nears it expiration date, it is sold, and a newer futures contract is bought. This can create capital gains inside the fund, which an investor would pay on an annual basis. These capital gains are taxed like futures, as explained in Chapter 8. With futures, 60 percent of the profits generated in a year are taxed as if they were long-term gains, a rate of 15 percent. The remaining 40 percent of the profits are taxed as short-term gains, or ordinary income, which can run as high as 35 percent.

Because futures only need a minimal investment to buy a contract, a lot of the fund's assets remain in cash or equivalents. These are invested in short term interest bearing notes or bonds to earn income. This interest is returned to the investors who must pay taxes on it. The interest is taxed as ordinary income. When investors sell their shares in the fund, the capital gains are taxed like a regular ETF. Shares sold after a year are taxed at the lower long-term capital gains rate.

Sapir cautions that investors need to understand that the short ETFs are designed to return the inverse performance of a given index on a daily basis.

"Over longer time periods, ProShares ETFs are unlikely to precisely double benchmark returns," Paul Mazzilli, the director of ETF research at Morgan Stanley, said in an October 2007 report. The interest income of inverse ETFs and fund expenses contribute to this discrepancy, he wrote.[9] The ProShares ETVs charge an expense ratio of 0.95 percent, one of the highest management fees in the ETF industry. ProShares says it needs to charge this because of the risk it takes by shorting inside the funds. The inverse ETFs from Rydex charge 0.7 percent.

Investors need to be aware that inverse ETFs are not to be core components of a portfolio that you buy and put away for 10 years. These are strategy tools. Even ProShares says it doesn't suggest investors put all their money into short ETFs and forget about it. It says these are tools that are appropriate for some investors at specific times. While you can hold a small sampling of short ETFs all the time to act as a hedge, large holdings should be limited to selected times when the market's downward move is pretty clear.

Options on ETFs

Another benefit trading makes possible is the ability to trade options on their ETFs. Options are derivative instruments that allow you to either buy or sell risk. This ability to transfer risk allows investors to execute sophisticated hedging and trading strategies at a fraction of the cost of owning ETF shares outright.

Unlike a future, which is an obligation, an option contract gives an investor the right to buy or sell a security at a specific price prior to the contract's expiration date. There are two basic types of options. A call option gives the holder the right to buy a security. You are calling the asset to you. The put option confers the right to sell the security at a certain price before the option expires. You are putting the contract to the other person. Option buyers are called holders, and sellers are writers. The call holder isn't obligated to exercise the options. But if he does, the options writers are obligated to sell shares at the strike price.

In exchange for this right the buyer of the option contract pays a premium. The premium, or nonrefundable price of an option, is just a fraction of the total value of the contract. The premium's price depends on the type of investment, its current price, and the time remaining before the option expires. Volatility also plays a part in option pricing. The more volatile the stock the greater chance the option will go into effect.

The premium is like an insurance premium. You pay a fee each month to continue your car insurance. If you don't have an accident or theft that month, the premium goes down the drain. You paid for "protection", but didn't receive anything. However, if you do have a crash, and you car needs extensive repairs, you would receive funds many times greater than the premium to help repair your care.

When the market moves in the opposite direction than expected, the option expires without being exercised and the call holder loses the premium. The writer of the option keeps the premium, no matter how the transaction goes.

The appeal of options is the investor doesn't need to commit a lot of capital. Options offer leverage, which is the ability to make a large profit on an investment smaller than the value of the asset. The profit can be hundreds or thousands times more than the original investment. Of course, leverage works on the downside too, and can create huge losses just as easily. If you expect the market to rise, you could buy a call option on the SPDR, the DIAmonds or the Qubes. The option gives you the right to buy the ETF at that price, which is called the strike or exercise price.

When the price of the underlying ETF increases, the call option becomes more valuable. If you buy a call to purchase 100 shares of the Vanguard

Health Care ETF (symbol: VHT) for $60 and the price of the ETF rises to $70 you are said to be *in the money*. You're in the money whenever the strike price is below the ETFs current price. This means it would be profitable to exercise the option. It's more advantageous to buy the ETF at $60 and sell it today at $70, than to buy it today at $70 on the stock exchange and hope it goes higher.

If the ETF's market price falls below the strike price, to $50, you are *out of the money*. It is cheaper to buy it on the exchange, than exercise the option and buy it for $60. When the option price and the price of the ETF's shares are the same the option is now *at the money*.

The situation is the opposite with puts. Puts, like shorts, gain in value when the price of the underlying ETF declines. However, with a put, the potential loss is limited to the premium, compared to the unlimited loss potential with shorting an ETF.

A put is in the money when the strike price is higher than the ETF's market price. If you bought a put for Vanguard Health Care at $70 and the ETF's shares fell to $60. It would be in the money. You could exercise the option to sell at $70 and buy the shares back at $60. If the share price rose to $80, the option would be out of the money. It would be more advantageous to sell at $80 than the option price of $70. To sell at the option price would put you at a $10 disadvantage.

Options allow you to speculate on the ETF's move outright. You are making a bet the ETF will either rise or fall in the specified amount of time. Options can also be used to hedge a position. For instance, say you hold an ETF that has seen a big rise in a short amount of time. You could sell now, but then you would have to pay short-term capital gain taxes. You don't want to sell now, but at the same time, you fear that the market will fall, pulling the price of your ETF lower. You can buy a put now, so that you can sell your option at today's price in the future should the market fall. This allows you to protect your gains. The option allows you to insure your profits against a broad based market decline.

Now you could place a stop loss order a few points below where the ETF trades. But if the market falls and triggers the stop loss, then you would have sold all your shares and incurred a short-term capital gain. The option allows you to capture the profit while still holding onto your shares.

In SmartMoney.com I explained how to use options as a way to bet on a rise in the market, or as a way to hedge against a fall in energy prices.

"Take the case of the Dow Jones Industrial Average. On Monday, Merrill Lynch lifted its target for the widely followed average to a range of 12400 to 12600 from 11300 to 11500. Instead of buying 100 shares of the DIAmonds Trust, the ETF which tracks the Dow, you could buy

100 shares of the DIAmond's December 100 call option. That day the industrials closed at 11643, and DIAmonds at $116.56. The option gives you, the call holder, the right to buy DIAmonds at $100 anytime before the contract expires in December. Each option share costs $18.70, so for 100 options you'd risk just $1,870 instead of the $11,656 you'd pay for 100 DIAmonds. If the Dow rallies to 12600, the options would pay about $2,600. That's an $730 profit, or 39 percent return on investment. Compare that to the DIAmonds rising to $12,600. That's a $944 profit, but only an 8 percent rate of return. That's the power of leverage. (Of course, if the Dow fell the contract would likely expire unexercised and you'd have nothing to show for the $1,800 premium that you paid.)

"Options can also protect portfolio gains, acting as insurance called a hedge. Say you own 100 shares of the Energy Select Sector SPDR Trust (Ticker: XLE), an ETF that tracks a basket of oil industry stocks. While bullish on energy, you fear oil's price will fall this summer. And you don't want to sell the shares, because you don't want to pay capital-gains taxes.

"You can limit your risk by buying put options. (Remember, the holder of a put has the right to sell shares at a specific price.) That day the XLE closed at $59.50. The premium for each XLE September 60 put costs $3.60, or $360 total. If oil falls and the XLE drops to $50, the ETF shares would lose $950 ($59.50 minus $50, times 100). But if you sell XLE at $60, as the put contract allows you to do, and buy back shares at $50, then you make $1,000. Subtract the $360 premium, and the option returns $640, protecting most of the fallen ETF's lost profit. If instead XLE rises above $60, you lose the $360, much like you lose car insurance premiums every year you avoid an accident. If you want to reduce the cost of the hedge, you could sell an XLE September 70 call, at 55 cents, or $55. This would reduce the hedge to $305. The downside of this is if XLE moves higher than $70, then you don't benefit because you have limited your upside gain to $70."[10]

Options can enhance returns through a variety of different strategies. Any option strategy available to equities is also applicable to ETFs. But, trading options isn't simple. This is just a brief overview of the possibilities that options offer to ETF investors.

If you want to know more about options, I recommend *The Option Advisor* by options guru Bernie Schaeffer (John Wiley & Sons, 1997). He is the chief executive of Schaeffer's Investor Research, which publishes a respected options newsletter called the "Option Advisor." He has a proven track record and provides market commentary and options advice daily on his Web site (http://www.schaeffersresearch.com).

Summary

Trading, the "T" in ETFs, provides a lot of the benefits these products have over mutual funds. Even investors who follow a buy-and-hold strategy need to understand the basics of trading because that is the only way to buy and sell ETFs.

It's possible to hire an financial advisor to make your trades for you, but this adds another layer of fees. To truly reap the low cost benefits of ETFs, you need to trade for yourself. It is recommended that investors trade through a discount broker. This will minimize trading costs.

Learning the basics of trading will prepare you for building your own portfolio of ETFs, which will be discussed in detail in Chapter 10. Learning trading strategies such as shorting and options gives you more flexibility in creating asset allocations and taking advantage of the market's trend.

The benefits of trading include:

- The ability to buy a diversified portfolio in one trade.
- The ability to buy a fund when it is most advantageous to you.
- Liquidity, the ability to buy and sell quickly.
- The ability to sell short.
- The ability to trade options on an ETF.

The downsides of trading:

- Stock Broker Commissions
- Bid-Ask Spread
- Temptation to day trade, or repeatedly buy and sell shares.

Another big advantage trading gives ETFs over mutual funds is the ability to short. Shorting is a trade that bets that the ETF's price will fall. Short selling is riskier than buying stocks, because the profit potential is limited, but the loss potential is unlimited.

Instead of shorting a particular ETF, there is now an alternative. You can buy an ETF that gives the inverse return of certain benchmark indexes. ProShares and Rydex Investments are the two companies selling inverse ETFs. They also sell Ultrashort ETFs, which give double the negative return of the index being tracked.

The advantage of buying an inverse ETF versus shorting an ETF:

- Avoids the risk of unlimited losses.
- Little difficulty buying, selling or finding shares of the inverse ETF.
- Don't have to set up a margin account

- Don't have to pay interest on borrowed shares.
- It's easier to hedge.
- Short ETFs are designed to return the inverse performance of a given index on a daily basis, not the exact inverse over a long period of time.

Options are another advantage afforded by trading ETFs. Options are derivative instruments that allow you to either buy or sell risk. This ability to transfer risk allows investors to execute sophisticated hedging and trading strategies at a fraction of the cost of owning ETF shares outright.

CHAPTER 10

Building Your Own ETF Portfolio

The best way to take advantage of the benefits of ETFs is to trade them and build a portfolio yourself. Hiring an investment adviser automatically adds a layer of fees. And sometimes, it can be very hard to determine what value or service you're getting for your money. If you've gotten through this much of the book, you can definitely build a portfolio by yourself.

You've learned the difference between an ETF and a mutual fund. You know that investing in ETFs is better than investing in single stocks because you get broad-based diversification with the flexibility and tax efficiency of equities, but without the single-stock risk. Diversification in one trade makes ETFs less expensive than buying individual stocks, and usually cheaper and more tax efficient than mutual funds. You also know you can invest in alternative asset classes with the same ease as investing in stock or bond ETFs.

Now it's time to put that information to good use and build your own investment portfolio. While I can recommend a certain investment strategy, readers will bring their own knowledge and preferences to how long they will hold ETFs and in what manner. You have to determine for yourself the amount of risk with which you feel comfortable. Like the title says, this book is about ETFs for the long run. The long run means buy and hold. Buy your investments, put them away, and let them grow; don't watch the daily machinations of the stock market. The main benefit of a buy-and-hold strategy is that you don't incur a lot of trading costs and you never have to worry about being out of the market during an up move. Since the U.S. market over the past century has been in a steady upward progression, betting on the market going up is a calculated bet.

When successful companies grow, so do their stocks. By holding and reinvesting the dividends given off by the stocks in your index, you increase the number of shares you own that can see their value grow. This compounds their value.

A buy-and-hold strategy does not mean buy and forget. Always remember: past results don't guarantee future returns. This means that even though the stock market has advanced over the past century, there's no guarantee it will in the future.

All investments experience down times. Sometimes these down periods last only months, sometimes they stretch out for years. I'm not recommending market timing, but it's good to be aware of the market and the outside world and see how they are affecting each other. Sometimes it's a very good idea to take profits off the table. If the economic mood is changing, you should reassess your asset allocation and possibly lower your exposure to stocks. The nice thing about ETFs is that they offer many products and opportunities that let investors take advantage of both an up and down market.

This chapter will offer concrete suggestions on how to build a portfolio as well as some complicated, more sophisticated strategies. Because I'm not a professional asset manager, I decided to ask some professionals for suggestions on how they put together ETF-only portfolios. It's rare for financial professionals to offer their portfolios for widespread public consumption like this. It's what they get paid to do—produce—so I greatly appreciate their contributions. Some are well-respected portfolio managers; others are people and firms I've used as sources of information for my articles. They all have a lot of ETF experience. I don't endorse any one strategy over another, but these are all people I respect.

James Kelly of Kelly Capital Management gives a very detailed road map to determine risk tolerance. I will then outline basic strategic asset allocations for conservative, moderate, and aggressive portfolios. These are precision allocations in that they break down the asset allocations into smaller categories in both the stock and bond allocations.

J. D. Steinhilber of Agile Investments created three easy-to-build strategic asset allocations—conservative, moderate, and aggressive—for the buy-and-hold investor saving for retirement. The portfolios take advantage of some strategic ETFs to grab a more diverse market exposure. These creative models provide a nice comparison to the first set of portfolios and show that even two similar strategies, with similar stock and bond ratios, can be constructed in very different ways.

Afterward, I provide two examples of portfolios that depart from the classic format of U.S. stocks and bonds. Ron DeLegge of ETF Guide.com provided his Contrarian Fox portfolio. This provides a good example of a tactical asset allocation and how to construct a portfolio that goes against conventional wisdom. Finally, Burton Malkiel offers a portfolio that is focused entirely on investing in the Chinese economy. Both of these portfolios are riskier than a classic strategic asset allocation.

Altogether, these examples show how ETFs offer investors a lot of opportunities to be creative in a wide range of portfolio construction possibilities.

The Simplest Portfolio

The easiest and most straightforward portfolio consists of two investments, maybe three.

The first would be an ETF of the entire stock market, such as the SPDR DJ Wilshire Total Market ETF (symbol: TMW) from State Street Global Advisors. This ETF follows the Dow Jones Wilshire 5000 Index. The second investment is an ETF that tracks 10-year U.S. Treasury bonds—for instance, the Vanguard Total Bond Market ETF (symbol: BND). It tracks the Lehman U.S. Aggregate Bond Index, which measures a wide spectrum of public, investment-grade U.S. government and corporate bonds. They all have maturities of more than one year, and an average maturity between five and 10 years.

This portfolio is fairly low risk. You adjust the percentages according to your age. The amount of fixed income you hold is equal to how old you are. A ten-year-old has the most time to recover from a financial disaster. He can afford to take on the most risk. So, his portfolio would be 10 percent bonds and 90 percent stock. A 40-year-old with a house, kids, and looming bills for college and retirement should put 40 percent in bonds and 60 percent in stocks. You're still young enough to take on risk in more than half your portfolio, but you're conservative enough so that while a financial disaster will hurt—a lot—it won't wipe you out. Then when you're seventy, you don't know if you might live to 90 years old. You still need to take some risk to grow your money, but you're not working any more and you need to make sure you have enough to live. This calls for at least 70 percent in bonds and 30 percent in stocks.

If you like it simple, stop reading. This portfolio will probably suffice.

Assessing Your Risk

James Kelly is the president of Kelly Capital Management in Philadelphia. In 2001 he became one of the first, if not the first, asset manager to make ETF-only portfolios for his clients. Kelly has an excellent track record and is always accepting new clients. He was kind enough to offer his insights on creating a portfolio. These are the questions he makes investors answer to determine their risk profile and what the most suitable investments would be for them.

These are the questions that a professional money manager asks when creating a portfolio. If you decide to create a portfolio on your own, these will be instrumental in preventing you from making disastrous investing decisions.

How Much Can I Invest, and Will It Be Held in a Taxable Account?

It's best to put securities that will be taxed the most in tax-exempt accounts such as individual retirement accounts (IRAs), 401(k) plans, or tax shelters. This would include taxable bonds and higher income securities. Securities expected to be sold in less than 12 months and one day should be in tax-sheltered accounts. If held in a taxable account, the capital gains from these investments would be charged at your base tax rate as ordinary income.

Taxable accounts should hold tax-free debt, unless your tax bracket is so low that the after-tax income is at least as good as the tax-free income from your home-state municipal bonds. Assets with a low turnover, those that won't be sold for a long time, should be in a taxable portfolio. When they are sold they will be taxed at the lower capital gains tax rate. Currently, this rate is 15 percent.

What Is My Risk Tolerance?

In order for a portfolio to return a profit, one must take on risk. The first variable of risk tolerance is the investment time horizon. How long will it be before you need this money? Can you lock up this money? Can you stay invested a long time if the investment goes through a rough patch?

- Can you invest for at least three years?
  - If the answer is no, don't invest in securities with a fluctuating market value, such as stock or bonds. Kelly recommends keeping these assets in money-market accounts and certificates of deposit (CDs).
  - If the answer is yes, then investing in securities with a fluctuating market value is acceptable.
- What is the goal for investing this money? Will it be for retirement, a child's education, a house, or another major purchase?
  - The longer the time horizon, the more "risky" assets you can use, such as stock ETFs instead of bond ETFs.

What Are My Liquidity Needs?

The second variable of risk tolerance is liquidity. Consider not only how long before you need the money, but your cash flow needs. How often do you expect to draw money from your investments? Will you need to access it immediately or on a regular basis? Liquidity is the ability to access your money quickly. Stocks are more liquid than a certificate of deposit. However, your stocks could be trading at a loss on the day you need to sell. Your liquidity needs will play an important part in determining what to invest in.

- Do you need to spend all or most of your money within the next three years?
  - If the answer is yes, then don't invest in "risky" assets.
  - If the answer is no, then you can invest in "risky" assets.
- When you begin to take the money out from your investments, how will you take it?
  - As needed, such as small lump sums on an ad hoc basis.
  - On a regular basis, such as an annual required distribution from an IRA account.
  - Like a pension, on a monthly basis. If so, fixed-income oriented ETFs may help smooth the cash-flow generation processes.
- Are there legal restrictions on what you can take, such as trusts paying out only income and a limited amount of principal?

If you don't expect to ever take money from the portfolio, then investing all of it in risky assets is appropriate. A good example of this kind of portfolio is one that will be donated to charity.

How Do I Feel about Losses?

Obviously, no one likes losing money. As described earlier, risk is the measurement of the likelihood of losing money. Risk is also the degree of volatility that the portfolio can be expected to experience. For only through volatility can a portfolio see great growth. The greater the volatility, the greater the moves up and down. A very risky investment is one that has high volatility. For taking on a large risk the investor has the potential to be compensated with huge returns. However, the large risk also means there is a great potential for a huge decline in the asset's value.

The best way to determine your tolerance of risk is the sleep factor. In short, how well can you sleep at night when your portfolio is experiencing large losses? Are you willing to tolerate fluctuations of 5 percent, 10 percent, 15 percent, 20 percent or more in the portfolio's value in a single year? Can you stay the course through a market downturn without becoming a nervous wreck? The greater the tolerance for risk, then the more stock ETFs you can use.

- Are you looking for a long-term inflation hedge? In this case, stock and real-estate ETFs are the best inflation hedges.
- Do you tend to look at your investments daily or less frequently? Curiosity is fine, but if you're a Nervous Nellie then don't invest much in stock, commodity, or real-estate oriented ETFs.

- Are you influenced by the talking heads on financial programs you see on television? These people are entertainers. Take what they say accordingly.

What Is My Tax Sensitivity?

Obviously, no one likes to pay taxes. But some people go absolutely crazy about paying taxes on investment income. If you've held long-term investments for many years, you've probably accumulated a lot of gains. And once they become realized, the government will want its share. So, the taxes that must be paid after selling assets must be factored into any strategy.

- Do you have substantial unrealized gains in low cost-basis securities? Do you have company stock acquired over many years of employment? If so, then set up a tax budget to limit the realized gains each year as you convert your low cost-basis stock into your ETF-based portfolio strategy.
- Did you inherit a security to which you are emotionally attached? For example, a parent or spouse may have left you some stock and you are reluctant to part with it.
- Is there an annual limit on how much tax you are willing to pay on capital gains? Generally 10 percent of your portfolio's market value is a reasonable limit for realized gains.
- From where will the funds come to pay the taxes on gains? The portfolio should pay its own taxes. It needs to keep enough liquidity to pay quarterly estimates to the IRS and your state revenue department.

Do Your Homework

ETF providers supply a lot of free information to investors, so look at their websites. A list of websites providing information and research can be found in the Appendix.

Some sites give you the means to assess your risk tolerance and create mock portfolios to match. In general, one should seek as much risk as one can tolerate and invest for the long term. Set up a tolerance band of about plus 5 percent and minus 5 percent around your long-term target asset mix. Rebalance this mix quarterly if it falls outside your tolerance band.

In general, unless you have a low risk tolerance, Kelly recommends that you place at least 70 percent of your assets in stocks, regardless of your age. Generally a limit of 30 percent foreign stock ETFs is comfortable for most investors with 10 percent being the minimum. The emerging-market stock ETFs give the greatest return, but are more volatile than developed market stock ETFs.

Real estate via ETFs, or specific REITS, should be limited to 10 percent of assets, which reduces the stock target by five percentage points and the fixed income target, if any, by five percentage points.

Commodities are a volatile asset class and a limit of 10 percent in commodities ETFs is tolerable for most individuals. This weighting further reduces the stock target by 10 percentage points.

A sample stock-only, aggressive portfolio might be 70 percent domestic stock ETFs and 30 percent emerging-market stock ETFs.

A sample balanced-aggressive account could be 60 percent domestic stock ETFs, 15 percent emerging-market stock ETFs, 10 percent real-estate ETFs and 15 percent fixed income ETFs.

Be Disciplined

Discipline is the ability to stick to your strategy in the face of strong head winds. Anybody can have a good strategy; it's the ability to stick with it even as the market goes against you that determines how disciplined you are. People who are not disciplined will take their money out of the market and then invest it back in at exactly the wrong times.

Most people don't sell at the beginning of a downturn. Instead, they typically suffer through months of declining asset values, hoping that the market will turn around and they will break even. Eventually, the pain of the losses becomes so overwhelming that the investor finally sells. Typically, this is near the bottom of the market, when he or she should be buying. He will get out at the bottom, and not be invested for the eventual upswing. Not believing the rally to be sustainable, the investor sits on his cash until the market proves to him the rally is real. If he invests at that time, he has to pay a higher price to enter the market. This increases the potential for buying just as the market is peaking.

- Develop a thick skin; don't overreact to short-term swings in market value.
- Control risk by rebalancing across the ETFs you have selected and across the asset classes they represent.
- Assess why things are going right and why they are going wrong. Don't change the asset mix target frequently.

Strategic and Tactical Asset Allocation

Two common strategies for creating portfolios are Strategic Asset Allocation (SAA) and Tactical Asset Allocation (TAA). According to Investopedia, strategic asset allocation is a method that establishes and adheres to what is a "base policy mix." This is a proportional combination of assets based on expected rates of return for each asset class. "Because the value of the assets can change given market conditions, the portfolio constantly needs to be re-adjusted to meet the policy. For example, if stocks have historically returned 10 percent per year and bonds have returned 5 percent per year, a mix of 50 percent stocks and 50 percent bonds would be expected to return 7.5 percent per year."[1]

Putting 60 percent of the portfolio in equities and 40 percent in bonds is your strategic asset allocation. This can be broken down further into many different stock and bond ETFs. Once you've researched the funds and created the asset allocation, you buy them. Then you hold them. This is a passive strategy.

Over the course of the year the weighting of each ETF in the portfolio changes depending on how the markets perform. At the end of the specified time period, usually the calendar year, the investor rebalances the portfolio to get back to the strategic asset allocation's original weightings. Most people wait until the end of the year to rebalance the portfolio and bring it back to its original allocations. For example, let's say your portfolio is 75 percent stocks and 25 percent bonds. Over the next year, you invest more into the fund and stock market rallies. The stock allocation grows to 85 percent of the portfolio, while bonds fall to 15 percent. To bring the allocation back into its proper weighting of 75 percent, you would sell some equity ETF shares. Then you take the money from selling stock ETF shares and buy enough shares in the bond ETFs to bring their allocation back up the model's desired 25 percent.

Rebalancing is a way of keeping your model at the appropriate risk level. In addition, it is a disciplined way to take profits in the investments that have been doing well and buy shares in the investments that are out of favor. Typically, these investments have been beaten down and trade at much cheaper prices. This is a systematic, disciplined way to force you to buy low and sell high.

The strategy is relatively rigid, but for many people that works. They want to set up their investments, then go about their daily lives. However, economic conditions often favor one asset class over another, creating unusual investment opportunities. In tactical asset allocation, the portfolios aren't passive. The investor, or asset manager, makes short-term, tactical deviations from the strategic mix to take advantage of these opportunities.

Tactical asset allocation, according to Investopedia, can be described as a moderately active strategy, since this flexibility adds a component of market timing to the portfolio. Tactical movements allow you to then make precise shifts in and out of the asset classes. This allows the asset manager to add value and reduce risk by taking advantage of "security misevaluations across the asset classes."[2]

TAA requires much more work and discipline than regular strategic asset allocation, because the portfolio must be rebalanced to the original long-term SAA when the short-term opportunities disappear. Such a strategy can be difficult for the individual investor. It will also add to your transaction costs.

A big problem with creating asset allocations with mutual funds is that you never really know what a mutual fund holds, so you never really know what your exposures are. ETFs bypass all that. The ETF's transparency allows for incredible risk management because ETFs offer the ability to create strategic allocations with great precision.

You can model these portfolios exactly or use them as a launching point. Feel free to add other ETFs in allocations appropriate to the model's benchmark ratio of stocks to bonds.

Classic Conservative Portfolio

A portfolio is considered conservative if it has an equity allocation of less than 50 percent. In this case conservative isn't a political philosophy, but an investing one. Conservative investors shy away from risk and are very concerned with not losing any of their principal investment. Many live off the income produced by their holdings.

In this portfolio, the strategic asset allocation is 40 percent equities, not including real estate trusts. This is a reasonable amount for a person with a fairly low risk tolerance. Most of the portfolio sits in bonds, about 51 percent. Unless you're nearing retirement, this is probably too little to be holding in stocks. But it's worthwhile to look at a conservative portfolio to give a base line for more aggressive portfolios.

The final 9 percent could be held in real-estate ETFs or commodity ETFs. For this example it won't hold commodities, because with expense ratios around 0.5 percent to 0.6 percent, these remain too high for the portfolio.

EQUITIES   The first thing to determine is how much of your stock portfolio will go to domestic stocks and how much to foreign stocks. Once the domestic allocation is determined, many investors choose to seek precision by breaking domestic stocks into three ETFs based on the size of the companies: large-cap stocks, mid-caps, and small-caps. Each one has different behavioral aspects and usually one sector will do better than the others. Small-caps usually lead bull markets, while large-caps are usually better during market turbulence and a good place to make defensive moves.

Another reason for breaking down stocks and bonds this way is for tactical asset management. This lets the investor or asset manager be more active in the portfolio management. They can take advantage of market opportunities by tactically tweaking the individual sectors up or down. If, for example, small stocks are doing better than large-cap stocks, the large-cap weighting of the portfolio could decrease by five percentage points while the small-cap portion could increase by the same amount. The three portfolios shown in Table 10.1 are suggested allocations from a variety of sources. Table 10.1 presents a classic conservative portfolio with 40 percent equity.

- In the strategic asset allocation (SAA), 15 percent of the equity portion is made up of large-capitalization stocks in the form of the SPDR Trust (symbol: SPY). This tracks the S&P 500 index, which holds about 75 percent of the U.S. stock market.
- Mid-caps comprise 5 percent of the portfolio in the form of the Vanguard Mid-Cap Index (symbol: VO). This ETF tracks the MSCI U.S. Mid Cap 450 Index. This index holds 450 stocks that comprise about 15 percent of the stock market.

TABLE 10.1   Classic Conservative Portfolio (40% Equity)

Asset Class	Fund	Symbol	Allocation	Expense Ratio
Large-Cap U.S. Stocks	SPDR Trust	SPY	15%	0.08%
Mid-Cap U.S. Stocks	Vanguard Mid-Cap ETF	VO	5%	0.13%
Small-Cap U.S. Stocks	iShares Russell 2000 Fund	IWM	6%	0.20%
Foreign Stocks	iShares MSCI EAFE Index Fund	ETF	14%	0.34%
Total U.S. Equity			26%	
Total Foreign Equity			14%	
Total Equity			40%	
Short-Term U.S. Bonds	Vanguard Short-Term Bond ETF	BSV	32%	0.11%
Long-Term U.S. Bonds	Vanguard Long-Term Bond ETF	BLV	4%	0.11%
Corporate Bonds	iShares Lehman Credit Bond Fund	CFT	5%	0.20%
Inflation-Adjusted Bonds	iShares Lehman TIPS Bond Fund	TIP	10%	0.20%
Total Fixed-Income			51%	
U.S. Real Estate	Vanguard REIT ETF	VNQ	9%	0.12%
Total Alternative Investments			9%	
Average Expense Ratio				0.17%

- Small-caps comprise 6 percent of the portfolio with the iShares Russell 2000 (symbol: IWM). This follows the Russell 2000 Index, the benchmark for the small-cap sector. The index holds the 2000 smallest companies, or about 10 percent, of the Russell 3000 Index.
- The international portion holds 14 percent of the portfolio and tracks the U.S. benchmark for the foreign market, the MSCI EAFE, with the iShares MSCI EAFE Index (symbol: EFA). It holds approximately 1,100 securities from 21 countries in Europe, Australasia and the Far East.

FIXED-INCOME The nonequity portion of the portfolio is generally divided among real estate, short- and long-term treasuries, corporate debt, and Treasury Inflation Protection Securities, better known as TIPS. These are U.S. Treasury bonds that adjust their principal and interest payments to protect investors from inflation. Fixed-income refers to bonds. It means these assets give off a steady stream of cash in the form of interest, also known as income.

- Short-term bonds mature within five years, and have less risk than long-term bonds. Short-term bonds make up 32 percent of the portfolio. The Vanguard Short-Term Bond ETF (symbol: BSV) is a good choice. It tracks the benchmark index, the Lehman 1–5 Year U.S. Government/Credit Index. This index includes all medium and larger public issues of U.S. government, investment-grade corporate, and investment-grade international dollar-denominated bonds that have maturities between one and five years. The average maturity shouldn't exceed three years, and is typically two years. The ETF holds about 700 securities.
- Long-term bonds typically have maturities greater than 10 years. The Vanguard Long-Term Bond ETF (symbol: BLV) follows the Lehman Long U.S. Government/Credit Index. It would hold 4 percent of the portfolio.
- The iShares Lehman Credit Bond Fund (symbol: CFT), which tracks the eponymous index, holds 5 percent. This index measures investment grade corporate debt and non-U.S. agency bonds with a maturity of greater than one year.
- The iShares Lehman TIPS Bond Fund (symbol: TIP) makes up 10 percent of the SAA.

ALTERNATIVE INVESTMENT A broad real estate ETF such as the Vanguard REIT ETF (symbol: VNQ) makes up 9 percent of the portfolio. This follows the MSCI US REIT Index, which covers about two thirds of the value of the entire U.S. real-estate investment trust (REIT) market. The fund invests 98 percent of its assets in REIT stocks and the rest in cash. In light of the current situation in the housing industry, an investor might be better off allocating this amount to a commodity fund, such as the PowerShares DB Commodity Index Tracking Fund (symbol: DBC).

Classic Moderate Portfolio

In this portfolio, equities make up 60 percent of the strategic allocation, fixed-income comprises 29 percent, and real estate holds 11 percent. This strategy uses the same ETFs, but in different allocations (see Table 10.2).

- The SPDR Trust is boosted to 24 percent from 15 percent in the ETF 40 Portfolio.
- The Vanguard Mid-Cap ETF rises to 8 percent from 5 percent.
- The iShares Russell 2000 climbs to 9 percent from 6 percent.
- The international component also gets much heavier, increasing the iShares MSCI EAFE Index to 19 percent from 14 percent.

TABLE 10.2   Classic Moderate Portfolio (60% Equity)

Asset Class	Fund	Symbol	Allocation	Expense Ratio
Large-Cap U.S. Stocks	SPDR Trust	SPY	24%	0.08%
Mid-Cap U.S. Stocks	Vanguard Mid-Cap ETF	VO	8%	0.13%
Small-Cap U.S. Stocks	iShares Russell 2000 Fund	IWM	9%	0.20%
Foreign Stocks	iShares MSCI EAFE Index Fund	ETF	19%	0.34%
Total U.S. Equity			41%	
Total Foreign Equity			19%	
Total Equity			60%	
Short-Term U.S. Bonds	Vanguard Short-Term Bond ETF	BSV	17%	0.11%
Long-Term U.S. Bonds	Vanguard Long-Term Bond ETF	BLV	7%	0.11%
Corporate Bonds	iShares Lehman Credit Bond Fund	CFT	5%	0.20%
Total Fixed-Income			29%	
U.S. Real Estate	Vanguard REIT ETF	VNQ	11%	0.12%
Total Alternative Investments			11%	
Average Expense Ratio				0.16%

- The real estate portion, in Vanguard REIT ETF rises to 11 percent from 9 percent.
- Among the fixed-income component, the Vanguard Short-Term Bond ETF gets sliced nearly in half to 17 percent from 32 percent.
- The Vanguard Long-Term Bond ETF, which takes on more risk because of the longer maturities, actually increases its allocation to 7 percent from 4 percent.
- The iShares Lehman Credit Bond Fund stays the same at 5 percent.
- The iShares Lehman TIPS Bond Fund is cut from the portfolio entirely.

Classic Aggressive Portfolio

This aggressive ETF portfolio (shown in Table 10.3) uses the same ETFs as the other two portfolios to hold 80 percent in equities, 10 percent in fixed-income, and 10 percent in real estate funds.

TABLE 10.3   Classic Aggressive Portfolio (80% Equity)

Asset Class	Fund	Symbol	Allocation	Expense Ratio
Large-Cap U.S. Stocks	SPDR Trust	SPY	30%	0.08%
Mid-Cap U.S. Stocks	Vanguard Mid-Cap ETF	VO	13%	0.13%
Small-Cap U.S. Stocks	iShares Russell 2000 Fund	IWM	13%	0.20%
Foreign Stocks	iShares MSCI EAFE Index Fund	ETF	24%	0.34%
Total U.S. Equity			56%	
Total Foreign Equity			24%	
Total Equity			80%	
Short-Term U.S. Bonds	Vanguard Short-Term Bond ETF	BSV	5%	0.11%
Long-Term U.S. Bonds	Vanguard Long-Term Bond ETF	BLV	3%	0.11%
Corporate Bonds	iShares Lehman Credit Bond Fund	CFT	2%	0.20%
Total Fixed-Income			10%	
U.S. Real Estate	Vanguard REIT ETF	VNQ	10%	0.12%
Total Alternative Investments			10%	
Average Expense Ratio				0.16%

- The SPDR Trust allocation climbs to 30 percent from 24 percent in the Moderate Portfolio.
- The Vanguard Mid-Cap ETF advances to 13 percent.
- The iShares Russell 2000 rises to 13 percent.
- The iShares MSCI EAFE Index jumps to 24 percent.
- The Vanguard REIT ETF slips to 10 percent from 11 percent.
- Meanwhile, among the bonds, the Vanguard Short-Term Bond ETF tumbles to 5 percent from 17 percent.
- The Vanguard Long-Term Bond ETF, drops to 3 percent from 7 percent.
- The iShares Lehman Credit Bond Fund sinks to 2 percent.

Foundation Portfolios

Another early adopter of the all-ETF portfolio, J. D. Steinhilber, contributed a series of model portfolios to this book. They are very straightforward, simple to understand, and easy to put together. Most investors can use these as a foundation for their own investments, or follow them exactly.

Previously an investment banker doing corporate finance at Nashville, Tennessee, regional bank J.C. Bradford & Co, Steinhilber started Agile Investments, his asset management firm, in 2001, following the popping of the Internet bubble. It was a bear market in full growl.

Building his business in the wake of the iShares launch, he decided he would never use single-company stocks for client portfolios, only ETFs. Once in a while, he adds a mutual fund to the ETFs. When he does, he chooses a fund that gives its portfolio manager wide latitude to add value to the fund.

The Nashville investment advisor likes the transparency of ETFs and believes their ability to track the market with broad indexes and low expense ratios is the best way to build a nest egg. But he doesn't call the firm Agile for nothing. Even though he uses passive vehicles, he employs an active management style called tactical asset allocation. That means the portfolios are fluid.

Depending on the economic backdrop and fundamentals at the asset class level, he re-evaluates different slices of the market, and tweaks the asset allocations to take advantage of the current market conditions. The strategy appears to work. The aggressive model portfolio he used from 2002 through 2007 saw an average annual return of 9.9 percent, in contrast with the S&P 500's 6.0 percent.

Steinhilber's belief in lower fees doesn't change when it comes to charging his own clients. He typically requires a client to have a minimum investment of $250,000 to invest with his firm. His fees start at a very reasonable 0.6 percent of assets for the minimum-sized portfolio, and decrease as the portfolios grow in size.

I asked him to design three fundamental strategies that a typical buy-and-hold investor could use as a foundation for a long-term portfolio. These models—conservative, moderate, and aggressive—are designed for an investor saving for retirement.

All three of these models are suitable for an average investor. All the ETFs are liquid. The average expense ratio is very low, with the two bond funds and the domestic REIT fund charging only 0.11 percent. The ETNs charge 0.75 percent or 0.85 percent, but they make up for it in tax efficiency. Which model you choose will be determined by your risk comfort level.

The buy-and-hold portfolios provided by Agile Investments are strategic asset allocations just like the classic portfolios, only these are more high concept. Instead of breaking up the stock portion into funds of different-sized companies, he buys a total market index, so that he can take advantage of ETFs that offer creative strategies.

While both the classic and foundation models are basically stock and bond portfolios, comparing the Agile portfolios with the portfolios in the previous section provides us with a great opportunity to see how two portfolios with similar risk tolerances and strategic asset allocations can be set up in completely different ways.

The Conservative Growth ETF Model

This model is good for investors with a low risk tolerance. They could be very wary of the stock market's direction or very concerned with protecting capital. Typically, people nearing or just entering retirement might like this model. Capital protection seems to be the overriding theme, but the equity components provide the potential to capture some outsized returns should stocks rally. (See Table 10.4.)

According to Steinhilber:

> *This portfolio is suitable for clients willing to assume a level of market risk and volatility typical of a traditional balanced investment portfolio. Although asset class weightings will vary based on our tactical asset allocation methodology, and alternative asset classes, such as real estate investment trusts or precious metals, may be employed, an appropriate benchmark for this portfolio is 60% equities and 40% fixed income.[3]*

The portfolio presented here breaks down into:

- Equities: 40 percent
- Fixed-Income: 45 percent
- Alternative Investments: 15 percent

TABLE 10.4   Agile Investments Conservative Growth ETF Model (40% Equity)

Asset Class	Fund	Symbol	Allocation	Expense Ratio
U.S. Stocks—Broad Market	Vanguard Total Stock Market ETF	VTI	15%	0.07%
U.S. Stocks—Dividend	iShares Dow Jones Select Dividend Index Fund	DVY	5%	0.40%
U.S. Stocks—Covered Call Writing	iPath CBOE S&P 500 Buy Write Index ETN	BWV	5%	0.75%
Foreign Stocks	Vanguard FTSE All-World ex-U.S. ETF	VEU	15%	0.25%
Total U.S. Equity			25%	
Total Foreign Equity			15%	
Total Equity			40%	
Short-Term U.S. Bonds	Vanguard Short-Term Bond ETF	BSV	25%	0.11%
Total U.S. Bond Market	Vanguard Total Bond Market ETF	BND	20%	0.11%
Total Fixed-Income			45%	
U.S. Real Estate	Vanguard REIT ETF	VNQ	3%	0.11%
International Real Estate	SPDR DJ Wilshire International Real Estate ETF	RWX	3%	0.59%
Energy MLPS	BearLinx Alerian MLP Select Index ETN	BSR	3%	0.85%
Diversified Commodities	Elements Linked to the Rogers International Commodity Index—Total Return ETN	RJI	3%	0.75%
Gold	streetTracks Gold Shares	GLD	3%	0.40%
Total Alternative Investments			15%	
Average Expense Ratio				0.34%

EQUITIES   The stock portion of the portfolio is broken into four ETFs, three domestic and one international.

Steinhilber starts with the Vanguard Total Stock Market ETF (symbol: VTI). This ETF tracks the performance of the MSCI U.S. Broad Market Index, which represents 99.5 percent of all the common stocks that trade on the U.S. stock market in terms of market capitalization.

The Vanguard Total Stock Market ETF makes up 15 percent of the portfolio. This ETF gives you almost the entire universe of U.S. stocks at the phenomenally low price of just 0.07 percent, or 70 cents for every $1,000 invested. This is definitely one of the cheapest ETFs on the market. Steinhilber likes it because of its low cost and very broad diversification. It has a high level of correlation to the S&P 500 Index, plus exposure to the small-cap and mid-cap markets.

He adds that you don't want to have too many moving pieces in a portfolio. All the slicing and dicing dilutes the impact of the individual components and gives a smaller premium when any single ETF advances.

In addition, Steinhilber likes that Vanguard uses a "full-replication strategy" to mimic the index rather than a "representative sampling" strategy. ETFs are designed to replicate the performance of the index they track.

Tracking error is the difference between the index's performance and the ETF's return. If the ETF holds the exact same securities, the tracking error should equal exactly the expense ratio, no more. But, the further away the ETF strays from the index holdings, the greater the tracking error.

For example, the Vanguard Total Stock Market ETF holds 3,607 stocks, while the MSCI U.S. Broad Market Index holds 3,807 stocks. It's a difference of 200 stocks, just a 5 percent differential. So the ETF captures 95 percent of the index. Compare that to the SPDR DJ Wilshire Total Market ETF (symbol: TMW) from State Street Global Advisors. It seeks to closely match the returns of the Dow Jones Wilshire 5000 Index. However, it holds only 1,012 stocks out of a possible 5,000, only 20 percent of the possible universe.

That can result in a sizeable difference in tracking error. For the 12 months ended Sept. 30, 2007, Vanguard Total Stock Market gained 14.97 percent in contrast to the MSCI U.S. Broad Market Index's return of 15.03 percent. Over the same period, the SPDR DJ Wilshire Total Market ETF rose 16.40 percent in contrast with the 16.97 percent gain in the DJ Wilshire 5000. So, the Vanguard Total Stock Market had a tracking error of 0.06 percentage points, also known as six basis points. That was one basis point less than the expense ratio. (One hundred basis points make up one percentage point.)

Meanwhile, the SPDR DJ Wilshire Total Market ETF had a tracking error of 57 basis points (0.57 percentage points), which was three times larger than its expense ratio of 20 basis points (0.2 percentage points), and 51 basis points, or more than half a percentage point, larger than the tracking error of the Vanguard Total Stock Market. If you hold only 20 percent of the index you track, it's very likely the other 80 percent is posting the best returns.

Granted the SPDR DJ Wilshire Total Market ETF had a better 12 months than the Vanguard ETF, by 1.43 percentage points. That's because the Wilshire 5000 had a better year than the MSCI index. But which index performed better isn't the issue here. The situation between these two indexes could easily reverse next year. The point is that, when you buy an ETF, you want to match the index you choose to follow as closely as possible. If it doesn't, it's taking money out of your pocket.

In the "full-replication strategy," the ETF holds all, or nearly all, the components in the index. This rewards the investor with minimal tracking error in contrast to ETFs holding fewer index components. And, just like transaction costs, tracking error is a drag on returns. The larger the error, the smaller the return.

Asked why he likes the Vanguard total market ETF over the SPDR total market ETF, Steinhilber says, "Vanguard has been doing this for a long time. They know how to run an index fund. So, I trust them and the expenses are the lowest. Why complicate things?"[4]

In fact, Vanguard's ETFs are not distinct funds from Vanguard's index funds. They are currently the only company in which the ETFs are a share class of the original mutual fund.

The next component to the domestic equity portion of Steinhilber's conservative growth ETF portfolio is the iShares Dow Jones Select Dividend ETF (symbol: DVY). This 5 percent holding is well suited for a conservative investor because dividend-paying stocks produce higher levels of current income than other stock investments and typically have lower volatility.

The last component of the portfolio's domestic equities portion is the iPath CBOE S&P 500 BuyWrite Index exchange-traded note (symbol: BWV) for 5 percent of the portfolio. The CBOE S&P 500 BuyWrite Index, commonly known as the BXM Index, measures the total rate of return of a hypothetical "buy-write," or "covered call," strategy on the S&P 500 Index. The index consists of a hypothetical portfolio that purchases all the common stocks in the S&P 500, then every month sells, at– or slightly out-of-the-money S&P 500 Index call options that are listed on the Chicago Board Options Exchange, or CBOE. The options offset the long portfolio, so that the majority of the index's return comes from the premium earned by writing the call options. It's called buy-write because you buy stocks and write call options against the stocks. This is a form of hedging where you give up some of the potential upside in the S&P 500 in exchange for the income generated from selling call options.

In a strongly rising market, the strategy underperforms the S&P 500 because it caps the upside potential by writing the covered calls. However, the index outperforms in a flat or down market, because the options premium that you're earning provides a positive return that may offset losses on the underlying index.

"Where the strategy pays dividends is in a flat market," says Steinhilber. "The security could earn 10 percent to 12 percent over the course of a year, when an investment in the S&P 500 would only earn the dividend yield on the index."[5]

Steinhilber says that over its 20-year history, the index has recorded a compounded annual return equal to the S&P 500, with about 60 percent of the volatility.

The final component of the equity portion is an ETF that tracks foreign stocks. It makes up 15 percent of this portfolio.

The Vanguard FTSE All-World ex-U.S. ETF (symbol: VEU) tracks the performance of the eponymous index. The index is a broad market benchmark of 47 countries, excluding the U.S. Developed markets comprise about 80 percent of the index, while emerging markets make up approximately 20 percent. The index holds approximately 2,200 stocks and the ETF holds about 2160 stocks.

FIXED INCOME The fixed-income section of the portfolio holds just two ETFs: The Vanguard Total Bond Market ETF (symbol: BND) makes up 20 percent of the portfolio and the Vanguard Short-Term Bond ETF (symbol: BSV) makes up 25 percent. The Total Bond Market ETF tracks the Lehman U.S. Aggregate Bond Index. This index measures a wide spectrum of public, investment-grade, taxable, fixed-income securities in the United States—including government, corporate, and international dollar-denominated bonds. It also holds mortgage-backed and asset-backed securities. All the securities have maturities of more than one year, and an average maturity between 5 and 10 years. The ETF invests at least 80 percent of its assets in bonds held in the index.

Vanguard Short-Term Bond ETF tracks the performance of the Lehman 1–5 Year U.S. Government/Credit Index. It is described earlier as part of the classic portfolios. The short-term bond ETF is a more conservative investment because it has less interest-rate risk and price volatility. The total market bond ETF gives a higher yield because it has a longer average maturity.

ALTERNATIVE INVESTMENTS The final 15 percent of the portfolio contains five investments that are neither stocks nor bonds. Each ETF makes up 3 percent of the total portfolio.

The Vanguard REIT ETF (symbol: VNQ) tracks the MSCI U.S. REIT Index, which covers about two-thirds of the value of the entire U.S. real-estate investment trust (REIT) market. It is described in detail in the previous section.

The SPDR DJ Wilshire International Real Estate ETF (symbol: RWX) tracks the Dow Jones Wilshire Ex-U.S. Real Estate Securities Index. This global equity index tracks real estate stocks from all over the world, except the United States.

"I think most asset allocators would agree that real estate is more of a separate asset class, rather than a sector of the economy," says Steinhilber.[6] The alternative section also holds BearStearn's exchange traded note, the BearLinx Alerian MLP Select Index ETN (symbol: BSR). This index tracks a very obscure asset class called master limited partnerships (MLPs). The ETN follows the Alerian MLP Select Index whose components are publicly listed energy MLPs engaging in the processing, production, storage or transportation of energy resources.

Steinhilber thinks of energy master limited partnerships as yield and infrastructure investments as opposed to commodity investments. He says the MLPs are not typically sensitive to the prices of commodities because they don't own the natural resources. The MLPs license their facilities, such as pipelines, to oil companies or whoever takes ownership of the commodities.

The MLPs have similar structures to the REITs, in that they pass through all dividends. Yet, they are less economically sensitive than real estate because energy is consumed every day, so demand is more consistent. With price appreciation and yield, this ETN is expected to produce double-digit annualized returns over time. The BearLinx ETN has many of the tax advantages of other ETNs, but it does give off an annual income distribution.

Last, but not least, are the commodities. The Elements Linked to the Rogers International Commodity Index Total Return ETN (symbol: RJI) tracks the broad commodities market, not any specific commodity. Jim Rogers founded the famous hedge fund, the Quantum Fund, with George Soros. He's also the author of *Hot Commodities*. His International Commodity Index has been a benchmark for the industry since 1998.

Late in 2007, a new consortium called Elements was founded to issue exchange-traded notes. The Swedish Export Credit Corporation and Merrill Lynch issued this ETN. This ETN doesn't hold commodities, but seeks to replicate the return of the index while producing greater tax efficiency than an ETF. For more information on ETNs, see Chapter 8.

"This is direct exposure to commodities," says Steinhilber. "The other commodity indexes are good, but I like this one because it tracks more commodities than the other ETFs. It has exposure to 36 different commodities, which is much more diversified than the others. And it gets the tax benefits unless the IRS changes its mind."[7]

The final piece of the puzzle is the streetTRACKS Gold Shares (symbol: GLD), which holds actual gold bullion. Its structure is fully explained in Chapter 8. Steinhilber likes the gold shares because gold is a hedge against inflation, which is very important in a climate when the dollar is falling in value. Pure gold also avoids the stock market risk inherent in the stocks of gold mining companies.

He says gold is a unique asset class and that this exchange-traded vehicle captures the benefits of owing the physical metal. However, it's a controversial investment: Gold is very volatile and can spend many years out of favor. He thinks gold will be a good investment for years to come and will increase in price, but he doesn't feel comfortable having it comprise as much as 10 percent of the portfolio. He doesn't hold more than 3 percent in the portfolio because it doesn't give off any income. He likes the streetTRACKS ETV over the comparable iShares product because it's the biggest and most liquid.

The Moderate Growth ETF Model

The Moderate Growth ETF Model and the Aggressive Growth ETF Model are variations on the theme. They both start with the Conservative Growth ETF Model then make a few adjustments to increase the profit potential by taking on more risk. The equity component makes up a greater proportion of the portfolio, while the total of fixed-income investments decreases. See Table 10.5.

Steinhilber describes the Moderate Growth ETF Model as "suitable for clients seeking potentially higher return opportunities and willing to assume a level of market risk and volatility somewhat higher than a traditional, balanced investment portfolio. Although alternative asset classes may be employed, an appropriate benchmark for this portfolio is 75 percent equities and 25 percent fixed income."[8]

The Moderate Growth ETF Model is the exact same basket of ETFs as the Conservative model, but the allocation of each ETF is different. In the Moderate Growth Model the total equity allocation jumps to 60 percent from 40 percent, while fixed-income's allocation drops to 25 percent from 45 percent. The proportion of Alternative Investments remains the same at 15 percent of the portfolio, with the same five ETFs each making up just 3 percent of the total portfolio.

In the equity portion of the moderate-risk model, the Vanguard Total Stock Market ETF allocation rises to 25 percent of the portfolio from 15 percent in the conservative portfolio. The iShares Dow Jones Select Dividend ETF and iPath CBOE S&P 500 BuyWrite Index ETN both remain at 5 percent, bringing the total domestic stock allocation to 35 percent. The Vanguard FTSE All-World ex-U.S. ETF remains the only international equity fund. It now comprises 25 percent of the portfolio, up from 15 percent.

In the fixed-income section, the Vanguard Total Bond Market ETF drops from 20 percent to 15 percent of the total model, while the Vanguard Short-Term Bond ETF takes an even bigger hit, falling to 10 percent from 25 percent.

TABLE 10.5   Agile Investments Moderate Growth ETF Model (60% Equity)

Asset Class	Fund	Symbol	Allocation	Expense Ratio
U.S. Stocks—Broad Market	Vanguard Total Stock Market ETF	VTI	25%	0.07%
U.S. Stocks—Dividend	iShares Dow Jones Select Dividend Index Fund	DVY	5%	0.40%
U.S. Stocks—Covered Call Writing	iPath CBOE S&P 500 Buy Write Index ETN	BWV	5%	0.75%
Foreign Stocks	Vanguard FTSE All-World ex-U.S. ETF	VEU	25%	0.25%
Total U.S. Equity			35%	
Total Foreign Equity			25%	
Total Equity			60%	
Short-Term U.S. Bonds	Vanguard Short-Term Bond ETF	BSV	10%	0.11%
Total U.S. Bond Market	Vanguard Total Bond Market ETF	BND	15%	0.11%
Total Fixed-Income			25%	
U.S. Real Estate	Vanguard REIT ETF	VNQ	3%	0.11%
International Real Estate	SPDR DJ Wilshire International Real Estate ETF	RWX	3%	0.59%
Energy MLPS	BearLinx Alerian MLP Select Index ETN	BSR	3%	0.85%
Diversified Commodities	Elements Linked to the Rogers International Commodity Index—Total Return ETN	RJI	3%	0.75%
Gold	streetTracks Gold Shares	GLD	3%	0.40%
Total Alternative Investments			15%	
Average Expense Ratio				0.34%

The Aggressive Growth ETF Model

The Aggressive Growth ETF Model takes on much more risk. Steinhilber describes the Aggressive Growth ETF Model as "suitable for clients willing to sustain substantial volatility and assume a high level of risk in pursuit of higher returns. Although alternative asset classes may be employed, an appropriate benchmark for this portfolio is 90 percent equities and 10 percent fixed income."[9]

In the aggressive model, the equity portion jumps to 73 percent of the total portfolio from 60 percent in the moderate portfolio, and just 40 percent in the conservative model. Bonds drop to just 7 percent of the total strategy. That's a huge decline from the moderate model's 25 percent and the 45 percent in the conservative one. Alternative investments jump to 20 percent from 15 percent (see Table 10.6).

Among the stocks funds, the Vanguard Total Stock Market ETF jumps to 35 percent from 25 percent in the moderate and 15 percent in the

TABLE 10.6 Agile Investments Aggressive Growth ETF Model (73% Equity)

Asset Class	Fund	Symbol	Allocation	Expense Ratio
U.S. Stocks—Broad Market	Vanguard Total Stock Market ETF	VTI	35%	0.07%
U.S. Stocks—Covered Call Writing	iPath CBOE S&P 500 Buy Write Index ETN	BWV	8%	0.75%
Foreign Stocks	Vanguard FTSE All-World ex-U.S.ETF	VEU	30%	0.25%
Total U.S. Equity			43%	
Total Foreign Equity			30%	
Total Equity			73%	
Total U.S. Bond Market	Vanguard Total Bond Market ETF	BND	7%	0.11%
Total Fixed-Income			7%	
U.S. Real Estate	Vanguard REIT ETF	VNQ	4%	0.11%
International Real Estate	SPDR DJ Wilshire International Real Estate ETF	RWX	4%	0.59%
Energy MLPS	BearLinx Alerian MLP Select Index ETN	BSR	4%	0.85%
Diversified Commodities	Elements Linked to the Rogers International Commodity Index—Total Return ETN	RJI	5%	0.75%
Gold	streetTracks Gold Shares	GLD	3%	0.40%
Total Alternative Investments			20%	
Average Expense Ratio				0.44%

conservative model. The iPath CBOE S&P 500 BuyWrite Index ETN increases to 8 percent from 5 percent in the other two models, and the iShares Dow Jones Select Dividend ETF disappears altogether from the portfolio. The Vanguard FTSE All-World ex-U.S. ETF gains another five percentage points to comprise 30 percent of the portfolio, up from 25 percent and 15 percent in the moderate and conservative models, respectively.

In the bond section, the Vanguard Short-Term Bond ETF is removed completely (it's considered too conservative), and the Vanguard Total Bond Market ETF now makes up the entire bond component. It sinks to just 7 percent of the portfolio from 15 percent and 20 percent in the two previous models.

Meanwhile, the amount of alternative investments increases. The Vanguard REIT ETF, the SPDR DJ Wilshire International Real Estate ETF, and the BearLinx Alerian MLP Select Index ETN all increase their allocations to 4 percent of the portfolio from 3 percent. The Elements Rogers International Commodity Index Total Return ETN jumps to 5 percent from 3 percent. However, the streetTRACKS Gold Shares remains at 3 percent for all three models.

Not Following the Herd

Contrarian investing is choosing to zig when the rest of the market says "zag"—or more precisely, trying to profit by doing the opposite of the market's conventional wisdom. Essentially, contrarian investing is defying the crowd.

One of the old sayings of Wall Street is that the market climbs a wall of worry. This means the best time to buy stocks is when people are fearful. When there is widespread optimism and most people believe the market will keep going higher, the contrarian investor says the securities are probably fairly priced or overpriced and now is the time to sell. On the other hand, when everyone decides to sell and market pessimism is at high levels, the contrarian finds that a perfect time to buy. Prices are low and if everyone has sold, they can't go much lower.

Value investing is a kind of contrarian investing because it looks for out-of-favor securities with low P/E ratios.

In this section are two portfolios that don't follow the herd. These are not the classic portfolios that consist predominantly of U.S. stocks and bonds. Both the Contrarian Fox and Active China Strategy are high-concept portfolios. They each take the idea that the broad U.S. stock market is not the best place to be invested. The Contrarian Fox picks a few under-the-radar sectors that it expects to outperform the U.S. market. The Active China Strategy essentially says China is where the best growth is, so why bother with the United States? Both of these portfolios are very risky, but they are presented to offer examples of the kinds of creative portfolios that ETFs make possible.

Contrarian Fox Portfolio

Ron DeLegge, the founder and editor of ETF Guide.com, a Web site focused on the ETF industry, offers sample portfolios to subscribers. DeLegge, a former portfolio manager, agreed to let me publish his contrarian portfolio to give people an idea of what such a portfolio might hold. DeLegge says the objective and strategy of the Contrarian ETF portfolio's is to "identify and select ETF asset classes that are out-of-favor or undervalued and which exhibit positive growth characteristics and a pending rebound."[10]

This is a snapshot of what the portfolio looked like in March 2008. At this time, the U.S. economy was said to be entering a recession. The U.S. stock market had already fallen 15 percent off its high. The bubble in the housing market had popped as the subprime mortgage crisis caused large amounts of homeowners to lose their homes in foreclosure. Across the country, the real estate market was falling in value. The financial sector, especially commercial and investment banks, suffered from the fall-out in the housing market. Many had taken on huge amounts of risk buying and selling mortgage-backed assets. By this time, many banks had written off losses in the billions of dollars. Meanwhile, the dollar continued its decline, sending the price of gold up 25 percent over the previous six months to $1,000 an ounce.

While a typical portfolio seeks to give an investor a broad overview of the stock market, this portfolio presents a different picture.

The Contrarian Fox model isn't a buy-and-hold portfolio. Instead, it is more of a tactical asset allocation model. The investor or portfolio manager buys and sells assets to take advantage of the changing market trends (see Table 10.7).

In buy-and-hold investing, you set your strategic asset allocation and stick with it, for the most part, in both up and down markets. The reason behind holding the same assets and allocation in a down market is that you never know when the market will rebound. You could be out of the market at the wrong time and miss a big move up. However, if you stay pat, you will catch the rebound.

The tactical asset allocation attempts to increase returns by taking advantage of changes in the market. These asset allocations can change often and it is not advisable to copy this portfolio exactly. However, it provides an example of how a portfolio can be structured in a declining stock market. For an up-to-date version of this portfolio, check out ETFguide.com.

TABLE 10.7   ETFGuide.com Contrarian Fox Portfolio (38% Equity)

Asset Class	Fund	Symbol	Allocation	Expense Ratio
U.S. Stocks—Healthcare Sector	iShares Dow Jones U.S. Healthcare Sector Index Fund	IYH	14%	0.48%
U.S. Stocks—Basic Industries Sector	Materials Select Sector SPDR ETF	XLB	9%	0.23%
U.S. Stocks—Financial Sector	Financial Select Sector SPDR ETF	XLF	5%	0.23%
Foreign Stocks	iShares MSCI Canada Index Fund	EWC	10%	0.59%
Total U.S. Equity			28%	
Total Foreign Equity			10%	
Total Equity			38%	
Inverse U.S. Stocks Sector	UltraShort Real Estate ProShares	SRS	8%	0.95%
Gold	streetTracks Gold Shares	GLD	16%	0.40%
Total Alternative Assets			24%	
Cash	Cash		38%	0%
Total Cash			38%	
Average Expense Ratio				0.48%

STRIKING DIFFERENCES   The first thing one notices when looking at this portfolio is the huge amount of cash. While cash can be a drag on a portfolio's performance, much like in a fund, it doesn't need to be in a down market. If the stock market is falling and cash earns interest of 3 percent to 5 percent that is a much better return than most stock ETFs in this environment. Also, having cash on hand makes it easy to take advantage of investing opportunities when they arise instead of having to sell off something in the portfolio. A large amount of cash in a down market means that when the investor thinks the time is right, he will be able to pounce quickly. I think this large allocation is not typical for the strategy.

The second unusual thing about this portfolio is that it holds no fixed-income ETFs. At the time of this snapshot, the U.S. Federal Reserve Bank had already cut interest rates over the previous seven months by 2.25 percentage points. One of the fundamental rules about bonds is that when interest rates, or the yield falls, the price of the bond rises. Since the Fed's target for short-term interest rates directly affects the yield on U.S. Treasury bonds, as the rate fell, the price of bonds climbed dramatically. The thinking behind holding no bond ETFs is the concern over whether there will be more rate cuts and, if so, how many? If not, then the price of bonds will probably not go much higher.

EQUITIES The iShares Dow Jones U.S. Healthcare Sector Index Fund (symbol: IYH) is the largest stock holding at 14 percent of the portfolio. It tracks the Dow Jones U.S. Health Care Index, which holds 141 stocks. About 64 percent of the index is comprised of pharmaceutical and biotechnology stocks, while 36 percent is in healthcare equipment and services. DeLegge liked this because health care is a good defensive move in a down market. That's because it's less of a discretionary purchase. Unlike buying cars or computers, when people get sick, they will spend money to get better, no matter how bad the economy. In a recession, the health care industry is one of the few places that makes money. In addition, of the nine S&P industry sectors, healthcare was an underperformer in 2007, says DeLegge, which means it's due for a rebound.

He fills out the portfolio with the Materials Select Sector SPDR (symbol: XLB) and the Financials Select Sector SPDR (symbol: XLF). The Select Sector SPDRs were created by dividing the S&P 500 into nine industry sectors indexes. Together the nine indexes represent the S&P 500 as a whole.

Any component change in the S&P 500 would also change in that specific industry index. At the time of publication, the Materials Select Sector SPDR was comprised of 28 companies in the basic materials industries: chemicals, construction materials, containers and packaging, metals and mining, and paper and forest products. DeLegge liked this ETF because it had been one of the best performing sectors of the S&P 500 in 2007. "If commodity prices remain firm, we think XLB will continue to perform well."[11]

That wasn't a true contrarian position, but buying the Financials Select Sector SPDR was. It represented 92 components in the very battered industries of financial services, such as investment banking, commercial banking, insurance, and investment management. DeLegge bought in after the index had fallen about 20 percent and he felt the valuations had begun to look good. Even though the financial sector continued to fall, he said, "Buying opportunities of this nature rarely come along and while others run and hide, we'll be opportunistic."[12] He used this time to add to his position.

ETF Guide offers six portfolios, including one called Strategic Balance, which is similar to the strategic asset allocations described earlier in the chapter. For example, for its international equity component, the Strategic Balance holds the Vanguard FTSE All World ex-U.S. ETF, the same as the Agile Investments models. However, the Contrarian Fox doesn't want exposure to the entire world. Because emerging markets may be peaking, it instead looks to one country, Canada. The iShares MSCI Canada Index

Fund (symbol: EWC) tracks the MSCI Canada Index, which holds 108 securities, most of which trade on the Toronto Stock Exchange. According to DeLegge, the Canadian economy is very dependent on natural resources, such as timber, mining, and oil/gas development. With the Canadian dollar strengthening against the U.S. dollar and a strong demand for commodities, this was one of DeLegge's favorite holdings.

ALTERNATIVE INVESTMENTS While the UltraShort Real Estate ProShare (symbol: SRS) tracks a sector of the stock market, I classify it as an alternative investment because it seeks to capture two times the inverse move of the sector. So, if the sector falls 1 percent, the ETF should rise 2 percent. This ETF shorts real-estate stocks. In light of the broad-based decline in the housing market, DeLegge decided that REITs, homebuilders, and banking stocks see a significant decline for the rest of the year.

In 2007, the Contrarian Fox model rose 17.3 percent, compared to the 3.5 percent return on its benchmark index. Since its inception in June 2005, the portfolio was up 44 percent.

The Active China Strategy

Wall Street is always searching for the next big thing. People speak in awe of the investors who, with either foresight or luck, bought into software giant Microsoft when it was a company of just ten people. These investors took a risk, bought early, held onto their shares, and became millionaires. For those with vision and a healthy appetite for risk, the potential rewards are endless.

Currently, China and India are considered the next big thing. Burton Malkiel is the author of *A Random Walk Down Wall Street* and the Chemical Bank Chairman's professor of economics at Princeton University. Recently he became the chairman of an investment committee to create a new portfolio called the Active China Strategy at Active Investment Advisors, a unit of Natixis Global Asset Management Advisors. This portfolio seeks to capture and profit from China's economic growth through an all-ETF portfolio.

"I'm an ETF supporter," says Malkiel. "I think there are real advantages to ETFs."[13]

According to Natixis, the main drivers for this economic growth are the urbanization and development of the middle and western regions of China. In May 2007, the World Bank pegged China's 2006 economic growth at 10.7 percent and forecast growth of 10.4 percent in 2007.[14] The Washington Post said that China's trade volumes were the third largest in the world.[15] In May 2007, the Organization for Economic Co-operation and Development predicted that if China continued with its double-digit trade growth, it would become the world's second-largest trader in 2007.[16]

However, there are plenty of challenges and risks to this investment scenario. Natixis lists an uneven distribution of income, an aging population, a weak banking system, corruption, political tensions with Taiwan and Japan, and environmental degradation. Investing in China is definitely a risky strategy. Coming from almost anyone else, this idea would make me leery. But Malkiel is a guru among the passive investing crowd. The idea behind it is that an investor can catch the fastest growing country in the world, a country with a growth potential similar to the United States in the 1950s. And the entire portfolio is built with ETFs.

The Active China Strategy invests 60 percent of the portfolio in ETFs, getting direct exposure to Chinese companies that trade on international markets, 30 percent in indirect exposure to China and 10 percent in the natural resources that China uses to grow its economy. There are two ways to directly invest in Chinese companies: The "A shares" and the "H shares" (see Table 10.8).

The A shares trade in Yuan, the Chinese currency, in a closed market on mainland China. Citizens of the People's Republic of China can't trade stock outside the mainland and few foreigners are allowed to buy in. Because Chinese investors have few options to grow their money, they've flooded the domestic market with cash, sending it soaring many times over.

The second way to invest in China, and the way most investors outside China participate, is to invest in H shares. These are securities of companies incorporated in mainland China, but which trade on the Hong Kong Stock Exchange in Hong Kong dollars.

While quite a few of these companies trade on both markets, their shares aren't fungible. That means the A shares can't be exchanged for an equal amount of H shares. Still, H shares have also rallied. However, since the Hong Kong market is open to anyone on the international market, it's only risen about half as much as the A shares. Red Chip shares are the securities of companies owned by the Chinese government, but which are incorporated in Hong Kong and trade in Hong Kong dollars.

The Active China Strategy offers direct exposure to Chinese companies that trade on international markets through three ETFs. This portfolio's single largest weighting, at 25 percent, is the iShares FTSE/Xinhua China 25 (symbol: FXI), which tracks the index of the same name. This index holds the largest 25 Chinese companies comprising H Shares and Red Chip Shares, ranked by total market capitalization. Index constituents are capped at 10 percent of the total index.

The remaining 35 percent of the Chinese direct investment is split equally at 17.5 percent between the PowerShares Golden Dragon Halter USX China Portfolio (symbol: PGJ) and the iShares MSCI Hong Kong (symbol: EWH).

TABLE 10.8   Natixis Global Associates Active China Strategy (90% Equity)

Asset Class	Fund	Symbol	Allocation	Expense Ratio
Chinese Stocks—large capitalization	iShares FTSE/Xinhua China 25	FXI	25%	0.74%
Chinese Stocks—Broad Market	iShares MSCI Hong Kong Index Fund	EWH	17.5%	0.52%
U.S. Stocks—Chinese ADRs	PowerShares Golden Dragon Halter USX China Portfolio	PGJ	17.5%	0.70%
Direct Equity Exposure to China			60%	
South Korean Stocks	iShares MSCI South Korea Index Fund	EWY	7%	0.68%
Japanese Stocks	iShares MSCI Japan Index Fund	EWJ	7%	0.52%
Taiwanese Stocks	iShares MSCI Taiwan Index Fund	EWT	5%	0.68%
Singapore Stocks	iShares MSCI Singapore Index Fund	EWS	5%	0.51%
Malaysian Stocks	iShares MSCI Malaysia Index Fund	EWM	3%	0.51%
Australian Stocks	iShares MSCI Australia Index Fund	EWA	3%	0.51%
Indirect Equity Exposure to China—Asia/Pacific Linked			30%	
Commodities—Broad Market	iPath GSCI Total Return Index ETN	GSP	7%	0.75%
Gold	streetTracks Gold Shares	GLD	3%	0.40%
Total China Linked Natural Resources			10%	
Average Expense Ratio				0.59%

The iShares MSCI Hong Kong ETF follows the MSCI Hong Kong Index. This is a basket of 55 stocks that trade in Hong Kong, which are considered representative of the Hong Kong market. Meanwhile, the PowerShares Golden Dragon seeks to replicate the Halter USX China Index. This index holds securities that trade on the U.S. exchanges, but which derive the majority of their revenues from the People's Republic of China. Most, but not all, of these are Chinese companies.

The portfolio also holds indirect exposure to China. It invests 30 percent of its holdings in country ETFs of its major trading partners, most of which have benefited enormously from China's growth. This also gives the investor a nice diversification throughout the Asia-Pacific economies, including some emerging markets.

iShares MSCI South Korea (symbol: EWY), which measures the performance of the South Korea equity market, and iShares MSCI Japan (symbol: EWJ), which tracks the performance of the Japanese equity market, each make up 7 percent of the portfolio, and about half of the indirect exposure. China is South Korea's largest export market.[17]

The iShares MSCI Taiwan (symbol: EWT) and the iShares MSCI Singapore (symbol: EWS) each comprise 5 percent of the total portfolio and a third of the indirect exposure. Finally, iShares MSCI Malaysia (symbol: EWM) and iShares MSCI Australia (symbol: EWA) are each 3 percent of the portfolio. All these ETFs follow the indexes of the same name, which MSCI uses to represent the stock markets in each individual country.

Then, because China has such a voracious appetite for raw materials, the final 10 percent of the portfolio consists of commodity ETVs. The iPath S&P Goldman Sachs Commodities Total Return Index ETN (symbol: GSP) receives 7 percent of the portfolio's cash, while the streetTracks Gold Shares (symbol: GLD) makes up the final 3 percent. (These ETFs were described in the Chapter 8.)

"That is an example of how you could put together a Chinese portfolio with ETFs," says Malkiel. "It's a way to get lower-risk exposure to China."[18]

Tax-Loss Harvesting

Tax-loss harvesting, also known as tax-loss selling, is the strategy of harvesting, or maximizing, capital losses to decrease the amount of annual net taxes paid, thus increasing the total return. It sounds odd that taking losses can increase a portfolio's returns. Yet, it's a proven strategy, though it can be a bit confusing.

If you hold an investment that has fallen in value, it remains a paper loss until you sell it. The idea behind tax-loss harvesting is that instead of just leaving paper losses on the table, you sell your fallen assets to realize a loss on the investment. By getting rid of losers now, you get out of a bad position and cut your future losses. In addition, you can use that loss to offset capital gains tax liabilities in another investment, thereby reducing your tax burden for the year. This is no small thing and can add up quickly, especially short-term capital gains. If this investment was held a short period of time, your capital gains taxes on any profits would be at your ordinary tax rate. If you're in the highest bracket, that can lop 35 percent off of your profits. A $10,000 profit becomes just $6,500 after taxes are paid. So, finding losses to offset your profits can save a lot of money. On top of that, you now can use the cash to buy investments with better prospects.

Many investors harvest their losses at the end of the year because then they have a better ideal of the gains they want to offset. But, many times they really don't want to be out that investment, be it a sector play, a country play, or a style play.

Obviously you bought this investment because you thought it had potential to increase in value. The danger with dumping your losers is that as soon as you sell they might begin to rise.

"Just jump back in and buy it back," you say. Well, it's not so easy. In the good old days you could sell the stock, then buy it back at another broker. This gave you a capital loss while leaving you in exactly the same place. That's called a "wash" because it leaves you no worse off, and potentially better off. If it doesn't sound fair, that's because it's not. In fact, it's illegal.

The Internal Revenue Service (IRS) now has the "30-day wash rule." This prevents the taxpayer from claiming the tax loss if they purchase the same investment either 30 days before or after the sale. So, as part of the harvesting strategy, instead of using the cash from the stock sale to buy the same investment, you buy something different, but similar enough that it should give similar performance. This way an investor should get the same pretax performance, but a small tax liability.

For instance, you own shares of Ford Motor Company. You decided to sell the Ford stock to realize the loss for tax purposes, but you still want to have an investment in the U.S. auto market. Because you don't know when the auto sector will rally, you don't want to risk it happening during the 30-day window you can't own Ford. So, you buy shares in something that you expect will have a similar performance, for instance, General Motors. This selling of one security, then buying a similar, but not identical, one is called a tax swap. You get to harvest the tax loss, while maintaining exposure to the auto sector.

This strategy can be easily applied to ETF portfolios, and actually works better than with single stocks. Kevin Maeda, the chief investment officer at Active Investment Advisors, does tax loss harvesting in his clients' accounts continuously. He offers the following strategy example for harvesting the losses, while not violating the IRS wash rule.

Buy something that is as similar as possible in order to get nearly the same exposure, but not the same index, even if it's a different ETF from another provider. Therefore, you can't sell the SPDR, which tracks the S&P 500, then buy the iShares S&P 500 Index Fund (symbol: IVV). You would end up owning the exact same stocks. Even though they are two different funds, they are identical.

On the other hand, if you sell the iShares S&P 500 Growth Index Fund (symbol: IVW) at a loss, you can buy another large-cap growth fund, such as the iShares Russell 1000 Growth Index Fund (symbol: IWF). In this case, they both track the same area of the market, large-cap growth companies, and probably have many of the same holdings. But, while the performance would be very similar, the index construction is not, and that's what matters.

This strategy can also be used to capture exposure given up by the sale of a mutual fund or individual stock. For example, if you own Microsoft or a technology mutual fund, at a depreciated price level, you can sell to capture the loss. But if you fear a rally in technology, you can purchase the Technology Select SPDR (symbol: XLK), an ETF that holds the 79 stocks that make up the technology component of the S&P 500. Microsoft makes up about 10 percent of the index. Any move by the Seattle software giant would be reflected in the Technology Select SPDR. At the end of the 30 days you could buy back Microsoft and sell the ETF to regain your full exposure.

The theory is fairly simple and something individual investors can do by themselves. However, it takes a lot of work to constantly watch the portfolio. There are many investment advisors who can do this kind of strategy. They are likely to examine every account on a daily basis looking for opportunities to harvest. However, this would be much more difficult for individual investors. Individual investors are more likely to do this annually or semi-annually at the end of the second and fourth quarters. It doesn't make sense for an individual to make small changes on a daily or weekly basis. The transaction costs alone can negate any potential profits. Most investors wait until the last three months of the year to harvest tax losses, and they do it as a part of their portfolio rebalancing.

Hiring an Investment Adviser

While you have the information to create your own portfolio, you may not feel comfortable doing it yourself. Many people do not have the time, skill, or inclination to take care of their financial matters.

The investment industry is built around the fact that most people would rather have someone else handle their finances. After coming home from their job, most people don't want to start pouring over financial reports, investment books, and websites comparing 12-month returns, risk levels, and the underlying holdings of potential investment vehicles. They want to relax and spend time with their friends or family. And if you're extremely wealthy or have complicated financial needs, running portfolios and minimizing taxes can be a full-time job. Unless your job is working in finance, you don't have the time to handle it.

John Bogle, the creator the first index mutual fund, points to the inherent conflict of interest the investment-management industry has with its clients. For the most part, investment managers make money when you buy and sell; this is known as a "Don't just stand there, do something" attitude. Bogle instead recommends, "Don't just do something, stand there."[19]

Still, a big reason for hiring a financial adviser is that you're just not comfortable making financial decisions. You might feel more comfortable leaving your money in the hands of an expert. Many people want advice from a professional, and advisers are professionals who give advice. People hire investment advisers because they want someone to talk with about ways to improve their portfolio. They like having someone they can bounce ideas off of, or with whom they can express their feelings about the market. They like working with someone who has a vested interest in listening to them. Your friends aren't likely to want to talk about your money, and do you want to take advice from someone who isn't involved with the market everyday? If you must hire a registered investment adviser, also known as an RIA, don't hire a stockbroker. There is a big difference between them. A stockbroker isn't a fiduciary. A fiduciary is like a trustee, someone who is legally obligated to look out for the investor's interests.

Stockbrokers are not fiduciaries. They're salespeople, and generally they are looking out for their best interests. A broker who is not a fiduciary isn't obligated to sell you the best investment for your needs. He's not even obligated to sell a good investment. Stockbrokers are not unlike car salesmen. They need to move product off the lot and are willing to sell you a car you don't want in order to make the sale and collect their commission.

If you decide to hire an adviser, don't pick just anyone. Financial advisors don't need to go to college or even get accreditation from a governing body, like the bar in the field of law. Anybody can hang a shingle outside their house and call him- or herself a financial adviser. So be wary. Do some investigative work to see if the SEC has reprimanded this adviser, or if this is a well-respected adviser constantly being quoted on CNBC or the financial press.

The best way to find an advisor is to get recommendations from friends and family. If that's not possible, make sure the adviser has some registered credentials. The top level of financial advisers is the Chartered Financial Analysts, the CFAs. Having the initials behind their name means they have taken courses and studied for a certain amount of time to become proficient in investments and advising people about them.

Next comes the Certified Financial Planner (CFP), a Registered Financial Consultant (RFC), the Chartered Financial Consultant (ChFC), and the Certified Fund Specialist (CFS). Each demarcation represents a certain amount of education and experience.

While you will have to pay for the advice, you should make sure he's not charging a commission for every transaction. Instead, you want an adviser who charges an annual fee to manage your portfolio. You should never, never, never pay more than 1 percent for an adviser's services. If he charges more, you should ask a lot of questions and make the adviser justify taking such a high fee. More often than not, you will walk out of his door never to return.

J. D. Steinhilber of Agile Investments says it's very hard for investors to constantly watch their portfolios and adjust them to changing conditions. Clearly, asset classes move around a lot and each one experiences periods of being overbought and oversold. If there is a bear market, the adviser can help restructure and rebalance the portfolio to take into account the volatile nature of the economy and the bear market.

It takes time to manage a portfolio as well as emotional and psychological discipline. Investors typically are overconfident in their own ability during bull markets and then panic, usually at the wrong time, in bear markets. Usually, they buy a lot at the top of the market and sell just as the market hits the bottom. Advisers hold investors' hands and steer them toward a more balanced course of action. In addition, advisers can maximize the harvesting of tax losses, while individuals may do it at a certain point of the calendar, which may not be the most opportune time for cashing out.

In particular, managing an ETF portfolio can be confusing. The industry is fluid, and so many new, innovative products are hitting the market that it can be difficult to gauge what products would be beneficial to your portfolio.

Summary

In conclusion, ETFs rock.

I'd like to think that I've proved to you that ETFs are one of the best investment vehicles, if not the best, for the individual investor.

They are, by far, the cheapest way to design a diversified portfolio. They offer the most diverse selection for asset allocation and are also one of the easiest investment vehicles to buy or sell. With the exception of a few index mutual funds, there is really nothing better out there.

There is no way I would suggest that this book is the end-all and be-all for investing in ETFs. There are other books that delve deeper into the mechanics of how ETFs work and portfolio construction. If you want to day trade or create a more exotic portfolio, I would suggest you do more research. However, if you want to create a buy-and-hold portfolio of the major asset groups, then this book should suffice.

The basic challenge for the individual investor is to achieve a broadly diversified portfolio for the least amount of money. Because past returns are no guarantee of future profits, investors can never know if their investment will return a profit or loss. However, the costs to own an investment can be easily determined. Thus, when individuals investigate investment products, they should focus on what they can control: costs, not returns.

For the individual investor creating his or her own portfolio, this book should provide a clear understanding of what ETFs are, how they came about, how they work and how they are a valuable, low-cost alternative for creating a diversified portfolio.

This summary presents the short version of why ETFs are the best investment vehicle for individual investors.

Creating a portfolio from individual stocks and bonds requires a lot of capital and incurs a sizeable amount of transaction costs. If you follow the premise that high fees are the bane of individual investor, then investment companies and fund-like structures are the best investing vehicles for the individual because they offer investors the ability to acquire a diversified portfolio for a small minimum investment with few transaction costs.

If you agree that investment companies are the best way to gain exposure to the stock and bond markets, then one needs to decide if he or she prefers passive management or active management. Passive management in the form of indexing creates a portfolio that changes little over time. Because of this, the costs of running the fund are small. Active managers have the freedom to buy and sell as often as they wish, creating the potential for high fees and many transaction costs. While active management offers investors the potential to beat the market, the odds are 3 to 1 against investors achieving market-beating returns. High fees and transaction costs typically prevent the active fund from even matching its benchmark. If you don't like those odds, and prefer the guarantee that you will earn the market's return minus a small management fee, then indexing is the style for you. ETFs are basically index funds that have the flexibility of being bought and sold during the trading day.

Index mutual funds and ETFs are both fine alternatives for individual investors. However, in most cases ETFs are the low cost alternative. They are also more transparent. Transparency is a benefit because it allows an investor to create strategic asset allocations with a precision not available with mutual funds. However, if one is investing a small amount of money each month in a dollar-cost averaging strategy, then index mutual funds may be the better choice because of the ETFs transaction costs.

ETFs are also a better vehicle because they offer investors the ability to make profits in both an up and down market. While there are a few mutual funds that make money in bear market, there are many ETFs that follow this strategy, Those ETFs that don't, can be shorted, which is impossible with mutual funds.

In addition, ETFs offer investors the ability to invest in a much wider range of asset classes, such as commodities and currencies, than mutual funds.

All those concepts have been discussed and led to this chapter, which provides you with the tools to create your own ETF portfolio. By now, you should be able to determine your risk tolerance and what kind of investments you would like to hold. The models presented offer concrete examples of the asset allocations needed to create conservative, moderate, and aggressive portfolios.

Even if you decide that you prefer to hire a registered investment adviser to build a portfolio for you, this book should give you the knowledge to fully understand the kind of products your adviser is recommending, their benefits, and their costs. With this knowledge, you will be well prepared to determine if these recommendations are the best products for your investing needs.

CHAPTER 11

The Future of ETFs

Compared to the mutual fund industry, the ETF industry's growth has been phenomenal. After only 14 years, there were 629 ETFs with $608.4 billion in assets under management. Including all exchange-traded products, the total was 657. If you consider the 1940 Act to be the start of the modern mutual fund industry, it took 44 years before there were that many mutual funds, and 46 years to accumulate the same amount of assets.

Comparatively, it took closed-end funds, which have been around the same amount of time, 66 years to reach that number. At the end of 2007, there were 668 closed-end funds, nearly the same as total ETPs, but with only half the assets.

After seeing ETFs eclipse the closed-end fund industry in assets, the broader mutual fund industry is finally waking up to the competitor in its house, with many investors now wondering "What is their ETF strategy?" The mutual fund industry likes to say ETFs aren't cannibalizing their cash inflows, but it's hard to imagine that if ETFs didn't exist all that money wouldn't end up in mutual funds. As more investors become aware of the ETFs and their benefits, it's hard to view this being anything but a negative trend for mutual funds.

With this rate of growth, it's easy to envision 1,000 exchange-traded products and $1 trillion in assets by the end of 2008. However, there are some headwinds hitting the ETFs that may cause the industry's growth to slow. Some of them are a function of the broader economy and a falling stock market, while some are unique to the industry.

While predicting the future is always a fool's game, some significant developments already underway have the potential to significantly change the marketplace:

- The NYSE-Amex merger
- Specialists and seed capital
- Actively-managed ETFs
- 401(k) plans.

The NYSE-Amex Merger

In the end it was all for naught.

After more than two hundred years of co-existence, on Jan. 17, 2008, the trailblazing American Stock Exchange succumbed to market pressures. NYSE Euronext, owner of the New York Stock Exchange, agreed to buy its smaller rival for $260 million, plus the proceeds from selling the Amex's headquarters in Lower Manhattan.

While the Amex remained the leader in ETF listings till the end, a confluence of factors combined to doom the exchange, starting even before the NASD sold the Amex back to its members in 2004.

In late 2003, a scandal erupted over the Amex's failure to supervise its options traders. Three years earlier, the Amex had received an enforcement order from the Securities and Exchange Commission requiring it to improve its regulation oversight. In the 2003 report, the SEC said the violations continued "to go undetected, unreviewed and unsanctioned."[1] The report found the Amex failed to police the specialists on its trading floor and ensure that they honor the quotes they posted. Not only that, but it tried to cover it up afterward, in what the SEC called a "deliberate attempt to conceal serious deficiencies."[2] This came on the heels of similar allegations on the NYSE.

During this time, the Amex's market share in the options market fell from 28.6 percent in 2000 to 20.6 percent in 2003.[3] Amex Chairman and Chief Executive Salvatore Sodano was forced to resign.

Weakened by the body blow to its reputation, the Amex was also dogged by technology problems—it didn't have the capability to perform the faster and cheaper executions of its electronic competitors. Suddenly, the Amex began to face serious competition for ETF listings from the New York Stock Exchange.

While the NYSE had launched its first ETF in 1996 with the Country-Baskets (dubbed CountryCaskets), that was a bust. It didn't launch another one until 2000, and even then that was mostly symbolic. In 2001, the NYSE began trading ETFs listed on the Amex through unlisted trading privileges. Still, it pretty much ignored ETFs until 2004 when it made a concerted effort to get new listings. In 2005, the Amex received another blow. Barclays Global Investors decided to move 81 of its ETF listings—all but one of the iShares and almost half the ETFs listed on the Amex—to the Big Board and the electronic Archipelago Exchange, which would soon merge.

"The NYSE had a hard time getting its hands around the ETF business in the beginning," said Lisa Dallmer, NYSE senior vice president of ETFs and indexes. "By 2005 it had gone beyond being an experimental idea and the NYSE recognized there was a cottage industry evolving that was in our business space of listings and trading products. It became apparent what the growth of the industry was going to be like and we wanted to be a part of it and help drive it."[4]

After the NYSE bought Archipelago and renamed it the NYSE Arca, the Big Board offered ETFs a hybrid trading system of both specialists on the trading floor and a faster electronic exchange, similar to the NASDAQ. That and the ability to trade with the most recognized brand in the financial world made it a formidable competitor.

Even so, the Amex had a big selling point. It provided a higher level of attention, service and support to ETF issuers. For new issuers, the Amex provided expertise in structural issues from inception to the launch date. This helped it garner the majority of new ETF listings from 2005 to 2007. At the time of the deal, the Amex listed 381 ETFs, while the NYSE Arca listed 240. But the new listings weren't enough to save the Amex. By the end of 2007, the Amex traded less than 5 percent of the shares it listed, while the NYSE and NASDAQ traded the rest.[5]

At the end of 2003, Amex reported a net loss of \$7.3 million.[6] That grew to a pre-tax net loss of approximately \$36 million by the end of 2007, despite operating revenues of \$178 million.[7] Even though the ETF proved incredibly successful, it just couldn't keep the innovative Amex alive.

Combining the Amex's stock options business with its own made the NYSE the third largest options marketplace in the United States. And the hundreds of small companies that still traded on the Amex would move to the NYSE trading floor. But, in the end, Nate Most's invention proved to be the Amex's most valuable asset. Probably the biggest reason for the deal was that the NYSE would now control about 95 percent of all ETF listings.

What does the NYSE-Amex merger mean for ETFs? With the two dominant players in the market combining into one powerhouse, there will be fewer options for new ETFs, which may make it tougher for smaller firms or unusual funds to get a listing. The NYSE isn't likely to give the same kind of attention to new ETF issuers that the Amex did, and this could be also be a problem for new players wanting to enter the industry. But possibly the biggest issue is with the specialists. All the Amex ETFs are expected to move to the electronic NYSE Arca exchange, which could prove to be a hurdle for the less liquid issues and small companies trying to bring new funds to market.

Specialists and Seed Capital

Even before the merger, the specialists, the elite floor traders on the both the New York and American stock exchanges, had seen their business decline sharply. Much like the Amex, the specialists suffered from a combination of factors that worked against their way of doing business. Some of these pressures came from outside participants in the financial industry, some were the specialists' own fault. The decline of the specialists has significant implications for ETFs, from raising the initial start-up funds to maintaining liquidity and small spreads.

In the stock market, the specialists are responsible for maintaining liquidity. They conduct the traditional open-outcry stock-trading system on the NYSE, the Amex, and other floor exchanges. Each specialist firm holds a book that contains the stocks in which it's responsible for making a market. As floor brokers and traders shout out bids and ask for a particular stock, the specialist verbally negotiates the auction until a price is agreed upon. This is called price discovery. If no one takes the trade, the specialist is obligated to use his own capital to make the deal.

When a company first goes public on the stock market it holds an initial public offering (IPO). It issues a fixed amount of shares to the stock market through a syndicate of investment banks. Before the IPO, the investment banks line up enough buyers to sell off the shares quickly.

Unlike a corporation, ETFs don't issue stock to the market. To have ETF shares on the first day of trading, typically 100,000, a specialist firm must put up its own capital. It buys the underlying stocks necessary to trade for the creation unit. These start-up funds are known as seed capital because they buy the shares that seed the fund, its first assets under management.

The specialist firm takes on more risk than an investment bank in an IPO, because the specialist doesn't line up buyers ahead of time. It assumes the risk for the ETF. If the ETF shares don't sell, the specialist is left holding them. As mentioned earlier, in return for providing the seed capital, the specialist received a monopoly for selling the ETF shares. The guaranteed order flow was the financial incentive for taking the risk. Because it didn't have to compete for trades, the specialist firm was willing to provide support for the fledgling fund. This support was a major reason ETF sponsors preferred to list on the Amex.

Business under Attack

The first driver of the specialist's decline was price. In 2001, the U.S. stock exchanges lowered the minimum stock quote from a sixteenth of a dollar, 6.25 cents, to a penny. This severely cut into the specialists' profits.

The next nail in the coffin was scandal. Like the options traders on the Amex, the specialist firms on the NYSE were accused of cheating investors out of millions of dollars on stock trades. Between 1999 and 2003, the "floor-trading firms routinely placed their own trades ahead of those by customers. The specialists withheld pricing information from the public or traded for their own accounts before filling public orders."[8] Charged with violating U.S. securities laws and exchange rules, the seven specialist firms paid a combined $247 million in fines and disgorgement penalties. Similar problems occurred with the specialists on other exchanges, including the Amex. The SEC eliminated the specialists' monopoly with the 2005 passage of the Regulation National Market System, or Reg NMS.

The third big pressure was the speed in executing a trade. Even before the scandal, institutional investors had complained about execution speed. They wanted the NYSE and the Amex to move to an electronic exchange like the NASDAQ, where trades took place in less than a second, instead of the 15-second average seen on the exchange floor. But after the scandal, the specialists were thought to have been taking advantage of the trade.

The Amex took a long time to acquire electronic trading technology, which even then failed to prove satisfactory. The NYSE solved the issue by buying the electronic Archipelago Exchange in 2006. Within the next two years, the specialists' ranks dropped by more than 30 percent.

The Dearth of Seed Capital

At the same time the specialist industry was shrinking, a plethora of ETFs began coming to the market. With fewer specialist firms to provide it, but more ETFs needing it, seed capital began to dry up. Many of the new issues were niche ETFs with a limited demand. So, on top of fewer specialist firms, the ones that remain are less willing to fund start-ups they believe unlikely to attract significant assets. This has caused a dramatic decline in the amount of seed capital a new ETF can expect to attract.

In 1999, NASDAQ attracted start-up funds of $150 million for the Qubes' launch (symbol: QQQQ). By the middle of 2007, seed capital allocations had fallen to between $3 million and $10 million.

Increasing difficulty in raising seed capital could sharply curtail the industry's growth rate. The large providers, such as Vanguard, State Street Global Advisors, and iShares, have little to worry about. They can fund their own ETFs. However, smaller ETF sponsors may have to come up with their own seed capital, which may prove difficult. Sponsors will be less willing to create interesting concept ETFs, like the PowerShares FTSE RAFI International Real Estate Portfolio (symbol: PRY), which creates an international real-estate portfolio based on the FTSE RAFI; the Claymore Clear Global Timber Index ETF (symbol: CUT), which tracks the global timber industry, or the MarketVectors Nuclear Energy ETF (symbol: NLR), which tracks the global nuclear and uranium industries.

While this will have the positive effect of forcing sponsors to create ETFs for which there is a demand, it will also curtail some of the innovation that has created very useful ETPs for investors.

Evaporating Liquidity

In addition to providing seed capital, specialists keep ETF share prices in line with the value of their underlying holdings, partly through the arbitrage process. When the ETF share price rises above the actual value of its index, the specialist buys the constituent stocks to create new shares, which it sells at a profit. If the stocks are worth more, the specialist redeems ETF shares to trade for the underlying stocks. This keeps the ETF shares liquid and the spreads tight.

As ETFs move their listings to the electronic markets, specialists will be less willing to make a market in smaller ETFs. These ETFs with sporadic demand could see their bid-ask spreads widen dramatically. As ETF prices become illiquid and move significantly out of line with their underlying portfolio, investors may find it difficult to sell shares when they need to. These ETFs may end up looking like closed-end funds, which trade at a large premium or discount to the net asset value. Already, this problem has been seen in the MacroShares products.

Jim Wiandt, publisher of IndexUniverse.com and editor of the Exchange-Traded Funds Report, encapsulated the issues in the wake of the NYSE-Amex deal:

> *The argument goes that with ETFs, because price discovery has already happened with the underlying, there's no better area to go fully electronic. And in theory this is true. In practice, however, the move toward electronic trading has not always been so smooth (see the NASDAQ-listed BLDRs when they came out). As with the BLDRs, my sense is that generally market forces have worked out and will continue working out the kinks in electronic trading. And overall, the more open markets are, the better that is for the end user. Look at how spreads have come down in the ETF industry. It's amazing. And that's largely attributable to the move toward electronic trading.*
>
> *Where I do have concerns, and the area the ETF industry has always downplayed is what happens in the most lightly traded ETFs. The line has always been that it's ALL about the underlying in terms of liquidity. And that's absolutely true if you're an investor of (say, creation-level) size. But if you're trading a couple hundred shares, if there's no one at the switch, you could get a market fill that's well off the NAV. Essentially, the financial incentive is just not there for larger players to competitively arbitrage at smaller size. I don't want to blow that issue up into something larger than it is, but it is an issue, and you see it in European electronic markets as well as in the U.S. This is an issue that is worth some study by us as things move forward. The first question will be whether all the Amex ETFs move to Arca, or whether some semblance of a specialist system stays in place."*[9]

While there have been problems and complaints about the specialist system, it has served ETFs very well. I think the NYSE-Amex merger, and transfer of all the ETFs to the NYSE Arca, will only hasten the decline of the specialist industry. This will have significant implications on the ETF industry by exacerbating the problems with seed capital and liquidity. This in turn could lead to small firms failing and the industry becoming more concentrated.

"The way the specialists operate in the ETF space is changing and will continue to change," says Arlene Reyes, chief operating officer of Exchange TradedFunds.com, a Web site that tracks the industry. "It will get harder for the small issuers to get seed money. They will have to become more imaginative and you are going to see issuers take a harder look at what they are issuing."[10]

Actively Managed ETFs

For the first 15 years, all the ETFs available in the U.S. were index funds of some sort. Even the "active" index funds, with their monthly rebalancings, were still index funds that needed to follow a rules-based formula.

However, a growing contingent of ETF providers have filed to produce actively managed ETFs. These funds would have the freedom to buy and sell what they want when they want. The claim has been made that by making ETFs active, they will be better able to compete for assets with mutual funds.

"Since 2002, ETF providers have struggled to come up with a formula that would pass muster with the SEC."[11] The process picked up steam in 2007 when regulators informally indicated to industry insiders a greater willingness to entertain the idea of an active ETF.

The idea of the actively traded ETF is anathema to the purity of the passively managed ETF. Going active removes some of the major benefits that come from following an indexing strategy. Active ETFs will cost more than passive ETFs for the same reasons active mutual funds cost more than index funds: higher research costs and managers trading more, leading to higher transaction costs and higher management fees. In addition, greater portfolio turnover will create more capital gains within ETFs, losing some tax efficiency. The funds also lose their transparency.

If the basic goal of the investor is to focus on what he can control, profit-eating costs, then the active ETFs pretty much go against nearly everything that make ETFs wonderful investment vehicles.

"Ron DeLegge, editor and publisher of *ETFGuide*, a Web site focusing on ETFs, said actively managed ETFs could trade out of line with their net asset values, much like closed-end funds. He questioned whether the firms planning these products have investors' best interests at heart. 'Who needs actively managed ETFs more—managers trying to distribute their actively-managed solutions or foolish investors who don't even know what an ETF is?"[12]

Obviously, the managers need them more. However, actively managed ETFs may be necessary for the industry to grow. After reading this book, you understand why passive investing beats active management. But, for ETF sponsors, there are only so many indexes that can draw a sizeable amount of assets. More than 30 years after the first index mutual funds, and ten years after their most phenomenal performance, only $1.5 trillion, or 12.5 percent, of all the mutual fund industry's assets are invested in index funds, according to Lipper. People like actively managed funds.

There are thousands of indexes, one for almost every tiny niche of the market, but many of them wouldn't draw many assets. Unlike mutual funds, in which many fund companies can track the same index, the first mover advantage precludes many ETFs from tracking the same index. Because of this, there will probably come a moment of index fatigue. The number of viable index ETFs will peak.

In 2007, a lot of narrowly focused, niche ETFs hit the market. However, many of them failed to generate a lot of assets quickly. In a hot market, investors are more willing to invest in interesting, offbeat ideas. But in a bear market they grow more conservative. New index ETFs will be launched, but won't be able to draw enough assets to make money. Unable to attract enough cash, they will slowly wither and die. Some people predict the market could see a long-overdue shakeout. This phenomenon has already claimed its first victims. In February 2008, Claymore Securities closed 11 ETFs that failed to garner enough assets to stay afloat. The 11 funds together equaled less than 2 percent of the firm's U.S. assets.

In addition, as more products compete for investor attention—and a limited pool of seed capital—while the existing ETFs continue to grow assets, the number of new index ETFs will potentially slow down to a crawl. For the industry to keep growing, it will need to launch active ETFs; but that doesn't mean you have to buy them.

The American Stock Exchange was a big proponent of the actively managed ETF. In an effort to be the first exchange to list them, the Amex worked intimately with ETF sponsors in devising systems to make trading easier. "It had received three patents for processes to trade actively managed ETFs without disclosing the portfolios and had five more patents pending."[13] Some suggested that the Amex thought that this could help it return to profitability. And while never mentioned when the NYSE offered to buy the Amex, it's highly likely that the patents were a major factor in the NYSE's decision.

The actively managed ETF will most certainly charge a higher expense ratio than a passive ETF. ETF sponsors will say you can't compare active ETFs to passive ETFs, but rather you should compare them to active mutual funds. The sponsors will then say active ETFs will be cheaper than active mutual funds. But, there's no reason you can't compare the costs to passive ETFs and see how much they will erode returns.

Transparency is also a incentive to buy ETFs. The transparency is necessary for the publishing of daily holdings, so that AP's can create and redeem shares. But will actively managed ETFs have to reveal their holdings? Most active mutual fund managers hate to let people know what they are buying and selling. They fear others will copy their strategies or get ahead of their trades, pushing the price higher. Some advocates for the active ETFs say transparency isn't an advantage, because it lets other investors know what you plan to buy and gives them the opportunity to front-run your trade. Front-running occurs when a trader who knows what you want to buy, buys the same shares before you, and then sells to you at a higher price.

Active funds might also be a product in search of a market. Whereas the original ETFs weren't *sold* so much as *bought* by interested investors, any sponsor of active ETFs will need a sizeable sales force to acquire shareholders and assets. New products charging higher fees and returning smaller profits will be a hard sell in a declining stock market.

"Jerry Moskowitz, president of indexing company FTSE Americas, said the big push for actively managed ETFs 'shows the industry is worried about running out of product ideas.' "[14]

"David Blitzer, chairman of the index committee at Standard & Poor's, has a similar view. 'I think about active ETFs the same way I think about active mutual funds: Index funds perform better.' Blitzer says he has no sympathy for potential issuers concerned about front running. 'We announce the changes to the S&P 500 three to five days ahead... and active mutual fund managers still can't beat us.' "[15]

Entering the 401(k) Market

Ironically, for all their similarities to mutual funds, ETFs haven't been able to conquer the lucrative 401(k) retirement plans. By garnering trillions of dollars on a regular basis, these tax-free defined contribution plans have been instrumental to the mutual fund industry's growth over the past 20 years.

ETFs have barely cracked this market for a variety of reasons, the biggest being competition. Mutual fund companies run some of the largest 401(k) plans and they haven't felt the need to offer ETFs, nor seen demand from their investors to include these low-cost products in their plans. The mutual funds' rebuttal is that they offer low-cost index funds and that 401(k) plans already offer a tax advantage.

"Fidelity Employer Services Company, a unit of mutual fund giant Fidelity Investments, is the leading provider of defined contribution plans, with 23 percent of the market. Still, 'with regard to ETFs in 401(k) plans, thus far, there has been virtually no demand for ETFs from our plan sponsor clients,' said Fidelity spokeswoman Jennifer Engle."[16]

Named after section 401(k) of the Revenue Act of 1978, the law allows employers to create retirement plans in which employees can contribute a pre-tax portion of their salary. Because employees contribute the funds, these are called defined contribution plans, as opposed to pensions, which are classified as defined benefit plans. As traditional pension plans disappear, defined-contribution plans have became the primary retirement-savings vehicle for most Americans.

The tax benefits of defined contribution plans are huge. Taking the money out before taxes lowers the individual's current income-tax bill. Then taxes on the pre-tax contributions, as well as subsequent earnings, are deferred until withdrawal. If the money is withdrawn during retirement, then most likely the individual saves by paying an income tax rate lower than what he paid while earning a salary. Employers can also help by adding pre-tax dollars that match employee contributions. The first half of 2007 ended with $4.4 trillion in all employee defined contribution plans, and $3.0 trillion of that held in 401(k) plans, according to the Investment Company Institute (ICI). Mutual funds managed $2.3 trillion, or 53 percent, of the total in all defined contribution plans. This amount represents 19 percent of the total mutual fund industry. Comparatively, these retirement plans held only $385 billion in assets in 1990, with just $35 billion, or 9 percent, held in mutual funds.

Meanwhile, the ICI doesn't even keep track of the amount of ETF assets in 401(k) plans because the number is so small.

Currently, the ETF industry is salivating over the growth potential from capturing just a fraction of that total. And 401(k) plans are the gift that keeps on giving: Employees make a contribution every pay period.

However, it's not only the mutual-fund–run 401(k) plans standing in the ETF's way. Two fundamental differences in the process of selling ETFs are bumping up against technological limitations: brokerage commissions and fractional shares.

Employees contribute a fixed amount of dollars to their 401(k) on a regular basis, typically a percentage of their salary. Because a mutual fund's NAV constantly changes, investing the same dollar amount will often result in the employee buying some fractional shares. However, ETFs can only be sold in whole numbers of shares, with no fractions. On top of that, mutual funds in 401(k) plans never charge a load; however, the purchase of ETFs always incurs a brokerage commission. Charging commissions in a 401(k) plan is problematic, not to mention that it eats into returns. These two features have been major stumbling blocks.

Initial attempts to offer ETFs in 401(k)s employed a bulky structure called a collective trust. The trust allows investors to buy fractional shares by pooling the plan's assets, like a mutual fund. But in the process, it negates two reasons for investing in ETFs: transparency and low cost. The collective trust is opaque. Plan participants can't view the holdings, nor can they determine the price paid for the shares. And on top of the ETF expense ratios, the trust adds another layer of fees to the retirement plan's expenses.

There have been a few significant attempts to move ETFs into 401(k) plans, but they've met with mixed results. Invest N Retire, a Portland, Oregon, company has been offering ETFs in 401(k) plans since 2004. In 2007, BGI's iShares teamed up with a 401(k) record-keeping firm named BenefitStreet. However, internal problems at BenefitStreet severely diminished that effort. Later that year, WisdomTree launched its own proprietary 401(k) platform featuring its family of fundamentally-weighted ETFs. "WisdomTree said it tackled the trading issue by eliminating the trading commissions through an omnibus account that allows for pricing at the close of the day, like a mutual fund."[17] While aiming the plans at small- and medium-sized firms, WisdomTree has found limited success.

The most likely way that ETFs will gain a foothold in the 401(k) market is through target-date funds. Typically target-date funds are funds of funds. The investments they hold are other mutual funds or ETFs. The target-date fund category, also known as lifecycle funds, is one of the fastest-growing segments of the retirement market. They provide one-stop shopping by blending stock funds and bond funds into a complete portfolio held in just one mutual fund.

Target-date funds have a year in their name, for example, 2030, indicating the year the investor plans to retire. Far away from the target date, the fund is aggressive with a large allocation of stocks. But with each succeeding year, it gets progressively conservative by selling some stock fund shares and buying more bond fund shares.

Mutual fund firms Federated Investors and J. & W. Seligman have both created target-date funds with ETFs as the underlying investments. However, these add a significant layer of fees that essentially removes the low-cost benefit. ETF firm Xshares, together with discount broker TD Ameritrade, in October 2007 launched target-date ETFs under the brand name TD Independence Funds. These ETFs don't hold other ETFs, but rather the actual stocks and bonds. However, these are not currently offered in any 401(k) plans.

"We expect to see in the near future the same proliferation of ETFs in the 401(k) market as we've seen in taxable accounts," said Lance Berg, principal, Barclays Global Investors. "Mostly due to increasing appetites for fee transparency given sponsors' fiduciary concerns and lower costs as compared to retail mutual funds."[18]

In Conclusion

No one doubts the ETF industry will continue to grow and challenge the mutual fund industry for assets and investors. However, the ETF industry faces a series of unprecedented headwinds that portend rough seas ahead. These headwinds have the potential to significantly temper that growth rate and change some of the fundamental ways the industry does business.

The implications for investors remains to be seen. However, the basics of investing in ETFs will remain the same for individuals. If investors focus on what they can control, they will continue to purchase index-based ETFs as the best way to build a low-cost, tax-efficient, transparent, diversified portfolio.

How to Decide Which ETFs Are Best for You

(This is an edited version of an article I wrote for TheStreet.com on December 4, 2007.)

With so many exchange-traded funds hitting the market, it's becoming tougher to compare them.

A small group of websites with screening tools and educational resources are vying to become the single go-to site for investors. To date, none offers true one-stop shopping. However, when used together, they can help you decide which ETFs are best for your portfolio.

ETFguide, an independent online resource, focuses on education. It also offers two proprietary functions that classify ETFs and let investors screen for funds that meet specific criteria. The education section compares ETFs to individual stocks, mutual funds, and closed-end funds, as well as describing advanced strategies in a simple, easy-to-understand format. There's also a subscription-based area with six model ETF portfolios. One of these, the Contrarian Fox, was explained in Chapter 10. The site produces original articles on industry developments, including the launch of new ETFs. One of its unique features is a quarterly survey of expense ratios.

One proprietary tool is a system for classifying funds. Essentially an adaptation of the classic mutual fund–style boxes, it looks at factors relevant only to ETFs. For example, instead of measuring a fund's investment style in terms of the asset class or size of company it holds, ETFguide classifies funds according to the way their benchmark indexes are weighted—by market-cap, fundamental criteria, or fixed weighting.

This makes a lot of sense. Index weighting and construction have been hot topics in the ETF industry for at least two years. For passively managed ETFs, benchmark weighting and construction are among the few ways they can differentiate themselves.

ETFguide's other great tool lets investors search for ETFs using between one and four criteria: asset class, fund provider, investment category, and index-weighting style. It also lets you easily compare two funds side by side. One tool ETFguide needs to add to its arsenal is a way to compare investment returns.

Nuveen Investments' **ETF Connect** has an education section that provides a broad overview of ETFs. It has some very good tools for comparing fund returns. However, this data is updated only once a month at the end of the month. That can be a drawback when the market takes a sudden, sharp turn.

The site does have some other interesting metrics such as data on dividend distributions and whether a fund's shares trade at a premium or discount to the value of its holdings. But half of the site is focused on closed-end funds, which Nuveen also considers to be ETFs because they trade on an exchange.

The Journal of Indexes' web site, **IndexUniverse.com**, offers timely news and features on the ETF industry. It also has the best tool for comparing 44 fund metrics, including historical returns, as well as alpha, beta, and Sharpe Ratio. Unfortunately, that's the site's only tool. In addition, while ETFs get a lot of space on the site, the majority of IndexUniverse is focused on the indexing industry.

Rydex Investments' **ETF Essentials Web site** offers information on how ETFs work in a simple, easy-to-understand format. While Rydex provides snapshots of its own funds, with performance returns, holdings, and taxable distributions, it doesn't have any functions that allow you to compare funds.

Exchangetradedfunds.com, which sponsors the Global ETF Awards, lists every ETF that trades on a foreign exchange. The site provides a lot of information that is aimed toward financial professionals rather than retail investors. But for people in the industry, it offers many resources, such as conferences and lists of index publishers, custodians, distributors, and law firms specializing in ETFs.

ETFtrends.com is one of the leading blogs watching the industry. It's owned by Tom Lydon, a money manager who sits on the board of Rydex Funds. Lydon links to ETF stories in the mainstream media and gives his personal opinions on what they mean.

Reuters' **Lipper Research Center** provides the latest stories on ETFs from the Reuters news service, as well as Lipper Research reports. The highlight of the site is the snapshot, which gives each fund a Lipper Leader rating in five categories: total return, consistent return, capital preservation, tax efficiency, and expenses. The snapshot also compares risk to return, provides in-depth performance numbers, and offers a breakdown of expenses.

Morningstar's website doesn't offer as much information about ETFs as it does about mutual funds. Still, the site is a number cruncher's dream. In addition to returns, tax analysis, and fees, it gives information on ETF options trading. It also rates ETFs.

You also can research ETFs at **TheStreet.com's ETF Center**. This has up-to-date news on the latest ETFs. TheStreet.com also rates ETFs in its ratings section. **TheStreet.com Ratings**' proprietary statistical models use key financial metrics and indicators to rate ETFs (as well as stocks, mutual funds, banks, insurance and other financial interests). You can also find an archive of ETF stories that I wrote for TheStreet.com.

SmartMoney.com has the best charts for ETFs and stocks. These Java-based charts allow you pinpoint your chart from any one day to any other day over the past five years. The chart can cover as much data as five years or as little as a week. You can also compare ETFs to indexes as well as other ETFs on the same chart. You can also find an archive of ETF stories that I wrote for SmartMoney.com.

The finance section of **Yahoo's** finance website is such an omnibus that it really doesn't deserve to be on this list, nor is its ETF section terribly impressive. However, it does offer something no one else has: The snapshots for individual ETFs provide historical prices and daily volumes that go all the way back to each fund's launch date.

Web Sites Mentioned in This Appendix

ETF Connect—http://www.etfconnect.com/
ETF Essentials—http://www.rydexinvestments.com/
InvestorResources/ETFessentials.shtml
ETF Guide—http://www.etfguide.com/
ETFtrends.com—http://www.etftrends.com/
Exchangetradedfunds.com—http://exchangetradedfunds.com/
IndexUniverse.com—http://www.indexuniverse.com/
Lipper Research Center—http://funds.reuters.com/lipper/retail/
reuters/overviewetf.asp?type=etf
Morningstar—http://morningstar.com/
SmartMoney.com—http://www.smartmoney.com
TheStreet.com ETF Center—http://www.thestreet.com/life-and-money/etf-center/index.html
TheStreet.com Ratings—http://www.thestreet.com/thestreet-picks/thestreet-ratings/index.html
Yahoo! Finance—http://finance.yahoo.com/

Additional links

> **My ETF blog and updates related to this book**
> http://www.etfsforthelongrun.com
>
> **My archive of ETF stories at TheStreet.com**—http://www.thestreet
> .com/author/1111789/LawrenceCarrel/articles.html
>
> **My archive of ETF stories at SmartMoney.com**—http://www.
> smartmoney.com/search/?story=author&authorName=Lawrence
> %20Carrel
>
> **My personal Web site**
> http://www.lawrencecarrel.com

Notes

Chapter 1: ETFs—The Newfangled Mutual Funds

1. John C. Bogle, "In Investing, You Get What You *Don't* Pay For," The World Money Show, 2 February 2005, Orlando, Fla.

Chapter 2: ETF History Lesson

1. Dow Jones Indexes, http://www.djindexes.com/mdsidx/index.cfm?event=showavgstats#no4.
2. Bob Tull, managing director at MacroMarkets, in an interview with the author, July 2007.
3. Steven Bloom, senior vice president for financial products, The NASDAQ Stock Market, formerly of the American Stock Exchange, in an interview with the author, June 2007.
4. Donald Katz, "Wall Street Rocket Scientists," *Worth*, February/March 1992. pp. 68–74.
5. Stuart Bruchey, *Modernization of the American Stock Exchange, 1971–1989* (New York: Garland Publishing, 1991), p. 8.
6. Ibid.
7. Ibid, p. 15.
8. Ibid, p. 17.
9. FINRA, http://www.finra.org.
10. Scott McMurray, "At a Crossroads: Continued Survival of Amex Is Threatened as Its Listings Decline—Thriving Options Business Slows Exchange's Slide; Merger with Big Board?—A Way to Meet with Reagan," *The Wall Street Journal*, 2 July 1985.
11. Ibid.
12. Ibid.
13. Ibid.
14. Anita Raghavan, "Curb Service: NASDAQ's Parent Is in Negotiations to Take Control of the Amex—Deal Would Alter Trading on a Storied

Exchange, Extend NASD's Reach—Uncertainty for Floor Brokers," *The Wall Street Journal*, 12 March 1998, p. A1.

15. Pat Wechsler Keefe, "Pressure on the Amex: No. 2 Stock Exchange Fights Increasing Competition," *Newsday*, 2 February 1986, p. 88.
16. Joe Stefanelli, Amex"s former executive vice president of derivative securities, in an interview with the author, July 2007.
17. Steven Bloom, senior vice president for financial products, The NASDAQ Stock Market, formerly of the American Stock Exchange, in an interview with the author, June 2007.
18. Ibid.
19. Jim Wiandt and Will McClatchy, *Exchange Traded Funds: An Insider's Guide to Buying the Market* (New York: John Wiley & Sons, 2002), p. 72.
20. Bloom, interview with the author, June 2007.
21. Laura Zinn and Marc Frons, "A Future? A Stock? Or Just a Good, Cheap Hedge," *BusinessWeek*, 3114, 10 July 1989, p. 98.
22. American Stock Exchange press release, "Record-Breaking First Day Volume for Derivative Securities Reported for Amex's Equity Index Participants," 15 May 1989.
23. Jeffrey Laderman, Joseph Weber, and Catherine Yang, "The Race to Bring a 'Missing Link' to Market," *BusinessWeek* 3065, 15 August 1989, p. 98.
24. Bloom, interview with the author, June 2007.
25. Ibid.
26. Ibid.
27. Joseph Keenan, managing director at Bank of New York Mellon, in an interview with the author, July 2007.
28. Doug Holmes, strategic advisor at Rydex Investments, formerly of State Street Global Advisors, in an interview with the author, June 2007.
29. "Exchanges' 'Basket' Plans Are off to Lethargic Start," *The Wall Street Journal*, 27 October 1989.
30. Sam Scott Miller, partner at Orrick, Herrington & Sutcliffe, in an interview with the author, July 2007.
31. Doug Holmes, strategic advisor at Rydex Investments, formerly of State Street Global Advisors, in an interview with the author, June 2007.
32. Tull, interview with the author, July 2007.
33. Bloom, interview with the author, June 2007.
34. Ibid.
35. Kathleen Moriarty, partner at law firm Katten Muchin Roseman, who worked on the SPDR while at Orrick, Herrington & Sutcliffe, in an interview with the author, July 2007.
36. Holmes, interview with the author, June 2007.
37. Bloom, interview with the author, June 2007.

38. Moriarty, interview with the author, July 2007.
39. Aaron Lucchetti, "Patent Poses Problem for Amex Exchange-Traded Funds," *The Wall Street Journal*, 20 September 2000. p. C1.
40. Bob Tull, managing director at MacroMarkets, formerly of Morgan Stanley, in an interview with the author, February 2008.
41. Keenan, interview with the author, July 2007.
42. Tull, interview with the author, July 2007.
43. Joseph LaCorte, chief executive officer of consulting firm S Network, formerly managing director of Deutsche Bank, in an interview with the author, July 2007.
44. "Webs Whip Country Baskets in Initial Exchange Trading," *Investment Dealers' Digest*, 12 April 1996.
45. "WEBS Looks to Succeed Where CountryBaskets Failed," *Bank Investment Product News* 3, no. 1, 13 (1997).
46. "DMG's CountryBaskets Set for Early Liquidation," *Funds International*. 1 January 1997.
47. Bob Tull, managing director at MacroMarkets, also formerly of Deutsche Bank, in an interview with the author, July 2007
48. LaCorte, interview with the author, July 2007.
49. Tull, interview with the author, July 2007.
50. Holmes, interview with the author, June 2007.
51. Greg Ip, "Amex Loses Times Listing, Market Share," *The Wall Street Journal*, 4 September 1997, p. C1.
52. John Jacobs, chief executive of NASDAQ Global Funds, in an interview with the author, February 2008.
53. Nicholas Bray, "Barclays to Buy Money Manager For $440 Million—Wells Fargo Nikko Purchase Is a Bid to Be Big Player In Fast-Growing Sector," *The Wall Street Journal*, 2 June 21995, p. A4.
54. Ibid.
55. J. Parson, iShares' head of sales in an interview with the author, July 2007.
56. Tom Lauricella, "Monthly Mutual Funds Review—How Barclays Became a Force in ETFs—Effort to Develop, Market Once-Obscure Funds Pays Off for the Firm," *The Wall Street Journal*, 1 November 2004, p. R1.
57. J. Parson, iShares' head of sales, in an interview with the author July 2007.
58. Ibid.
59. Cliff Weber, American Stock Exchange executive vice president, formerly Amex head of ETF Marketplace, in an interview with the author, July 2007.
60. Paul J. Lim, "39 Fund Strategies 'Basket' Securities, an Alternative to Traditional Mutuals," *Los Angeles Times*, 30 November 1999, p. C8.

61. Sandra Ward, "New Spiders, New Webs: New Spiders, New Webs Fund Companies Consider Creating Their Own Exchange-Traded Replicas," *Barron's*, 15 November 1999, p. F3.
62. Jim Wiandt and Will McClatchy, *Exchange-Traded Funds: A Insider's Guide to Buying The Market* (New York: John Wiley & Sons, 2002).

Chapter 3: The Evolution of the ETF

1. Securities and Exchange Commission, http://www.sec.gov/answers/mfinvco.htm.
2. Securities and Exchange Commission, http://www.sec.gov/about/laws.shtml#invcoact1940.
3. *2008 Investment Company Fact Book, 48th Edition* (Washington, D.C.: Investment Company Institute, 2008), p 11.
4. Jack P. Friedman, *Barron's Dictionary of Business Terms* (Hauppauge, N.Y.: Barron's Educational Series, 2007), p. 582
5. *2007 Investment Company Fact Book, 47th Edition*, Washington, D.C.: Investment Company Institute 2007, p. 4.
6. ICI Research Department, "Trends in Ownership of Mutual Funds in the United States, 2007," Investment Company Institute, November 2007.
7. *2008 Investment Company Fact Book, 48th Edition* (Washington, D.C.: Investment Company Institute, 2008), p. 8.
8. Ibid, p. 9.
9. Kathleen H. Moriarty and Jeffrey McCarthy, "So You Want to Launch an ETF?," *Journal of Indexes*, July/August 2006.
10. Ibid.
11. Scott Ebner, senior vice president, ETF Marketplace, American Stock Exchange, in an interview with the author, April 2007.
12. Jack P. Friedman, *Barron's Dictionary of Business Terms* (Hauppauge, N.Y.: Barron's Educational Series, 2007), p. 33.

Chapter 4: Index Fund-amentals

1. Steven A. Schoenfeld. *Active Index Investing: Maximizing Portfolio Performance and Minimizing Risk through Global Index Strategies* (Hoboken, N.J.: John Wiley & Sons, 2004), p. 59.
2. Burton G. Malkiel, *A Random Walk Down Wall Street: The Time-Tested Strategy for Successful Investing* (New York: W.W. Norton & Company, 2007), p. 362.
3. Index Fund Advisors, Inc., http://www.ifa.com/12steps/step2/step2page2.asp.

4. Steven A. Schoenfeld, *Active Index Investing* (Hoboken, N.J.: John Wiley & Sons), p. 17.
5. Eugene F. Fama, "Random Walks in Stock Market Prices," *Financial Analysts Journal*, September/October 1965.
6. Eugene Fama, "One-on-One Interview with Eugene Fama" by Financial Engineering News http://www.fenews-digital.com/fenews/.
7. Steven A. Schoenfeld, *Active Index Investing* (Hoboken, N.J.: John Wiley & Sons), p. 18.
8. Ibid.
9. Ibid.
10. Ibid., p. 21.
11. Ibid.
12. Standard & Poor's 500, http://www2.standardandpoors.com/portal/site/sp/en/us/page.topic/indices_500/2,3,2,2,0,0,0,0,0,0,0,0,0,0,0,0.html.
13. Ibid.
14. Russell Investments, http://www.russell.com.
15. FTSE UK Index Series, http://www.ftse.com/Indices/UK_Indices/index.jsp.

Chapter 5: Fee Bitten

1. John C. Bogle, author and founder of The Vanguard Group, in an interview with the author, May 2007.

Chapter 6: The Better Mousetrap

1. James Pacetti, president of ETF consulting company ETF International, in an interview with the author, July 2007.
2. Investment Company Institute http://www.ici.org/issues/dir/bro_mf_directors_2.html.
3. Lawrence Carrel, "SEC Tackles Fund Fees," TheStreet.com, http://www.thestreet.com/story/10351983/2/sec-tackles-fund-fees.html (23 April 2007).
4. Christopher Cox, SEC Chairman, "Address to the Mutual Fund Directors Forum," Seventh Annual Policy Conference, 12 April 2007, Washington, D.C. http://www.sec.gov/news/speech/2007/spch041207cc.htm.
5. Ibid.
6. Jason Karceski, Miles Livingston, and Edward O'Neal, "Portfolio Transaction Costs at U.S Equity Mutual Funds," 2004. http://bear.cba.ufl.edu/karceski/research%20papers/Execution_Costs_Paper_Nov_15_2004.pdf.

7. Roger M. Edelen, Richard B. Evans, and Gregory B. Kadlec, "Scale Effects in Mutual Fund Performance: The Role of Trading Costs," 17 March 2007. http://papers.ssrn.com/sol3/papers.cfm?abstract_id=951367.
8. Bob Tull, managing director at MacroMarkets, formerly of Amex, in an interview with the author, July 2007.
9. Hank Belusa, the DTCC's vice president of product management for equities, in an interview with the author, August 2007.

Chapter 7: The New Indexers

1. *2008 Investment Company Fact Book, 48th Edition* (Washington, D.C.: Investment Company Institute, 2008), p. 121.
2. Bruce Bond, president and chief executive officer of PowerShares, formerly of Nuveen Investments, in an interview with the author, November 2007.
3. Ian Salisbury, "Did Nuveen Miss ETF Gold Rush?—Amid a Personality Clash, Firm Ended Plan for Funds, but Alumni Are Performing," *The Wall Street Journal*, 18 Oct. 2006, p. C11.
4. Investopedia.com, http://www.investopedia.com/terms/b/beta.asp.
5. Gary Gastineau, managing director of ETF Consultants, formerly of Nuveen Investments, in an interview with the author, October 2007.
6. Bond, in an interview with the author, November 2007.
7. Ibid.
8. Dave Hooten, chairman and chief executive officer of Claymore Securities, formerly of Nuveen Investments, in an interview with the author, November 2007.
9. *2008 Investment Company Fact Book, 48th Edition* (Washington, D.C.: Investment Company Institute, 2008), pp. 120, 121.
10. Yuka Hayashi, "Exchange-Traded Funds Take Off—Fast-Growing Segment of Industry Is Undeterred by Punishing Bear Market," *The Wall Street Journal*, 8 August 2002, p. D9.
11. Ian Salisbury, "Small ETF Firms Have a Tough Go against Goliaths—One Newcomer's Vision—and Failure—Illustrates the Importance of Backing," *The Wall Street Journal*, 23 October 2006, p. C10.
12. Bruce Bond, president and chief executive officer of PowerShares, formerly of Nuveen Investments, in an interview with the author, November 2007.
13. Cliff Weber, American Stock Exchange executive vice president, formerly Amex head of ETF Marketplace, in an interview with the author, July 2007.

14. Richard A. Ferri, *The ETF Book: All You Need to Know about Exchange-Traded Funds* (Hoboken, N.J.: John Wiley & Sons, 2007), p. 98

15. Bond, interview with the author, November 2007.

16. Peter Elkind, Christopher Tkaczyk, and Doris Burke, "The Secrets of Eddie Stern: If You Think You Know How Bad the Mutual Fund Scandal Is, You're Wrong. It's Worse," *Fortune*, 19 April 2004, p. 106.

17. Ibid.

18. Ibid.

19. Ibid.

20. Cliff Weber, American Stock Exchange executive vice president, formerly Amex head of ETF Marketplace, in an interview with the author, July 2007.

21. Lawrence Carrel, " 'Godfather' of Fundamental Indexing Faces Challenge," TheStreet.com, http://www.thestreet.com/story/10362121/1/godfather-of-fundamental-indexing-faces-challenge.html (13 June 2007).

22. Lawrence Carrel, "Index Wars," SmartMoney.com, http://www.smartmoney.com/etffocus/?story=20060816b (16 August 2006).

23. Ibid.

24. Rob Arnott, chairman and founder of Research Affiliates, in an interview with the author, January 2008.

25. Kevin Burke, "Among Giants," Registered Rep.com, http://registeredrep.com/mag/finance_among_giants_200708100523/, (7 April 2007).

26. Kevin Burke, "Among Giants," Registered Rep.com http://registeredrep.com/mag/finance_among_giants_200708100523/, (7 April 2007).

27. Luciano Siracusano, WisdomTree director of research, in an interview with the author, November 2007.

28. Lawrence Carrel, "A WisdomTree Grows on Wall Street", Smartmoney.com, http://www.smartmoney.com/etffocus/?story=20060628 (28 June 2006).

29. Luciano Siracusano, WisdomTree director of research, in an interview with the author, November 2007.

30. Ibid.

31. Burke, "Among Giants."

32. Jeremy Siegel, "The 'Noisy Market' Hypothesis," *The Wall Street Journal*, 14 June 2006, p. A14.

33. Lawrence Carrel, "Index Wars," SmartMoney.com, http://www.smartmoney.com/etffocus/?story=20060816b (16 August 2006).

34. Ibid.

35. Robert D. Arnott, Jason Hsu, and Philip Moore, "Fundamental Indexation," *Financial Analysts Journal*, 61, no. 7, (2005), p. 83.

36. Lawrence Carrel, "Index Wars," SmartMoney.com, http://www.smartmoney.com/etffocus/?story=20060816b (16 August 2006).

37. Jeffrey Feldman, chairman and founder of Xshares Group, in an interview with the author, November 2007.
38. Jen Ryan, "Xshares Reinvented as ETF Hawker," TheStreet.com, http://www.thestreet.com/story/10339788/1/xshares-reinvented-as-etf-hawker.html (20 February 2007).
39. Lawrence Carrel, "Target-Date ETFs Could Make or Break Xshares," TheStreet.com, http://www.thestreet.com/story/10382343/1/target-date-etfs-could-make-or-break-xshares.html (2 October 2007).
40. Lisa Matza, director of sales and marketing at Ziegler Capital Management, in an interview with the author, November 2007.

Chapter 8: The ETFs That Aren't ETFs

1. Securities and Exchange Commission, http://www.sec.gov/about/laws.shtml.
2. Mary Van Leuven, "Variable Prepaid Forwards: Are Stock Loans Possible in Light of TAM 2?," *The Tax Advisor* 37, no. 6 (2006).
3. Kathleen Moriarty, partner at law firm Katten Muchin Roseman, in an interview with the author, August 2007.
4. Lawrence Carrel, "Looking for the Silver Lining," http://www.smartmoney.com/etf-focus/index.cfm?story=20060503, SmartMoney.com, 3 May 2006,
5. Kenneth M. Morris and Alan M. Siegel, *The Wall Street Journal Guide to Understanding Money & Investing* (New York: Lightbulb Press, 1993), p. 124.
6. Ibid.
7. Ibid.
8. Lawrence Carrel, "Contango and Cash", SmartMoney.com, http://www.smartmoney.com/etf-focus/index.cfm?story=20060412, 12 April 2006.
9. Ibid.
10. Ibid.
11. Ibid.
12. Index Universe Staff, "Make Way for Macros," IndexUniverse.com, http://indexuniverse.com/sections/breaking-news/10/889.html, (29 November 2006).
13. Lawrence Carrel, "Paired Oil ETFs Prepare for Split," TheStreet.com, http://www.thestreet.com/story/10384306/1/paired-oil-etfs-prepare-for-split.html (15 October 2007).
14. IndexUniverse Staff, "Make Way for Macros,", IndexUniverse.com, http://indexuniverse.com/sections/breaking-news/10/889.html (29 November 2006).
15. Ibid.

16. Kenneth M. Morris and Alan M. Siegel, *The Wall Street Journal Guide to Understanding Money & Investing* (New York: Lightbulb Press, 1993), p. 28.
17. Lawrence Carrel, "More Currency ETFs to Debut", SmartMoney.com, http://www.smartmoney.com/etf-focus/index.cfm?story=20060621 (21 June 2006).
18. Ibid.
19. Lawrence Carrel, "Exchange-Traded Notes' Tax Perks Under Attack," TheStreet.com, http://www.thestreet.com/story/10394918/1/exchange-traded-notes-tax-perks-under-attack.html (18 December 2007).

Chapter 9: Putting the "Trade" in Exchange-Traded Funds

1. Todd Lofton, *Getting Started in Exchange Traded Funds* (Hoboken, N.J.: John Wiley & Sons, 2007).
2. Jim Wiandt and Will McClatchy, *Exchange-Traded Funds: An Insider's Guide to Buying the Market* (New York: John Wiley & Sons, 2002), p. 12.
3. Warren Buffett, quoted in John C. Bogle, *The Little Book of Common Sense Investing* (Hoboken, N.J., John Wiley & Sons, 2007), p. 5.
4. John C. Bogle, author and founder of The Vanguard Group, in an an interview with the author, May 2007.
5. Lawrence Carrel, "Not as Easy to Short ETFs as You May Think," TheStreet.comhttp://www.thestreet.com/s/not-as-easy-to-short-etfs-as-you-may-think/funds/etftuesday/10372694.html?puc=_tscs (7 August 2007).
6. Ibid.
7. Ibid.
8. Ibid.
9. Lawrence Carrel, "An Easier Way to Short Emerging Markets," TheStreet.com http://www.thestreet.com/s/an-easier-way-to-short-emerging-markets/funds/etftuesday/10387179.html?puc=_tscs (30 October 2007).
10. Lawrence Carrel, "ETF Options Strategies," SmartMoney.com, http://www.smartmoney.com/etf-focus/index.cfm?story=20060510 (10 May 2006).

Chapter 10: Building Your Own ETF Portfolio

1. Jason Van Bergen, "Asset Allocation Strategies," http://www. investopedia.com/articles/04/031704.asp, Investopedia.com.
2. XTF Global Asset Management, www.xtf.com.

3. J. D. Steinhilber, president of Agile Investing, in an interview with the author, November 2007.
4. Ibid.
5. Ibid.
6. Ibid.
7. Ibid.
8. Ibid.
9. Ibid.
10. Ron DeLegge, www.etfguide.com.
11. Ibid.
12. Ibid.
13. Burton Malkiel, professor of economics at Princeton University and chairman of and consultant to an investment committee to create the Active China Strategy at Active Investment Advisors, a unit of Natixis Global Asset Management Advisors, in an interview with the author, November 2007.
14. World Bank (Beijing office), Quarterly Update, May 2007.
15. "China's Trade Time Bomb," *Washington Post*, 9 May 2007.
16. "OECD predicts double-digit economic growth for China," *China View*, 25 May 2007.
17. World Trade Organization Annual Report, 2006.
18. Malkiel, interview with the author, November 2007.
19. John C. Bogle, *The Little Book of Common Sense Investing* (Hoboken, N.J.: John Wiley & Sons, 2007), p. 5.

Chapter 11: The Future of ETFs

1. Kopin Tan, "Amex Is Facing Fresh Questions On Handling of Options Orders," *The Wall Street Journal*, 30 September 2003, p. C12.
2. Bloomberg News , "Amex Is Accused Of Breaking Pact," *The New York Times*, 30 September 2003.
3. Kopin Tan, "American Exchange's Chairman on Hot Seat for Retirement Pay," *The Wall Street Journal*, 10 October 2003, p. C11.
4. Lisa Dallmer, NYSE senior vice president of ETFs and indexes, in an interview with the author, November 2007.
5. Aaron Lucchetti, "NYSE Euronext Is in Talks to Buy Amex As Its Old Rival's Market Share Erodes—Deal Could Carry $350 Million Value; Some Hurdles Loom," *The Wall Street Journal*, 10 January 2008, p. C3.
6. Jed Horowitz and Kate Kelly, "Moving the Market: NASD Completes Its Sale of Amex to Member Group," *The Wall Street Journal*, 4 January 2005, p. C3.

7. American Stock Exchange, press release, "NYSE Euronext to Acquire the American Stock Exchange," 17 January 2008.

8. Deborah Solomon, Kate Kelly, and Gaston F. Ceron, "Moving the Market—Regulation: SEC Prepares to Charge the NYSE—Exchange Is Likely to Settle, Boost Specialist Oversight; Spear's Luckow Is Banned," *The Wall Street Journal*, 13 January 2005, p. C3.

9. Jim Wiandt, "Speaking of the NASDAQ..." IndexUniverse.com, http://www.indexuniverse.com/component/content/article/31/3575.html?Itemid=3 (18 January 2008).

10. Arlene Reyes, chief operating officer at ExchangeTradeFunds.com in an interview with the author, December, 2007.

11. Lawrence Carrel, "A Push Is on for Actively-Managed ETFs," TheStreet.com, http://www.thestreet.com/story/10396662/4/a-push-is-on-for-actively-managed-etfs.html (2 January 2008).

12. Ibid.

13. Ibid.

14. Lawrence Carrel, "Financial Planners Aren't Sold on Active ETFs," TheStreet.com, http://www.thestreet.com/s/financial-planners-arent-sold-on-active-etfs/funds/etf/10398983.html?puc=_tscs (16 January 2008).

15. Ibid.

16. Lawrence Carrel, "Barclays Boosts Inclusion of ETFs in 401(k)s," TheStreet.com, http://www.thestreet.com/story/10359257/1/barclays-boosts-inclusion-of-etfs-in-401ks.htmlb (29 May 2007).

17. Lawrence Carrel, "WisdomTree Breaks into 401(k) Market," TheStreet.com, http://www.thestreet.com/story/10384628/1/wisdom-tree-breaks-into-401k-market.html (16 October 2007).

18. Lance Berg, principal at Barclays Global Investors, in an interview with the author, February 2008.

About the Author

After working as a newspaper reporter and editor, Lawrence Carrel got in on the ground floor of the online publishing business when financial news entered the Internet age. As a founding staff member of The Wall Street Journal.com, he was one of the original writers of its "Cyber Investing" column and among the first to write about small stocks for the Web. Later at SmartMoney.com, his daily market story covered the period leading up to the popping of the dot-com bubble and the crash of 2000. A year later, he created Smart Money's daily online hot stocks column, "The One-Day Wonder." Carrel originated SmartMoney.com's ETF Focus column in 2006 just as the ETF industry began its era of explosive growth. In 2007, he took over the weekly ETF and mutual funds columns at TheStreet.com. He has been a guest commentator on MSNBC, CNN, and many others. A native of Buffalo, N.Y., he is a graduate of Cornell University and has lived in Washington, D.C. and London. He currently resides in Manhattan with his two sons. This is his first book.

Index

Note: The abbreviation of ETF in the index refers to exchange-traded funds.

Accountants, 103
Active China Strategy, 262–265
Actively managed ETFs, 84, 279–281
Actively managed funds, 69–70, 72–74, 75,
   90–92, 126–127
Administrators, 102
Aggressive portfolios, 247–248, 256–258
Agile Investments, 236, 248–258
Alpha, 133–134
American depositary receipts (ADRs), 48,
   137–138
American Stock Exchange (AMEX):
   commodities and, 17–18
   DIAmonds on, 34
   ETF development by, 12–13, 21–26
   ETF fees and, 32
   history of, 13–16
   index creation by, 82–83
   index participation contracts and, 18–20
   Intellidex and, 139
   NASDAQ merger with, 35–37, 39, 41, 49
   NYSE and, 13–14, 45–46, 274–275
   patents and, 27–29
   SPDR on, 26–27
Ameristock, 165–166
Amvescap, 148–149
Arbitrage, 66
Arnott, Rob, 155–158, 161–163
Asset allocations, 6–7, 71, 241–248
Asset-based fees, 126
Asset managers, 30–33
Authorized participants:
   electronic transactions and, 117
   ETF share creation by, 39–40, 64–66,
      111–112, 225
   ETV share creation by, 182, 194, 201
   transaction costs and, 114–115, 118–119

Bachelier, Louis, 76
Back-end loads, 97

Backwardation, 189
Baker, Jay, 26
Balanced funds, 59
Bank of New York, 22, 29–30, 48, 137–138
Barclays Global Investors, 33, 42–45,
   176–177. *See also* iPaths; iShares
Baskets of Listed Depositary Receipts
   (BLDRS), 48, 137–138
Bear Stearns, 177–178
Benchmarks, 70–72, 131
Beta, 133–134
Bid-ask spreads, 108–109, 122–123
Black Monday, 11
Bloom, Steven, 13, 22, 26, 27–28, 38
Board of directors, 99–100
Bogle, John, 46–47, 78, 161
Bond, Bruce, 132–135, 138–140, 144, 148
Bonds, 59, 133–134, 136–137, 165–166. *See
   also* Fixed-income securities
Brokers:
   as authorized participants, 111
   certified financial planners as, 45
   commissions of (*see* Commissions)
   discount, 219–220
   fiduciaries *versus*, 268
   share lending by, 223–226
   transfer agent services by, 67, 122
   12b-1 fees to, 101–102
Buttonwood Agreement, 13
Buy-and-hold strategy, 218, 235–236
Buy-write strategy, 251–252

Call options, 229–230
Capital gains taxes:
   in actively *versus* passively managed
      funds, 75
   ETFs and, 5, 64–65, 115–116, 119–122
   ETNs and, 179
   ETVs and, 175
   futures and, 190–191

Capital gains taxes (*Continued*)
  mutual funds and, 5, 104–105
  short trades and, 228
Cash:
  dividends, 19, 113
  in down market, 260
  drag, 27, 30, 62, 105, 112–113, 145
  ETF trades and, 218
  index participation contracts and, 19–21
  in-kind trades *versus*, 115
Cash Index Participation contracts (CIP
    shares), 18–20, 115
Certified financial planners, 45
Chicago Board of Trade, 19
Chicago Board Options Exchange (CBOE),
    16, 19
Chicago Mercantile Exchange, 19
Classic portfolios, 243–248
Claymore Securities, 134, 144, 152–153,
    198–199
Closed-end investment companies, 57
Collective trusts, 282–283
Commissions:
  dollar cost averaging and, 124–126
  ETFs and, 7–8, 114, 122
  ETVs and, 175
  401(k) plans and, 282
  mutual funds and, 96–99, 107–108
  soft dollars and, 109
Commodity Futures Trading Commission
    (CFTC), 19–20, 186
Commodity indexes, 191–192
Commodity markets, 7, 17–18, 149–150,
    171–173, 180–199, 210–213, 254–255
Commodity pools, 186–187
Conservative portfolios, 243–246, 249–255
Consistency, 87–88
Contango, 189
Contrarian investing, 258–265
Costs. *See also* Expense ratios; Fees; Loads
  actively managed funds and, 74, 90–92
  currency ETVs and, 201
  ETFs and, 4–5, 7–8, 88–92, 95–96,
    110–123, 218
  401(k) plans and, 282–283
  futures and, 188
  hidden, 105–110
  index funds and, 75, 88–92
  market timers and, 145
  mutual funds and, 61–63, 89–92, 95–110
CountryBaskets, 31–33
Covered call strategy, 251–252
Creation process/units, 65, 110–114,
    117–118, 182, 194, 201
Credit risk, 177

Cubes, 4, 40–41, 168
Currency markets, 7, 149–150, 171–173,
    199–204, 213–214
Custodians, 61–63, 103, 107–108, 182

Day orders, 223
Defined contribution plans (DCPs), 53,
    123–124, 281–283
DeLegge, Ron, 236, 259
Depository receipts, 4, 26–27, 30, 35, 48,
    115, 137–138, 174–176
Depository Trust & Clearing Corporation
    (DTCC), 111, 116–118
Depository Trust Company (DTC),
    116–117
Deregulation, 15
Deutsche Bank, 31–32, 149–150, 192,
    202–203
DIAmonds, 4, 34
Discipline, 241, 242–243
Disclosure, 52. *See also* Transparency
Discount brokers, 219–220
Distributors, 103
Diversification, 53–55, 113–114
Dividends, 19, 30, 104, 113, 123, 179, 224
Dividend-weighted stock indexes,
    158–162
Dollar cost averaging, 124–126
Dot-com bubble, 33, 41, 146
Dow Jones Industrial Average (DJIA), 34,
    79–80
Dow Jones Wilshire 5000 Total Market
    Index, 80
Down Trusts, 194–196

Ebner, Scott, 139
Efficient Market Hypothesis, 76–78, 160
Electronic stock exchanges, 83–84,
    167–168, 277
Electronic transactions, 116–118, 278
Equal weighting, 141, 166–167
Equities, 243–245, 250–252, 261–262. *See
    also* Stock funds; Stocks, prices of
Equity Index Participations (EIPs), 19–21,
    114–115
ETF Advisors, 136–137
ETF Guide.com, 236, 259
ETFs (exchange-traded funds):
  actively managed, 84, 279–281
  creation of, 63–67, 110–114, 117–118
  definition of, 1–2
  future of, 273–284
  growth of, 129–131, 148, 150–154,
    163–168, 273
  history of, 11–13, 21–26

international, 31–33, 150–152, 166–167, 263–265
inverse, 226–228
portfolio creation (*see* Investment strategies)
short, 153–154, 223–228
trading, 217–231
ETNs (exchange-traded notes), 172–173, 176–179, 203–204, 206–210
ETVs (exchange-traded vehicles), 149–150, 171–176, 180–199, 200–203, 205–214
Exchange Stock Portfolios, 23
Exemptions, 33–34, 63–64, 135, 139–140, 164
Expense ratios:
 ETFs and, 4–5, 89–92, 119, 134
 ETNs and, 178
 ETVs and, 175, 181, 195, 201
 mutual funds and, 61–63, 89–92, 99–101
 tracking errors and, 250–251

Face-amount certificate companies, 56
Fama, Eugene, 76–77
Fees. *See also* Costs; Loads
 asset-based, 126
 asset management, 32–33
 fund managers and, 52, 92, 97–98, 100–101
 management, 32–33, 100–101, 269
 transfer agent, 116–118
 12b-1, 97, 101–102
Feldman, Jeffrey, 163–165
Fiduciaries, 98, 99, 268
Financial Regulatory Authority (FINRA), 14
First-mover advantage, 32, 130, 136–137
First Trust Portfolios, 132
Fixed-income securities, 47–49, 245, 252, 260–261. *See also* Bonds
Fixed-Income Treasury Receipts (FITRs), 137
Flexibility, 3–4, 242
Focus Shares, 168
Foreign Exchange (Forex) market, 199
40-Act investment companies, 23, 33–34, 151
401(k) retirement plans, 53, 123, 281–283
Fractional shares, 124, 282
Front-end loads, 96
Front-running, 281
FTSE International, 81–82, 156–157
FTSE RAFI, 156–157, 161–163
Full-replication strategy, 250–251
Fulton, Ben, 132–135, 144, 150
Fundamental Analysis, 76–77
Fundamental indexing, 155–163

Fund managers, 52, 62–63, 72–74, 92, 97–98, 100–101, 107–108
Funds of funds, 60, 283
Fund sponsors, 99, 103
Futures, 12, 17–18, 185–191, 228

Gastineau, Gary, 132–137
Gold, 150–152, 180–185, 197–198, 200, 254–255
Goldman Sachs, 177–178
Good-'til-cancelled orders, 223
Grantor trusts, 174, 181, 184, 195, 201

Healthcare sector, 164–165, 261
Hedge funds, 145–146
Holding Company Depository Receipts (HOLDRs), 174–176
Holmes, Doug, 23, 27–28
Hooten, Dave, 132–135, 144
Hundred Index Participation Units (HIPS), 24

Indexes:
 benchmark, 70–72, 131
 commodity, 191–192
 composition changes of, 120–122
 definition of, 69
 ETFs tracking, 85, 250–251
 fundamental, 155–163
 intelligent, 138–140, 144–145, 190
 international equity, 81–82
 Major Market, 16, 17
 MarketGrader, 166–167
 niche, 150
 providers of, 79–82, 103, 158–159
 quantitative analysis and, 131
 from stock exchanges, 82–84
 weighting in (*see* Weighting)
Index funds:
 benefits/value of, 76–78, 85
 definition of, 69
 dollar cost averaging and, 124–125
 ETFs as, 4–5
 index composition changes and, 121–122
 inverse, 140, 153–154
 no-load, 98–99, 122, 124–126
 passive management of, 74–75
 purchase and sale of, 105
 retail investors and, 33–34, 78
 transparency of, 72
Index participation contracts, 18–20
Individual investors. *See* Retail investors
Inflation, 182–183
In-kind trades, 115

Institutional investors, 12, 27, 171–172, 218, 225
Intellidexes, 138–140, 144–145
Interest, 223–224
International equity indexes, 81–82
International ETFs, 31–33, 150–152, 166–167, 263–265
Internet, 33, 37–38
Inverse funds, 140, 153–154, 226–228
Investing style, 69, 73, 113
Investment advisors, 125–126, 267–269
Investment banks, 32–33, 176–177
Investment companies, 23, 33–34, 38, 51–52, 55–58, 104, 151
Investment Company Act of 1940, 51–52, 62–64, 135, 139–140, 164. *See also* 40-Act investment companies
Investment Company Institute (ICI), 129
Investment strategies:
    asset allocation and, 241–248
    building ETF portfolios, 235–237
    contrarian investing as, 258–265
    investment advisors and, 267–269
    model portfolios of, 248–258
    risk assessment and, 237–241
    tax-loss harvesting as, 265–267
    transparency of, 6–7
iPaths, 176, 178–179, 193–194
iShares, 42–45, 47–49, 130, 136–137

Jacobs, John, 38

Kelly, James (Kelly Capital Management), 236, 237
Kranefuss, Lee, 42–43

Large-capitalization stocks, 54, 243–245
Late-day trading, 146–147
Leverage, 140, 154, 187, 229
Licensing, 34, 46–47
Limit orders, 108–109, 221–222
Liquidity, 238–239, 276, 278
Loads, 96–99, 125–126. *See also* No-load index funds
Losses, 239–240, 265–267

MacroShares, 194–196
Major Market Index, 16, 17
Malkiel, Burton, 161, 236, 262
Management fees, 32–33, 100–101, 269
Management styles, 69–70, 72–76
Market. *See* Stock market
Market capitalization, 54, 74, 80, 131, 155–157, 160, 243–245
MarketGrader indexes, 166–167

Market makers, 109
Market orders, 109, 221
Market timers/timing, 145–147, 218
Market Vectors, 150–152, 197–198
Master limited partnerships, 254
Micro-capitalization stocks, 54
Mid-capitalization stocks, 30, 243–245
Miller, Sam Scott, 24–25
Moderate portfolios, 246–247, 255–256
Money market funds, 59–60
Mopex, 29
Morgan Stanley, 29, 31–33, 81
Morningstar, 59
Most, Nathan, 12–13, 16, 17–18, 22, 27–28, 49, 115–116
Mutual funds:
    actively managed, 69–70, 72–74, 75, 90–92, 126–127
    costs of, 61–63, 89–92, 95–110
    ETFs *versus,* 2–7, 65, 110, 143, 217–218
    401(k) plans and, 281–283
    industry scandal, 145–147, 217–218
    inverse, 226–228
    as open-end investment companies, 56–57
    operation of, 60–63
    passively managed, 69, 74–75
    popularity of, 55–56
    reasons to purchase, 123–127
    structure of, 99–101
    types of, 58–60

NASDAQ (National Association of Securities Dealers Automated Quotations), 14–16, 35–41, 48, 49, 83–84
Nathan, Ranga, 138–139
National Futures Association, 186
National Securities Clearing Corporation (NSCC), 116–117
Net asset value (NAV), 3, 56–57, 65, 107
New York Stock Exchange (NYSE), 13–14, 31, 45–46, 83, 167–168, 274–275
Niche indexes, 150
No-load index funds, 98–99, 122, 124–126
Nuveen Investments, 132–136

Oil, 185–189, 194–197
Open-end funds, 30–33
Open-end investment companies, 56–57
Operating expenses, 102–103. *See also* Costs; Fees
Optimized Portfolios as Listed Securities (OPALS), 29

Options, 12–13, 16, 229–231
Order types, 108–109, 220–226

Passively managed funds, 69, 74–75
Patents, 27–29, 156, 163, 280
Performance measurement, 71–72
Philadelphia Stock Exchange, 18–20
PowerShares Capital Management:
 BLDRS sale to, 48
 ETVs by, 192, 202–203
 fundamental indexing and, 157
 growth of, 144–145, 147–148
 ownership of, 138–140, 142, 148–150
 Triple Q, 4, 40–41
 water ETFs by, 198–199
Premiums, 229–230
Prepaid forward contracts, 176–177
Price discovery, 276, 278
Prices:
 of commodities, 183–186
 dollar cost averaging and, 124
 of ETFs, 65–66
 of mutual funds, 106–109
 options and, 229–231
 order types and, 221–226
 of purchases *versus* sales, 121
 spot, 188
 of stocks, 76–77
 strike, 229–231
 value *versus*, 160
Price weighting, 79
Principle underwriters, 99, 103
Private funds, 52
ProShares (ProFunds Group), 153–154,
 226–228
Purchase and sale:
 of ETFs, 3–4, 65–66, 107, 110–123
 of index funds, 105
 of mutual funds, 3–4, 60–63, 95–110
 of options, 229–231
Put options, 229–230

Quantitative analysis, 131
Qubes, 4, 40–41, 168

Random Walk Theory, 76–77
Real-estate investment trust (REIT) market,
 245–246, 252–254
Registered investment advisors (RIAs),
 125–126
Regulated Investment Company (RIC), 38,
 104
Regulation National Market System, 40
Representative sampling strategy, 250–251
Research, 219, 240–241

Research Affiliates, 155–157
Retail investors:
 buy-and-hold strategy for, 218
 commodities and, 171–173, 180–181,
  197
 currency ETVs and, 171–173, 202
 diversification by, 53–55
 ETFs and, 12, 31, 270–271
 hedge funds *versus*, 146
 index funds and, 33–34, 78
 investment companies and, 51–52
 marketing to, 42–45, 97–98
 short trades and, 225
Retirement-savings accounts, 53, 123,
 281–283
Rich, Kevin, 150
Risk:
 age *versus*, 237
 alpha or beta, 133
 credit, 177
 diversification and, 53–55
 fund structure and, 75–76
 healthcare sector ETFs and, 164
 investment strategies and, 237–241, 243,
  249, 255–256
 limit orders and, 221–222
 mutual funds and, 59–60
 short trades and, 224
Russell Investment Group, 81
Ryan, Ron, 165–166
Rydex Investments, 140–142, 200–201, 226

Samuelson, Paul, 76
Schaeffer, Bernie, *The Option Advisor*, 231
Schoenfeld, Steven, *Active Index Investing*,
 70
Securities Act of 1933, 174
Securities and Exchange Commission
 (SEC):
 AMEX enforcement order from, 274
 on ETFs, 24–25
 exemptions by, 33–34, 63–64, 135,
  139–140, 164
 on index participation contracts, 20
 on Intellidexes, 139–140
 on 12b-1 fees, 101–102
Securities Exchange Act of 1934, 23, 64
Seed capital, 39–40, 99, 276–277
Shareholders, 103–105, 117–118, 120–122,
 143, 145–146, 174, 217–218
Shares:
 authorized participants and, 39–40,
  64–66, 111–112, 182, 194, 201, 225
 borrowing/lending, 30, 223–226,
  225–226

Shares (*Continued*)
  CIP, 18–20
  fractional, 124, 282
  A *versus* H, 263
Shiller, Robert, 194
Short ETFs, 153–154, 223–228
Siegel, Jeremy, 159–160
Silver, 184–185
Siracusano, Luciano, 158–160
Small-capitalization stocks, 54, 243–245
Soft dollars, 109
Southard, John, 138–139, 144
SPA ETFs, 166–167
Specialists, 39–40, 64, 108–109, 111,
  275–279
Spitzer, Eliot, 145–147
Spot prices, 188
Standard & Poor's, 46–47
Standard & Poor's Depositary Receipt
  (SPDR), 4, 26–27, 30, 35
Standard & Poor's (S&P) 500 Index, 80–81
State Street Global Advisors, 22–23, 35
Steinberg, Jonathan, 158–160
Steinhart, Michael, 159–160
Steinhilber, J. D., 236, 248–258
Stock brokers. *See* Brokers
Stock exchanges, 56–57, 64–65, 82–84,
  167–168, 277. *See also specific stock
  exchanges by name*
Stock funds, 58–59
Stock market, 3–4, 11–12, 70–72, 76–78
Stocks, prices of, 76–77. *See also* Equities
Stop-loss orders, 222
Strategic asset allocation, 241–242
Strike prices, 229–231
Style drift, 113
Super Trusts, 24
Swap agreements, 228

Tactical asset allocation, 242–243, 259
Target-date funds, 165, 283
Taxes:
  account types and, 238
  capital gains (*see* Capital gains taxes)
  defined contribution plans and, 282
  ETFs and, 5–6, 64–65, 115, 119–120,
    137, 143
  ETNs and, 178–179, 203–204
  futures and, 190–191
  investment strategies and, 240, 265–267
  mutual funds and, 103–105
  short trades and, 228
  tax-loss harvesting, 265–267
Technical Analysis, 71
Technology stocks, 38, 146, 167. *See also*
  Dot-com bubble

Termination dates, 58
Ticker symbols, 40
Time orders, 222–223
Toronto 35 Index Participation Units
  (TIPS), 24
Tracking errors, 72, 89, 178, 250–251
Transaction costs. *See* Costs; Fees; Loads
Transfer agents, 61, 67, 103, 116–118, 122
Transparency. *See also* Disclosure
  of ETFs, 6–7, 112, 137, 243, 280–281
  hidden costs *versus,* 105–110
  of index funds, 72
  of mutual fund costs, 96–105
Triple Qs, 4, 40–41, 168
Trustees, 29–30, 182
Tull, Bob, 139
12b-1 fees, 97, 101–102

Underwriters, principle, 99, 103
United States Oil Fund (USO), 186,
  188–191
Unit investment trusts (UITs), 21, 30,
  57–58
Unlisted trading privileges, 45–46
Up Trusts, 194–195

Value investing, 258
Value of Index Participations (VIPs), 19
Van Eck, 150
Vanguard 500 index fund, 4–5, 25–26
Vanguard Group, 46–47, 78, 142–143
Vanguard Index Participation Equity
  Receipt (VIPERs), 47, 142–143
Volatility, 239

Warehouse receipts, 17–18, 21, 115
Wash, 266
Water market, 198–199
Weber, Clifford, 34, 139
Weighting:
  dividend, 158–162
  equal, 141, 166–167
  fundamental indexing and, 155–163
  market-cap, 54, 74, 80, 131, 155–157,
    160, 243–245
  price, 79
  strategic asset allocation and, 242
Wells Fargo, 21–22, 78
Wilshire 5000 Index, 80
WisdomTree, 157–163
World Equity Benchmark shares (WEBS),
  31–33, 42–43

XShares, 163–165

Ziegler Capital Management, 167–168